# DID YOU KNOW

**THAT SAMUEL A. MAVERICK, a 19th-century cattle rancher who refused to brand his calves, gave birth to an English word meaning nonconformist, or one who does not follow the herd . . . that the man who discovered hypnotism, Friedrich A. Mesmer, is responsible for the rather sinister word mesmerize . . . that mishmash is an Old English word dating back to the early 15th century?**

Authors Nurnberg and Rosenblum go after a word the way James Bond went after Dr. No. Once they have a word nailed down— its origin, development, use, misuse—it is nailed forever. They include everything, from the first English words derived from Anglo-Saxon (the word *word*, for instance) to flash words like *astronaut* which come into being overnight.

**Here's a brilliant new way to learn and remember words—and have fun, too— as you power your speech with more punch, pertinence, and perspicuity.**

# ALL ABOUT WORDS:

## An Adult Approach To Vocabulary Building

*by Maxwell Nurnberg
and Morris Rosenblum*

A MENTOR BOOK

**NEW AMERICAN LIBRARY**

NEW YORK AND SCARBOROUGH, ONTARIO

MENTOR TRADEMARK REG. U.S. PAT. OFF. AND FOREIGN COUNTRIES
REGISTERED TRADEMARK—MARCA REGISTRADA
HECHO EN WINNIPEG, CANADA

SIGNET, SIGNET CLASSIC, MENTOR, PLUME, MERIDIAN AND NAL
BOOKS are published *in the United States* by
New American Library,
1633 Broadway, New York, New York 10019,
*in Canada* by The New American Library of Canada Limited,
81 Mack Avenue, Scarborough, Ontario M1L 1M8

FIRST MENTOR PRINTING, FEBRUARY, 1968

14  15  16  17  18  19  20  21  22

PRINTED IN CANADA

## ABOUT THE AUTHORS

Maxwell Nurnberg is Adjunct Associate Professor of English at New York University and Chairman of the English Department at Abraham Lincoln High School in Brooklyn. He is the author, among other books, of *What's the Good Word*, and co-author with Dr. Rosenblum of *How to Build a Better Vocabulary*.

Dr. Morris Rosenblum is Lecturer in Classical Languages and Comparative Literature at the City College of City University, New York. He is the author of an award-winning book—a translation and study of the Latin poet Luxorius—as well as other works on literature, the classics, and language.

*To Rose and Dora*

# Acknowledgments

For the many excerpts from the daily press, we are especially indebted to the writers—many of them anonymous —of *The New York Times* and the New York *Herald Tribune*, from whose pages we have gathered most of our citations. We have also used material from the New York *World-Telegram and Sun*, and the New York *Post*, as well as short excerpts from *Saturday Review, Life, Time, Newsweek,* and the *Nation*.

Since we have used so much current material—sometimes of a controversial nature—we wish to make the usual disclaimer: The opinions expressed in these excerpts do not necessarily represent either our views or those of our publisher.

For material other than newspaper excerpts we should like to make the following acknowledgments:

To *Saturday Review* for permission to reprint excerpts from John G. Fuller's "Trade Winds," Martin Levin's "Phoenix Nest," and "Your Literary I. Q.," where some of the material for exercises called "Triple Threat" first appeared under our names.

To "Pleasures in Learning," publication of New York University's Division of General Education, in which some of the material in Chapter 1 first appeared, and which, in its March 1966 issue, printed an abridged version of Chapter 8.

And to the following publishers for permission to reprint: Holt, Rinehart, and Winston, Inc. and The Society of Authors as the literary representatives of the Estate of the late A. E. Housman, and Messrs. Jonathan Cape Ltd., publishers of A. E. Housman's *Collected Poems* for "Loveliest of Trees."

Alfred A. Knopf for the sestet from Elinor Wylie's sonnet "Pretty Words."

Cassell and Company, Ltd. and Doubleday Anchor Books for excerpt from Robert Graves' *Goodbye to All That*.

Harvard University Press for excerpts from Plutarch's "Life of Aristides," "Life of Solon," and "Life of Lucullus" in the

Loeb Classical Library edition of *Plutarch's Lives,* translated by Bernadotte Perrin.

Harcourt, Brace and World for the excerpt from David Garnett's *The Golden Echo.*

Merrill Lynch, Pierce, Fenner & Smith for paragraph about Confucius.

The Macmillan Company for excerpt from Sean O'Casey's *I Knock at the Door* (1939).

*Ellery Queen's Mystery Magazine* and the author, Michael Harrison, for excerpt from "The Mystery of the Fulton Documents."

Doubleday for excerpt from "Poet in a Valley of Dry Bones" in Robert Graves' *Mammon and the Black Goddess* (1965).

The New York *Herald Tribune* and Judith Crist for excerpt from a film review.

To check derivations and definitions, we have used the Oxford English Dictionary, Webster's New International Dictionary Second Edition Unabridged, as well as Webster's Third New International Dictionary Unabridged (hereafter referred to as Webster's Second and Webster's Third), and Webster's New World Dictionary of the American Language.

Those who wish to continue the study of words—words rather than vocabulary—will find the works of the following authors enjoyable and helpful: Ivor Brown, Mario Pei, Eric Partridge, and Ernest Weekley.

# Contents

# A Word to Our Readers

Why still another book on vocabulary?

Frankly, because we thought we could write a better one. Even better than our own *How to Build a Better Vocabulary* (Prentice-Hall, 1949)? Yes, for in the intervening years we have learned a great deal more about words and we're ready to share this information with you.

If you read this book we do *not* guarantee:

1. that you will become the leader of your community because of a newly acquired fluency or ease in conversation or

2. that because of an increased vocabulary you will be able to sell your ideas to the boss and be made vice president by a grateful company and its equally grateful stockholders or

3. that you will marry the attractive, charming, and utterly worshipful heir or heiress to millions.

Arrant nonsense! (You'll find the word *arrant* in Chapter 7.)

*But* we do guarantee—if you read this book:

1. that you will develop a keener interest in words,

2. that you will obtain a greater insight into words—into their wonder and magic,

3. that you will acquire many, many new words and *hold on to them longer,* and

4. that, if you are preparing for an examination in which a question on vocabulary figures large, you will find this book a valuable aid.

We hope, too, that you will have a good time reading the text and doing the exercises. We have interjected what the English call "asides"—stray bits of related information, revealing sidelights, *obiter dicta.* (You'll find *obiter dicta* explained in Chapter 12, "Much Latin, Less Greek.")

Nor have we hesitated to include poetry, anecdotes, fillers, and word games—always provided they had something to do with the subject at hand. For we have tried to make the study of words pleasant and easy and as readable as a story. The book has been designed for your enjoyment as well as instruction.

Have fun!

# ALL ABOUT
# WORDS

A word is dead
When it is said,
    Some say.
I say it just
Begins to live
    That day.

EMILY DICKINSON

# 1. A Funny Thing Happened on the Way Through the Dictionary

MR. TAFT:    *What does the Senator mean by*
*supererogation?*

MR. CONNALLY:    *The Senator can look in the dic-*
*tionary for it. I do not have time to*
*educate the Senator from Ohio.*

THE CONGRESSIONAL RECORD,
MAY 25, 1950

A friend of ours was talking to a theatrical agent who was not particularly distinguished for the range or choice of his vocabulary. He was therefore a little startled to hear the word *eclectic* suddenly pop out.

"Joe! Where did you get hold of that elegant word?"

"*Eclectic?* Oh, I just happened to come across it in the dictionary."

"What do you mean you just happened to come across it in the dictionary?"

"Well, you see, I was looking up the word *egregious* and on my way to *egregious*, my eye caught the word *eclectic* and I liked it."

"Okay. But wait a minute, Joe. How did you *happen* to be looking up the word *egregious*?"

"I always look up the word *egregious*!"

What word are you always looking up? *Jettison? Charismatic? Panache? Suborn?* Long ago our word was *factitious*. It was a little hard to sort out *factitious* from among such words as *factious, fractious, factual,* and *fictitious*. One got confused. But this time we resolved once for all to nail down the meaning in one of several ways—by getting at the derivation, by associating it with other words we knew, or by tying it in with a story. So we turned to the dictionary.

There it was: *factitious*, from the Latin *factus*, past participle of *facere*, "to make, to do." In other words, *factitious* refers to something "made up," not natural, therefore "artificial." We had gotten to the root of it. We had made an association with *artificial*. We didn't have to look up *factitious* again.

Or *factious*. We pinned that down by noting that it is related to *faction* and therefore means tending to promote internal dissension.

Or *fractious*. That comes from the Latin element *fract*, broken, and means refractory or unruly. And doesn't "being unruly" mean breaking a law?

Perhaps that was the approach to vocabulary building that a friend of ours wanted her class of youngsters to learn. They had been asked to bring in words from the newspapers of the day before, words whose meanings they weren't sure of. All went smoothly until the word *euphoria* came up. No one knew what that meant.

Deftly, the teacher asked, "Does any one of you have one of those large dictionaries at home?"

Proudly, several hands went up.

"Henry," the teacher smiled, "for tomorrow look up the word *euphoria* for us and bring in not only the meaning of the word but also the derivation."

"The derivation?"

"Yes, Henry, the derivation, too."

"Oh boy, that's two words I'll have to look up!"

But Henry was wrong. If he had a real interest in words, he would be finding many more than two words, because on the way to *euphoria*—as happened to Joe, the theatrical agent—his eye would be caught by other words: *eugenics, eulogy, eupeptic, euphemism,* and *euphonious.* And he would learn that all was "well" (*eu*) with words like these.

If Joe had used this method to try to fix the meaning of *egregious*, he wouldn't "always" have to be looking it up. For *Webster's New International Dictionary, Second Edition, Unabridged*, after telling him that *grex, gregis* means herd, would have instructed him to "see *gregarious*." At *gregarious* he would have been referred to *aggregate, congregate, egregious,* and *segregate.* And, like Henry, he would have come back holding a fistful of words.

Of the flock of *greg* words, *egregious* is the black sheep. Once it meant standing out (*e*) from the flock and therefore eminent, distinguished, etc. (In Italian it still means that. A writer friend of ours was relieved to find that *Egregio Signore* in the salutation of a letter he received from an Italian admirer meant "Distinguished Sir.") But now we use *egregious* only for anything outstandingly bad—"an egregious blunder, an egregious fool." It always has this derogatory, belittling, or pejorative meaning. There are many words like *egregious* that are now used only in a pejorative sense. Such words are dealt with in Chapter 10.

In vocabulary building, the problem is not so much finding new words or even finding out what they mean. The problem is to remember them, to fix them permanently in your mind.

For you can see that if you are merely introduced to words, you will forget them as quickly as you forget the names of people you are casually introduced to at a crowded party—unless you meet them again or unless you spend some time with them.

In this book you will again meet some of the more difficult words—seen in their contexts, looked at from other angles—and you will spend some time with them. Your meeting will not be a casual one. Some association, we hope, will be established between you and the words. We hope to help you file away permanently in your mind words that are now on the tip of your tongue—precariously perched. We hope to bring into sharp and permanent focus those words that are now on the blurred fringe of your mind.

How do we propose to do this? It must be obvious that we believe that getting at the roots of words—taking words apart—is *one* of the effective ways of *fixing* the meaning of words. Though it is only one of the ways, we are nevertheless going to attack the left flank (prefixes), the right flank (suffixes), and—most important—the center (roots). We are going to find out what makes a word tick and how we can make it stick.

But—and this is a big *but*—we advocate this method for tying down the word only *after* you know its meaning. We hesitate to advocate using the prefix-root method to *get at* the meaning of a word, because there are just too many booby traps around. A bright student in one of our classes neatly fell into one of them when he was confronted on a test with:

*amenable*      (a) contemptible   (b) religious   (c) submissive
                (d) stubborn

He checked (b) as the right answer. When asked how he had arrived at that answer, he replied triumphantly, "By derivation! The suffix *able*, of course, means 'able' and *amen* means what it says, 'amen'; so if you're able to say 'amen,' you're religious!"

Yet through derivation—the proper derivation—he could have found the key to unlock the right answer. For the root of the word *amenable* is found in the French verbs *mener* and *amener*, meaning to lead, to bring to; and so *amenable* means "able to be led," or submissive, responsive, docile. You just have to have the right key!

Not all roots, unfortunately, are as amenable as *greg* or as easily recognizable after their long leap from Latin (or Greek) to English. The Latin root for *to leap*, for example, appears in various guises: as *sal* in *salient*, *sil* in *resilient*, *sault* in *somersault*, *sail* in *assail*, *sult* in *desultory*—and in still another disguise in the word *exult*.

Sometimes, too, confusion arises because roots may look alike. The *ped* of *expedite*, "to get the foot free (*ex*, out of, as from a trap)," to speed up things, comes from the Latin word for *foot*, as do *impede*, *pedestrian*, *pedal*, etc. But the *ped* in *pediatrician* comes from a Greek word for *boy* or *child*, as do *pedagogue*, *orthopedic*, and *encyclopedia*.

Despite these various traps and difficulties in identifying and handling roots, there are compensations. In addition to helping us fix the meaning of words, derivations offer us three fringe benefits:

(1) We often come back with a cluster of words.

(2) We get insights into familiar words. For example *reveal* means "to draw back (*re*) the veil"; a *companion* is one "with (*com*) whom we break *bread* (*pan*, from Latin *panis*)"; to *doff* is "to do off," and to *don* is, of course, "to do on"; *dearth* is nothing more than the word *dear* plus the suffix *th* as in *health*, *wealth*, *truth*, *warmth*, etc. We see, too, how a word that now means only scarcity once meant both dearness and scarcity, thereby suggesting that the law of supply and demand is old—what was scarce soon became dear.

Or let us take a more difficult word like *ineluctable*. It breaks up into *in*, not + *e*, out of + *luct*, struggle or fight + *able*. Put them all together again and we have "not able to struggle out of," hence, inescapable, inevitable. And so the word *ineluctable* has been illuminated, as is the word *reluctant*, which has in it the idea of fighting back (*re*) or struggling against.

(3) Finally, we may learn what a rewarding experience it can be to thumb a ride through a good dictionary. All desk dictionaries are good. The only bad one is the one that isn't used.

As far as the use of dictionaries is concerned, this book has a double purpose: to make you use the dictionary less often but more frequently than you do now. A paradox? Yes. We want you to make fewer trips to the dictionary for words you have looked up before, but we want you to use the dictionary much more often in enlarging your vocabulary and building it much more effectively.

If all you know about a word is its meaning, you do not know the word. If you meet someone unusual, you want to know more than his name; you want to know where he comes from, what he does. It's the same with words. If you know where they come from (their source or provenance, their derivation) and what they do in a sentence, then you know the words. A dictionary sometimes gives you this information. Avail yourself of it every time you can. It is our belief that this is a fascinating and permanent way to learn words.

Though we don't believe in learning lists of words—the hit-and-run method—we nevertheless realize that there are those who have an immediate use for this book because they are preparing for civil service, college board, or teachers' examinations, tests in which vocabulary items loom large. We have therefore devoted a generous portion of this book to word lists, exercises, sentence fill-ins, and analogies in order to satisfy the needs of just such readers. Even they will profit from a careful reading of the body of this book.

When we meet new words we meet them in context, in the company of other words. This context usually gives a clue to the meaning. We are going to say a good deal more about this in the next two chapters, but at this point, to ease you into the tests at the end of this chapter we have selected four sentences that offer no difficulty in comprehension but that include words you might have some trouble in defining if they were presented to you by themselves. To help you even more we will sketch in the background of these sentences. Test yourself on the italicized words, selecting from the four choices given the one that most nearly corresponds in meaning to the word as it is used in the sentence.*

Reporting a baseball game in which the last-place Kansas City Athletics, wearing colorful new uniforms, refused to roll over and play dead for the Yankees, sportswriter Joseph M. Sheehan of *The New York Times* decided to make his opening sentences colorful too:

> With an *unwonted* display of *truculence,* the lowly Athletics thoroughly spoiled the homecoming of the Yankees last night. The vividly *caparisoned* visitors from Kansas City whaled four home pitchers for fourteen hits, while hard-throwing Diego Segui held the Bombers to nine *innocuous* singles.

1. *unwonted*      (a) unaccustomed (b) uncalled for (c) carefree (d) unexpected
2. *truculence*    (a) servility (b) savagery (c) impatience (d) honesty
3. *caparisoned*   (a) flamboyant (b) adorned (c) helmeted (d) outlined
4. *innocuous*     (a) scattered (b) short (c) protected against (d) harmless

The next sentence, from the lively sports column of Arthur Daley, also of *The New York Times*, deals with a tennis controversy.

> The *capitulation* of the Aussie authorities would seem to indicate that any player can *flout* its rules with *impunity* as long as he's also careful enough to star at Wimbledon and thereby prove himself a *sine qua non* for Davis Cup play.

5. *capitulation*  (a) greed (b) headstrong action (c) surrender (d) brief statement
6. *flout*         (a) boast about (b) make a mockery of (c) defend (d) display proudly
7. *impunity*      (a) safety (b) boldness (c) mischievousness (d) embarrassment
8. *sine qua non*  somebody who is (a) disqualified (b) available (c) indispensable (d) remarkable

* Answers to all exercises at ends of chapters and to pretests like this one can be found in the answer section at the back of the book. Answers are identified by chapter and page numbers.

The last sentence, from the *Times* editorial page, deals with a political situation:

> In sharp contrast to the *vituperations*
> of a Vishinsky and the shoe-pounding of
> Premier Khrushchev, Mr. Gromyko was
> mild in tone and, except for a *vitriolic*
> attack on West Germany, *eschewed* the
> language of the cold war.

9. *vituperations*    (a) wild charges (b) insincerities (c) lively exchanges (d) abusive language

10. *vitriolic*    (a) shattering (b) restrained (c) acidulously biting (d) lively

11. *eschewed*    (a) avoided (b) carefully chosen (c) softened (d) denied

## TAKING INVENTORY

And now here is the kind of test that is presented to you on practically all civil service, college board, and teachers' examinations—one hundred words with no context to help you. We took these words from our newspaper reading of the past two years. They do not come from the editorial pages or from music or book or theater or film reviews. We found them all on the sports pages! The fifty in Section A are somewhat easier than the fifty in Section B.

When multiple-choice questions in naked vocabulary are given, as here, you must be careful. Since short definitions (often one-word synonyms) are attempted, what is given may sometimes be only an approximation. That is why this type of question is usually preceded by an instruction like this: "Select the word that you think comes closest to the meaning of the word tested." Sometimes the correct answer is not an exact definition—but it is, of the choices given, the one closest in meaning to the word tested.

Many of the words in this test, especially the more difficult ones, are dealt with in depth elsewhere in this book. All you have to do is look in the index. The word you want may be there.

### A.

1. abjure    (a) curse (b) renounce (c) misjudge (d) disagree

2. adulation    (a) howling sound (b) sincere greeting (c) excessive admiration (d) religious ceremony

3. anachronistic    (a) rebellious (b) timely (c) outdated (d) subversive

4. arbiter    (a) umpire (b) adviser (c) worker (d) tree doctor

5. assiduously    (a) sensitively (b) diligently (c) eagerly (d) bitterly

6. avarice    (a) greediness (b) stinginess (c) meanness (d) wealth

7. beatific    (a) avant-garde (b) helpful (c) blissful (d) smiling

8. bilk    (a) accuse (b) browbeat (c) antagonize (d) swindle

9. bona fide    (a) honorable (b) remunerative (c) well-made (d) genuine

10. colossal    (a) epic (b) gigantic (c) breakable (d) superb

11. conglomeration    (a) exciting display (b) varied mixture (c) deceptive appearance (d) difficult enterprise

12. desultory    (a) useless (b) desperate (c) aimless (d) insulting

13. dexterity    (a) genuineness (b) correctness (c) skill (d) sugar content

14. diffident    (a) shy (b) indifferent (c) fearful (d) lifeless

15. divested    (a) squandered (b) denounced (c) stripped (d) bankrupt

16. doughty    (a) valiant (b) severe (c) devout (d) not thoroughly baked

17. dour    (a) stingy (b) embittered (c) gloomy (d) mean

18. duress    (a) cover (b) difficulty (c) compulsion (d) hardship

19. emanate    (a) disappear (b) issue from (c) give prominence to (d) regurgitate

20. epitome    (a) review (b) criticism (c) written praise (d) embodiment

21. execrable    (a) exceptional (b) abominable (c) painful (d) unbelievable

22. gregarious    (a) talkative (b) generous (c) bold (d) sociable

23. imprecation    (a) evil effect (b) insult (c) forecast (d) curse

24. inarticulate    (a) unable to put into words (b) unclear (c) unesthetic (d) disorganized

25. indomitable      (a) uncomfortable (b) invincible
                     (c) resentful (d) unstable

26. ingenuity        (a) naiveté (b) inventiveness (c) scheme
                     (d) natural wisdom

27. ingratiating     (a) pleasing (b) ungrateful (c) thankful
                     (d) ungracious

28. innate           (a) unfeeling (b) yearly (c) clever
                     (d) inborn

29. maladroitness    (a) dexterity (b) clumsiness
                     (c) wickedness (d) severe illness

30. martinet         (a) small bird (b) teacher (c) severe
                     taskmaster (d) mild disciplinarian

31. mesmerist        (a) sleepwalker (b) ringleader
                     (c) mastermind (d) hypnotist

32. minimal          (a) moderate (b) decreasing
                     (c) simplified (d) least possible

33. mishmash         (a) hodgepodge (b) cooked cereal
                     (c) riffraff (d) helter-skelter

34. moribund         (a) dying (b) delaying (c) malingering
                     (d) pessimistic

35. nemesis          (a) pet abomination (b) avenger
                     (c) threat (d) forgetfulness

36. nostalgia        (a) rheumatism (b) indescribable feeling
                     (c) childish dream (d) sentimental
                     yearning

37. paladin          (a) companion (b) champion of a cause
                     (c) avenger (d) Robin Hood character

38. pariah           (a) false god (b) faithful servant
                     (c) outcast (d) heathen

39. penchant         (a) inclination (b) weakness
                     (c) uncertainty (d) amulet

40. perennial        (a) enduring (b) every other year
                     (c) tough (d) flowery

41. plummeting       (a) flying away (b) sliding (c) feathering
                     (d) plunging

42. pragmatic        (a) unyielding (b) practicable
                     (c) mathematical (d) logical

43. preposterous     (a) absurd (b) enormous (c) vexing
                     (d) putting off

44. rancor           (a) slow decay (b) sadness (c) violence
                     (d) deep-seated hatred

45. redoubtable      (a) unconquerable (b) unquestionable
                     (c) formidable (d) remarkable

46. schism           (a) canyon (b) confusion (c) split
                     (d) hostility

47. sinecure         (a) carefree (b) easy job (c) focus of
                     attention (d) irremediable

48. succinct         (a) concise (b) sullen (c) strict (d) tense

49. tirade    (a) resentment (b) fatigue (c) harangue (d) modest appeal

50. vituperative    (a) lively (b) abusive (c) excessive (d) repetitious

## B.

1. abstruse    (a) hard to understand (b) stupid (c) scattered about (d) thrown away

2. aegis    (a) outlet (b) sponsorship (c) vigilance (d) ancient times

3. apocryphal    (a) temporary (b) exaggerated (c) not genuine (d) fantastic

4. bellwether    (a) flatterer (b) leader (c) mimic (d) humidifier

5. bucolic    (a) rustic (b) seasonal (c) foolish (d) sickly

6. burgeoning    (a) beating up (b) struggling (c) budding (d) uprooting

7. cacophony    (a) climax (b) harsh sound (c) choir (d) strangeness

8. canard    (a) jest (b) coward (c) scoundrel (d) hoax

9. carping    (a) scraping (b) yelling (c) rugged (d) faultfinding

10. chauvinistic    (a) fanatically patriotic (b) boastful (c) irritating (d) hotheaded

11. contretemps    (a) fantasy (b) antagonism (c) embarrassing occurrence (d) timelessness

12. cosset    (a) pamper (b) coax (c) coerce (d) anger

13. coterie    (a) funeral escort (b) elegance (c) sufficiency (d) clique

14. eleemosynary    (a) extravagant (b) slow-moving (c) slimy (d) charitable

15. enclave    (a) peninsula (b) deserted place (c) special enclosed area (d) meeting place

16. esoteric    (a) private (b) strange (c) indifferent (d) selfish

17. euphemism    (a) compliment (b) wise saying (c) pleasanter expression (d) good intention

18. fortuitously    (a) by chance (b) surprisingly (c) entertainingly (d) powerfully

19. furbelow    (a) trick (b) ruffle (c) continued trill (d) weak trait

20. gargantuan    (a) awkward (b) gigantic (c) distorted (d) hoarse

21. gaucherie    (a) awkwardness (b) misery (c) embarrassment (d) stupidity

22. ignominy    (a) frustration (b) disgrace (c) foolishness (d) disguise

23. ineffable    (a) fanciful (b) unpopular (c) untouchable (d) unspeakable

24. inexorable    (a) improbable (b) unavoidable (c) relentless (d) powerful

25. insouciant    (a) unsmiling (b) selfish (c) persistent (d) carefree

26. inviolate    (a) guarded (b) unharmed (c) undecided (d) uncrossed

27. lachrymose    (a) sorry (b) overabundant (c) tearful (d) insufficient

28. machination    (a) signal (b) rigid regulation (c) experiment (d) scheming

29. malefic    (a) evil (b) frightening (c) antagonistic (d) badly organized

30. mendicant    (a) liar (b) beggar (c) pharmacist (d) repairman

31. nascent    (a) significant (b) increasing (c) being born (d) pearly

32. nefarious    (a) tricky (b) completely incredible (c) negligent (d) very wicked

33. neophyte    (a) beginner (b) orthodox follower (c) stranger (d) caveman

34. obfuscation    (a) opposition (b) illusion (c) frustration (d) purposeful confusion

35. ornithology    science dealing with: (a) fish (b) birds (c) spiders (d) domestic animals

36. panache    (a) kind of pastry (b) coat of arms (c) heroic flourish (d) sweet mixture

37. panegyric    a speech that is: (a) all-inclusive (b) laudatory (c) abusive (d) soothing

38. pantheon    (a) hall of fame (b) Greek architecture (c) world court (d) nature worshiper

39. penultimate    (a) final (b) next to last (c) closely related (d) demanding

40. prescience    (a) poise (b) foresight (c) tact (d) punctuality

41. pristine    (a) antiquated (b) unforgettable (c) unspoiled (d) delicate

42. purview    (a) oversight (b) summary (c) panorama (d) jurisdiction

43. ratiocination     (a) communication (b) agreement (c) logical reasoning (d) mathematical concept

44. recondite     (a) obscure (b) penitent (c) forgiven (d) recounted

45. serendipity     (a) tranquility (b) sympathy (c) lucky discovery (d) pleasure

46. supernal     (a) springlike (b) lofty (c) excellent (d) overflowing

47. tenuous     (a) secure (b) slim (c) stubborn (d) shaded

48. transitory     (a) impatient (b) rapid (c) enduring (d) temporary

49. trencherman     (a) ditchdigger (b) hearty eater (c) faithful retainer (d) professional fisherman

50. vernal     (a) majestic (b) green (c) springlike (d) truthful

If you didn't do too well on this test, don't be discouraged. There are several hundred more pages and they all deal with the problem at hand—vocabulary building.

If you did do well, don't go away. There are many more difficult words coming along.

And, oh yes, did you look in the dictionary for the meaning of *supererogatory?* If you didn't, look in the word index of this book.

## ADD AN INITIAL LETTER

Just to relax you after the strenuous test you've just finished, here's a little vocabulary word game for devotees of Scrabble.

Place a letter before each of these words to form the word that has the meaning asked for:

EXAMPLES:    —love    = a spice      ANSWER:   clove
            —edition = treason      ANSWER:   sedition

1. —ache = hide away
2. —action = partisan group
3. —align = slander
4. —allow = left idle
5. —antic = prophetic
6. —arrow = to distress
7. —aunt = haggard
8. —creed = lengthy speech
9. —enchant = inclination
10. —ensure = blame
11. —hard = fragment of pottery
12. —hasten = punish
13. —light = predicament
14. —lithe = joyous
15. —lout = defy
16. —oath = reluctant
17. —pate = a flood
18. —poor = trace
19. —rate = angry

20. _raven = coward
21. _relate = church dignitary
22. _rite = hackneyed
23. _rivet = metal stand
24. _rode = wear away
25. _roll = amusing
26. _rope = figure of speech
27. _toll = coral island
28. _trident = harsh sounding
29. _trophy = wither away
30. _thwart = across

# 2. One Day with a Newspaper

> POLONIUS: *What do you read, my lord?*
> HAMLET: *Words, words, words.*
> POLONIUS: *What is the matter, my lord?*
> HAMLET: *Between who?*
> POLONIUS: *I mean the matter that you read, my lord.*
>
> WILLIAM SHAKESPEARE, *Hamlet*

The words that follow appeared in one column (page 8) of *The New York Times* of December 12, 1963. The headline of the news item was CONGRESS DEFERS REFORMING ITSELF.

See how well you can do with these words stripped of their context (arranged in the order in which we met them). It might be a good idea to reread the instructions given in Chapter 1 about these multiple-choice tests.

1. defers — (a) rejects (b) considers (c) postpones (d) disagrees about
2. cumbersome — (a) restful (b) unwieldy (c) inflexible (d) permissive
3. ironically — (a) paradoxically (b) stiffly (c) firmly (d) heatedly
4. proponents — (a) separate parts (b) advocates (c) followers (d) instigators
5. peripheral — (a) sentimentally important (b) circumstantial (c) fleeting (d) marginal
6. arcane — (a) mysterious (b) ancient (c) unintelligible (d) frightening
7. impede — (a) speed up (b) destroy (c) weaken (d) block
8. truncated — (a) stowed away (b) elaborated (c) curtailed (d) rigid
9. unassailable — (a) honorable (b) unquestionable (c) hard to figure out (d) remarkable

28

10. prerogative    (a) privilege (b) duty (c) obligation
                           (d) former assignment
11. germaneness    (a) sterility (b) strangeness (c) respect
                           (d) pertinence
12. derided    (a) envied (b) shouted down (c) ridiculed
                           (d) offset

Don't look now to find out how many of these definitions you got right. Later in this chapter we're going to put these words back in their context and you will see how much easier it will then be to select the correct answer. Right now just go on reading.

When Paul Bessel was thirteen, he had a problem. He stated it in a letter to the New York *World-Telegram and Sun*.

"Recently my English teacher," he wrote, "gave me an assignment to find the words *lengthy* and *pragmatic* fifteen times each by the end of this week. Please use these words immediately. I will be counting on you. Thank you very much."

On April 27, 1962, there appeared the following headline in the newspaper Paul had appealed to:

**Homework Problem Solved**
**We Wouldn't Fail You, Paul, For Words**
Yes, Paul, you may count on us, though the time limit fixed by your English teacher imposes on you and our writers and columnists a heavy burden. Pragmatic men and women they are but given to lengthy consultations.

The writer then went on ingeniously to ring fourteen more changes on *lengthy* and *pragmatic*, although the fifteenth attempt, "How many times, Paul, did you have to find *lengthy* and *pragmatic?*" wasn't exactly cricket.

Though we dissociate ourselves from the kind of assignment given (except to point out that the teacher did want to have the children see the words used), there is something to be said for Paul's appeal to a newspaper to help bail him out.

Because that's exactly what we have done. We had a problem, too. We had to find words for this book, words of some difficulty, words that were being *used*. So we took to heart the English teacher's assignment and gave it to ourselves. We decided to read what most of you were reading over the past few years but we read with a purpose other than that of merely getting the news. Equipped with red pencils, scissors, and index cards, we set out on a safari to hunt down useful words—most useful, because wherever possible, we were going to present them in the sentences in which we found them. We wanted to bring them back alive in their natural habitat. For we believe with Emily Dickinson in the poem reprinted at the beginning of this book that a word "just begins to live when it is said" (or written) in a meaningful context.

We had another reason for going to the newspapers. We wanted to bring back sentences illustrating the unself-conscious use of words in authentic experience. To use a word significantly in a sentence—on demand—when neither the need nor the situation exists is not easy. You have to create a situation. You become self-conscious. A mental censor steps in to save you from committing yourself, and you come up with a flat, neutral, bland, bloodless, and noncommittal sentence like, "Have you seen any aborigines lately?"

By the way, the answer to that question is, "Yes, we've seen a great many aborigines lately." In a dispatch from Darwin, Australia, appearing in *The New York Times* on January 9, 1964, under the headline

### Ranchers Fight Move to Let Australia Aborigines Get Liquor

the word *aborigines* appears exactly fifteen times. How happy this would have made Paul and his English teacher. Fifteen times! The explanation for this frequency is easy. There just is no substitute for *aborigines* in this context. Some Australians interviewed in the news story used the word *native,* but *native* is not really a synonym for *aborigine.* In this particular case a native is anyone who is Australian born (from Latin *natus,* meaning born, yielding such words as *innate,* inborn; the *Nativity,* Christ's birth; *naive,* as innocent as on the day when one is born). But an *aborigine* is one whose ancestors were there *ab origine,* Latin for "from the beginning." Again you can see how useful derivation can sometimes be.

Thus we are very happy that we can use sentences from newspapers, because even authors of books on vocabulary become self-conscious when they make up their own illustrative sentences. In the treatment of the meaning of the word *fatuous,* for example, we have come across this sentence made up as an illustration:

"His fatuous behavior made me dislike him intensely."

Not quite so bad as, "Have you seen any aborigines lately?"

How much better are these two sentences from *The New York Times:*

> He also warned that it was "quite fatuous to suppose that all is well with the world simply because Communist China and the Soviet Union are now at odds."

* * *

> For ten years candidates have been going through the big food bazaars grinning fatuously and shaking hands with astounded females in the dubious belief that somehow this would assure the women's vote.

*Fatuous,* as can be seen from this context, means silly, foolish, but Webster's Third adds the qualification "especially marked by ill-founded hope or desire." The word comes alive in the newspaper sentences quoted. Why? Because the speaker in one case or the writer in the other wanted to express his thought. He did not make up a fatuous sentence on demand. The word in the sentence from the vocabulary book was factitious (remember?), artificial, made up. There's a certain free-flowing immediacy about words used in newspapers. Ideas have to be banged out quickly, precisely, and, if possible, vividly.

No matter how old the news in the sentences we use may have become by the time you read this book, the words will still be alive. Besides there may be some left-over, residual interest or perhaps a stray bit of interesting information—all of which will serve as so much lagniappe.*

Now let's get back to the dozen isolated words you tested yourself on and see how much easier they become when we restore them to the words in whose company they appeared in the news column, for words, like people, are known by the company they keep.

## 1. CONGRESS DEFERS REFORMING ITSELF

The first sentence begins, "Among the important items of unfinished business that Congress is putting over until next

---

* Whenever we use an unusual word that may not be known to you, you can turn to a dictionary or to the index of this book. Such words generally receive special treatment somewhere in this book.

year. . . ." In the context, "putting over until next year" takes care of *defers.*\*

2. Many critics contend that Congress's methods of doing business, which have not been modernized in a century, are too *cumbersome.*

3, 4. *Ironically,* such instances of one-man or minority control of the legislative process are among the conditions that (4) *proponents* of reform most wanted to correct. (Farther down, the phrase "advocates of reform" occurs.)

5. They declared that the action exempted the main targets of any reform effort and left for study only such *peripheral* subjects as relationship between the two houses. . . .

6. The rules and parliamentary procedures of the two houses are a complex and *arcane* code that has been built up without substantial modification or systematization in more than a hundred years.

7. In the hands of a determined minority, the right to unlimited debate can be used to *impede* the work of Congress.

8. Senator Clark agreed reluctantly that the *truncated* version of their measure was better than none at all.

9, 10. They were referred to the House Rules Committee and there pigeonholed—a virtually *unassailable prerogative* of the committee chairman.

11. One proposal would enforce a rule of *germaneness* in Senate debate for a limited number of hours each day.

12. It was *derided* by Everett McKinley Dirksen of Illinois as an attempt to force "second-class citizenship" on Senators.

It is obvious that reading will help you to increase your vocabulary—even without resort to a dictionary—because the context often helps to reveal the meaning. That's the way most of us have acquired whatever vocabulary we have. It is a slow process, but it can be accelerated if—but that *if* will be developed in the next chapter.

## I.  ONE DAY'S BAG OF WORDS

Meanwhile here is one day's bag of words—when the hunting was good—from the pages of *The New York Times* (Monday, January 13, 1964). Lest you think we've done all our hunting on the editorial pages or in book or drama reviews, we are giving the page (in parentheses) on which each word

---

\* After each sentence, look back at choices given in the pretest and check your answers.

appeared. As a matter of interest, seven of the more difficult words appeared on the sports pages (28–31). Because we are giving you context wherever it is helpful, you may find the definitions a little more difficult and you may have to be more selective in your choice because you will have to define each word as used in the passage given.

Before you begin this exercise, it may help you to know that the major news items published on this day included the Panama crisis, the revolution in Zanzibar, the rising tensions between the Arab states and Israel over pumping water from the Sea of Galilee, an account of the economic depression areas in the North Woods region, and the publication of the Federal report on the harmful effects of cigarette smoking, along with the reactions of the tobacco industry, the retailers, and the consumers.

Alphabetically we begin with this lovely sentence—an answer a cigarette-smoking woman gave to a reporter who had asked her whether she intended to stop smoking:

1. My husband bugs me *ad infinitum*.   (p. 21)
   (a) at home (b) at will (c) forever (d) occasionally

2. Irrigational canals provide *arable* land.   (p. 34)
   (a) abundant (b) plowable (c) suitable (d) desertlike

3. demanded amendment of the existing *archaic* situation (p. 34)
   (a) confused (b) principal (c) antiquated (d) worsening

4. *atavistic* return to the cook-fire at the mouth of the cave (p. 34)
   (a) ancestral (b) religious (c) invisible (d) senseless

5. the most *bellicose* of the rowdy crowd   (p. 31)
   (a) attractive (b) intractable (c) noisy (d) pugnacious

6. Is it not dangerously easy to become *bemused* by the facile appeal?   (p. 34)
   (a) subdued (b) entertained (c) stupefied (d) distracted

7. the *blighted* villages tucked away in the folds of Kentucky's Cumberland mountains   (p. 22)
   (a) ruined (b) uninhabited (c) fortunate (d) isolated

8. There was something *charismatic* about Keats. His family idolized him; his friends, including his publishers, were consistently loyal.   (p. 33)
   (a) unctuous (b) religious (c) enigmatic (d) appealingly attractive

9. action *contingent on* two conditions  (p. 1)
    (a) adjacent to (b) provided for (c) improving
      (d) dependent upon

10. enthusiastic preparations for a *convivial* meeting of East and West at the 25th International Skoal Congress.  (p. 12)
    (a) festive (b) friendly (c) joking (d) cooperative

11. The split *culminated* in the banning of the left-wing group. (p. 9)
    (a) fell apart (b) interfered (c) reached its climax
      (d) instigated

12. Today there is no *dearth* of candidates for relief.  (p. 22)
    (a) fear (b) care (c) need (d) paucity

13. stripped of its timber and facing *depletion* of its iron ore (p. 1)
    (a) doubling (b) total destruction (c) expropriation
      (d) exhaustion

14. ghostly and silent over the *desolate* land  (p. 1)
    (a) arid (b) sunless (c) forsaken (d) congealed

15. Once again the *dichotomy*—what a university seems to be and what the university really is—has been made sadly apparent.  (p. 26)
    (a) comparison (b) betrayal (c) doubt (d) two-part
      division

16. being *dilatory* with problems in our own backyard  (p. 34)
    (a) careless (b) procrastinating (c) inflated (d) diverted

17. Moscow appears *discomfited* because the Panama crisis broke out just as Premier Khrushchev had initiated a major new peace offensive.  (p. 15)
    (a) uncomfortable (b) peevish (c) disconcerted
      (d) disappointed

18. There has also been a sharp increase in the amount of *disinterested* research into smoking.  (p. 20)
    (a) impartial (b) apathetic (c) unproductive
      (d) contradictory

19. so *egregious* an oversight  (p. 31)
    (a) trifling (b) important (c) flagrant (d) socially wrong

20. The distance from the border led to *erroneous* interpretations.  (p. 14)
    (a) exaggerated (b) mistaken (c) untruthful (d) biased

21. a blunt *exhortation* to remember  (p. 25)
    (a) reminder (b) message (c) denunciation (d) urging

22. the political *exigencies* of the Presidential year   (p. 17)
    (a) pressing needs (b) extremities (c) poor excuses
    (d) unnecessary delays

23. by the *facile* appeal of the term "internationally guaranteed access route to Berlin"   (p. 34)
    (a) artificial (b) glib (c) sensitive (d) seductive

24. The creation of a new public agency to take over community services is both *feasible* and desirable.   (p. 34)
    (a) fashionable (b) attractive (c) inexpensive
    (d) practicable

25. midst the din of divorce statistics and headline *hedonism* (p. 21)
    (a) lack of religious feeling (b) pleasure-seeking (c) rioting
    (d) sensationalism

26. *immutable* as the tide   (34)
    (a) outspoken (b) restless (c) unchanging (d) stubborn

27. her *impeccable* vocal technique   (p. 26)
    (a) displeasing (b) remarkable (c) unbelievable
    (d) flawless

28. suspected of having *incited* riots or looting   (p. 14)
    (a) participated in (b) secretly planned (c) incorrectly quoted (d) fomented

29. the conflict between the Arabs, who make up about 15 per cent of the 307,000 population, and the *indigenous* Africans (p. 9)
    (a) native (b) wicked (c) lazy (d) poverty-stricken

30. to assist the defense of *indigent* criminal suspects   (p. 12)
    (a) native (b) wicked (c) lazy (d) poverty-stricken

\*      \*      \*

31. censorship in its most *insidious* form   (p. 26)
    (a) wily (b) objectionable (c) unsettled (d) frightening

32. One of the *ironies* of the relationship between TV programming and tobacco advertising is that all of the medium's highly popular "medical shows" are sponsored at least in part by cigarette companies.   (p. 21)
    (a) surprises (b) solid virtues (c) seeming contradictions
    (d) solutions

33. to underline its support of South Vietnam's military *junta* (p. 11)
    (a) ruling council (b) segment (c) one-man rule
    (d) director

34. allowed *latent* trouble to fester   (p. 34)
    (a) dormant (b) delayed (c) obvious (d) unknown

35. The Rockefeller Foundation has been *maligned* and our casts and directors insulted.   (p. 26)
    (a) embittered (b) threatened (c) slandered (d) cursed

36. The primitive campfire has *metamorphosed* into an infra-red device that cooks without perceptible heat.   (p. 34)
    (a) vanished (b) been enlarged (c) been eliminated
       (d) been transformed

37. a *miniscule* bit of research   (p. 31)
    (a) negative (b) basic (c) untrustworthy (d) insignificant

38. The *mystique* of the criminal, the worshiper of evil, is not new in French literature.   (p. 33)
    (a) enigma (b) special mysterious aura (c) religious fervor
       (d) puzzling characterization

39. Their rhythms are generally tidy; their *nuances* are agreed upon.   (p. 25)
    (a) disturbances (b) cloud formations (c) shadings
       (d) innovations

40. helped to make some fans *oblivious to* the cold   (p. 28)
    (a) stupefied by (b) unmindful of (c) eager for
       (d) satisfied with

41. rapidly becoming *obsolescent*   (p. 34)
    (a) outmoded (b) unsolvable (c) fixed (d) disintegrated

42. This tower [judges of candidates for election to baseball's Hall of Fame] of *omniscience*   (p. 31)
    (a) confusion (b) integrity (c) infinite knowledge
       (d) significance

43. what Big Steel calls *onerous* iron-ore taxation   (p. 22)
    (a) worthy (b) unfair (c) burdensome (d) possessive

44. a joyous *paean* of emancipation   (p. 25)
    (a) song of celebration (b) symbol (c) praise (d) example

45. The chopped feathery green leaves of fennel add color and *piquancy* to sauces.   (p. 27)
    (a) pleasantly sharp flavor (b) daintiness (c) fragrance
       (d) nutty flavor

46. sang the *poignant* spiritual "Is Massa Gwine to Sell Us To-morrow?"   (p. 25)
    (a) bellicose (b) deeply moving (c) tender (d) sentimental

47. a *portent* that despite all conciliatory U. N. efforts the Middle East remains a dangerous powder keg   (p. 34)
    (a) omen (b) promise (c) charge (d) possibility

48. often *pretentious* and silly    (p. 33)
    (a) ostentatious (b) false (c) childish (d) petty

49. A cigarette has become a small *procrastination* before a difficult task.    (p. 20)
    (a) forewarning (b) problem (c) postponement
       (d) incentive

50. the haunting, *pungent* and pleasant flavor of anise    (p. 27)
    (a) strange (b) delicate (c) sharp (d) overpowering

51. a general *recapitulation* of earlier findings    (p. 1)
    (a) withdrawal (b) restatement (c) denial (d) surrender

52. Mr. Price's *resonant* baritone    (p. 25)
    (a) polished (b) powerful (c) sonorous (d) strained

53. keeping tight control over a *restive* population    (p. 3)
    (a) remaining (b) apathetic (c) detained (d) balky

54. touched on a *salient* issue in French politics    (p. 10)
    (a) troublesome (b) touchy (c) outstanding (d) wholesome

55. the first *salvo* [on the cigarette issue] was expected to come from the Federal Trade Commission.    (p. 10)
    (a) volley (b) soothing word (c) safeguard (d) attention

56. out of consideration of American, if not Arab *sensibilities*. (p. 6)
    (a) good sense (b) sensitivity (c) consent (d) sentiments

57. Their [Arab states'] dream of annihilating Israel in a second combat round is still a pet Arab *shibboleth*.    (p. 34)
    (a) objective (b) fear (c) slogan (d) desire

58. lock themselves in for their one-week *simulated* voyage to the moon    (p. 7)
    (a) hoped for (b) likely (c) instigated (d) exactly imitated

59. one killed and another wounded by *sporadic* firing    (p. 14)
    (a) accidental (b) nervous (c) full-fledged (d) occasional

60.       **Symposium* on the Theater
          Set Monday at the Lambs**    (p. 24)
    (a) wild party (b) discussion (c) lecture (d) reading

61. *Tentative* agreement on the plan was disclosed.    (p. 1)
    (a) definitive (b) attempted (c) provisional (d) slight

62. urging the Legislature to *transcend* political considerations (p. 17)
    (a) bow down to (b) rise above (c) ignore (d) reconsider

We know that some of the words given as definitions are more difficult than the words to be defined. But that's just another way of increasing your stock of words—if you consult a dictionary.

## II. A NEWSPAPER IS SOMETIMES A DICTIONARY

When an unusual word appears in a newspaper headline or news story you will often find that its meaning is made clear —or some clue to its meaning is given—in what immediately follows.

For example here's a headline from *The New York Times* of August 27, 1964:

> **Pontiff Says Some *Tenets*
> of Peace Are "Crumbling"**

And here's the first sentence of the news story:

> Pope Paul VI, in a vibrant appeal for
> peace, said that "some of the basic prin-
> ciples of peace were crumbling."

It's very easy to see that *tenets* equals "basic principles."

Sometimes only a clue—but a very definite one—may be given.

> **NATO Is Cautious
> on New *Detente***

> The Western allies are in a cautious
> mood about the possibility of agreement
> with the Soviet Union in further moves
> to reduce East-West tensions.

The clue words are obviously *reduce* and *tensions* so that *detente* means relaxation, or easing, of tensions.

But on occasion—especially when a new word or one just coming into prominence is being used—the news story will actually supply a definition.

> The doctors also told of other promis-
> ing uses of *cryosurgery*—that is, tech-
> niques involving use of extreme cold to
> "kill" diseased tissue instead of cutting it
> away.

*Cryosurgery* appears in neither Webster's Second nor Webster's Third. From the Greek combining form *cry(o)*, icy cold, also comes *cryotherapy*, treatment of pain by use of cold.

Here are twenty fairly unusual words so presented. Select from the passages given the word or words that make clear the meaning of the words italicized. You can check your answers, as usual, in the back of the book.

1.              **Senators Bitter
              at Debate Limit**

An air of *acrimony* pervaded the usually placid Senate today as Senators chafed under an unusual limitation of debate.

2.              In his lighter moments T. S. Eliot was an unabashed *ailurophile*. He kept cats at home, bestowing upon them such names as Man in White Spats.

3.              His play was attracting and repelling the customers in that not infrequent *ambivalence* which fills theaters.

4.              ***Amnesty* Is Announced**

Perhaps the best news was that several thousand prisoners had been pardoned.

5.              He is so reactionary a conservative as to be a political *anachronism* out of step with the times we live in.

6.              I am attracted to *autodidacts*. We must all, without exception, educate ourselves.

7.              The evidence of such fraud was indisputable. We are going to see that such *chicanery* doesn't happen again.

8.              **De Gaulle Shakes Off
              Potential *Contretemps***

President De Gaulle averted a potentially embarrassing diplomatic incident last night by ignoring it.

9.
### *Distaff* Drivers
### Called Terrifying

A Briton has been following women drivers around for three months studying female driving habits.

"Terrifying," he reports.

10.
### Sullen Strikers
### Return in Spain

Today 4,000 more *dour*-faced miners returned to their pits.

11.
### A Land of *Euphemism*

There are elaborately genteel phrases for every delicate subject. Repressive actions without court proceedings are "administrative measures."

12.
### Thailand Official *Exhorts* U.S.
### to Hold Firm in Vietnam Crisis

Thanat Khoman, Foreign Minister of Thailand, urged today that the United States stand firm against the Communist insurgents in South Vietnam.

13.
### Council at *Impasse*
### on Cyprus Proposal

A deadlock over the terms of a proposed resolution prevented the Security Council today from taking action on the extension of the mandate.

14.
### Rare *Incunabula*
### Offered for Sale

Rare early printed books—books printed in Italy in the 1480's—will be auctioned tomorrow at the Parke-Bernet Galleries.

15.

He was placed under an *interdict*—forbidden to receive the sacrament—by Archbishop Michael Gonzi.

16.          He called both *"lethal"* because "they
             play deadly games on the brink of dis-
             aster."

17.                   **Coin Collectors**
                    **Gather in Jersey**

             *Numismatists* from twelve states
             gathered yesterday at the underground
             auditorium of the Bergen Mall.

18.          Here was the *panacea* they long had
             sought. Here was the one formation [in
             football] that could cure all ills.

19.          **Soviet Cadet a *Scion* of Prince**

             A descendant of Prince Michael Bar-
             clay de Tolly, one of Czar Alexander I's
             generals who defeated Napoleon in 1812,
             is a Soviet Army student officer.

20.          **Political *Tyro* Finds Zeal Alone**
             **Is Not Enough for a Campaign**

             This is particularly true for the rookie
             who has neither an established organiza-
             tion nor a name that commands news-
             paper space.

*I still consult the O. E. D. at least four or five times a day,
never letting a doubtful word go by; I need to know its derivation, its first occurrence, its change of meaning down the centuries, and the sort of people who used it in different contexts.*

      Robert Graves, "The Poet in a Valley of Dry Bones,"
                Horizon, March 1963

*One may become fascinated by a dictionary. One turns up
one word, and then finds oneself following, as it were, a chain
of thought.*

Michael Harrison, "The Mystery of the Fulton Documents,"
Ellery Queen's Mystery Magazine, September 1965

## 3.   A Week with a Book

> *Every line bristled with many-syllabled
> words he did not understand. He sat up in
> bed, and the dictionary was in front of him
> more often than the book. He looked up so
> many new words that when they recurred,
> he had forgotten their meaning and had to
> look them up again. He devised the plan of
> writing the definitions in a note-book and
> filled page after page with them.*
>
> JACK LONDON, *Martin Eden*

How did you acquire the words you now know? Most of
you probably learned them from the sense they made in sentences you read or heard. By sheer weight of encounter, repetition, and association, the words gradually sank into your
consciousness. Words came to you. You learned them pas-
sively. But you can also learn them actively. You can go out
in search of them.

If you're really serious about increasing your vocabulary,
you will have to make vocabulary building a hobby, an absorb-
ing interest, or even an obsession as it was with Martin Eden
and, understandably, with his creator, Jack London. In *Sailor
on Horseback*, Irving Stone tells us how for Jack London "one
of the greatest things in the world was words, beautiful words,
musical words, strong and sharp and incisive words." London
always had a dictionary at hand. He would write new words
on pieces of paper and hang them where he could see them
while dressing or string them on a line with clothespins so he
could study them. Jack London wanted aggressively to increase
his vocabulary. He thought he needed to learn words to
become a writer. Words were his stock in trade.

## WORD COLLECTORS

But even those who merely make a hobby of word collecting sometimes develop interesting techniques. There's Mrs. Chester Hargreaves of Severance, a small village in the Adirondacks, in whose kitchen we stepped one day last summer. Over her kitchen sink was a slate, the kind that housewives might use to remind them of purchases to be made, but on the slate we didn't find the expected "potatoes," "flour," "lamb chops." What Mrs. Hargreaves was looking at while she washed her dishes was:

> chimera—an impossible or foolish fancy
> chimerical—imaginary, fantastic, unreal, visionary, impossible
> endemic—prevalent in a particular nation, group or locality, indigenous, native
> cabal—a small group of persons joined in a secret design or scheme, junta, a plot

Fascinated, we asked her where she had got the words for her slate.

"Oh, generally from my reading."

"*Cabal*, too?"

"No, I got *cabal* from a speech made the other night at the Republican convention."

"And your definitions?"

"I copied them from my desk dictionary—a good one—which I got with green stamps!"

Her interest in words, she added, had rubbed off on her husband, who pasted words on the bathroom mirror so he could study them while shaving. (He uses an electric razor.)

Then, too, there's the method used by a friend of ours. When he reads, he folds a large sheet of paper into a book to serve both as a bookmark and as a place for listing—with their page and line numbers—words that he has some question about. After he has finished reading for the day, he looks up the words, relates them to their context, and tries in some way to fix them in his mind.

Therefore, if you want to add to your store of words, you too must read with a purpose. When you come across new or unfamiliar words, STOP. Then LOOK around to see whether the text helps to reveal their meaning. If the context doesn't give

you first aid, LIST THEM. Sometimes perhaps, you will LOOK
them up in a dictionary. When you do, find some way to fix
their meaning or your trip to the dictionary will be wasted. It
might even be a good idea to LIST THEM after you've looked
them up. The list you make of words you've actually met in
your reading is worth a great deal more than any list made
for you. It's connected with your interests; it's associated with
your ideas; it's yours. And it will stick. STOP, LOOK, AND LIST
THEM.

In the judgment of all authorities, the three best ways of
improving your vocabulary are:

Read!        READ!!        READ!!!

To which we want to add one bit of advice: Read with a pencil
nearby and a dictionary in the offing.

We have done this kind of reading for you, in a classic written over a hundred years ago, and we made note of some of
the useful words. If you have read Dickens's *Great Expectations*, you may nostalgically recognize some of the names and
situations; if you haven't read it, we strongly recommend that
you do. Meanwhile all you have to do is add a little thought
and ingenuity and see how many right answers you can give
in the test based on *Great Expectations*.

## I. WORDS FROM *GREAT EXPECTATIONS*
### A.

Here are ten words arranged in alphabetical order. Put
them back into the context Dickens gave them:

| | |
|---|---|
| a. ablutions | f. disparagement |
| b. adjured | g. ignominiously |
| c. choleric | h. refractory |
| d. contumaciously | i. suppliants |
| e. cupidity | j. vicariously |

1. All the times she had wished me in my grave, and I had
_____ refused to go there.
2. He knew all kinds of things to my _____, if he
only chose to mention them.
3. Hereupon, a _____ gentleman flew into a most
violent passion.
4. I _____ Provis to sit quite still, wrapped in his
cloak.
5. I soon found myself heavily bumped from behind and having
my face _____ shoved against the kitchen wall.

6. My _____ completed, I was put into clean linen.
7. Mr. Wemmick and I parted at the office where
   _____ for Mr. Jagger's notice were lingering about as usual.
8. My sister, having so much to do, was going to church
   _____. That is to say Joe and I were going.
9. These people [the hopeful heirs of Pip's patroness] hated me with the hatred of _____ and disappointment.
10. This part of course was lightened by several single combats between Biddy and [her] _____ students.

## B.

Here are forty more words with partial context from *Great Expectations.* You are to select among the choices given the one that most nearly gives the meaning of the italicized word *as used in the excerpt.*

1. in some gloomy *aberration* of mind
   (a) injury (b) wandering (c) misunderstanding (d) change

2. pledged myself to comfort and *abet* Herbert in the affair of the heart
   (a) console (b) advise (c) assist (d) have confidence in

3. My obstinacy was *adamantine.*
   (a) primitive (b) immovable (c) misunderstood (d) temporary

4. My depression was not *alleviated* by the announcement.
   (a) lessened (b) completely cured (c) increased (d) curtailed

5. remarking that things that are man-traps were not among the *amenities* of life
   (a) religious manifestations (b) dangers (c) civilities (d) excitements

6. most strongly *asseverates*
   (a) separates (b) denies (c) affirms (d) believes

7. greatly *augmented* my curiosity
   (a) aroused (b) satisfied (c) diverted (d) increased

8. *beguile* the time . . . with conversation
   (a) drag out (b) pass pleasantly (c) waste (d) bedevil

9. Biddy was never *capricious,* or Biddy today and somebody else tomorrow.
   (a) changeable (b) enchanting (c) wild (d) willfully obstinate

10. for which *cogent* reason I kept Biddy at a distance
    (a) plausible (b) clearly defined (c) convincing (d) characteristic

11. *commiserating* my sister . . . for the trouble I was to her
    (a) making miserable (b) praising (c) rebuking (d) pitying

12. exhausted by the *debilitating* effects — (a) destructive (b) enfeebling (c) immoral (d) uncertain

13. supervising me with a *depreciatory* eye — (a) supercilious (b) disparaging (c) disappointed (d) profound

14. *descrying* traces of Miss Havisham and Stella all over — (a) objecting to (b) following (c) observing (d) drawing

15. a stately house . . . but *dolefully* in want of painting — (a) hardly (b) desperately (c) only slightly (d) woefully

16. without *evincing* any inclination to come in again — (a) overcoming (b) shrinking from (c) manifesting (d) directing

17. where the *festooned* sails might fly in the wind — (a) badly torn (b) garlanded (c) tied down (d) rigid

18. lived *frugally* and paid my debts — (a) lavishly (b) fearfully (c) austerely (d) selfishly

19. a *gibbet* with some chains hanging to it which had once held a pirate — (a) scaffold (b) mainmast (c) platform (d) gallows

20. considered the subject of the day's *homily* ill chosen — (a) discussion (b) entertainment (c) fable (d) sermon

21. I became *imbued* with the notion. — (a) angered (b) distressed (c) inspired (d) emboldened

22. muttering impatient *imprecations* at [his fetters] — (a) curses (b) objections (c) vulgarities (d) epithets

23. a keen sense of *incongruity* — (a) humor (b) revulsion (c) inappropriateness (d) consistency

24. proceeded to *indite* a note to Biddy — (a) prepare (b) write (c) send (d) promise

25. In a sulky triumph Drummle showed his *morose* depreciation of the rest of us. — (a) bitter (b) silent (c) enlarged (d) sullen

26. quite still and silent and apparently quite *obdurate* — (a) adamant (b) uncertain (c) resentful (d) hostile

27. The articles were carried *ostentatiously*. — (a) with difficulty (b) conspicuously (c) symmetrically (d) strangely

28. in a *paroxysm* of terror — (a) convulsion (b) chill (c) fever (d) pretense

29. acquisition of *plebeian* domestic knowledge — (a) unpleasant (b) rudimentary (c) complete (d) common

30. with *prolix* conversations about nothing — (a) agreeable (b) dull (c) intense (d) long-winded

31. with a *ravenous* intensity     (a) maddening (b) bold (c) voracious (d) selfish

32. scratching his head in a *rueful* manner at sight of his accumulating figures     (a) puzzled (b) mournful (c) troubled (d) indecisive

33. Joe said after some *rumination*     (a) hesitation (b) compensation (c) reflection (d) concentration

34. a favorite *supposititious* case of his     (a) underhand (b) hypothetical (c) desirable (d) controversial

35. "Why don't you know?" said Mr. Pumblechook *testily*.     (a) proudly (b) irritably (c) pompously (d) quizzically

36. not a *tithe* or a twentieth part     (a) tenth (b) infinitesimal (c) significant (d) indefinite

37. to be a *toady* and a humbug     (a) rogue (b) mimic (c) impostor (d) sycophant

38. *vacillating* weakly     (a) journeying (b) attempting (c) wavering (d) concealing

39. indulged in other *vagaries*     (a) wild behavior (b) diversions (c) odd actions (d) indefinite procedures

40. a house which I then quite *venerated*     (a) remembered clearly (b) visited often (c) suspected (d) revered

## II. FROM A CONTEMPORARY NOVEL

When you read some contemporary novels, you will find the words we selected from Dickens almost elementary. For example, here are some words we found in *Night and Silence Who Is Here?* by Pamela Hansford Johnson:

*anorexia, hebephrenia, houselled, meiosis, mescalined, nayword, mesomorphically,* and *peridot.*

We thought these and some more like them too "far out" for this book, but from the listing we made we have salvaged the following words, principally for those who are preparing for difficult academic or civil service tests:

1. avatar     (a) temple (b) embodiment (c) ancestor (d) flying object

2. dimity     (a) obscurity (b) half portion (c) cotton fabric (d) consistency

3. effete    (a) effeminate (b) wornout (c) athletic (d) cowardly

4. glaucous    (a) smooth (b) sticky (c) pale green (d) bright

5. lubricious    (a) lecherous (b) oiled (c) glowing (d) determined

6. minatory    (a) reducing (b) trivial (c) amenable (d) menacing

7. objurgation    (a) objection (b) taking of an oath (c) obstacle (d) violent criticism

8. ogival    (a) eight-sided (b) of a former era (c) Gothic in style (d) dovetailed

9. phthysical    (a) tubercular (b) catlike (c) muscular (d) philosophical

10. pusillanimity    (a) mean-spirited cowardice (b) ill health (c) frivolity (d) lack of agreement

11. putative    (a) thoughtful (b) rightful (c) commonly supposed (d) respected

12. susurrated    (a) enclosed (b) guaranteed (c) sweated out (d) whispered

(Some of these words will be taken up in later chapters. You will find similar repetitions of a number of words treated in different ways throughout the book.)

## III. FROM VARIOUS SOURCES

As a final exercise, here, in partial context, are forty more words from our recent reading of books and magazine articles.

1. an *admonitory* gesture keeping them back    (a) violent (b) stern (c) warning (d) conciliatory

2. after an hour of *bootless* attempts    (a) barefoot (b) unavailing (c) unceasing (d) frustrating

3. *burnishing* the statuette with affectionate hands    (a) polishing (b) singeing (c) cleaning (d) brushing

4. his long *cadaverous* face    (a) wrinkled (b) haggard (c) sensitive (d) somber

5. *cajoling* him away from the sandpile    (a) coercing (b) rudely brushing (c) politely asking (d) coaxing

6. characteristically
   *chimerical* schemes
   (a) tentative (b) scientific (c) visionary (d) miraculous

7. an intolerable and
   *consummate* rascal
   (a) complete (b) scheming (c) overbearing (d) grasping

8. listening with *corrugated* brows
   (a) anxious (b) narrow (c) lifted (d) furrowed

9. a *craven* abandoning his post
   (a) sentinel (b) base villain (c) coward (d) supernumerary

10. speaking softly and *deferentially*
    (a) carelessly (b) indifferently (c) respectfully (d) apologetically

11. *dexterously* parrying the thrust
    (a) rightly (b) adroitly (c) viciously (d) revengefully

12. a huge book, *diffuse* and formless
    (a) unusual (b) rambling (c) argumentative (d) incisive

13. a complete *dossier* of his activities
    (a) analysis (b) repudiation (c) failure (d) documented file

14. his weak, *emaciated* body
    (a) badly scratched (b) paralyzed (c) skinny (d) partly healed

15. great legal and *forensic* skill
    pertaining to: (a) prophecy (b) public debate (c) outdoors (d) mechanics

16. laughing at our incredible *gullibility*
    (a) stupidity (b) credulity (c) objective (d) cupidity

17. hoping for world *hegemony*
    (a) regimen (b) vastness (c) dominance (d) popularity

18. accepting their *homage* very modestly
    (a) hospitality (b) respect (c) ovation (d) flattery

19. a *homogeneity* of outlook
    (a) diversity (b) unspoiled freshness (c) similarity (d) stubbornness

20. safe in his *impregnable* fortress
    (a) impressive (b) unmolested (c) lofty (d) unassailable

21. *inferring* much from the look on her face
    (a) concluding (b) imagining (c) not understanding (d) interrogating

22. propaganda *inundating* the people
    (a) misleading (b) deluging (c) influencing (d) not reaching

23. *inviolable* right of free people
    (a) sacred (b) inherited (c) intangible (d) permanent

24. "Reckon," he replied *laconically*.
    (a) tersely (b) insultingly (c) mysteriously (d) incredibly

25. driving along the North Sea *littoral*
    (a) peninsula (b) coastal region (c) highway (d) surface

26. a mechanical and *meretricious* melodrama
    (a) well-planned (b) tawdry (c) worthy (d) stupid

27. ashamed of his brother's *parsimony*
    (a) stinginess (b) piety (c) wickedness (d) strangeness

28. a *patently* unconvincing motive
    (a) obviously (b) deviously (c) contradictory (d) totally

29. the *polyglot* tumult of New York's East Side
    (a) foreign (b) overwhelming (c) many-languaged (d) multitudinous

30. a woman's voice droning *querulously*
    (a) insistently (b) complainingly (c) questioningly (d) quietly

31. the grass bending *resiliently* under one's feet
    (a) forever (b) backwards (c) elastically (d) unchangingly

32. denouncing her in *scurrilous* terms
    (a) contemptuous (b) vague (c) sly (d) abusive

33. the *secular* interests of the common man
    (a) spiritual (b) worldly (c) selfish (d) secret

34. the *strident* sound breaking the silence
    (a) amplified (b) long-drawn-out (c) shrill (d) unesthetic

35. his face *suffused* with joy
    (a) transfixed (b) atremble (c) overspread (d) delirious

36. *surreptitiously* pocketing the fragments of food
    (a) shamelessly (b) speedily (c) stealthily (d) nervously

37. under rigid, restricted *surveillance*
    (a) imprisonment (b) legal search (c) appraisal (d) close watch

38. *taciturn*, icy, aloof
    (a) silent (b) nervous (c) indifferent (d) touchy

39. experiencing it *vicariously*
    (a) with enthusiasm (b) religiously (c) intimately (d) by proxy

40. a half-consumed *wizened*-looking candle
    (a) shriveled (b) waxen (c) bedraggled (d) bright

**A Final Word**

Yes, you can accelerate the building of your vocabulary by spending a week with a book . . . provided that you also consult the book that you can spend a lifetime with—an unabridged dictionary.

Sometimes a smaller dictionary will do the work for you almost as well. We'd like to make special mention of the pocket-sized paperback edition of Webster's New World Dictionary of the American Language, published by Popular Library. It has derivations, excellent definitions, and a very helpful pronunciation key.

## VOCABAGRAMS

After the difficulties you have just encountered, we think you need a change of pace. Here's a little game based on anagrams (Greek *ana*, backward, and *gram*, letter). Because we have introduced variations and because we believe that this game will painlessly increase or sharpen your vocabulary, we have coined a new name for it: Vocabagrams.

All you have to do is take the letters of the word given—we'll begin with short ones—and rearrange them backward and forward to form the word we define for you.

| EXAMPLES: | wary = twisted | ANSWER: awry |
| | atom = a ditch surrounding a castle | ANSWER: moat |

| | | | |
|---|---|---|---|
| 1. rave | = declare to be true | 11. navel | = mercenary |
| 2. tore | = mechanical memory | 12. glide | = ice-cold |
| | | 13. drain | = lowest point |
| 3. tory | = rookie, beginner | 14. finer | = draw a conclusion |
| 4. sure | = a trick | | |
| 5. tome | = speck of dust | 15. talent | = lying hidden |
| 6. mire | = hoarfrost | 16. trance | = take back publicly |
| 7. fire | = widespread | | |
| 8. said | = raised platform | 17. wither | = twist in pain |
| 9. gore | = a grotesque monster | 18. coiled | = teachable, submissive |
| 10. attic | = unspoken | 19. conical | = brief |
| | | 20. relating | = essential |

If you're having trouble with some of these, here are the initial letters: 1. a, 2. r, 3. t, 4. r, 5. m, 6. r, 7. r, 8. d, 9. o, 10. t, 11. v, 12. g, 13. n, 14. i, 15. l, 16. r, 17. w, 18. d, 19. l, 20. i.

# 4. Getting at the Roots

*At 12:56 P.M. they will fire their solid
fuel retrorockets, dropping their ship still
lower. In 45 seconds they will jettison the
whole retropack and prepare for re-entering
the atmosphere.*

NEW YORK HERALD TRIBUNE, JUNE 7, 1965
(story of "landing" preparations of Gemini
4)

\*          \*          \*

*The plane reported that the astronauts
successfully jettisoned the 84-foot parachute
and were floating on the water.*

NEW YORK POST, DECEMBER 18, 1965 (story
of "landing" of Gemini 7)

In this space age of jet propulsion the word *jettison* may
well become a word of common, everyday usage. Yet we remember when on vocabulary tests it was a bête noire for many
of our students. Only after we were able to tie the word *jettison*
to the French verb *jeter,* to throw, were we able to fix it in
their minds as a word that means to throw overboard. We had
forged a link between *jettison* and *jeter.* We went on to associate *jettison* with *jetsam,*\* goods thrown overboard to
lighten the load of a vessel in distress, and with *jetty,* a structure thrust out into the sea to serve as protection or as a landing pier.

Through the Latin verbs *jactare* and *jacere,* to throw, we
ultimately associated these words with the word element *ject,*

---

\* Generally found with its twin *flotsam,* the wreckage of a ship or its
cargo found floating in the sea.

thrown, or to throw. When we called for words in which *ject* was central—with prefixes fore and suffixes aft—a blackboard was soon filled with a column of words: *abject, adjective, conjecture, dejected, eject, inject, interjection, objective, projectile, reject, subjective, trajectory.*

And all of them had the idea—literally or figuratively—of throwing. Even *adjective*, which can by a stretch of the imagination be defined as a word that throws itself toward or at (*ad*) a noun—or, in more restrained language, that modifies or "is added to" a noun. When man *conjectures*, he throws his thoughts together (*con*) and comes up with a calculated guess.

In other words, *after* you know the meaning of a word you can somehow make room for the root* in your definition.

Would that all roots were as accommodating as *ject!* In each of the twelve words the spelling of *ject* remains constant and the meaning of the word does not stray too far from the idea of throwing.

But a warning has already been sounded—in Chapter 1— on the unreliability of roots. Just how misleading roots may sometimes be can be seen in the twelve *ven, vent* words we have gathered here. The root *ven(t)* of the Latin verb *venire* means to come. Yet only two of the twelve contain the *ven* or *vent* that means to come. Which two are the genuine ones?

| | | |
|---|---|---|
| 1. adventitious | 5. veneer | 9. venomous |
| 2. avenge | 6. venerable | 10. venous |
| 3. provenance | 7. venial | 11. ventilate |
| 4. venal | 8. venison | 12. ventricle |

* Under the term *root* we are including another word element, the stem, which may at times coincide with the root but which is usually slightly different. Thus, *ject* is the stem of the past participle of compounds of *jacere*, whose root is *jac*, as in *ejaculation*, an exclamation. A linguistic difference exists between root and stem, but for practical purposes nontechnical books of this kind generally use the single word *root* for both, and some books even include a full word under the term *root*.

In this chapter we shall deal with roots coming from Latin (including French and other Romance languages) and Greek. Such roots, according to a count made by Roland G. Kent, help us to form more than 60 percent of the 20,000 English words most commonly used. Other counts of larger numbers of words show a higher percentage, according to Stuart Robertson and Frederic G. Cassidy, *The Development of Modern English* (Prentice-Hall, 1960). See the second note in Chapter 11 of this book.

Puzzling, isn't it? The correct answers are 1 and 3. Now that we know that *adventitious* is one of them, let's try to analyze it. The prefix *ad* means to, the root *vent* means come, and the suffix *itious* shows that the word is an adjective. So, you come up with something like "having to do with coming to," which is certainly not a satisfactory or illuminating definition. It is only after you know that *adventitious* has the general meaning of *accidental* that you can see how it took on that meaning: "having come (*vent*) as something additional (*ad*, to)," therefore accidental.

Or take the second *ven, vent* word: *provenance* (alternate form *provenience*). Analyzing it, you realize that it has to do with something that comes forth (*pro*, forward, or forth). But if you know that *provenance* means source or origin, you can say—with hindsight and confidence—"Ah, yes, it comes from the root *ven*, come, plus *pro*, forward, but in this instance closer to *from*, so that *provenance* means the place from which something comes, in other words, the source, the origin."

Such a method of analysis may be used fairly safely with words whose workable definitions correspond to the literal meanings of their parts as in *reject*, "throw back," *projectile*, "something thrown forward." However, more often, as with *adventitious* and *provenance*, we may have to work backward to see how the meaning is arrived at from the elements forming the word.

Despite the dangers, despite the mental gymnastics and gyrations involved, we do recommend a judicious and circumspect study of roots. (*Circumspect* means cautious. How? Knowing the meaning we can readily see that, if we look [*spect*] around [*circum*] before we act, we are being cautious!)

In this chapter, we are not going to ask you to learn a list of roots by rote, to memorize a long list of nonwords. We are here presenting only a selected sampling, because throughout the book emphasis has been placed on the root as a guide to revealing the meaning or as a way of remembering it.

## SOME DEPENDABLE ROOTS

Quotation marks around a definition indicate that the definition so marked is a literal translation of the prefix, root, and suffix. We have done this because we think it is interesting as well as helpful to see either how the original meaning has been retained or how the present meaning has evolved from the literal meaning. Whenever the literal meaning is not a workable definition we have supplied an explanation or synonyms.

**flu, flux,** flow

**affluent**    "flowing to"; abundant; rich.

**confluence**    "a flowing together"; junction of two rivers; a gathering; a crowd. The city at the junction of the Rhine and Moselle Rivers in Germany is called Coblenz (German, Koblenz), a Teutonic adaptation of the Latin word *confluentia*.

**fluctuate**    waver, vacillate.

**flume**    a narrow gorge or ravine through which a stream flows.

**flux**    a constant flow.

**influence**    "a flowing in"; power to affect persons or events. The meaning of the word *influence* comes from an early astrological belief that from the stars there flowed, or emanated, a fluid that affected the lives and characters of men. From the Italian form *influenza* comes the name of the epidemic more familiarly known as "the flu." Apparently it was once believed that an outbreak of an epidemic was due to the influence of the stars.

**influx**    "a flowing in"; a coming in like a stream; arrival of a great number.

**mellifluous**    "flowing with honey"; dulcet; honeyed; smooth; sweet.

**superfluity**    "a flowing beyond and above"; an overflow; an oversupply; excess.

**lat,** from *latus,* past participle of *ferre,* to carry, to bear.

**collate**    "brought together"; to compare for the purpose of verification and orderly arrangement. A collation is a comparison of manuscripts and texts. At one time this word also designated a conference at which monks read or discussed books. A light repast after the conference was also called a collation; hence, the word *collation* came to mean a light meal.

**dilate**    "brought apart (*di*)"; expand; widen; speak at length; expatiate.

**dilatory**    "carried apart." The Latin verb *differre* can mean to defer, carry over to another time, postpone; hence *dilatory* means delaying, putting off, or procrastinating.

**elation**    "act or state of being carried outside oneself"; great joy; exultation.

**oblation**    "something brought in, to, or toward (*ob*)"; an offering, usually a religious offering.

**prelate**    "preferred," from *praelatus*, "carried or placed (*latus*) before (*pre* for *prae*)." In Medieval Latin *praelatus* appears as a title of honor for a noble; the word was taken over by the church to designate a high church official or dignitary.

**relate**    The everyday meanings of this word are simple. However, the word has been entered because it has become a vogue word meaning to communicate with others in a meaningful way, to understand and be understood. So it was said of a baseball manager: "Despite his inarticulateness, he relates well to players."

**CAUTION:** In words like *latent*, *lateral*, and *latitude*, the root is not this *lat*. In *latent*, *lat* means to hide; in *lateral*, the root is *later*, meaning side; and in *latitude*, *lat* means wide!

**locut, loqu,** speak, from the verb *loqui*, speak, talk.

**circumlocutory**    "speaking around"; said in a roundabout way; long-winded.

**colloquial**    "relating to speaking together"; used in conversation; informal in speech or writing. When a dictionary entry is labeled [Colloq.] it does not mean that the word or phrase so designated is slang or substandard but that it is used in informal writing or speaking. The noun *colloquialism* indicates such an informal word or expression.

**colloquy**    "a speaking together"; conference; conversation; dialogue. A colloquy refers to a somewhat formal talk. When the talk is chatty, less formal, a word for it is *confabulation* (Latin *fabula*, a story, "something spoken").

**grandiloquence**    "lofty (*grandi*) speech"; use of lofty words; pompous speech; magniloquence.

**interlocutor**    "one who speaks between"; a participant in a dialogue; the middle (*inter*, between) man who asked the questions in the old-fashioned minstrel show. An interlocutory decree is one that is not final, that is spoken (*locut*), or pronounced, during the course (*inter*) of the proceedings, hence provisional.

**loquacious**    talkative; garrulous.

**obloquy**    "act of speaking against (*ob*)"; abuse; strong condemnation; calumny; vituperation.

**ventriloquist** "one who talks from his stomach." A ventriloquist was so called because it was believed that he projected speech from his stomach (*ventr*).

**rog, rogat,** from the verb *rogare*, ask, ask for.

**abrogate** "ask away (*ab*)." The Latin verb *rogare* had a special meaning: to ask the people about a law, hence, to propose a law or introduce a bill. *Abrogare* had the opposite idea, to propose the annulment of a law. Hence, *abrogate* means to abolish, to rescind, to repeal.

**arrogance** "an asking to (*ar* for *ad*, to) or for oneself"; a taking to oneself of great pride or a feeling of superiority; haughtiness; overpowering pride; hubris.

**arrogate** "ask to or for oneself"; to claim as one's right; to assume unduly.

**derogatory** "asking for less"; belittling; disparaging; decrying.

**prerogative** "something asked for before (*pre*)"; special privilege; inherent right of one's position, rank, or office.

**prorogue** "ask before or ahead," from *prorogare*, to prolong; to defer; postpone; adjourn a legislative body.

**supererogatory** "asking for more (*super*) from (*e*)." This word will be understood better if we go back to its Latin ancestor, the verb *erogare*, which means to spend money from the public treasury after having asked for and received permission from (*e*) the people. In Late Latin the prefix *super* was added, and the verb came to have a general meaning of to spend in addition (*super*), to make an extra disbursement. The English adjective *supererogatory* has the still broader meanings of doing something over and above what is required, beyond the call of duty, superfluous.

**surrogate** "asked under (*sur* for *sub*, under, lower)." Here the prefix *sub* has the special meaning of "in place of," so that a surrogate is somebody chosen (asked for) in place of another, a substitute, a deputy. In some states of this country the title *surrogate* refers to an official who deals with wills and estates. The word *surrogate* is also an adjective, meaning substitute, standing in place of another.

## PARALLEL ROOTS AND WORDS

Another way of using roots as an aid to vocabulary building is to couple a word of Latin origin with one of Greek origin, whenever the meanings of the words themselves and the roots correspond. For example, *circumlocutory* may be teamed with *periphrastic*, "speaking around," from the Greek root *phras*, speak, from which we also get *phrase* and *paraphrase*.

A few examples are given below. You will find many more in subsequent chapters. The Latin roots and words are put first; their Greek counterparts come after the colon.

**fer: phor**　　bear, carry

　　**circumferential : peripheral**　　going around; encircling. *Peripheral* also means marginal, around the border.

**scrib, script : graph**　　write

　　**superscription : epigraph**　　"something written above or upon."

The excerpt that appears at the head of each of our chapters is called an epigraph.

**sacer, sacr : hiero**　　holy

　　**sacerdotal : hieratic**　　"priestly"; relating to a priest or his duties.

**spect : scop**　　look

　　**conspectus : scope**　　range; survey

**tempor : chron**　　time

　　**contemporary : synchronous**　　"happening at the same time."

## WORD CLUSTERS

We have given *adumbrate*, the first word in our list, full treatment. For the other words—with the exception of *recreant* —we are merely suggesting what can be done if you go where the dictionary leads you. (See *egregious* in Chapter 1. That chapter merely adumbrated what we are discussing here.)

**adumbrate**　　In *Lochiel's Warning* the English poet Thomas Campbell wrote, "Coming events cast their shadows before."

"To cast a shadow" is the literal meaning of the verb *adumbrate*, which comes from the Latin verb *adumbrare* (*ad*, to, and *umbra*, shadow) and means to foreshadow, suggest, and predict, as well as to outline, to sketch lightly.

*Penumbra* is another word formed from *umbra*. A penumbra is a shadow cast, as in an eclipse where an intervening body cuts off the light partly (*pen, paene*, almost, which also appears in *peninsula*, "an almost island," and in *penultimate*, "almost the last," next to last).

There's nothing bright or gay about *somber*, "under a shadow," from Latin (via French) *sub*, under + *umbra*, hence dark, gloomy. A *sombrero* (Spanish) is, understandably, a broad-brimmed hat.

*Umbrage*, another word derived from the root of *umbra*, is generally met in the expressions *to give umbrage* and *to take umbrage*, where the word means annoyance, displeasure, resentment.

**bellicose**   "warlike"; aggressive; combative; pugnacious; from *bellum*, war, root *bell*. *Belligerent*, another of its synonyms, contains the same root. In the cluster with *bellicose*, we find also *rebel, rebellious, ante bellum* and *post bellum*.

**contravene**   "come against"; act in a contrary way; break or disregard a law or order; from *contra*, against, and *ven*, root of *venire*, to come. There are many other words formed from *ven, vent*, some of them easy, like *convene, convention, invent, invention;* some more difficult like *circumvent* and *supervene*.

**diffident**   "not (*dis*) having faith"; lacking faith in oneself; modest; shy. The root is *fid* from Latin verb *fidere*, to trust. Hi-fi is a short way of saying *high fidelity. Diffidence* is the noun for *diffident;* Yum-Yum couples the former word with its synonym in *The Mikado* by Gilbert and Sullivan:

> The moon's Celestial Highness;
> There's not a trace
> Upon her face
> Of diffidence or shyness.

Clustering around the word *diffident* are *confident* and *confidence, infidel* and *perfidy*.

**exacerbate**   "to make more bitter," from *ex*, intensive, and *acer*, sharp, root *acr*. To *exacerbate* means to aggravate, irritate, exasperate. With *exasperate* (*asper*, rough, bitter) we can associate *asperity*, and with *exacerbate*, the words *acerb, acerbity, acrid*, and *acrimonious.*

**impugn**   "fight against," from *pugn*, root of verb *pugnare*, to fight, and *im(in)*, against; to attack with words or argument; call into question; make insinuations against.

With *impugn* we can associate *inexpugnable, pugnacious*, and *repugnant*.

**presentiment**      "that which is felt before," from *pre*, before, and *sent, sens*, root of *sentire*, to feel. Words we can learn with it are *dissent, resentment, sentient*.

**propensity**      "quality of leaning forward," from *pro*, forward, *pend, pens*, root of *propendere*, "to hang forward," to be inclined + suffix *ity*, indicating quality, condition. *Propensity* means a bent, disposition, inclination, proneness, strong tendency. Besides *propensity*, the words that gather around the root *pend* are *append, appendage, impending, pendant, pendulum*, and *penthouse, depend* and *independence*, in all of which the idea of hanging, that is, leaning upon, comes through.

**recreant**      "going back on one's belief"; cowardly; craven; false; unfaithful. The root of this word is one that can fool you on first sight; it is not related to the root in *create* or *recreation*, but is a much-changed form via French of *cred*, from Latin *credere*, to believe, which yields among others such words as *credit, credible, credulous, credulity*.

There's a story in the two sets of meanings of *recreant: cowardly* and *false*. The term was applied to a knight who renounced his cause because of defeat, who gave up and cried for mercy. He was considered not only a coward but also a backslider (*re* of *recreant* = back), one who went back on his faith, an apostate, a deserter.

With *recreant*, we can couple the word *miscreant*, which also has two sets of derogatory meanings: one who holds a false (*mis*) religious belief, a heretic, an infidel, and also one who is a villain. As an adjective *miscreant* means depraved, vicious, villainous, as well as unbelieving.

**redundant**      "overflowing," from *re* and *unda*, a wave; superfluous; surplus; excessive; tautological; pleonastic; prolix. In England the word is applied to a worker who has been let go because technological advances or automation have rendered him superfluous or unneeded. *Redound, inundate, undulate, undulation*, and *undulatory* are other words formed from *unda*, as is the name *Ondine*, or *Undine*.

**tergiversation**      "act of turning the back," from *tergum*, back, and *vert, vers*, found in the verb *vertere*, to turn; desertion; changing of sides; going one way and then another; equivocation. From the root of *vertere* come a large number of words, among them *animadversion, controvert, diversity, divers* and *diverse, perverse, traverse,* and *versatility.*

**venal, venial**    These words are sometimes confused. A knowledge of their roots can help to keep them apart. *Venal* literally means "salable," hence capable of being bought, open to corruption and bribery, mercenary. *Venal* comes from the root *ven,* which is part of the Latin verb *vendere,* to sell, from which also come the words *vend,* to sell, and *vendor,* one who sells.

*Venial,* coming from Latin *venia,* pardon, means pardonable, excusable, slight, trivial. As another way of avoiding confusion with *venal,* we can associate *venial* with *trivial,* for the two words are synonyms and end in *ial.*

## I. MATCHING

Match each word on the left with the word on the right closest to it in meaning.

| | | |
|---|---|---|
| 1. adventitious | a. honeyed |
| 2. circumspect | b. traitorous |
| 3. circumvent | c. overcome, outwit |
| 4. dilatory | d. defer |
| 5. hieratic | e. wary, careful |
| 6. mellifluous | f. priestly |
| 7. oblation | g. accidental |
| 8. obloquy | h. an offering |
| 9. prorogue | i. delaying |
| 10. recreant | j. calumny, disgrace |

## II. MULTIPLE CHOICE

From the group after the letters select the word that is closest in meaning to the word after the number.

1. adumbrate    (a) clothe (b) shelter (c) insult (d) suggest
2. affluent    (a) volatile (b) wealthy (c) vanishing (d) ill
3. circumlocutory    (a) long-winded (b) surrounding (c) bypassing (d) indirect
4. collation    (a) light repast (b) indirect reference (c) source book (d) serious reflection
5. colloquy    (a) condemnation (b) convenience (c) conference (d) concerted attack

6. exacerbate            (a) drive out (b) point out
                          (c) exaggerate (d) aggra-
                          vate

7. prelate               (a) close connection (b) church
                          dignitary (c) early form of
                          life (d) a foreboding

8. prerogative           (a) firm belief (b) difficult
                          question (c) advance
                          notice (d) special privilege

9. provenance            (a) advance (b) source
                          (c) anthology (d) fitness

10. surrogate            (a) substitute (b) presumption
                          (c) willfulness (d) testa-
                          ment

## III.  LIKE AND UNLIKE

In which pair are the words of similar meaning, and in which
pair are they of unlike or almost opposite meaning?

1. bellicose    — pugnacious        6. jettison    — salvage
2. contravene — obey                7. recreant    — backslider
3. diffident    — shy               8. redundant   — terse
4. impervious — impassable          9. venal       — honest
5. impugn      — attack            10. venial      — inexcusable

## IV.  ASSOCIATED WORDS

This exercise and all the following exercises are partly review, partly "Do-It-Yourself."

1. acerbity              a. turn aside from
2. animadversion         b. treachery
3. appendage             c. accrue
4. deviate               d. distasteful
5. obviate               e. rolling
6. perfidy               f. unfavorable criticism
7. redound               g. sourness
8. repugnant             h. conscious
9. sentient              i. make unnecessary
10. undulating           j. attachment

## V.  IN TWO LANGUAGES

Each word on the left comes from Anglo-Saxon or a related source. On the right is the first letter of a word of Latin
origin; the meaning of the roots of both the Anglo-Saxon and
the Latin words is the same on each line, and the word on
the right is a synonym of the word on the left. Complete the
word on each line; each bar represents a letter.

EXAMPLES:  filled  c _ _ _ _ _ _ _  ANSWERS:  complete
           to free  l _ _ _ _ _ _              liberate

1. behest        c _ _ _ _ _ _
2. believable    c _ _ _ _ _ _ _
3. embody        i _ _ _ _ _ _ _ _
4. forewarning   p _ _ _ _ _ _ _ _
5. friendly      a _ _ _ _ _ _ _
6. healthful     s _ _ _ _ _ _ _ _ _ ; s _ _ _ _ _ _ _
7. inborn        i _ _ _ _ _
8. outcome       e _ _ _ _ _ _ _ _
9. spotless      i _ _ _ _ _ _ _
10. tireless     i _ _ _ _ _ _ _ _ _ _ _

## VI.  VARIATION ON A BILINGUAL THEME

This time the words of Latin origin are on the left. The completed words must be of Anglo-Saxon origin.

EXAMPLE:  tedious  i _ _ _ _ _ _  ANSWER:  irksome

1. accretion      g _ _ _ _ _
2. adumbrating    f _ _ _ _ _ _ _ _ _ _ _ _
3. avarice        g _ _ _ _
4. eminent        o _ _ _ _ _ _ _ _ _
5. impending      o _ _ _ _ _ _ _ _ _
6. lassitude      w _ _ _ _ _ _ _ _
7. mundane        w _ _ _ _ _ _
8. unpredictable  u _ _ _ _ _ _ _ _ _ _ _
9. veracity       t _ _ _ _
10. verbose       w _ _ _ _

## VII.  DOUBLETS AND COLLAPSED FORMS

There are many pairs of words with different spellings and sometimes different meanings, which came into the English language in different ways and at different times from the same source. Examples of such doublets are *regal, royal; legal, loyal; fealty, fidelity*. If one of the two words is shorter, we call the shorter form "a collapsed form."

Each word after the number is either a doublet or a shorter, collapsed form of one of the words after the letters. Select the correct word.

EXAMPLE:  sexton  (a) sacristan (b) secondary (c) secularist
ANSWER:  sacristan

1. alms    (a) alimony (b) alimentation (c) eleemosynary
2. amble   (a) ambulate (b) ramble (c) amenable

3.  avow      (a) avuncular (b) advocate (c) asseverate
4.  benison   (a) benefaction (b) benediction (c) benevolence
5.  blame     (a) blaspheme (b) emblazon (c) blemish
6.  costive   (a) accosting (b) constipated (c) costliest
7.  desire    (a) desperate (b) deserving (c) desideratum
8.  flail     (a) flagellate (b) fluctuate (c) flagitious
9.  kiln      (a) calumny (b) kindle (c) culinary
10. limn      (a) eliminate (b) illuminate (c) liminal
11. maim      (a) malign (b) manumit (c) mayhem
12. manure    (a) manufacture (b) maneuver (c) manipulate
13. melee     (a) medley (b) mingling (c) melody
14. palsy     (a) pulsation (b) paroxysm (c) paralysis
15. proxy     (a) approximate (b) proctor (c) procuracy

## VIII.  TRIPLE THREAT

The Greeks had a word for it; the Romans had a word for
it; the Anglo-Saxons had a word for it. That is why, in English,
we can foretell, or predict, or prophesy. It's the Anglo-Saxon,
the Latin, and the Greek of it. Supply the missing word in
each set of "triplets"; the first letter has been given to start
you off. Each blank represents a letter.

EXAMPLE:  forecast  p_ _ _ _ _ _  prognosticate
ANSWER:    predict *or* presage

| Anglo-Saxon | Latin | Greek |
|---|---|---|
| 1. teamwork | c_ _ _ _ _ _ _ _ _ _ | synergy |
| 2. rim | margin | p_ _ _ _ _ _ _ _ |
| 3. b_ _ _ _ | origin | genesis |
| 4. top | summit | a_ _ _ |
| 5. odd | e_ _ _ _ _ _ _ _ | idiosyncratic |
| 6. song | chant | a_ _ _ _ _ |
| 7. belief | t_ _ _ _ | dogma |
| 8. ghost | specter | p_ _ _ _ _ _ |
| 9. h_ _ _ _ _ _ _ | celestial | ethereal |
| 10. a saw (saying) | a_ _ _ _ | apothegm |

## IX.  A ROOT GAME

Supply the word that will satisfy the definition after each
root. Each blank represents a letter.

EXAMPLE:  *ced, cess,* go.  A noun meaning a mild depression:
_ _ _ _ _ _ _ _ _  ANSWER:  recession

1. *aud, audit,* hear. An adjective meaning pertaining to hearing:
_ _ _ _ _ _ _ _

2. *cap, capt,* take. An adjective meaning quick to take exception, to find fault: _ _ _ _ _ _ _

3. *cred, credit,* believe. An adjective beginning with the prefix *in,* not, meaning unwilling to believe, skeptical: *in* _ _ _ _ _ _ _ _ _

4. *curr, curs,* run. An adjective meaning "running together," happening together in time or place: _ _ _ _ _ _ _ _ _ _

5. *gen, genit,* give birth to. A noun meaning offspring: _ _ _ _ _ _ _

6. *mon, monit,* warn. A verb meaning to warn, advise, reprove mildly: _ _ _ _ _ _ _ _

7. *scind, sciss,* cut. A verb meaning "to cut back," to cancel, or abrogate: _ _ _ _ _ _ _

8. *sed, sid, sess,* sit. An adjective beginning with *as* for *ad,* to, meaning diligent, persevering: *as* _ _ _ _ _ _ _

9. *tang, tact,* touch. An adjective meaning not easily touched, impalpable, vague: _ _ _ _ _ _ _ _ _ _

10. *tempor,* time. A verb meaning to gain time by putting off: _ _ _ _ _ _ _ _ _

11. *vert, vers,* turn. An adjective meaning unfavorable: _ _ _ _ _ _ _

12. *vid, vis,* see. A noun meaning something composed and recited without preparation: _ _ *pro* _ _ _ _ _ _ _ _

## X. WORDS IN CONTEXT

Choose the meaning closest to that of the italicized word in each passage. After making your choice consult a dictionary to see how the meaning of the word developed from the root.

1. Only those who are planning aggression could have objected so strenuously to the sane call that states in the Middle East *abjure* the use of military force.

    (a) deprecate (b) renounce (c) discuss (d) reconsider

2. West Germans were found *apathetic* on aiding the emerging nations.

    (a) compassionate (b) unrealistic (c) indifferent
    (d) dilatory

3. If the word is spread that we are very much concerned with the well-being and behavior of these youngsters, our reputations stand to be enhanced rather than *denigrated.*

    (a) unnoticed (b) denied (c) deplored (d) sullied

4. Punishment as a *deterrent* may be justified where it serves to protect a country and its people.

    (a) discourager (b) lesson (c) safeguard (d) form of
    vengeance

5. Twenty-one victories in a season is an unusual *deviation* in the pattern of young pitchers.

   (a) occurrence (b) record (c) bit of luck (d) departure from normal pattern

6. The United States is embarking on a program for the *eradication*, in this country, of the mosquito that spreads yellow fever.

   (a) wiping out (b) total control (c) quarantine (d) deactivating

7. The high cost of living is hard enough to bear, even in the knowledge that it is borne aloft by certain *ineluctable* forces of inflation.

   (a) unforeseen (b) uncontrolled (c) inescapable (d) cyclic

8. A fickle fandom has let itself become enamored of the Mets with their *propensity* for getting involved in the bizarre, the unexpected, the unusual, and heroics in reverse.

   (a) tendency (b) talent (c) ineptitude (d) destiny

9. No madman's bullet can stop the *inexorable* march of human rights; no murder, however tragic, can make it falter.

   (a) progressive (b) relentless (c) foreordained (d) hard-won

10. He is and has always been a radical individualist, indeed a *solipsist*, whose books are self-revelatory to a degree that is often embarrassing.

   (a) theorist (b) egoist (c) nonconformist (d) crusader

## VOCABAGRAMS: 1

As in Chapter 3 you are given the definition and you are asked to form a word that corresponds to this definition by rearranging the letters of the numbered word. Now there will be a variation in the procedure. You are asked to add or to subtract one letter as you rearrange the word to meet the definition given.

EXAMPLES: (1) Rearrange only: marital = warlike
           ANSWER: martial
          (2) Add a letter: overeat + n = to make new
           ANSWER: renovate
          (3) Subtract a letter: caper − r = step
           ANSWER: pace

Every answer must be a word of Latin origin, as in the examples given.

1. brace         = sour
2. dormant     = bitter
3. editing       = set afire (past tense)
4. misers        = negligent
5. quieter       = repay
6. refining      = violate
7. voter         = open
8. amulets  + i = feign
9. desire    + r = crowded together
10. dried     + e = to ridicule
11. drive     + t = turn aside
12. eager    + l = entertain
13. lines     + a = salty
14. mental   + b = flickering
15. parses   + e = to slander
16. scale     + o = comfort
17. scene    + r = container for burning incense
18. bromide  − e = diseased
19. entrails   − r = outstanding
20. jumping  − j = to attack

Here are the first letters of the most difficult ones: 3. i, 6. i, 8. s, 9. s, 14. l, 15. a, 19. s, 20. i.

## VOCABAGRAMS: II

This time answer only with a Latin word that you have met in this chapter.

    EXAMPLE: race = sharp    ANSWER: acer

1. refer     = carry
2. refuel    = flow
3. decree + r = believe
4. entire + s = feel
5. fried  + e = trust
6. nape   + e = almost
7. never  + i = come
8. revert + e = turn
9. vain   + e = pardon
10. crease − e = holy

As a help, here are the first letters of the answers: 1. f, 2. f, 3. c, 4. s, 5. f, 6. p, 7. v, 8. v, 9. v, 10. s.

*Many a treasure besides Ali Baba's is unlocked with a verbal key.*

                   HENRY VAN DYKE

*Ella went over to rummage among the books left behind as unsalable out of her father's fine store. She brought back a*

*Superseded Spelling-book by Sullivan, who held that by learning affixes and suffixes, Latin and Greek roots, you could net words in hundreds, as against the old method of fishing one word up at a time. . . .*

SEAN O'CASEY, *I Knock at the Door*

# 5.   Syllables That Start the Word Going

> *In Winnipeg, Canada, Marian Forer stares*
> *at the ceiling, wondering how, if lawyers are*
> *disbarred, and priests unfrocked, other peo-*
> *ple in the other walks of life might be read*
> *out of their callings.*
>
> *Examples: Electricians get delighted; mu-*
> *sicians denoted; cowboys deranged; models*
> *deposed; judges distorted. What's more,*
> *mediums are dispirited; dressmakers un-*
> *biased; Far Eastern diplomats disoriented;*
> *office workers defiled.*
>
> JOHN G. FULLER's "Trade Winds,"
> SATURDAY REVIEW, NOVEMBER 28, 1964

A prefix sits up front in the driver's seat. It can determine where the word is going—backward or forward, in or out, up or down. It can signal the turn the word will take for better or worse, for good or ill. It can enlarge or diminish. It can count the ways.

It is therefore worthwhile to learn about these little determinants that so often control the destiny of a word. How significantly prefixes affect the meanings of words can be seen in this fairly easy pretest, in which you are asked to change the direction the word takes by substituting another prefix for the one now appearing in the word. The word you supply should have a meaning opposite to the one given. Watch your spelling.

EXAMPLES:   attract — distract      import — export

1. antemeridian          3. converge
2. assent                4. deficient

5. deflate
6. demote
7. destructive
8. eject
9. epilogue
10. immigration
11. include
12. introvert

13. prefix
14. prenatal
15. presence
16. proponent
17. prospect
18. regenerate
19. subjective
20. synonym

## DIRECTION SIGNALS

We generally list words in alphabetical order for ready reference, but if we were to list prefixes in that way, they would go off haphazardly in different directions. Instead, we shall assemble prefixes in groups according to where they direct you.

**In, On, Upon, Into, Within**
**in** (Latin)     For the sake of euphony, *in* changes its spelling before certain letters—to *il* before *l*, as in *illogical*, to *im* before *b*, *m*, or *p*, as in *imbibe*, *immediate*, and *implant*, and into *ir* before *r*, as in *irradiate*. Such a change, in which the last letter of the prefix blends with the first letter of the word or element to which it is attached, is called *assimilation*, itself an example of the change (*ad*, to, changed to *as* before *similis*, like). Especially in words of French origin, *in* appears as *en*, as in *encroach* (intrude on), *encumber* (load down), and *engender* (beget, produce).

    **immure**     "wall in"; enclose within walls (*mur*, from Latin *murus*, wall, as in *mural*).
    **inject**     "throw in or into."
    **inscribe**     "write in or on"; engrave upon.
    **invade**     "go into"; enter in a hostile manner.
**en** (Greek), in, into
    **encaustic**     "burnt in"; fixed by heat; term applied to a method of painting in which the paint is mixed with melted beeswax and fixed by heat. This Greek prefix is changed to *em* by assimilation in words like *emblem* and *empathy*, and to *el* in words like *elliptical*.
**epi** (Greek), upon
    **epigraph**     an inscription; a quotation at the head of a work or a chapter to suggest the theme.
    **epitaph**     an inscription, as on a tomb (*taph*) or gravestone.

**intra** (Latin), within

   **intramural**    "within the wall"; occurring within the limits of a state, community, organization, institution; among the members of an institution, as in *intramural athletics*.

**intro** (Latin), within

   **introspection**    "the act of looking within"; self-examination.

**end(o)** (Greek), within

   **endocrine**    pertaining to internal secretions, as in *endocrine glands*.

## To, Toward

**ad** (Latin)    This prefix undergoes assimilation, changing to *ac, af, ag, al, an, ap, ar, as,* and *at,* as in *accord, affable, aggressive, alleviate, annotate, appal, arrogant, assume,* and *attract.*

   **annihilate**    to reduce "to nothing"; destroy completely.

**pros** (Greek)

   **proselyte**    "come to, gone to"; one who has gone over to another faith; a convert.

## Away From, Out Of

**ab** (Latin)

   **abnormal**    "away from the normal."

   **abstain**    "keep from"; refrain. There are two noun forms: *abstinence* and *abstention.*

**apo** (Greek)    This prefix appears as *aph* in words in which the Greek element to which it is added starts with an *h* sound, as in *aphorism,* a terse formulation of a truth, an adage, or maxim.

   **apocryphal**    "hidden away"; false; spurious; fictitious.

   **apogee**    the point in the orbit of a satellite at the greatest distance away from (*apo*) the center of the earth (*gee,* from Greek *ge,* "earth"). The opposite is *perigee.*

**e, ex** (Latin), out, out of    *Ex* may change to *ef,* as in *effete, effluvium, effective,* etc.

   **exorbitant**    "out of the usual track"; excessive.

   **extirpate**    "tear out by stock or stem, trunk or root"; eradicate (*radic,* root), "tear out by the roots"; wipe out.

**ec, ex, eco** (Greek), out of, outside of

   **ecstasy**    a state of rapturous delight in which one is standing (*stas*) outside (*ec*) oneself; a state of transport or exaltation (Latin *altus*, high); perhaps stronger than *exultation*, in which one has "jumped" (Latin *sult*, leap, jump) outside (*ex*) oneself.

**exorcise**    "to swear out"; to drive away an evil spirit by a solemn oath; to relieve someone of an evil spirit.

**extro** (Latin, from *extra*), outside, outward

**extrovert**    "turned outward"; one who is chiefly concerned with what is happening outside oneself; more popularly, one who is uninhibited in expressing oneself; opposed to *introvert*.

**se** (Latin), away, aside, apart

**secede**    "go away"; withdraw from.

**seclude**    "hide away"; to withdraw from others.

**sedulous**    "apart from (i.e., without) guile or deceit"; diligent; industrious; assiduous.

## Below, Down

**de** (Latin), down

**dejected**    "thrown down"; downcast; depressed.

**depository**    place where things are "put down" for safekeeping.

**cata, cath** (Greek *kata*), down

**cataclysm**    "a washing down"; tremendous flood; catastrophe; disaster.

**catapult**    "hurl down or against."

**infra** (Latin), below, lower    Its opposite is *ultra*.

**infrared**    lying outside or below the red end of the visible spectrum.

**infrasonic**    below the level of human audibility.

**sub** (Latin), under    This prefix also occurs as *suc, suf, sug, sup*, and *sur*, as in *succeed, suffer, suggest, support*, and *surrogate*.

**subliminal**    "below the threshold"; influencing thought below the level of personal awareness.

**surreptitious**    "seized from under"; taken away suddenly and secretly; marked by fraud and stealth; "underhanded."

**subterranean**    "beneath the earth."

**subter** (Latin), beneath    In *subterranean*, the prefix is *sub; ter* is part of the Latin word *terra*, earth.

**subterfuge**    Here the prefix has the connotation of "secretly" and "underhanded." Hence, a subterfuge is a bit of deception, an excuse to get out "from under," to evade or escape from a duty.

**hypo** (Greek), under

    **hypocaust** "burned under"; ancient heating system with underground furnace.

    **hypodermic** "beneath the skin" (*derm*, from Greek word for skin).

## Above, Over, Beyond, Outside Of

**extra** (Latin), beyond, outside of

    **extrasensory** beyond the ordinary senses. ESP stands for *ExtraSensory Perception.*

    **extravagant** "wandering beyond"; beyond reasonable limits; spending beyond what is necessary.

**ultra** (Latin), beyond

    **ultramundane** situated beyond the world or the limits of the solar system.

    **ultrasonic** beyond the limits of human audibility.

**trans** (Latin), beyond

    **transcend** "to climb beyond"; rise above; exceed.

**super** (Latin), above, beyond In words derived from French this prefix may appear as *sur*, as in *surplus*, an amount over that required, and in *surplice*, name of an ecclesiastical garment, so named because it was once worn *over* fur coats in churches in northern countries.

    **supernumerary** "above the number"; superfluous; extra.

    **surrealist** "above realism"; producing imagery by unnatural combinations.

**hyper** (Greek), above, beyond

    **hyperbole** "a throwing beyond"; an exaggeration, especially figuratively, as in poetry.

    **hyperborean** "beyond the North"; relating to the Far North; arctic; frozen.

**over** (Anglo-Saxon), beyond

    **overweening** from Anglo-Saxon *ween*, think; unduly confident; arrogant; unrestrained.

**out** (Anglo-Saxon), above, beyond, surpassing

    **out-Herod** to exceed in violence or blustering. Herod, ruler of Judaea at the time of Christ's death, was depicted as a blustering despot in medieval mystery plays: hence, the expression "to out-Herod Herod."

## Across, Through

**per** (Latin), through

    **peregrination**    a wandering through many lands. *Pilgrim* and *pilgrimage* are derived from the same root.

**dia** (Greek), through, across

    **diaphanous**    allowing light to go through; transparent.

    **diathermy**    "heating through"; application of heat to body tissue by electric currents.

**trans** (Latin), across

    **transient**    "going across"; transitory; fleeting; short-lived; ephemeral. As a noun it means one who has not come to stay, one who is merely "passing through."

    **transmigration**    the passing or "going across" of the soul into another body, whether human or animal. The equivalent word from Greek elements is *metempsychosis*, in which the prefix *met*, from *meta*, indicates a change of condition.

**meta** (Greek), across, beyond

    **metamorphosis**    change of form or shape; transformation.

    **metaphor**    a figure of speech or trope in which one thing is spoken of as if it were another, e.g., "All the world's a stage,/And all the men and women merely players."

**inter** (Latin), between, among

    **interpolate**    to insert words in a text as additional or explanatory matter.

## After, Behind, Back, Backward

**re, retro** (Latin), back, backward

    **recede**    "to go back"; withdraw

    **retrogress**    "to step backward"; to revert to an earlier condition. This prefix is useful in "getting back to earth" with *retropack* and *retrorocket*.

**palin** (Greek), back

    **palindrome**    a word, verse, or sentence that reads or runs (Greek *drom*) the same backward or forward, like the words *level* and *tenet*, the names Anna, Eve, and Otto, and the sentence "A man, a plan, a canal, Panama."

## Before, In Front Of, Forward

**ante** (Latin), before

    **antechamber**    a room before the main apartment; a waiting room or foyer.

    **antepenult**    "before almost the last"; the syllable coming before the next to the last syllable in a word.

**pre** (from Latin *prae*), "before, in front of"

    **predilection**    "act of choosing ahead (from many)"; inclination; a liking; preference.

    **preposition**    "placed before"; a word usually coming in front of a noun or pronoun.

**pro** (Latin), before, forward

    **propel**    "drive forward."

**pro** (Greek), before

    **proscenium**    part of the stage (*skene*) in front of the curtain.

### Around, About

**circum** (Latin), around

    **circumambient**    "going around"; encircling; surrounding; encompassing.

    **circumlocution**    "talking around"; a roundabout way of saying something.

**peri** (Greek), around

    **peripatetic**    "walking around"; itinerant; walking from place to place.

    **periphrastic**    talking in a roundabout way; circumlocutory.

## OF TIME AND AGE

In the section on direction signals we have discussed only true prefixes. From now on we shall also treat those combining forms that come at the beginning of a word. A combining form is a word or word element that is attached, or affixed, to another word or word element. It may occur at the beginning or the end of a word. For example, the Greek combining form *phil(e)*, meaning love, comes at the beginning of *philharmonic*, where it acts as a prefix, and at the end of *Anglophile*, where it serves as a suffix.

**arch(a)eo, archa(e)** (Greek), old

    **archaeology**    the study in depth of ancient peoples and their culture.

    **archaic**    belonging to an earlier time; old-fashioned; belonging to the language of earlier times.

**neo** (Greek), new    This may be attached to show that a movement or tendency is springing up anew, as in *neo-classic*, referring to a revival of interest in the Greeks and the Romans.

    **neologism**    a newly coined word.

    **neophyte**    "new shoot"; novice, novitiate (from Latin *novus*, new); beginner; new convert; tyro.

**ante** (Latin), before

    **antediluvian**    "before the flood"; antiquated; behind the times.

**palim, palin** (Greek), again

    **palimpsest**    "rubbed again"; a manuscript in which an earlier text was rubbed off so that the parchment could be used again and again for later writings.

**pre** (from Latin *prae*), before

    **prelude**    "before the play"; introductory matter; preliminary part; preface.

    **premeditate**    "to think on beforehand"; plan in advance.

**pro** (Greek), before, ahead

    **prognosis**    "a knowing before"; act of foretelling the progress of a disease; forecast; "projection," a word that has come into vogue with the use of computers.

**post** (Latin), after

    **postscript**    "written after"; often something that is written as an afterthought; what P.S. (*post scriptum*) stands for.

**re** (Latin), again

    **recapitulate**    to repeat the principal points; restate; sum up.

## BIG AND LITTLE, MANY AND FEW

Most of these are combining forms. The comforting thing about them is that their meanings remain fairly well-fixed. Whether they tell us about the size or the number, we can count on them. However, the combining forms for specific numbers are so numerous that they are given detailed treatment in the next chapter.

**macro** (Greek), large

    **macrocosm**    "the large world"; the universe; a complex regarded as a world in itself.

**meg(a), megal(o)** (Greek), great, large

    **megalith** "great stone"; one of the huge unadorned stones found in prehistoric structures, as at Stonehenge, England, or Carnac, France.

    **megalomania** disease characterized by delusions (*mania*) of grandeur.

    **megaton** "large ton"; the explosive force of a million tons of TNT.

**micro** (Greek), small

    **microcosm** "small world"; miniature world, an epitome of a larger unity.

**multi** (Latin), many

    **multilingual** expressed in several languages; able to speak many languages.

**poly** (Greek), many

    **polyglot** multilingual; composed of different languages.

**omni** (Latin), all

    **omnipotent** "all-powerful."

    **omnivorous** "all-devouring"; eating everything.

**pan** (Greek), all

    **panacea** "all-healing"; cure-all; universal remedy.

**holo** (Greek), wholly, entire, complete

    **holocaust** complete destruction by fire; widespread devastation and destruction.

    **holograph** "wholly written" in the hand of the author.


## ACCENTUATING THE NEGATIVE

These prefixes have a firm hold of the steering wheel. You can be fairly sure that words beginning with Latin *contra, dis, non,* and Greek *a(n), anti,* and *dys* are generally traveling down a road marked "No." For all these prefixes and the combining forms in this section may in varying degrees give a negative shading to the words they lead, though only *non* and *in* (Latin), *a(n)* (Greek), and *un* (Anglo-Saxon) give an unqualified No!

**a** (Greek), not     appears as *an* before vowels and usually before *h*, as in *anomaly* and *anhydrous*.

    **amorphous** "shapeless, formless."

    **anodyne** "without pain"; anything that relieves pain.

**in** (Latin)

**inexorable**    not to be moved by prayer or entreaty; inflexible; unyielding; relentless.

**intangible**    "untouchable"; vague; imperceptible; having no physical substance.

**non (Latin)**

**nonage**    "not of an age"; condition of being under required legal age for certain transactions; youth, childhood, infancy.

**nonpartisan**    politically independent; impartial; objective.

**un (Anglo-Saxon)**

**unstinting**    giving generously; not holding back.

**ant(i) (Greek), against**

**antagonism**    "suffering or struggling against"; enmity; hostility; antipathy.

**antonym**    a word that is opposite in meaning to another.

**contra, contro (Latin), against**    In words derived from French, these prefixes may appear as *counter.*

**contravene**    "come against"; act contrary to; contradict; infringe; obstruct.

**controversy**    "turned against; disagreement; dispute; strife.

**countermand**    "order against"; cancel; rescind.

**countervailing**    putting up an equal "opposing force"; counterpoising; offsetting.

**with (Anglo-Saxon), against**

**withstand**    "stand against"; oppose; resist.

**dis (Latin), apart, away**    This prefix changes to *dif* before a word element beginning with *f*, as in *diffuse,* and drops the *s* before *g, l,* and *v,* as in *digress, dilute,* and *divert.*

**digress**    "step away"; to turn off (from the main subject in speech or writing).

**discrepancy**    "a rattling differently" (from same Latin verb that gives us *decrepit*); difference; disagreement; inconsistency.

**disparate**    "not made equal"; different.

**disperse**    cause to break up; scatter.

**divert**    "to turn aside"; distract; entertain.

**ob (Latin), against**    This prefix changes to *oc* before a word element beginning with *c,* as in *occlusion,* to *of* before *f* as in *offensive,* and to *op* before *p,* as in *opponent.*

**obloquy**    "a talking against"; censure; disgrace.

**obstruct**    "build against"; block; hinder; place an obstacle in the way of.

**mal(e)** (Latin), bad, badly

**malefactor**    "evil doer"; felon; criminal.

**malfunction**    to work badly or imperfectly.

**dys** (Greek), badly

**dyspepsia** "bad digestion."

**caco** (Greek), bad

**cacophony**    "bad sound"; harsh, discordant sound; opposite of *euphony*.

**mis** (Greek), hate

**misogynist**    "one who hates women." *Gyne* is a Greek word for woman; it appears in *gynecology* and *gynecologist*.

**mis** (Anglo-Saxon), badly, wrongly, mistakenly

**misfeasance**    "act of doing wrongly"; improper conduct in public office.

**hetero** (Greek), unlike

**heterogeneous**    opposite of *homogeneous;* dissimilar; unlike; made of different parts that are not unified.

**pseudo** (Greek), false    Attached to a word, *pseudo* indicates something spurious masquerading as the real thing, as in "pseudo-freedom."

**pseudonym**    "a false name"; pen name; fictitious or assumed name.

## ON THE OTHER SIDE OF THE ROAD (POSITIVE)

**co, com, con,** together with    *Com* is used before *b*, *m*, and *p*, as in *combat, commiserate,* and *compensate; col* before *l* as in *collaborate* (work together) and *cor* before *r* as in *correlate*.

**coagulate**    curdle; clot; gather together in a mass.

**collusion**    "act of playing together"; secret agreement for fraudulent or illegal purposes; in "cahoots."

**concomitant**    accompanying; attending.

**syn, sym** (Greek), together

**symmetrical**    "measuring together"; having corresponding opposite sides; having a pleasing, harmonious balance.

**synthesis**    "act of putting together"; combination of parts to form a whole.

**bene** (Latin), well

**benediction**   "act of saying well"; blessing; best wishes; benison.

**beneficent**   "doing well"; doing good; performing acts of kindness.

**eu** (Greek), well

**euphony**   a pleasant sound.

**euphoria**   a feeling of well-being, often without good reason.

**phil** (Greek), love

**philanthropist**   "one who loves mankind" well enough to invest money in its welfare.

**homo** (Greek), like

**homogeneous**   of the same kind or structure; consisting of similar (Latin *similis,* same) parts throughout.

**ortho** (Greek), straight, right, true

**orthodox**   "holding the right opinion"; conforming to practices and opinions, especially in religion.

**rect(i)** (Latin), straight, right

**rectitude**   "rightness, straightness"; righteousness; strict observance of standards of honesty and integrity.


## INTENSIVES

A number of the prefixes by extension of their meaning or by their figurative use become intensifiers of the words they're attached to. It is easy to see, for example, how *de* can become "down and out,"; *per,* "through and through"; *con,* "with it"; *in,* "enforced," all of them essentially meaning "very."

The prefix *in* does not mean *not* in *inflammable, incensed,* or *incandescent.* It merely serves to intensify the flame. The *cor* in *corroborate* fortifies the word and makes it stronger (*robor,* from a Latin word meaning strength). The *de* in *decrepit* gives the word the meaning of being completely feeble (Latin *crepare,* to crack, to break). The *ex* in *exhilarate* makes the gladness (*hilarity*) greater. The *per* in *perfervid* heightens the fervor, zeal, or passion (Latin *fervere,* to boil).


## ODDS AND ENDS

**auto** (Greek), self

**autochthonous**   native (Greek *chthon,* earth); aboriginal; indigenous.

**be** (Anglo-Saxon)        a prolific prefix (*bedevil, bedim, be-friend, belittle, beseech, beside*) with many meanings but serving chiefly, as can be seen from the words cited, as an intensive, causal, or positional (like *by* in *bystander*) prefix.

   **bedight**        bedecked; accoutered; arrayed. Although archaic, the word is listed because Poe's "El Dorado" begins with:

> Gaily bedight, a gallant knight
> In sunshine and in shadow . . .

   **bedizen**        to dress gaudily—in a cheap, ostentatious manner.

   **berate**        to scold or criticize severely.

**crypt(o)** (Greek), hidden        The words to which *crypto* is attached denote something or somebody hidden and secret, like *crypto-Communist, crypto-Nazi;* a "crypto-anything" is one who is accused of working secretly for an objective he is unwilling to declare.

   **cryptogram**        message with a hidden or secret meaning; a writing in cipher or code.

   **cryptic**        hidden; occult; secret.

**par(a)** (Greek)        This prefix, which is being placed in front of more and more words, has many meanings, but we can simplify things by thinking of it as meaning close (alongside, nearby) or close (not exactly, resembling).

   **paramilitary**        close to being military, in the sense of serving as an auxiliary group, though not officially designated as a fighting force.

   **paranoia**        (Greek *nous,* mind); a mental disorder marked by delusions of persecution. The word *nous* (adjective *noetic*) is coming into use as a vogue word meaning the highest intellect, sometimes with the additional idea of expertise.

> *Bad Boys* is directed by Susumu Hani
> with considerable Freudian nous.

   In E. M. Forster's *The Longest Journey* (1907), Mr. Pembroke, complaining about Rickie's absent-mindedness, says, "Really, the lower classes have no nous."

   **paraphrase**        to get close to the original by stating it in one's own words; as a noun—a rephrasing or rewording.

   **parasite**        "taking food alongside"; an organism or person that lives on or off someone else.

**paronomasia**    a play on words, in which one uses words whose sounds are "closely" alike but whose meanings are different; a pun. One usually "perpetrates" a pun, so low is it in the scale of humor. A famous pun by Sydney Smith, the well-known nineteenth-century British wit, deals with two women, living on opposite sides of the street, who engaged in daily loud disputes as they leaned out of their windows. It was Sydney Smith's reasoned conclusion that they could never come to any agreement because they were "arguing from different premises."

By the way, the Greek word *onoma* (variant form *onyma*) means name and appears in such other words as *antonym, synonym, anonymous, pseudonym, and eponymous* (a long shortcut for "from the book of the same name"). For example, Tom Jones is the eponymous hero of Fielding's great novel.

**para** (Latin)    The combining form *para* comes from a Latin verb *parare* meaning to prepare; to guard or to protect against; "to parry."

**parachute**    a protection against a rapid fall (French *chute*). Paratroopers are parachute troops.

Often seen and heard today is the expression *drogue chute (parachute)*. The word *drogue* is probably another way of saying *drag*. The function of the drogue parachute is given in this *New York Times* item of December 19, 1965:

> At an altitude of about eight miles, the small drogue parachute unfurled to brake the craft's fall to 200 miles an hour. A minute later, the main chute billowed and Gemini 7 began dropping horizontally.

**parapet**    (*pet* from Latin *pectus*, through Italian *petto*, chest) "breastwork"; a protecting wall; a rampart.

**parasol**    a protection against the sun (*sol*). The French also have a *parapluie* to protect against the rain (*pluie*). Our umbrella (Latin *umbra*, shade) serves both purposes.

**quasi** (Latin), as if    Placed before words to indicate that the writer or speaker is qualifying that word, as if to say it's almost but not quite the thing. One example is sufficient for all.

**quasi-stellar** almost like a star. From *quasi* comes the newly formed word *quasar,* of which *The New York Times* of April 13, 1965, wrote:

> The most recently discovered class of celestial objects is the quasar—a body that looks like a star but is apparently millions of times larger and billions of times brighter.

**vice** (Latin), in turn In English this form means instead of, in place of. It comes from a Latin word meaning "a turn, a change, a time" from which the Italian *vece,* the Spanish *vez,* and the French *fois* are derived. It is not related to *vice* (a sin), which comes from *vitium,* the source of *vitiate* and *vicious.* In words like *vice president, vice* is generally separated from its noun, but occasionally it forms an integral part of the word, as in the next word:

**viceroy** "in place of the king"; a monarch's representative.

**vicar** a substitute; a deputy; one acting as representative of God on earth; a parish priest. The play known here as *The Deputy* is called *Le Vicaire* in France.

**vicarious** experienced imaginatively through someone else, as when one reads a book or sees a play or moving picture.

**vicissitudes** "the turns of fortune"; change of circumstances in life; the ups and downs of life.

**xeno** (Greek), strange, foreign

**xenophile** one who likes or is friendly to foreigners.

## I. PREFIXES PRO AND CON

In the left-hand column is a list of words whose meanings are given only in the sense that the component parts (prefix and root) are literally translated. You are asked to place a prefix before the decapitated word on the right that will produce a meaning *more or less opposite* to that of the corresponding word on the left. In the process you will learn the meanings of some important Latin and Greek roots.

1. <u>ac</u>celerate     "speed up"     ——celerate
2. <u>bene</u>volent     "well wishing"     ——volent
3. <u>con</u>fident     "having faith with (strongly)"     ——fident

| | | |
|---|---|---|
| 4. consecrate | "make holy" | ___secrate |
| 5. consonance | "sounding together" | ___sonance |
| 6. dyspeptic | "having bad digestion" | ___peptic |
| 7. encourage | "put heart into" | ___courage |
| 8. euphony | "pleasant sound" | ___phony |
| 9. exhibit | "hold out" for display | ___hibit |
| 10. explicit | "unfolded" for all to see | ___plicit |
| 11. homogeneous | "of the same kind" | ___geneous |
| 12. inculpate | "place blame upon" | ___culpate |
| 13. ingress | "a stepping in" | ___gress |
| 14. intramural | "within the walls" | ___mural |
| 15. macrocosm | "large world" | ___cosm |
| 16. malefactor | "evildoer" | ___factor |
| 17. persist | "to stand through" thick and thin | ___sist |
| 18. persuade | "urge thoroughly" | ___suade |
| 19. philanthropist | "lover of mankind" | ___anthropist |
| 20. progression | "a stepping forward" | ___gression |

## II. ANGLO-SAXON AND LATIN SIDE BY SIDE

In most of the pairs of words below the Anglo-Saxon and the Latin roots have substantially the same meaning, as have many of the prefixes. You are asked to supply the missing prefix (Anglo-Saxon or Latin) that will complete the word so that it becomes a synonym of the word alongside it.

EXAMPLES: bewildered —fused  ANSWERS: confused
        —draw   depart           withdraw

| | | | |
|---|---|---|---|
| 1. forgive | ___done | 6. ___look | disregard |
| 2. ___cast | dejected | 7. bewitch | ___chant |
| 3. ___seer | supervisor | 8. undermine, | ___vert |
| 4. becloud | ___fuscate | overturn | |
| 5. ___guile | deceive | | |

## III. LATIN AND GREEK PARALLELS

For each word in the left-hand column, derived from Latin elements, there is a corresponding word derived from Greek elements in the right-hand column. In almost every pair even the root and the prefix have substantially the same meaning. You are asked to pair the words off.

1. ambulatory     a. adamant
2. circumference   b. anomalous

|   |   |
|---|---|
| 3. circumlocution | c. eclectic |
| 4. experiential | d. empirical |
| 5. indomitable | e. metamorphosis |
| 6. irregular | f. metaphysical |
| 7. multilingual | g. peripatetic |
| 8. selective | h. periphery |
| 9. transcendental | i. periphrasis |
| 10. transformation | j. polyglot |

## IV.   SYNONYMS AND ANTONYMS

Here you will meet either prefixes already taken up or some words included in the discussion of prefixes. In each group choose a pair of words that are either synonyms (of same or like meaning) or antonyms (of opposite or unlike meaning).

1. (a) prognosis (b) premonition (c) ambiguity (d) foretelling (e) contravention
2. (a) short poem (b) proem (c) preface (d) advance (e) prolongation
3. (a) modern (b) antediluvian (c) prominent (d) miraculous (e) transitory
4. (a) neglect (b) pardon (c) glory (d) shame (e) ignominy
5. (a) panacea (b) hyperthyroidism (c) transmigration (d) propulsion (e) metempsychosis
6. (a) provide (b) pursue (c) purblind (d) purvey (e) peruse
7. (a) eulogy (b) apogee (c) perigee (d) apocalypse (e) perimeter
8. (a) inability to speak (b) nervous ailment (c) aphorism (d) temporary stoppage (e) adage
9. (a) sad (b) secluded (c) spiteful (d) sedulous (e) industrious
10. (a) good posture (b) rectitude (c) dishonorable conduct (d) orthodoxy (e) recollection

## V.   IN CONTEXT

In each of the following passages we have removed the prefix from one word. Restore the prefix so that the word corresponds to one of the following meanings:

| | | |
|---|---|---|
| (a) guardedly | (d) unwelcome | (g) relic |
| (b) rises above | (e) strolling | (h) inducing well-being |
| (c) freak | (f) confident | (i) secretly |

1. The notion that a Rockefeller would ever have to prove an energetic practitioner of the old Horatio Alger maxim of "strive and succeed" is an ——omaly of American politics.

2. The intellectual and artistic community in Hungary is exerting its pressure on the Government and party leadership more ___spectly than its counterpart in Poland.

3. Although the practice, which can be habit-forming, causes no organic illness, it produces a ___phoric state that can be dangerous.

4. Harry S. Truman is a particularly lively elder statesman; having been President of the United States, he is now historian, teacher, ___patetic philosopher and—by no means least—a politician.

5. *The Trojan Women* is a play that ___cends the age it was written in. It's universal in spirit.

## VI. FUN WITH WORDS

The missing word in each of the numbered passages given can be found in this list of terms dealing with words and language:

| | | | |
|---|---|---|---|
| (a) | acronym | (f) | hyperbole |
| (b) | adage | (g) | onomatopoeia |
| (c) | anagrams | (h) | palindrome |
| (d) | cryptogram | (i) | paronomasia |
| (e) | euphemism | (j) | simile |

Select the one that will correctly complete the blank space in the sentences below; and as an extra task, a sort of "Do-It-Yourself," look up the meanings of the terms in the above list that you do not yet know.

1. In a certain kind of word game, a player changed *malice* to *climate* by rearranging the letters of *malice* and adding a *t*. This game is called _____.

2. Speaking English for the occasion, Napoleon allegedly declared, "Able was I ere I saw Elba." A group of words reading the same backward and forward is called a(n) _____.

3. Calling older persons "senior citizens" is an example of a(n)

_____.

4. At Ophelia's grave, Hamlet exclaims:

> I loved Ophelia: forty thousand brothers
> Could not, with all their quantity of love,
> Make up my sum.

This kind of poetic exaggeration is called _____.

5. In the story "The Gloria Scott" Sherlock Holmes decoded the following apparently harmless but actually sinister message:

> The supply of game for London is going steadily
> up. Head-keeper Hudson, we believe, has been now

told to receive all orders for fly-paper and for preservation of your hen pheasant's life.

A message that contains a hidden meaning that must be decoded is known as a(n) _____.

Incidentally, how did Holmes pluck forth its hidden meaning? If you do not care to match your deductive powers with his, the answer is:

> *The game is up. Hudson has told all. Fly for your life.*

(Every third word tells the story—counting hyphenated words as two words. Elementary!)

## VOCABAGRAMS

As in Chapters 3 and 4, you are given the definitions and you are asked to form a word that is a synonym of that definition by rearranging the letters, or by adding or subtracting the letter indicated and then rearranging the remaining letters. We give you the prefix with which the word to be formed begins.

Here is an example of each type of operation:

| | | | | | |
|---|---|---|---|---|---|
| A. timer | | = to send back | re_____ | ANSWERS: | remit |
| B. green | + e | = go back on a promise | re_____ | | renege |
| C. retain | − a | = inactive | in_____ | | inert |

| | | | |
|---|---|---|---|
| 1. counters | | = interpret | con_____ |
| 2. discern | | = cancel | re_____ |
| 3. ruined | | = hardened | in_____ |
| 4. sausage | | = lessen, allay | as_____ |
| 5. boar | + h | = shrink from | ab_____ |
| 6. clout | + c | = hidden | oc_____ |
| 7. dieter | + u | = learned | e_____ |
| 8. fruits | + e | = excess | sur_____ |
| 9. legal | + e | = assert | al_____ |
| 10. mobile | + r | = involve in dispute | em_____ |
| 11. pint | + e | = clumsy | in_____ |
| 12. respite | + g | = renown, influence | pre_____ |
| 13. simple | + i | = hints at | im_____ |
| 14. tale | + x | = lift up | ex_____ |
| 15. tramp | + i | = communicate, give to | im_____ |
| 16. bending | − d | = kind | ben_____ |
| 17. escalating | − t | = pain-soother | an_____ |
| 18. mailing | − i | = to slander | mal_____ |
| 19. murder | − r | = to object | de_____ |
| 20. sanguine | − a | = following | en_____ |

*It is said that Confucius, when asked what his first deed would be if he were to be made Emperor of China, replied, "I would re-establish the precise meaning of words."*

*There is a great deal to be said for his idea. Whenever language loses its accuracy, it loses some of its ability to communicate and, in turn, some of its reason for existence.*

INVESTOR'S READER,
Merrill Lynch, Pierce, Fenner and Smith, Inc.

# 6.  Take a Number

> *Numbers have a legendary and mystic significance. It is not only the mathematician that has been fascinated by them. The poet, the philosopher, the priest have pondered over their changeless relations to each other, have come to look upon numbers and their symbols as in some sort a revelation from on high, things to be dealt with reverently and awesomely. And so, almost every number has been given an esoteric meaning.*
>
> WILLIAM S. WALSH, *Handy Book of Literary Curiosities*

Students of words have also pondered over numbers, especially when the words by which they are designated have been used as elements to form other words. For example, a number from 1 to 10 is contained in each of the words listed below. Tell what the number is in each one.

a. decade
b. duplicity
c. hebdomadal
d. monolithic
e. novena
f. octopus
g. pentathlon
h. quadrille
i. semester
j. trident

When you read more about these pretest words in the verbal countdown we have enumerated below, you will see that all ten come from Latin and Greek roots. The names of our numbers, whether cardinal ("counting off," telling us how many) or ordinal ("in order," telling us which one), are with only two exceptions (the number *million* and its multiples and the ordinal *second*) of Anglo-Saxon origin. However, words that have a numerical element in them, like *principal*, "taking

*89*

first place," are formed principally from Latin and Greek names of numbers.

Below is an important fraction of the large number of such words in the English language—words that have an interest, a fascination, and a magic of their own—verbally speaking!

## FROM 1 TO 10

1 The combining form *uni* from the Latin word *unus*, one, is easily recognizable in words like *unit*, *unity*, and *union*. A form of this word appears in our national motto *E pluribus unum*, "Out of many [states] one [country or government]." The Unisphere, symbol of the 1964–65 World's Fair in New York, stressed the idea that different peoples all over the world form "one world" after all. Unilateral action is "one-sided," undertaken by one side only. *Unison* means "one sound," that is, singing with one sound; hence, to act in unison is to act harmoniously. *Unique* means the only one of its kind; therefore, the word *very* is not needed to qualify it, for uniqueness is absolute. The universe is the sum total of existing things, earth and space considered as one.

The number *one* was invested with a sacred quality, being indivisible and forming a part of all other numbers. The sacred and awesome connotation of the Anglo-Saxon word *one* appears in the beautiful words *atone* ("at one") and *atonement* ("act of being at one"), which in religious doctrine contain the idea of the oneness between man and God or the reconciliation between them. In general use the words refer to expiation and reparation, making amends, or "making up" for wrongs or for things that should have been done.

The Latin word *prior* means former or preferable. Hence, *priority* means precedence. As a title, *prior* refers to a monastic superior, the head of a priory, a religious house ranking below an abbey. The superlative (in Latin) of *prior* is *primus*, first. A primate is a churchman of high rank, like a bishop. The idea of *first* occurs in another use of *primate* when it denotes the highest order of mammals—man and especially monkeys. *Primacy* is the state of being first.

*Primitive* is a synonym of *primeval*, well-known from "This is the forest primeval," the opening words of Longfellow's "Evangeline." Something primitive or primeval goes back to the first ages (*aevum* is Latin for *age*, as in *medieval*, or *mediaeval*, *coeval*, occurring at the same time, contemporary, and *longevity*). Another synonym is *primordial*, existing from the first "order." *Premier*, foremost, and *premiere*, first appearance, debut, come from *primus* via French. A more difficult word from *primus* is *primogeniture*, the right of inheritance by the firstborn.

From the Greek adjective *monos*, meaning single, solitary, come a great many English words containing the idea of oneness. How often do we encounter *monolith* and *monolithic* used to convey the idea of vastness and solidity! A monolith is a single huge stone (*lith* means stone, as in *lithograph*, a print of a design first produced on a flat stone). Because of the rocklike solidity implied, *monolith* and *monolithic* are preferred by some writers and speakers to *unity* and *unified* in speaking of organizations and alliances.

> We will not have a monolithic world
> —all Communist or all democratic but a
> world of great diversity.

*     *     *

> The great alliance which once made a
> monolith of the Moscow-Peking axis will
> be ended.

Of the many English words containing the combining form *mon(o)* we list a few here:

**monarch**    originally a supreme ruler (*arch*, chief, ruling).

**monastery**    a residence of monks. A monk (from *monachus*, "alone") is one who originally retired from the world for religious meditation.

**monism**    a system of thought seeking to deduce all phenomena from a single substance.

**monocle**    a glass for one eye (*oculus*, eye).

**monogamy**    state of being married (Greek *gamos*, marriage) to only one person at any one time.

**monogram**    the combining of two or more letters to form one, like the design made by intertwining two or more initials.

**monograph**    a treatise or piece of writing (Greek *graph*, write) on a single subject.

**monologue**    a long talk or speech (Greek *logos*, speech) by one person while others listen but do not participate. A monologue is also a dramatic sketch performed by one actor or actress—a "one-man" show. The word *soliloquy* is etymologically equivalent, from Latin *solus*, alone, and *loqui*, speak. An actor delivers a soliloquy when he utters his thoughts aloud in a long "aside," supposed to be heard only by himself and the audience.

**monomania**          form of insanity in which the sufferer is irrational on only one subject.

**monophobia**          morbid dread of being left alone.

**monopoly**          exclusive possession or control.

**monotheism**          doctrine or belief that only one god (Greek *theos*, god) exists.

The Greek word for *first* is *protos*, combining form *prot(o)*. It may indicate the first of a group to whose name it is attached. Thus, *proto-Hellenic* refers to the "first, or earliest" Greeks, and *proto-martyr* denotes the first martyr in a cause. *Prototype* is the general word for "first of its kind," the original.

From *proto* comes *protocol*, a word with an interesting history. Its literal meaning is "a first gluing" (Greek *kollon*, glue, from which is also derived *collage*, a gluing together of materials to form a picture). Originally, *protocol* was connected with the use of rolls of papyrus, which consisted of sheets glued together. The *protocol* was the first sheet, which bore the authentication and date of manufacture. The word came to mean an original draft or memorandum from which official copies were made and also a formal statement of a transaction or proceeding. Today the word *protocol* is used in a different sense; it refers to the etiquette to be observed by the head of a state in dealing with representatives or heads of other countries, to a code of procedure prescribing the order of precedence at functions, to official duties fixed by custom and tradition.

> According to protocol, the Vice President is the President's replacement at important ceremonies.

The word *protagonist* was the technical name of the first actor in a Greek drama, the one with the leading role. It also meant the chief contender (Greek *agon*, struggle). Hence, it came to mean also the chief character in a novel, the one about whom the action revolves. In modern usage, the meaning of *protagonist* has been extended to indicate a champion or proponent of a cause.

**1½** Between the combining forms for *one* and *two* we are placing the Latin prefix *sesqui*, which is formed from two parts, *semis*, for *semi*, half + *qui*, for *que*, and. *Sesqui* means literally "and a half (more), (more) by a half"; in effect its meaning is one and a half, or one and a half times. *Semi* itself is attached to hundreds of English words, as in *semicolon*, *semiconscious*, and *semicircle*. Also meaning half are *hemi* (Greek), as in *hemicycle* and *hemisphere*, and *demi* (Latin via French), as in *demitasse*, *demigod*, and *demimonde*, the shady "half-world." *Sesqui* is found in a number of English words, among them:

**sesquicentennial**    "pertaining to 1½ × 100"; the 150th anniversary; *sesquicentenary* celebrates the same thing.

**sesquipedalian**    "a foot (*ped*) and a half long"; a term used to characterize unusually long words. This word goes back to the phrase *sesquipedalia verba* ("sesquipedalian words") with which the Roman poet Horace described the use of bombastic language and multisyllabic words by writers of tragedies. The noun that names such language is *sesquipedalianism*, or *sesquipedality*.

**2** Two may be company, but the idea of twoness may also cause division, breaking unity into two opposing (*di*) parts. When doubt enters, a person is of two minds about something, a condition that the Germans call *Zweifel* (from *zwei*, two). *Doubt* and *dubiety*, *doubtful* and *dubious*, *double* and *duplicity* (double-dealing, deception), are derived from *duo*, the Latin word for *two*. *Indubitable*, "not able to be doubted," means certain, unquestionable.

Other Latin word elements containing the idea of *two* are *bi* and *bini*, combining form *bin*, which sometimes have a distributive force—they tell us how many times. Some words with these elements are:

**biannual**    occurring twice a year; semiannual. It is better to use *semiannual* and avoid *biannual*, a dangerous word because of possible confusion with:

**biennial**    happening every two years or lasting for two years.

**bicameral**    having two houses or chambers (Latin *camera*, room), like the American Congress.

**bifurcate**    to branch into two parts or "forks" (Latin *furcus*).

**bigamy**    state of being married to two persons at the same time, as opposed to *monogamy*.

**binary**    consisting of two things or parts.

**binocular**    adapted for the use of two eyes at the same time.

**binomial**    consisting of two terms or names.

**combine**    to put together two or more things; to unite.

From Greek we get the combining form *di* meaning twice or double. A diploma originally meant something doubled over, a paper folded in two. Taken over into Latin, the word came to mean not only a document conferring an honor but also a paper of credentials. So, a diplomat is an accredited representative of a country sent to another country. Another interesting word of Greek origin containing *di* is *dilemma* (*lemma*, an assumption), an argument presenting two choices. A choice of unsatisfactory alternatives is said to impale a person "upon the horns of a dilemma." In modern usage, *dilemma* has come to mean any difficulty, a course of action that promises no satisfactory solution.

A Greek adverb related to *di* is *dicha,* combining form *dich(o)*, meaning in two, apart. Where there is a *dichotomy* there are two divisions, two opposing schools of thought, a bifurcation. The terminal combining form of *dichotomy* means a cutting, from *tom,* a Greek root meaning to cut. (See *tomy* in the next chapter.)

**3**    In the system of the ancient philosopher Pythagoras, the number three was the perfect number, expressive of a beginning, middle, and end. Among the word elements used to form English words with *three* in them are the Greek *tri,* three, and the Latin *tri, ter,* three at a time, thrice, *tert,* from *tertius,* third, and *trini,* three each. Of course, the word *three* itself is also used as in *threefold* and *three-ply,* but such words present no vocabulary difficulty.

Here are some representative words formed with the Greek and Latin word elements:

**Greek**

**triad**    a group of three.

**trilogy**    work of literature or music in three parts, like the *Oresteia* of Aeschylus, which consists of three separate plays on a unified theme.

**tripod**    three-footed stand (*pod,* foot).

**triptych**    picture or carving in three compartments; a three-part picture; figuratively, a work in three contrasting or matching parts.

## Latin

**tercentenary**    a 300th anniversary.

**travail**    hardship, suffering, from French word for *work*, assumed to come from a Latin word meaning three stakes used as an instrument of torture—*tripalium*, from *palus*, a pole, from which we get *impale*, to pierce as if with a stake, or pole.

**trellis**    a lattice work frame or screen, originally meaning a fabric of triple thread.

**trident**    three-pronged (*dent*, tooth) spear of sea gods in classical mythology; a symbol of power; a scepter.

**trimester**    name given to a college term where the academic year is divided into three regular terms (see *semester*, under the entry for the number *six*).

**Trinity**    the union of three to form a single godhead; without a capital first letter the word means any group of three.

**triumvirate**    an official group of three men (*viri*) in ancient Rome, now used to mean any group of three men or even countries. Recently, the Russian word *troika*, the name of a vehicle drawn by three horses abreast, came into vogue, and being shorter than *triumvirate*, has often replaced it in the daily press, especially in headlines.

**trivet**    a three-footed stand for holding a kettle; a stand with short legs for a hot plate. Etymologically, *trivet* is akin to *tripod*, for *vet* stands for Angle-Saxon *fēt*, feet, as in *fetters*, shackles for the feet.

Three other words with an interesting history dealing with the number three are *trivial*, *trivium*, and *untrammeled*.

**trivial**    In Latin the place where three roads meet was called a *trivium* (*via*, road). The meaning of this word was extended to include any crossroad, highway, or public square. Since, like our marketplace talk, the gossip and chatter in these places was held to be commonplace and ordinary, the adjective *trivialis*, whence the English *trivial*, was used to characterize such unimportant talk, and by extension anything of little consequence.

**trivium**    On the other hand, in the medieval universities *trivium* was elevated, for it denoted three roads to learning—

grammar, rhetoric, and logic—which formed one division of the seven liberal arts (the other four are given under *quadrivium*).

**untrammeled**　　This word is derived from *trammel*, a net for catching fish or birds, or a shackle regulating the motions of a horse. The number *three* is concealed in *trammel*, which comes from the Latin *tres*, three, and *macula*, a mesh; the word designates a certain kind of three-layered net. As a verb *trammel* means to enmesh, to tie up and hold fast as in a net, as when Macbeth soliloquizes about the contemplated murder of Duncan, King of Scotland:

> If the assassination
> Could trammel up the consequence, and catch
> With his surcease success.

*Trammeled* means impeded or hampered; *untrammeled* means unimpeded, unshackled, and unfettered.

**4**　The number four was venerated by the followers of Pythagoras, as the first square after one. It has also been considered sacred because of the four ancient elements—earth, air, water, and fire—and the four cardinal points.

The Latin word for the number four is *quattuor;* its combining form is *quadr(i)*. The ordinal is *quartus*, fourth. *Quadr(i)* may also mean a square, as in *quadrate*.

**quadrangle**　　a figure with four sides or a four-sided court of a building.

**quadrant**　　an instrument with an arc of 90 degrees, which is one-fourth of a circle.

**quadratic**　　refers to an equation in which the highest power of the unknown term is a square, like $x^2$.

**quadrennial**　　held every fourth year; a fourth anniversary.

**quadrille**　　(from French) an old form of square dance.

**quarto**　　size of a piece of paper cut four from a sheet.

**quatrain**　　a four-line stanza, like the ones composing the *Rubáiyát* of Omar Khayyám. (*Rubáiyát* is the plural of the Arabic *rubái*, a quatrain.)

The word *square* acquired the s from the final sound of *ex* in the Latin expression *ex quadra*, "from a square." *Squadron* and *squad* originally referred to men arranged in a square. *Cadre*, a core group, a nucleus about which an organization is built, a dedicated cell of indoctrinated leaders, is a word of Italian and French origin ultimately related to square.

Two additional interesting words with the idea of *four* in them are *quadrivium* and *quadricentennial*. Higher than the trivium in the medieval courses of study, the quadrivium consisted of four subjects: arithmetic, astronomy, geometry, music. The word *quadricentennial*, the 400th anniversary or a celebration of that anniversary, flashed across the world in 1964, because that year marked the 400th anniversary of the birth of William Shakespeare. The English preferred the word *quatercentennial* in celebrating that event.

The word *quattrocento* is met in studies of Italian art and literature. Literally, it means 400, but actually it refers to the fifteenth century, for it is an abbreviation of the Italian word for 1400. In the same way, our own word *fortnight*, meaning a period of two weeks, is a shorter form of an earlier English expression meaning fourteen nights.

The Greek combining form *tetra*, four, is used in English chiefly to form scientific words. However, there is one very interesting word derived from it: *tessel(l)ated*, which comes to us via Latin *tessera*, diminutive form *tessella*, a small piece of marble or glass usually cut into squares or rectangles. These pieces were used in the making of mosaics, patterns using small tiles, an art that was highly cultivated in various periods and parts of the Roman world. *Tesselated* means made into, or like, a mosaic, or like a checkerboard.

**5** Five fingers, five toes, five senses—magic powers were also once imputed to the number five. The five-pointed star was used as a magical symbol. Because it can be drawn continuously without lifting pencil from paper, it is called the endless knot. The technical name for it is *pentacle* or *pentagram*, from *pente*, Greek word for *five*, combining form *penta*.

Some additional English words with *penta* in them are:

**pentagon**      a five-sided plane figure.

**pentameter**      a line of poetry having five metrical feet.

**Pentateuch**      the first five books of the Old Testament.

**pentathlon**      an athletic contest in which each contestant participates in five different events.

The Latin word for *five* is *quinque*, ordinal *quintus*, fifth, from which we get such simple words as *quintet* and *quintuplets*. Here are a few others, not so simple.

**quinquennium**      "a five-year period."

**quintessence**      "the fifth essence." This word also means the highest essence, because in ancient and medieval philosophy there was thought to be a fifth or higher essence above earth, air, water, and fire, permeating all nature and forming the substance of the heavenly bodies. When Hamlet in pessimistic mood speaks of man, "the paragon of animals," he says, "And yet, to me, what is this quintessence of dust?" The adjective *quintessential* means highest and purest of its kind, embodying perfection.

From French *cinq(ue)* derived from *quinque* come the words *cinquain*, a five-line stanza, and *cinquefoil*, a figure enclosed by five joined foils, which one can see in Gothic tracery. The Italian *cinquecento*, 500, short for 1500, is used to mean the sixteenth century, especially in art and literature (like *quattrocento* for the fifteenth century).

**6** Six was considered a perfect number representing equilibrium because it denoted the number of sides in two equilateral triangles placed base to base. Whatever may be its supposed magic properties, the Latin word *sex*, meaning six, and its ordinal, *sextus*, sixth, give us a number of interesting words, of which these are a sampling:

**sestet**    a stanza of six lines, or the last six lines of the Italian form of the sonnet.

**sextant**    a navigator's instrument, so named because its arc is 60 degrees, one-sixth of a circle.

**sextet(te)**    a group of six, especially six voices or instruments singing or playing together, as in the celebrated sextet in Donizetti's opera *Lucia di Lammermoor*.

The Latin word for *six* is somewhat concealed in the next two words to be considered. *Semester* comes from a Latin adjective, *semestris*, "every six months" (*sex*, six + *mensis*, month). Originally, *semester* meant a period of six months, then it came to mean any of the two terms into which a school year is generally divided, without reference to the number of months.

Disregarded also is the number six in the word *siesta*. This name for an afternoon nap or a break in the day's routine is derived via Spanish from the Latin phrase *sexta hora*, referring to the sixth hour after sunrise, which is set at six in the morning for the purpose of reckoning time. The *siesta* began, therefore, at noon. However, as far as the time is concerned, the original significance of the word has been lost but the word itself has been kept to refer to any rest period at any hour of the day.

From *hex*, the Greek word for *six*, come only a few English words. (Incidentally, *hex*, a Pennsylvania-German word dealing with enchantment and witchcraft, has nothing to do with the Greek word but is derived from German *Hexe*, a witch.) The appearance of *hex* in *hexameter*, a line of verse containing six metrical feet, and in *hexagon*, a six-sided plane figure, is plainly visible, but not so in *samite*. This rich medieval fabric woven in silk with at times an interweaving of silver or gold was made with six threads to the warp. The name comes from Medieval Greek *hexamiton* (*hex*, six + *mitos*, thread).

> So flash'd and fell the brand Excalibur:
> But ere he dipt the surface, rose an arm
> Clothed in white samite, mystic, wonderful,
> And caught him by the hilt, and brandish'd him
> Three times. . . .
>
> ALFRED, LORD TENNYSON,
> *The Passing of Arthur*

**7** Seven ages of man, seven days of the week, Seven Wise Men, seven seals—in all ages and creeds, the number seven has had a symbolic, mystic character. However, there are few English words in which the number seven is significant.

Of course, there is always September. By derivation September should be the seventh month of the year. So it once was among the ancient Romans until the year 153 B.C. Until then their year had started with March. When January was made the first month, September, of course, became the ninth month but the name was kept without regard for its numerical significance. We have seen this phenomenon over and over again—the original meaning is lost, as in the case of *siesta*, but the word is kept. The names of the months following September were also retained, although the numbers in them no longer referred to the correct order in the calendar: October, from *octo*, eight, November, from *novem*, nine, and December, from *decem*, ten.

*Septet* and *septicentennial* are easy to figure out; not so easy is *septentrional*, meaning northern, a word derived from the Latin name of the Great Bear, or Great Dipper, *Septentriones*, "seven plow oxen," referring to the seven stars near the North Pole of the heavens.

*Hepta,* the Greek word for seven, appears in many words used in the sciences and music. We pass over such words as *heptane, heptagon,* and *heptachord* to consider *heptarchy,* a government by seven persons. Capitalized, the word refers specifically to the confederacy of seven Anglo-Saxon kingdoms of the seventh and eighth centuries.

Via Latin from the Greek ordinal *hebdomos,* seventh, comes the word *hebdomadal,* which means occurring every seven days, that is, weekly. The word is also used to mean a publication appearing weekly. The *Heptameron* is a collection of medieval stories attributed to Marguerite, Queen of Navarre, and published in 1558. It received its name from the fact that the stories were supposed to have been told in seven (*hepta*) days (Greek *hemera,* day); see *Decameron* under the number *ten.*

**8** The Pythagoreans considered eight the number of justice, for it divides evenly into four and four, which divide evenly again into two and two, which in turn divide into one and one. In addition, eight is the first cube after one.

The Latin word for *eight* is *octo,* ordinal, *octavus.* A few words formed with these elements are:

**octave**     in music, the eighth full tone above or below any given tone, or the interval embracing eight tones in the diatonic scale; the eighth day following a church festival, or the period between the day of the festival and the eighth day; any group of eight.

**octavo**     page or piece of paper cut eight from a sheet; its abbreviation is 8vo.

**octet**     any composition for eight voices or instruments; the first eight lines of the Italian form of the sonnet—completed by the sestet; any group of eight.

**October**     Look under *September.*

From Greek *okto,* transliterated as *octo,* come:
**octagon**     an eight-sided plane figure.

**octopus**     a mollusk with eight arms or tentacles (*pus,* from *pous,* foot). The plural of this word has three forms: *octopuses, octopi,* an erroneously Latinized plural form, and *octopodes,* Greek plural form. By an extension of meaning *octopus* is used to designate an organization that has many branches and exercises control over other groups. This use of the word was made famous by Frank Norris in 1901 when he gave the name *The Octopus* to a novel, in which a railroad company symbolizes organized business strangling the country, like an octopus squeezing its prey.

**9** Nine, representing three equilateral triangles, was considered a lucky number indicating the equilibrium of the three worlds. Although there are a number of English expressions with *nine* in them like "a nine days' wonder," "dressed to the nines," "nine points of the law," and "every cat has nine lives," the concept of *nine* appears in only a few words. Among them are *November, novena,* a nine days' period of devotion, and *nonagon,* a nine-sided plane figure—all from Latin *novem,* nine, or *nonus,* ninth.

*Noon* is ultimately derived from *nonus;* it originally referred to the ninth hour of the day, or *nona hora* in Latin. As we have seen in the case of *siesta* (under the number *six*), the hours were reckoned from 6 A.M., so that the ninth hour meant 3 P.M. A church office recited at that hour was called the *nones.* Although the hour of this service was pushed up (some say so that the hungry monks could eat earlier), the name *noon* was kept for the hour in which the nones were recited, even though it was now closer to twelve than to three. So, twelve o'clock noon bears a name which means three o'clock. *Noon* joins the company of *siesta, September, October, November,* and *December*—the number in each word tells an interesting story of something now all but forgotten.

**10** Ten was considered a perfect number; the fact that man learned to count on his ten fingers and ten toes gave this number its mathematical importance.

*Decem* is the Latin word for *ten;* its ordinal is *decimus.* The Greek word for *ten* is *deka,* written *deca* in English words.

A *decade* of words with *ten* in them are:

**dean** from Latin *decanus,* originally a chief over ten men; now a high officer in religious and academic circles; the senior member of a professional group. In the last meaning given, the French word *doyen,* from the same root, is often used instead of *dean,* especially in the sense of a person eminently qualified because of long experience.

**decade** a period of ten years; any group of ten.

**decagon** a ten-sided plane figure.

**Decalogue** the Ten Commandments; with a small *d* it means any set of binding rules.

**Decameron** name of the collection of 100 stories written in 1353 by Boccaccio. They were told in ten days by ten storytellers, each relating a tale a day, during the plague in Florence (1348). (Look back to *Heptameron* under *seven*.)

**decathlon**    an athletic contest in which each entrant participates in ten different events.

**December**    See *September*.

**decibel**    A bel is a scientific unit for measuring the volume of sound. A *decibel*, one-tenth of a bel, is just about the smallest degree of difference in loudness that the human ear can distinguish. There are about 25 decibels (abbreviated to *db*) in the softest note of the violin and about 100 in the *fortissimo* of a full orchestra. The word *decibel* is often used in nonscientific writing to imply loudness, as in this opening of a description of a play: "Amid the din of a high-decibel delivery on the part of the performers. . . ." The word *bel* itself is a tribute to Alexander Graham Bell, inventor of the telephone.

**decimal**    a number expressed in scales of tens; as an adjective, *decimal* means based on tens. In fractions, it refers to 10 as a denominator, as 3/10.

**decimate**    Originally, this meant to execute one chosen by lot out of ten; as now used, *decimate* means to kill or destroy totally or almost totally.

The original meaning of *dime* is one-tenth, from *decimus* via French. Another word for *one-tenth* is the Old English word *tithe* so often met in the Bible. It means a tax of one-tenth of a person's income or property, or a contribution of that amount, usually to a church or religious organization.

## BEYOND 10 TO 10,000

**12**    The Latin word for *twelve* is *duodecim;* the Greek, *dodeka* (*dodeca*). Twelve, of course, makes a dozen, a word that comes from *duodecim* via French *douzaine*. The duodecimal system refers to a reckoning by twelves. The first, shortest, and widest part of the small intestine measures about ten inches in man, but is called the duodenum (from *duodeni*, twelve at a time) because its length is about the breadth of twelve fingers. A dodecahedron is a solid with twelve plane faces. The Dodecanese Islands are a group of twelve (if one does not count Rhodes, which once belonged to Italy) Greek islands in the Aegean off the coast of Asia Minor. Among them are the newly discovered tourist havens of Cos and Patmos.

**40** From the Latin word *quadraginta,* forty, we get via French *quarante* the word *quarantine,* a period of forty days. It was applied to the period during which a ship suspected of carrying contagion was not allowed to have contact with the shore. As used today, it indicates the restriction itself, without any reference to the specific number of days, or the isolation of persons and animals carrying or suspected of carrying contagious diseases, or the place of seclusion itself. Figuratively, the verb *quarantine* means to isolate or to cut off somebody or even a nation from normal relations with society or other nations.

The Latin word for *forty* raises an interesting set of questions. Is there any one word for "a ten-year-old," or "a twenty-year-old" or "a thirty-year-old"? Not that we can think of. But there is a word for a forty-year-old—*quadragenarian,* from *quadraginta.* From there on, a single word of Latin origin will do the trick through the age of one hundred:

| | |
|---|---|
| *quinquegenarian* | fifty-year-old |
| *sexagenarian* | sixty-year-old |
| *septuagenarian* | seventy-year-old |
| *octogenarian* | eighty-year-old |
| *nonagenarian* | ninety-year-old |
| *centenarian* | hundred-year-old |

**50** *Pentecost* is derived from the Greek word for *fifty.* It is the seventh Sunday after Easter, that is, the fiftieth day. The name *Pentecost* may also refer to the Jewish festival of Shabuoth, or Shavuoth, which occurs on the fiftieth day after the second day of Passover.

**70** The famous translation of the Old Testament into Greek was said to have been made by seventy (or seventy-two) scholars some time in the third century B.C. in Alexandria. It is called the Septuagint because of the traditional number of scholars who worked on the translation. (According to modern scholars the story is spurious—but the name *Septuagint* remains.)

**100** Most of the words derived from Latin *centum,* 100, are fairly obvious, like *centenarian, centennial, centipede,* and *centurion* (originally a commander of 100 men in the Roman army). In the metric system, *centi,* a combining form, means ¹⁄₁₀₀; for 100 the Greek combining form *hecto* is used. So, a centimeter is ¹⁄₁₀₀ of a meter, whereas a hectometer is 100 meters. A hectograph is a duplicating machine able to turn out at least 100 copies. Nowadays the word *hecatomb* is used to mean a slaughter of a great number of persons; its Greek original, met so often in Homer, means (etymologically) the sacrifice of 100 animals, chiefly bulls or oxen. The final *b* is all that is left of the Greek word-ending formed from *bous,* bull, ox, cow, from which we get *bucolic,* pastoral.

**1,000**    From Latin *mille,* 1,000, we get *mile* (there were 1,000 paces in a Roman mile), *millipede,* "having 1,000 feet," *millimeter,* $\frac{1}{1,000}$ of a meter, generally written mm., *millennium* (*mille + annus,* year). This last word may be used simply to mean 1,000 years, a future period of happiness, peace on earth, or the realization of an ideal state on earth, based on the prophecy in Revelation 20:6 of a thousand years during which holiness shall triumph.

The two different meanings of *millennium* are brought out in these excerpts:

> For millennia, man has been haunted by the fate of Icarus, who flew too high and fell too far.

\*         \*         \*

> It would mean the end of revolutionary movements, thereby leaving the field open for peaceful evolution. It would mean the lion lying down with the lamb, the millennium.

The plural of *millennium* is either *millenniums* or *millennia,* a direct borrowing of the Latin plural form.

Sometimes the word *chiliad,* from *chilioi,* the Greek word for 1,000, is used instead of *millennium.* Its transliterated combining form, *kilo,* is used in the metric system to denote 1,000. Thus, a kilogram is 1,000 grams, whereas a milligram is $\frac{1}{1,000}$ of a gram.

**10,000**    Strictly counting, myriad, from the Greek word for 10,000, should mean only that number. However, both the ancient Greek word and its English descendant may mean a large, indefinite number. In *Biographia Literaria* Samuel Taylor Coleridge paid tribute to the multitudinous aspects of Shakespeare's genius by calling him "our myriadminded Shakespeare."

To many the word *myriad*, because of its evocation of the past and its mystical suggestiveness, may seem to be a more poetic word than *ten thousand*. Yet, in two of the most anthologized passages of English poetry we find the words *ten thousand* making their own music.

Wordsworth, describing a hill of daffodils, writes:

Ten thousand saw I at a glance
Tossing their heads in sprightly dance.

And Byron, apostrophizing the sea in *Childe Harold*, says:

Roll on, thou deep and dark blue Ocean—roll!
Ten thousand fleets sweep over thee in vain.

## I. ASSORTED NUMBERS

Fill in the blanks with the correct word or word element that indicates a number.

a. There are _____ sides in a nonagon.
b. Three men form a _____virate.
c. A hexapod is a _____-footed creature.
d. A kilometer contains one _____ meters.
e. A person who has reached his seventieth birthday has become a _____.
f. The celebration of a 200th anniversary is called a _____-centennial.
g. A quadrilingual hotel clerk can speak _____ languages.
h. Primogeniture is the right of inheritance by the _____-born.
i. The fifth or highest essence is the _____essence.
j. The *Decameron* is the title of a book of stories told over a period of _____ days.

## II. FIGURE THESE OUT

Answer the questions below by using numbers.

a. The status of Berlin was established on the basis of a quadripartite accord.
   How many countries made the accord?
b. Abraham Lincoln was born in 1809.
   In what year was the sesquicentennial of his birth observed?
c. John Masefield's poem "Cargoes" opens with this line:
   Quinquireme of Nineveh from distant Ophir.

One theory is that the number in words like *bireme, trireme,* etc., refers to the banks of oars; another theory is that it indicates the number of rowers to a bench. No matter which belief is correct, the number in such words is not affected. Therefore, how many banks of oars (*rem,* oar, from Latin word *remus*) or rowers to a bench did a quinquireme (also written *quinquereme*) have?

d. Someone wrote that the Pan American Building in New York is the work of one of the most unlikely architectural troikas ever harnessed.

How many architects designed the building?

e. In how many events do the athletes take part if they are competing in a decathlon?

## III. COUNT OFF!

Each of the following words contains a number. Rearrange the words in numerical instead of their present alphabetical order.

| | | |
|---|---|---|
| a. | bireme | i. nonce |
| b. | centime | j. noon |
| c. | cinquefoil | k. octachord |
| d. | duodenal | l. quarantine |
| e. | farthing | m. samite |
| f. | fortnight | n. septentrional |
| g. | kilowatt | o. tierce |
| h. | myriad | p. tithe |

## IV. ELIMINATE THE IMPOSTOR!

After each number, four of the words contain an element that corresponds to the number itself. The fifth word looks like a word of the same numerical family but it is only an impostor. Throw out this word in each group that does not count.

EXAMPLE: 1. (a) monogram (b) universal (c) atone
(d) onerous (e) protoplasm

ANSWER: (d) onerous    All the others contain a word element meaning *one* or *first; onerous* does not.

1. (a) onion (b) unison (c) monopoly (d) monitor (e) primacy
2. (a) dupe (b) dubious (c) combine (d) dilemma (e) duologue
3. (a) ternary (b) tertiary (c) tripe (d) trammel (e) Trinity
4. (a) square (b) cadre (c) quadrant (d) quarrel (e) tesselate

5. (a) quinquennium (b) pentameter (c) quince (d) cinquain
   (e) pentacle
6. (a) sextant (b) siesta (c) sestet (d) sextuplet (e) sexton
7. (a) septet (b) heptarchy (c) Heptameron (d) septum
   (e) September
8. (a) octagon (b) octave (c) oculist (d) octet (e) October
9. (a) Nones (b) nonagon (c) noon (d) November
   (e) nonentity
10. (a) decibel (b) dean (c) decadent (d) Decalogue (e) decuple

## V.  MATCHING

Match the words on the left with those on the right.

1. atonement          a. transitory
2. decimate           b. person playing a leading role
3. dichotomy          c. four-line stanza
4. ephemeral          d. great slaughter
5. hecatomb           e. very long
6. protagonist        f. expiation
7. protocol           g. agony
8. prototype          h. established code of ceremonial procedure
9. quatrain           i. destroy a large part of
10. samite            j. division into two parts
11. sesquipedalian    k. first of its kind
12. travail           l. heavy silk fabric

## VI. ANALOGIES

From the pairs after the letters select the one that best completes the analogy. (For detailed instructions see pages 329–332; 335.)

EXAMPLE:  PENTATHLON : DECATHLON : : (a) ten : five
          (b) four : two (c) five : ten (d) score : decade
ANSWERS   (c) because there are five events in a pentathlon and
          ten in a decathlon; the other ratios are not 1 : 2

1. PRIMORDIAL : PROTOCOL : : (a) primitive : etiquette
   (b) decibel : sound (c) declare : expostulate
   (d) bifurcate : fork
2. COEVAL : CONTEMPORARY : : (a) medieval : paleolithic
   (b) volume : scroll (c) defend : protect (d) arduous : difficult
3. DEAN : TEN : : (a) centurion : 100 (b) millipede : 1,000
   (c) admiral : fleet (d) prototype : first
4. MONOGRAPH : ENCYCLOPEDIA : : (a) giant : giant
   (b) dwarf : giant (c) dwarf : dwarf (d) giant : dwarf
5. NONAGENARIAN : NINETY : : (a) century : 100
   (b) centipede : 100 (c) centenarian : 100 (d) centimeter : 100

## DO-IT-YOURSELF DEPARTMENT

Answer the following questions—the story is told by the numbers in the words.

1. The following terms are often heard and seen today in reference to sound, music, recording, and broadcasting:
    (a) binaural (b) monaural (c) dodecaphonic.
First tell what number is contained in each word, and then look up the meaning of the words.

2. Why is a very large and powerful wave sometimes called a decuman wave?

3. What does each of the following have to do with the number two?
    (a) Deuteronomy (b) dimity (c) twilight (d) twill
    (e) twine (f) twist.

4. What kind of figure is a hexagram?

5. What is the relationship between *onion* and *union?*

6. To what numerical element are *prim* and *primp* related?

7. What number is said to be contained in the name of the drink called punch?

8. What is the relation of *primer, primrose, protein,* and *proton* to "first"?

9. What number is contained in each of the following words?
    (a) trapeze (b) trapezium (c) trapezoid.

10. Why are the Unitarians so called?

Since the purpose of the Do-It-Yourself Department is to have you do independent research, no answers to these questions or to the other Do-It-Yourself exercises throughout this book are given in the back.

### *VOCABAGRAMS*

This is a variation of the game that you met in Chapters 3, 4, 5—now you will work with two words at a time. Put together the words in the left-hand and center columns; rearrange the letters to form a word that corresponds to the definition in the right-hand column. Each answer will be a word with a number in it.

EXAMPLE:   quit + net = a set of five    ANSWER:   quintet

1. buy   + tied  = doubt
2. cheat + mob   = great sacrifice
3. cool  + port  = ceremonial procedure
4. day   + rim   = at least 10,000
5. mad   + mile  = quandary
6. moan  + creed = title of a famous book
7. set   + set   = last six lines of a sonnet
8. sit   + sea   = afternoon nap
9. ten   + dirt  = Neptune's scepter
10. tip  + mare  = high churchman
11. top  + rid   = three-legged stool
12. vat  + lair  = great suffering

# 7.   End Pieces That Shape the Word

***The Ize Have It***

*Iron is galvanized, rubber vulcanized, salt iodized, people hypnotized. But we agonized when President Kennedy utilized and Merriam-Webster dictionary authorized the word finalized.*

*We would have criticized this ominous trend were it not for the conviction that whatever is bureaucratized must also be gobbledegookized.*

ST. LOUIS POST-DISPATCH, DECEMBER 10, 1961

Suffixes come at the end of a word. Unlike prefixes, they play a small role in influencing the meaning of the word they're attached to. Most of the time, they serve as tags to identify the word as a Noun or Verb, Adjective or Adverb.

It is safe to assume, for example, that words ending in the free-wheeling suffix *ize* (seen in action in the epigraph that heads this chapter) are verbs, that such suffixes as *ism* and *ness* lock in nouns, and that the suffix *ous* announces the presence of adjectives. However, we cannot always depend on individual suffixes to form verbs, nouns, or adjectives exclusively. Nor is it always easy to assign precise meanings to them. Nevertheless, we have several reasons for devoting a chapter to suffixes:

1. Such a discussion may serve as a review of the terminology of grammar.
2. It may help solve some terminal spelling problems.
3. Most important, it offers us an opportunity to slip in some

difficult or interesting words. Where else could we list a lovely upcoming word like *numinous*?

## SOME VERB ENDINGS

Throughout this chapter—except where otherwise noted—the suffix comes from Latin. We shall give the meaning only when the suffix has a fairly constant meaning. As before, quotation marks around a definition indicate the literal meanings of the prefix, root, and suffix. Synonyms and definitions will generally follow.

**ate**    (also used as an adjective ending)
   **ameliorate**    "to make better"; to improve.
   **attenuate**    "to make thin"; to weaken.
   **consummate**    "to bring to the highest (*summus*) point"; to bring to fulfillment; to complete. When accented on the first syllable, CON'summate, this word is a verb; when the accent shifts to the second syllable, consum'mate, it is an adjective meaning complete in every detail, out-and-out, perfect. The noun form is *consummation,* fulfillment, as in Hamlet's soliloquy: " 'Tis a consummation/Devoutly to be wish'd."
   **desiccate**    "to dry up"; dehydrate. This is a spelling demon; you can remember the one *s* and the two *c*'s from the derivation: Latin prefix *de,* intensive + *siccus,* dry.
   Two adjectives ending in *ate* are:
   **disparate**    unlike; different; dissimilar; unequal.
   **importunate**    urgent in demands; annoyingly insistent.
**esce**    The Latin verb ending *escere* means to begin to, to become. English adjective and noun suffixes from it are respectively *escent* and *escence.* Some English words derived from the same root show all three forms:
   **effervesce**    "to begin to boil over"; to bubble.
   **effervescent**    "boiling over"; bubbling; ebullient.
   **effervescence**    "a boiling over"; a bubbling; excitement.
   For a few others we shall give only a representative form:
   **coalesce**    "to grow together"; to unite. The noun form is *coalition.*
   **evanescent**    "beginning to *van*ish" almost as soon as it appears; ephemeral; fleeting.
   **deliquescence**    "becoming a fluid"; a melting away.

**obsolescence**    the condition of becoming outdated or outmoded.

**recrudescence**    "a becoming raw (*crudus*) again," that is, starting all over again; a new breaking out of anything; a revival.

## en (Anglo-Saxon)

**dishearten**    "to discourage"; to depress.

**enlighten**    "to bring light to"; inform; instruct.

**h(e)arken**    "to listen"; to heed. This verb is used a great number of times in the King James version, as in Numbers 21:3: "The Lord hearkened to the voice of Israel."

## fy

**deify**    "to make a god of"; exalt.

**rectify**    "to make right"; correct; adjust.

**stultify**    "to make foolish"; to cause to appear foolish or ridiculous.

**edify**    to enlighten; uplift.

**ize**    As examples of this suffix, you have your choice of those offered in the epigraph.


## SOME NOUN ENDINGS

Most of these have the generalized meaning of the result of, the act of, the quality of, the condition of.

## age (French)

**montage**    process of combining several pictures or parts of pictures to produce a single composition. (This suffix occurs in many words we have borrowed from the French: *barrage, mirage, sabotage, voyage*.)

## ance, ence (adjective forms *ant, ent*)

**appurtenance**    something accessory to or derived from something more important.

**arrant**    thoroughgoing (usually in a pejorative sense); out-and-out; unmitigated.

**emollient**    "making soft"; soothing; also something that soothes.

## ion

**manumission**    "sending away from the master's hand" or power, originally referring to the liberation of Roman slaves; emancipation (the act of releasing from the master's hand, or power).

**mutation**    a basic change or alteration.

And thousands of other words ending in *ion!*

**ism** (Greek via Latin)        By itself *ism* is a word meaning a doctrine or system. It can, therefore, easily be attached as a suffix to the name of any religious, political, or national entity.

 **aphorism**        a concise statement containing wisdom or truth; maxim; adage; apothegm.

**ity, iety**        (often equivalent to Anglo-Saxon suffixes *hood* or *ness*)

 **amenity**        "pleasantness"; in the plural, courteous acts.

 **propriety**        "properness"; appropriateness; behavior that is socially acceptable.

 **sobriety**        "soberness"; seriousness; temperance.

**ment**

 **arbitrament**        authoritative or final judgment.

 **escarpment**        steep slope or cliff.

**mony**

 **parsimony**        extreme frugality; stinginess.

**ry**

 **bigotry**        extreme intolerance.

 **gimmickry**        gadgetry; use or collection of ingenious mechanical devices.

 **mimicry**        act of mimicking or imitating. Note that the suffix is *ry;* this word has nothing to do with crying out.

 **ribaldry**        coarse or indecent language.

**tude**

 **beatitude**        "blessedness"; happiness.

 **hebetude**        "dullness"; lethargy.

 **turpitude**        "baseness"; vileness.

**ture**

 **aperture**        "an opening."

 **suture**        a surgical "sewing."

 **tonsure**        "a clipping"; shaving of the head.


## SOME ADJECTIVE ENDINGS

Most of these adjective endings have the general sense of marked by, having to do with, pertaining to, relating to, tending to, resembling, and such "like" meanings.

**al (ical)**

 **connubial**        relating to marriage; conjugal; nuptial.

 **inimical**        "unfriendly"; hostile.

**an, ane**

    **sylvan**    "wooded"; characteristic of or belonging to the forest.

    **germane**    pertinent to what is being discussed or explained; closely connected.

**ar, ary**

    **annular**    "ring-shaped."

    **sanguinary**    "bloody"; accompanied by much bloodshed; bloodthirsty.

    **tutelary**    "watching over"; serving as a guardian; protecting.

With *ary* nouns are also formed, such as *aviary* (a place where birds are kept), and *apiary* (a place where bees are kept).

**fic**    from *facere,* make, do.

    **malefic**    exerting unfavorable or evil influence.

    **soporific**    inducing sleep.

**ic** (Greek via Latin)

    **ascetic**    austere; practicing rigorous self-denial.

    **aseptic**    surgically sterile.

    **didactic**    teaching a moral lesson; giving instruction.

    **kinetic**    "pertaining to motion."

**id**

    **sapid**    "flavorsome"; savory.

    **insipid**    "not sapid," hence tasteless, flat, dull.

    **limpid**    perfectly clear (like water), used literally of a stream and figuratively of one's style in writing.

**ine**

    **bovine**    "like a cow"; dull.

    **vulpine**    "like a fox"; crafty.

**ish** (Anglo-Saxon)

"Let's eat at eightish, shall we? I'm feeling peckish," is something you might hear any day in England. *Eightish* means at about eight and *peckish* means "feeling like pecking," hence somewhat hungry. *Ish* is one of those suffixes you can add humorously to almost any word, as was done in "Something Sort of Grandish," the delightful song from *Finian's Rainbow.* Or you can use it in a more straightforward way, as in *childish, boyish, mannish, English.*

    **brackish**    somewhat salty (of water); undrinkable.

**ive**

    **furtive**    "like a thief"; stealthy; secret.

**palliative**    "like a cloak"; acting to soothe pain or distress temporarily; alleviating.

Some *ive* words become nouns: *alternative, conservative, diminutive.*

**ory**

**dilatory**    tending to put off; causing delay.

Nouns are also formed with *ory*, such as *refectory* (a dining hall), *laboratory*, and *repertory* (both adjective and noun).

## SOME ADVERBIAL ENDINGS

**ly** (Anglo-Saxon)

Since almost any adjective can be made into an adverb by adding *ly* and since only a comparatively few adjectives are formed by adding *ly* to a noun (*friendly, saintly, leisurely*), it can be seen that the great bulk of *ly* words are adverbs.

When *ly* is added to a word ending in *l*, there are two *l*'s: *Occasionally, beautifully.* Note the spelling of *accidentally— accident + al + ly.*

**ward(s)** (Anglo-Saxon)

As a suffix indicating direction, *ward(s)* appears in *backward(s), upward(s), forward(s), sideward(s), homeward(s),* etc. Many of these (without the *s* ending) are also adjectives.

Here are two other interesting words ending in *ward:*

**froward**    "in a direction from" (*fro* as in *to and fro*), hence contrary, perverse, willfully stubborn.

**untoward**    *un + to + ward:* unfavorable; inconvenient.

**wise** (Anglo-Saxon)    The word *wise* meaning way or manner is found today in such expressions as *in no wise, in this wise,* and as a suffix in such words as *otherwise, likewise, lengthwise,* etc.

There is a tendency today, however, to attach *wise* to any noun and make an adverb of it, at, it must be admitted, a saving of words. "Taxwise and healthwise," you might hear someone say, "I'm better off living in Connecticut, but transportationwise and entertainmentwise, I'm a loser." Translation: I pay less in taxes and feel healthier in Connecticut, but the daily commuting and lack of entertainment are getting me down.

The last and the definitive word on the use of this catch-all suffix appeared in *The New York Times* of March 1, 1965, in an item in "Random Notes":

### Good Head, Shoulder-Wise

> Overheard in a Washington elevator, one man speaking to another about a girl friend: "She's not so smart, wisdom-wise!"

That wraps it up neatly!

## SOME MEANINGFUL SUFFIXES

There are some suffixes that affect the meaning of the word in a more definite way than those already cited. We group them here according to meaning.

### Showing Capability or Fitness

**able, ible**
>   **feasible**     "workable"; practicable.
>   **inexpugnable**     "unable to be outfought"; unconquerable; impregnable; unconciliatory; relentless.

**ile**
>   **nubile**     "marriageable"; voluptuous.
>   **prehensile**     "fit or adapted for grasping."

### Chiefly Medical

**ma, oma** (Greek)     originally meaning the result of an action; now usually indicating a tumor.
>   **carcinoma**     a type of cancer.
>   **trauma**     a wound.

**osis** (Greek)     originally meaning a condition; now usually a disease.
>   **hypnosis**     induced sleeplike condition.
>   **neurosis**     nervous disorder characterized by obsessions and anxiety.

### A Man Who

**ary**
>   **antiquary**     one who studies ancient things.
>   **lapidary**     one who cuts precious stones.

**ard** (Anglo-Saxon)
>   **dastard**     one who is cowardly, meanly so. Lochinvar's "rival" was "a laggard in love and a dastard in war."
>   **sluggard**     one who lies abed and does nothing; lazy, idle person.

**er** (Anglo-Saxon)

    **broker**   one who negotiates contracts (marriage, stocks).

**eur** (French)

    **amateur**   one who participates for love of the sport, not for money.

**ian**   When a word ends in *ic*, the suffix *ian* seems to be preferred to *ist* for "one who": *physician, magician, statistician, tactician,* etc. *Physicist, publicist, polemicist* are exceptions.

**ist** (Greek via Latin)

    **hedonist**   one who believes pleasure is the chief goal of life.

**ite**

    **anchorite**   "one who withdraws from the world"; a religious recluse; hermit.

**or**

    **impostor**   one who deceives; pretender; fraud.

**nik** (Russian and Yiddish)

We see this suffix in its pure Russian form in the word *sputnik,* "one who (*nik*) on the path (*put*) with (s)," hence a "co-traveler," a satellite. This is not a new Russian word. An illustrative sentence given in a Russian etymological dictionary tells about nine *sputniks,* or satellites, of Saturn.

However, when used as an English attachable, *nik* has come to us via Yiddish (cf. *nudnik,* a nagging bore), and it almost always forms a word of ridicule or contempt. Besides the well-established *beatnik,* we have the recent contemptuous coinages of *peacenik* and *folknik* (a guitar-playing ballad singer). *Time* pointedly emptied both barrels when it coined the word *Vietnik* as an epithet for those demonstrating against United States involvement in Vietnam.

## DIMINUTIVES

**cle, cule, le**   The Latin form is *culus.*

    **corpuscle**   "a little body (*corpus*)"; minute particle; a body cell.

    **homunculus**   "a little man"; dwarf; manikin.

    **minuscule**   "less + small"; very small; infinitesimal.

    **nozzle**   "little nose"; spout of a hose.

**ette** (French)

    **dinette**   small dining area near the kitchenette.

    **superette**    a small supermarket
**kin(s)** (Anglo-Saxon)
    **manikin**    "a small man"; pygmy; a skeletal model.
This diminutive is found in English surnames, where it means descendant or son of and is seen in such names as Adkins, Atkins ("little Adam" or son of Adam), Dickens (Richard), Hodgkins (nickname for Roger), Hopkins (from Hob, an ancient nickname for Robert), Jenkins (John), Perkins (Peter).
**less** (Anglo-Saxon)    Really a negative suffix meaning "without."
    **dauntless**    fearless; intrepid; undaunted; indomitable.
    **feckless**    "without effect"; ineffectual; incompetent.
**ock** (Anglo-Saxon)
    **hummock**    a little hill; a hillock.

## THE FEMININE MYSTIQUE

**ette** (French)
    **suffragette**    a female fighter for the right to vote.
**euse**    French feminine of *eur*.
    **masseuse**    female masseur.
**ine**    *Ine* is found chiefly in girls' names formed from their masculine counterparts, some of which are Bernardine, Geraldine, Josephine, Maxine, and Pauline, and in such odd words as *chorine,* a female member of a chorus.
**ster**
    **spinster**    "one who spins"; this word has, of course, acquired a more specific meaning.
Family names like Baxter, Brewster, and Webster indicate that women in earlier times were bakers, brewers, and weavers. In time *ster* lost its strictly feminine meaning and we have such masculine words as *teamster* and *huckster* (one who hawks or sells his wares).
**trix**
    **aviatrix**    female flyer.

## WORDS OF PLENTY

**acious, icious** (compound suffixes)
    **voracious**    having a huge capacity for devouring food; gluttonous.

**ful** (Anglo-Saxon)
>    **bountiful**      full of generosity; abundant; bounteous.
>    **guileful**       full of deceit.

The *ful* in adjectives is always spelled with one *l*, and in almost all nouns: cupful, pocketful, mouthful.

**ious, ose, ous**
>    **adipose**       "full of fat."
>    **impecunious**      not having one's pockets full of money; penniless.
>    **numinous**       as used today, most often means filled with a divine presence; like a god.

Note that in medicine and in good usage the nouns are *callus, fungus, mucus* and the adjectives *callous, fungous, mucous.*

**some** (Anglo-Saxon)
>    **awesome**       "full of awe"; inspiring awe.
>    **mettlesome**       "full of metal"; spirited; fiery.

**y** (Anglo-Saxon)
>    **rimy**      characterized by hoarfrost; frosty.

## TAIL-END COMBINING FORMS

We're going to treat as suffixes those combining forms that usually come at the end of a word. All the combining forms treated here are of Greek origin except *cide*.

**arch, archy**      ruler, rule.
>    **anarchy**       "lack of rule"; disorder.
>    **oligarchy**       "rule by a few."
>    **tetrarch**      ruler of one-fourth of a Roman province, like Herod of the New Testament.

**cide** (Latin)      kill, killer.
>    **genocide**      When a new word was needed to name the Nazi crime of wiping out national, ethnic, or religious groups, Dr. Raphael Lemkin added *cide* to a Greek word element meaning nation or group and produced the all too familiar word genocide.
>    **homicide**       "killing of one's fellow man."
>    **suicide**       "self-slaughter."

**cracy**      form of government.
>    **gyneocracy**       "rule by women."
>    **plutocracy**       "rule by wealth."

**iatric, iatry**    "medical treatment"; Greek *iatreia*, healing; *iatros*, physician.

    **geriatrics**    branch of medicine concerned with treatment of the elderly.

    **psychiatry**    branch of medicine concerned with disorders of the mind (Greek *psyche*, soul).

**nomy**    law, rule, systematized knowledge.

    **astronomy**    "science dealing with the stars" and other heavenly bodies. *Astrology* is also concerned with stars (Greek *astron, star*) but it is a pseudo-science that presumes to tell the influence of stars and planets on human life and affairs. The word *disaster* ("contrary to the stars") shows how strong this connection was once thought to be—and by many still is.

**ology**    from Greek *logos*, word, study, science.

    **entomology**    study of insect life.

    **etymology**    science dealing with origin and development of words, actually the study of the true (Greek *etymos*) meaning.

**phile**    Greek *philos*, loving.

    **bibliophile**    a lover of books.

    **Francophile**    a lover of France or things French.

**phobe, phobia**    Greek *phobos*, fear.

Mankind is beset by a host of fears and there is a name for practically every one of them. Here is one which is not in Webster's Third but is in the medical dictionaries, which list some two hundred phobias!

> Not long ago, a New Yorker suffering from aichomophobia—a morbid fear of pointed objects—reacted to the sight of his dentist reaching for a drill by hurling himself through a window.

The word *aichomophobia* comes from the Greek word *aichme*, a spearpoint, and refers to the fear of being touched by any other pointed objects, including the index finger!

    **acrophobia**    fear of high places.

    **xenophobia**    "fear of strangers."

**tomy**    Greek *tomos*, slice, a piece cut off.

The form *tomy* cuts away the need for using many words "to talk about your operation," for *tonsillectomy* is much shorter than "a cutting away of the tonsils." The *ec* in words like *tonsillectomy* and *appendectomy* is the Greek prefix *ec* (out).

The following words come from the same root as *tomy:*

**atom**    something "not cuttable"; at least until modern scientists split the unsplittable.

**epitome**    a condensation, having the nonessentials cut away; embodiment or distillation of characteristic qualities; the quintessence.

## I.  ELEMENTARY GRAMMAR

### A

Change the following verbs to corresponding nouns and adjectives by using the proper suffixes. Watch your spelling in these exercise. Words ending in *er, or, ist,* or *ing* are not allowed.

EXAMPLE:   inflate (verb), inflation (noun), inflationary (adj.)

1. acquire
2. analyze
3. antagonize
4. contend
5. corrode
6. eulogize
7. pursue
8. resent
9. reveal
10. subvert

### B

Supply the corresponding nouns for these verbs; words ending in *ing* are not allowed.

EXAMPLE:   secede (v.), secession (n.)

1. allege
2. allot
3. demolish
4. deprive
5. enjoin
6. exist
7. maintain
8. pronounce
9. repeat
10. rescind

### C

Supply the corresponding adjectives for these nouns.

EXAMPLE:   category (n.), categorical (adj.)

1. analogy
2. apathy
3. climax
4. crux
5. enemy
6. heresy
7. miscellany
8. portent
9. presumption
10. prodigy

## II. LANGUAGE INTERCHANGE

### A

The words in the left-hand column end with the Anglo-Saxon suffix *hood* or *ness*, and with the exception of *falsehood* are formed from Anglo-Saxon roots. On the other hand, all the words in the right-hand column end in the suffix *(i)ty*, from Latin, and are formed from Latin roots. Match each word on the left with its Latin counterpart.

| | | | |
|---|---|---|---|
| 1. brotherhood | | a. asperity |
| 2. falsehood | | b. cupidity |
| 3. fatherhood | | c. fraternity |
| 4. fewness | | d. mendacity |
| 5. greediness | | e. paternity |
| 6. hardihood | | f. paucity |
| 7. harshness | | g. possibility |
| 8. holiness | | h. sanctity |
| 9. likelihood | | i. temerity |
| 10. liveliness | | j. vicinity |
| 11. manhood | | k. virility |
| 12. neighborhood | | l. vivacity |

### B

This time the words on the left are all of Latin origin and all end in the suffix *tude*, also from Latin. The words on the right are all with the exception of *baseness* of Anglo-Saxon origin; all contain the Anglo-Saxon suffix *ness*, which corresponds to *tude*. Match as before.

| | | | |
|---|---|---|---|
| 1. certitude | | a. awkwardness |
| 2. hebetude | | b. baseness |
| 3. ineptitude | | c. comeliness |
| 4. lassitude | | d. dullness |
| 5. pulchritude | | e. likeness |
| 6. quietude | | f. loneliness |
| 7. rectitude | | g. righteousness |
| 8. similitude | | h. stillness |
| 9. solitude | | i. sureness |
| 10. turpitude | | j. weariness |

### C

Match the words on the left (all except *bulgy* of Anglo-Saxon origin), all ending with the Anglo-Saxon suffix *y*, with the words on the right (all coming from Latin), all ending in the suffix *id*, from Latin *idus*.

| | |
|---|---|
| 1. bulgy | a. fetid |
| 2. filthy | b. gelid |
| 3. gloomy | c. gravid |
| 4. heavy (with child) | d. humid |
| 5. icy | e. morbid |
| 6. muddy, murky | f. sapid |
| 7. smelly | g. squalid |
| 8. steamy | h. turbid |
| 9. sticky | i. tumid |
| 10. tasty | j. viscid |

## D

Match the words on the left ending in Anglo-Saxon *ful* or *some* with the words on the right ending in *(i)ous*, derived from or related to Latin *us* or *osus*. In a general way, all these suffixes mean full of.

| | |
|---|---|
| 1. burdensome | a. contentious |
| 2. careful | b. deleterious |
| 3. fretful | c. hideous |
| 4. gruesome | d. iniquitous |
| 5. harmful | e. lachrymose |
| 6. loathsome | f. lugubrious |
| 7. mournful | g. meticulous |
| 8. quarrelsome | h. odious |
| 9. sinful | i. onerous |
| 10. tearful | j. querulous |
| 11. tiresome | k. salubrious |
| 12. wholesome | l. tedious |

## III. TERMINAL AFFIXES

In the left-hand column there are the beginnings of ten words. Add the missing suffix or combining form so that the completed word corresponds to its synonym or definition on the same line in the right-hand column. Each bar represents a letter.

## A

| | |
|---|---|
| 1. cardi _ _ _ _ _ _ | heart specialist |
| 2. deliqu _ _ _ _ _ _ | melting; becoming liquid |
| 3. dicho _ _ _ _ | division into two parts |
| 4. gastro _ _ _ _ | art of good eating |
| 5. ossi _ _ | to change or make into bone |

6. pen _ _ _ _ _      study of prisons
7. peon _ _ _      servitude
8. pleni _ _ _ _      fullness
9. predat _ _ _      characterized by plundering
10. rest _ _ _      impatient; unruly; balky

## B

1. anthrop _ _ _ _ _      study of mankind
2. contigu _ _ _      adjoining
3. decrepi _ _ _ _      state of being worn out by old age
4. discomfit _ _ _      embarrassment; frustration
5. escarp _ _ _ _      cliff; steep slope
6. gustat _ _ _      having to do with the sense of taste
7. phrase _ _ _ _ _      choice of words
8. recrud _ _ _ _ _ _      becoming active again
9. reincarnat _ _ _      rebirth in another body
10. venture _ _ _ _      daring

## IV. TWO KINDS OF RULE

Match the name of the form of government in the left-hand column with the appropriate word in the right-hand column.

### A

| Type of Rule | Ruled by |
|---|---|
| 1. aristocracy | a. God or religious officials |
| 2. autocracy | b. elders |
| 3. bureaucracy | c. mob |
| 4. gerontocracy | d. principle of love of honor |
| 5. gyneocracy | e. wealthy |
| 6. kakistocracy | f. officials and administrators |
| 7. ochlocracy | g. "best"; privileged class |
| 8. plutocracy | h. women |
| 9. theocracy | i. one person with absolute power |
| 10. timocracy | j. worst men |

### B

| | |
|---|---|
| 1. anarchy | a. a few |
| 2. autarchy | b. church officials |
| 3. dyarchy | c. landed gentry |
| 4. heptarchy | d. two individuals or powers |
| 5. hierarchy | e. no government or law |
| 6. matriarchy | f. women as head of the family |
| 7. oligarchy | g. absolute sovereign |
| 8. squirearchy | h. seven |

## V.  SPECIALISTS

Match each specialist on the left with his specialty on the right.

| | |
|---|---|
| 1. entomologist | a. ears |
| 2. etymologist | b. fossils |
| 3. horologist | c. birds |
| 4. neurologist | d. origin of words |
| 5. ophthalmologist | e. poisons |
| 6. ornithologist | f. earthquakes |
| 7. otologist | g. insects |
| 8. paleontologist | h. time; timepieces |
| 9. seismologist | i. eyes |
| 10. toxicologist | j. nerves |

## VI.  IT'S A MAD, MAD, MAD, MAD WORLD

*Mania,* used here as a combining form, means a madness, sometimes a hatred. Match the madness on the left with the cause, type, or subject on the right.

| | |
|---|---|
| 1. arithmomania | a. fire |
| 2. bibliomania | b. impulse to steal |
| 3. dipsomania | c. desire to pluck one's hair |
| 4. dromomania | d. preoccupation with numbers |
| 5. kleptomania | e. lying and exaggerating |
| 6. megalomania | f. delusions of grandeur |
| 7. monomania | g. craving for alcoholic drink |
| 8. mythomania | h. books |
| 9. pyromania | i. "running about," wandering |
| 10. trichotillomania | j. irrationality on one subject |

## VII.  WHO'S ZOO

The words in the left-hand column pertain to animals. The animals are lined up on the right. Join each animal on the right to its appropriate adjective on the left.

| | |
|---|---|
| 1. anserine | a. horse |
| 2. aquiline | b. pig |
| 3. bovine | c. bull |
| 4. canine | d. goat |
| 5. equine | e. bear |
| 6. feline | f. eagle |
| 7. hircine | g. cow |
| 8. leonine | h. sheep |
| 9. lupine | i. lion |

| 10. ovine | j. sparrow |
| 11. passerine | k. fish |
| 12. piscine | l. wolf |
| 13. porcine | m. dog |
| 14. taurine | n. cat |
| 15. ursine | o. goose |

## VIII.  KILLERS

Match the name of the crime or killing in the left-hand column with the name of the victim on the right.

| 1. apicide | a. sister |
| 2. avicide | b. wife |
| 3. canicide | c. worms |
| 4. filicide | d. dogs |
| 5. fratricide | e. viruses |
| 6. herbicide | f. children |
| 7. ovicide | g. weeds |
| 8. regicide | h. brother |
| 9. sororicide | i. king |
| 10. uxoricide | j. eggs |
| 11. vermicide | k. bees |
| 12. viricide | l. birds |

## *VOCABAGRAMS*

This time we supply the suffixes. By rearranging the letters as directed, you are to form a synonym for the definition appearing after each word. For detailed instructions, see "Vocabagrams" at ends of Chapters 3, 4, 5.

EXAMPLE:   entrusting − u = strict   _____ent
ANSWER:    stringent

| 1. bleating | | = palpable | _____ible |
| 2. plane | | = relating to punishment | _____al |
| 3. angel | + i | = kindly | _____al |
| 4. blare | + a | = plowable | _____able |
| 5. clears | + u | = worldly, not religious | _____ar |
| 6. fails | + c | = financial | _____al |
| 7. gale | + i | = nimble | _____ile |
| 8. noise | + l | = injury | _____ion |
| 9. printed | + i | = fearless | _____id |
| 10. rcal | + f | = wild | _____al |
| 11. rooms | + e | = gloomy | _____ose |
| 12. scoured | + o | = showing good taste | _____ous |
| 13. toils | + d | = unexcitable | _____id |
| 14. toxic | + e | = strange | _____ic |

15. uncrate    + t = shorten                              _____ate
16. entrusting − t = rebellious                           _____ent
17. estimating − m = incite                               _____ate
18. license    − c = doddering                            _____ile
19. medicine   − i = prevalent in a region                _____ic
20. unmanned   − n = worldly, commonplace                 _____ane

*In Brooklyn the same year he [the late Magistrate J. Roland Sala] reigned as Lorenzo the Magnificent at a costume ball and proceeded to tell the masqueraders that City Hall was afflicted with "pusillanimity, asininity, torpidity, futility, perversity, impropriety and cupidity," and saw himself as an ideal candidate who would bring to City Hall "pertinacity, assiduity, ideality, propriety, and magnanimity."*

NEW YORK HERALD TRIBUNE, NOVEMBER 3, 1963

# 8. Words All About and Around Us

> *When the doomsters prophesy*
> *Atomic holocausting, I*
> *Only hope that somehow they*
> *Find new wordings to convey*
> *Their repetitious, honest dread*
> *And coin fresh usages instead*
> *Of those two clichés piping shrill*
> *"Escalate" and "Overkill."*

CHARLES POORE, "A Few Hopes
and Promises for 1965" *
THE NEW YORK TIMES, DECEMBER 31, 1964

Most statesmen, candidates, and officials no longer worry about the impression they make on the world; they are concerned about their "image." They no longer attend conferences, carry on discussions, or engage in debates. They take part in "dialogues." Nothing builds up or increases, it "escalates." Nothing spreads like wildfire, it "burgeons" or "proliferates." Anyone in the public eye whose personality is especially attractive has "charisma." Those with special skills and knowledge have "expertise." And they no longer offer suggestions or draw blueprints, they lay down "guidelines." Someone who assumes an enthusiastic "posture" about the Civil War, opera, or horse racing is a "buff" or "aficionado." A newborn babe, an emerging nation, a country's economy—you name it—that seems likely to survive is "viable" and probably has its own "mystique."

These are a few of the words you will come across—with startling frequency—in your reading and listening. These are today's vogue words.

We had a lengthy dialogue about what posture to take toward including a segment on such words. At first we felt it might spoil the image of a book on vocabulary for adults or alienate those readers who might regard it as an unworthy ploy. And then too one of us felt that some of these words might not prove viable. However, since we wanted to present a broad spectrum of the world of words that might serve as guidelines for vocabulary buffs and since we wanted your vocabulary to burgeon and proliferate and your knowledge of words to go up, up, up—pardon us, escalate—we finally decided to share our expertise with you and therefore opted for inclusion.

## WHAT MAKES A VOGUE WORD?

Pretty much the same forces that create vogues in clothes, hobbies, dances, entertainment. Someone influential displays it, Madison Avenue runs the word up a flagpole and everybody who's anybody salutes it.

Such words, we feel, are not merely passing fancies. Most of them *are* viable, because when used discriminatingly they often offer us a shortcut in communication. They are able to express in one word what might often have taken three or four words to express as forcefully. They contribute a little something that wasn't in the word or words they replace.

Let us take *proliferate* as an example. Instead of having to use a cliché such as "spreading like wildfire" or an awkward succession of words like "sprouting all over the place at an ever-increasing pace" we use the one word *proliferate* and we've said it all.

Besides, *proliferate* is an interesting word. It comes from the Latin word *proles*, offspring, plus the root *fer*, to bear, and so has the idea of multiplying, spreading, expanding. Words containing the same basic root are *prolific* (abundant, profuse), and *proletariat*. Because *proles* is the Latin word for offspring and because the poor were *prolific* and served the state not with their property but with their offspring, they were given the name *proletarii*, from which come our words *proletarian* and *proletariat*. But not the word *prolix*, which by derivation means "pouring forth (*pro*) like a liquid (*lix*)," and is a synonym of *diffuse*, *long-winded*, and *verbose*.

Even the much overused word *dialogue* has something in its favor. It's more formal than a conversation, less formal than a debate, and probably less boring than a conference. What's more, it guarantees an exchange of ideas which none of the other words do.

## FROM THE FRENCH

Besides our faith in many of these overworked words, we believe that learning them in this context may help you to remember them better. We'll begin with nine vogue words that we have "borrowed" from the French.

**accolade**     From its original meaning of "embrace," the word *accolade* has swung into a modern figurative meaning of "crowning praise." In this meaning this overworked word has become a vogue word, used instead of *award, praise, honor*.

In the example given below the word *accolade* has risen above the word *ovation*, which refers to the ultimate in enthusiastic celebration, like the triumph of a Roman general:

> He was not just applauded. He received ovations followed by accolades.

Originally, *accolade* was the name of the final step in conferring knighthood. The early kings of France were etymologically correct when they placed their arms around the neck (Latin *collum*, neck) of the newly-named knights in order to kiss them. French generals and officials still keep the custom of the accolade when they kiss the cheeks of the man on whom they bestow an award. Another form of the accolade is a tap on the shoulder with a sword.

**ambiance, ambience**     The second is the more usual English spelling. *Ambience* has taken over some of the duties of *environment* or *milieu*, but it says more. It adds the idea of a pervading atmosphere, an aura, a setting.

> The ambience of the present colloquy differs vastly from that in the spring of 1955 when Khrushchev first flew to Yugoslavia.

**burgeon**     (once spelled *bourgeon* like its French original) meaning to bud, is used as a weaker and more poetic form of *proliferate*. The Oxford English Dictionary notes that the noun and verb forms "seem to have died out in ordinary and even in poetic use before the 18th c., but to have survived as technical terms in gardening. In the 19th c. they have been revived in poetry." To which we can add that the verb form has begun to burgeon (especially in the adjective form *burgeoning*) as a vogue word in our own time. The cover article of the *Saturday Review,* December 19, 1964, is called "The Burgeoning Community College."

> Stamford's speedy solution of its burgeoning high school segregation problem this week has raised some new questions.

**cachet**    a lovely word that generally is used to mean the seal of approval, the status that goes with complete acceptance.

> Of course, it is strictly lightweight clowning, wholly dependent on the archness of Peter Sellers to give it a cachet.

Readers of Dickens's *A Tale of Two Cities* may remember the *lettres de cachet,* letters containing the King's seal, used by the nobility for arbitrary orders of arrest, as in the case of Dr. Manette.

**detente**    a one-word way of saying "relaxation of tensions." *Rapprochement* is the next step toward friendlier coexistence, or accommodation.

> And in the months and years ahead, we intend to build both kinds of strength—during times of detente as well as tension, during periods of conflict as well as cooperation—until the world we pass on to our children is truly safe for diversity and freedom.
>
> JOHN F. KENNEDY

**echelon**    Coming through French from the Latin word *scala*, ladder, it is now used chiefly to indicate a level of rank or grade—a rung of the ladder, upper or lower, as the case may be.

> He suggested that there was awareness on the part of some second-echelon Chinese Communist officials and intellectuals that Peking's dogmatic policies were unrealistic.

Another word—of Greek origin—*hierarchy* (*hiero*, sacred + *archy*, rule) is now used in very much the same way as *echelon* to indicate levels of rank.

> He said that physicians who experimented on others, not on themselves, were building up a human "hierarchy" with themselves on top.

**expertise**    This is often used showily when only knowledge or expertness is meant. It means expert knowledge in a special field, not only know-how but know-what; it characterizes one who is at once an expert and a connoisseur in the field.

> For just as experience and expertise make for reliable judgments about Congressional procedures, so also experience and expertise in the arts and sciences make for reliable judgments in those fields.

**mystique**    A difficult word to define, it carries its own mystery with it. It doesn't appear in Webster's Second, and Webster's Third takes forty-one words to define one meaning of it. The word *mystique* implies a complex of mysterious beliefs or skills gathered around an idea, a feeling, or a person that magically form a whole—an occult cult, so to speak. Two recent titles exploit this word: *The Feminine Mystique* by Betty Friedan and *The Southern Mystique* by Howard Zinn. A leading article in *Show* Magazine is titled "The Success Mystique," and contains the sentence "There is an aura of magic, a curious mystique," which helps to give added meaning to the word, as do the excerpts below.

> Mexico is one of the leading nations of Latin America and her revolutionary mystique is still strong.

>         *        *        *

> The new men will not be quite like the "New Frontier." The idea, the mystique, the style will go, and, in time, the men will go, too.

**panache** (French word for plume or bunch of feathers) Anyone who has read Edmond Rostand's *Cyrano de Bergerac* knows that *panache* refers to the white plume on Cyrano's hat.

However, the word today carries its symbolism—the sweep and flourish that Cyrano could make with it in the face of death. And so today *panache* has come to mean a heroic gesture, a splendid swagger, flamboyance, brio, dash, verve. Rostand, in a long explanation of the word to the French Academy, said in part: "A little frivolous perhaps; a little melodramatic certainly, the *panache* is no more than a charming gesture. But this charming gesture is so difficult to make in the face of death and supposes so much strength (for isn't wit that soars the most graceful triumph over the body that trembles?) that it is a charming gesture I would wish for us all."

> She has lived her life as an expatriate
> in Paris, with flourish, with panache.

## FROM MEDICINE

Four of our list of "vogue words" were for a time merely terms in medical literature.

**proliferate**      This word, already noted, was originally restricted to biology and medicine. Now the gates are wide open.

> High school courses on Communism
> are proliferating.
> The radicals on the right who seem to
> proliferate in California. . . .

> \*        \*        \*

> Not only are teenagers proliferating,
> but they are also doing more and spending more.

**syndrome**      From its Greek elements, this word means "a running (*drome*) together (*syn*)," a concurrence, a cycle of symptoms or manifestations that occur together. It is used loosely, as can be seen from the excerpt below, to mean any cycle, any combination or complex.

> A careful examination of the Horatio
> Alger syndrome would be illuminating.

A recent novel deals with "the characteristic American syndrome of urgency, energy, and waste."
*The New York Times* of October 10, 1964, told how Harvey Smith, a lawyer defending twenty-two New Jersey state

troopers charged with moonlighting, wrote his brief in rhymed couplets. *The Times* goes on to say:

> Mr. Smith's entire brief runs 38 lines
> and covers a page and a half. His closing
> lines are:

> > What is the object of this
> > simple tome?
> > To establish by trauma, a
> > reversal syndrome.

> In a lone footnote to the brief, the
> rhyming lawyer explained that an ap-
> pellate judge had once commented that
> every good brief should contain the
> words "trauma" and "syndrome."

And, we assume, every good book dealing with vocabulary should, too.

**trauma, traumatic**    The Greek word for wound is *trauma,* but these words are now used chiefly and loosely for emotional wounds—any scarring or scaring emotional experience.

> But working with the Harper editors,
> he said, had been free of the traumas an
> author is supposed to have with editors.

**viable, viability**    once referred only to the chances of an organism's survival, but their use has burgeoned, escalated, and proliferated. As used so frequently, *viability* is a synonym for *durability*, and even *success*, as well as for *survival*.

> Critics of the operation say that the
> strategic hamlets are over-extended and
> are neither politically nor militarily
> viable.

## AND MANY OTHERS

Without any attempt at classification here is an alphabetical listing of other vogue words.

**alienation**

> From literature, philosophy, psychol-
> ogy, poetry and personal narrative, more
> than 90 selections explore the universal
> problem of identity and alienation.

So reads an advertisement in *The New York Times Book Review* describing the contents of *Alienation: The Cultural Climate of Our Time,* a book edited by Gerald Sykes.

*Alienation* is a word much seen these days, when novels are written about nonheroes who feel lost in the troubled world outside them and can find no identity in the turmoil inside them. The use of the word in this sense is beautifully illustrated in a description by a former resident of the New York City Women's House of Detention as quoted by James A. Wechsler in the New York *Post* (June 8, 1965):

> "We had friends outside, we had lives to go back to—yet we felt an immediate loss of identity. . . . Everything done seemed almost designed to create a feeling of alienation and hopelessness and humiliation."

The verb *alienate* does not always have this psycho-sociological extension of meaning as can be seen in the following excerpt from a letter in *The New York Times:*

> On a continent seething with social unrest and rising nationalism, such a policy can only alienate us more and more from those who are most anxious to bring about social change within a democratic framework.

**arcane**      from Latin *arcanus,* "closed, secret," mysterious, hidden, recondite, as contrasted with something clear, lucid and direct.

> To get something off his chest, he invariably chose the most devious and arcane expression conceivable.

**bellwether**      is a word beloved of writers for the sports and financial pages. It's another way of identifying the leader in a particular sport or in a stock market trend. The word itself identifies the male sheep (*wether*) which has a *bell* tied around its neck. The others, being sheep, follow him.

*Bellwether* is gradually developing an additional meaning (probably influenced by the word *weathervane*) to indicate which way the wind is blowing—a kind of barometer, something from which a prediction can be made, as seen in the following headline and news story:

**Election Splits Two Bellwether Counties**

> One of New Hampshire's two weather-vane counties could lose its reputation for pointing to national trends after the election on Nov. 3.
>
> \* \* \*
>
> On the trading floor of the New York Stock Exchange, brokers like to keep their eyes on several bellwether issues in order to judge the tone of the general market.

This meaning has not yet reached the dictionaries.

**charisma, charismatic** (*k* sound for *ch*) a relative new-comer, is probably *the* vogue among vogue words today. It cannot be found in Webster's Second, where only *charism* appears and is there defined as "a special divine gift," along with its adjective *charismatic*, which has the same restricted meaning. In Webster's Third *charisma* has the additional meaning that we find so frequently today of personal magnetism, people appeal, charm (if you consider both its meanings). Indeed, *charisma* breaks down anagrammatically into *is a charm*.

An ad for *Woman's Day* tells us that its editor "spreads her charisma over a greater ratio of editorial to advertising than anybody else in the field."

> But the experts describe the movement's posture as one of "contained aggressiveness," largely because of the concepts of its charismatic leader.

**-cum-** is the Latin preposition meaning "with." It is stylish to make it a connective between two words with a hyphen on each side, thus replacing two words—*combined with*. In England it is found in local combined parish names such as Stow-cum-Quy.

> A Heritage trail leaves Hartford for two weeks of sightseeing-cum-luxury.
>
> \* \* \*
>
> It is a mystery-cum-comedy affair.

We can see little except ostentation in the use of -cum- except that, with the hyphen on each side, it makes a tie-in or package deal where *with* would form a three-word sequence.

**enclave**    in one word tells that an area is an enclosure within alien territory, a landlocked island, a place set apart. West Berlin, which is more than one hundred miles inside East Germany, is the most famous territorial enclave.

> The 64 residents of Patchin Place and Milligan Place have a common cause—the desire to keep their quiet enclave the way it is.

Here *enclave* almost means an isolated place. (*Isolated* has Italian *isola*, island, within it; etymologically, it is a cousin of *insulated*, from Latin *insula*, island.)

*Enclave* itself comes from the Latin word *clavis*, key, the root of which we also find in *conclave*, "locked in together (*con*) with a key," literally so when it refers to the assemblage of cardinals choosing a new Pope (though it ordinarily means a private meeting, one "behind closed doors," or a meeting of some special group); in *clavicle*, a bone near the neck resembling a key; in *autoclave*, a hermetically sealed chamber used for sterilizing or pressure cooking; in *clavichord*, the earliest type of stringed keyboard instrument, the predecessor of the harpsichord and piano.

**epiphany**    comes from a Late Greek word meaning appearance or manifestation (*epi*, upon + *phan*, show). The feast of Epiphany, celebrating the manifestation of Christ to the Magi, is also called Twelfth Night or Twelfth Day. In France, it is called *le jour* ("the day") or *la fête des Rois* ("the feast of the Kings"); in Italy, this religious feast is celebrated as a second Christmas. It is similarly observed in other lands.

> In emulation of the Magi of the Bible, who carried their offerings to the Christ child 12 days after his birth, Italians present gifts to their children on Epiphany.

In literary use, *epiphany* also means a manifestation, sometimes a sudden manifestation of some essential truth or self-discovery.

> Sebastian tells his story in a series of flashbacks, crucial scenes of epiphany and self-discovery.

Other words that contain the Greek element found in *epiphany* are *cellophane*, *diaphanous*, "showing through (*dia*)," *fantasy*, *phantom*, *phantasmagoria*, *phenomenon*, and *sycophant*.

**escalate, escalation**    Along with *proliferate*, these two are probably the most frequently encountered vogue words. Like *echelon*, *escalate* comes from Latin *scala*, "ladder," and it means "to go up the ladder" higher and higher, "to step up." It's a very strong word for *increase, heighten, build up*.

> But a direct line between the two
> major capitals of world power could
> avert escalation of an untoward inci-
> dent into a nuclear holocaust.

Webster's Third gives only the following definition of *escalate:* "to ascend or carry up on or as if on a moving staircase or conveyor belt," while Webster's Seventh New Collegiate Dictionary (1963), based on Webster's Third, has no entry for either *escalate* or *escalation!*

In an editorial, *The New York Times* of April 22, 1965, coined the word *descalation*. The headline reads **'Descalation' Needed.** In the body of the editorial appears the sentence, "We think . . . a 'descalation' of the war is needed, rather than the escalation that we now see imminent." In the next paragraph the editorial speaks of "a scaling down of the bombing"—"scaling down," a literal and perfect definition of "descalating." This is an example of how new words arise to meet new needs.

**hubris**    is defined in this excerpt from *Life* (January 4, 1963):

> But in the very pursuit of excellence
> the Greeks forever overreached them-
> selves and had to suffer for hubris, or
> excessive pride. "For when arrogance
> blooms," wrote the tragedian Aeschylus,
> "it reaps a harvest rich in tears . . .
> and god calls men to a heavy reckoning
> for overweening pride."

Put the words *excessive pride, arrogance,* and *overweening pride* together and you have a definition of *hubris*, which is a strong and useful word.

**opt**    means choose, often when there are only two choices, as the excerpt from *Time* (August 19, 1963) illustrates.

> Since the day when Hitler opted for
> guns rather than butter, West Germany
> has known near starvation, austerity, and
> for the past decade, such heady abun-
> dance that it has become the Adipose
> Society.

**ploy**     has had a big play recently. It is related to the
word *employ* and is used as a synonym for device, tactic,
maneuver (replacing in popularity a former vogue word
*gambit*).

> Guestmanship involves ploys and ma-
> neuvers so delicate that most people
> simply throw up their hands after a
> few days and say, "Next time we stay
> home."

We have even found *ploy*—with an attached prefix—used as a
verb:

> To outploy them, the Seabees and
> Cuban workers laid out a circular con-
> crete slab on which they painted the
> anchor-globe-and-eagle emblem of the
> Marines in red, gold and white.

**serendipity**     A lovely word is *serendipity*. Its origin is discussed in Chapter 14; it means a lucky discovery made while
looking for something else. Today it's just the happy discovery
that is emphasized and the word itself has been a happy discovery for many. A flourishing restaurant in New York has
taken it as its name. A headline tells us that **Serendipity Takes
Horse Show Title**. A successful group of folk balladeers call
themselves the Serendipity Singers. And a mystery novel bears
the title of *The Real Serendipitous Kill*.

> Sam Spiegel, one of the canniest, most
> ingenious, and most resourceful produc-
> ers in the world today, has a consistent
> serendipity that is the envy and despair
> of lesser men.

**spectrum**     has replaced *gamut* (which ran the whole
musical scale from *gamma* to *ut;* see entry for this word in
Chapter 15) and has much the same meaning: the whole
range or scope. It is often used with *broad*, as in *broad-spec-
trum antibiotics*.

> These children represent the broad spectrum of educational ability, from the severely retarded to the intellectually gifted.

**tendentious**     means promoting a particular tendency; hence, biased and often controversial.

> Portugal's mission accused the African-Asian group today of "bare tendentious propaganda" in charging Portuguese atrocities in Angola.

**value judgment**     often appears as a two-word pomposity for *opinion*. But in philosophical and literary *dialogues*, it may mean something more, as it does here:

> Professor Carney also said that the word "oligarchy," which he had used to describe the business leadership, was a neutral sociological term and did not imply a value judgment.

We cannot end this section without mentioning a newcomer that has suddenly jumped at us from the printed page.

**paradigm**     is a word whose practice used to bedevil pupils who numbly recited, "I am, you are, he is, we are," etc., or "amo, amas, amat," etc., without knowing that they were presenting a paradigm of the verb *to be,* or of the Latin verb *amare,* to love. Used otherwise, *paradigm* means a model, a pattern, an example.

> Indeed, McCarthy has posthumously been made the paradigm of political demagoguery and irresponsibility in the 1950's.

## PUT THEM BACK

Fill in the blanks in the sentences below with the word that best completes the sense from the group of words that appear at the head of each section.

### I.  From the French

(a) accolade            (f) echelon
(b) ambience            (g) expertise
(c) burgeon(ing)        (h) mystique
(d) cachet              (i) panache
(e) detente             (j) rapprochement

1. Western officials here are attempting to determine whether this new Soviet line is a short-term tactical maneuver or a switch in policy that contemplates a long_____in the cold war.

2. Can we share, and share in time, the vast reserves of our wealth and our _____ to put nearly a billion adults and adolescents and children into school?

3. Taipei is a sad place of refuge for those intellectuals, educated Chinese, and even small shopkeepers and tradesmen who knew the _____ of Shanghai.

4. Despite the dignity and grace of the promenade and the luxury buildings dotting portions of the Concourse, the area is quietly losing its _____, its magic.

5. Government salaries are low even judged by the standards that prevail in the lower _____s of private industry.

6. I liked Milne's gallop toward the goal line; it had style, it even had _____.

7. The _____ student expansion and shrinking college faculty made it imperative that the colleges try new methods of solving the crisis.

8. Grover A. Whalen leaves as a legacy the nation's prime _____—the ticker tape parade up Lower Broadway.

## II.  From Medicine

(a) proliferate       (d) traumatic
(b) proliferation     (e) syndrome
(c) trauma            (f) viable
          (g) viability

1. Mia Farrow dresses in Greenwich styles that an ordinary actress would find _____.

2. Although the Communist regime opposes _____ of private cars, the streets of Moscow now feel the beginning of a traffic problem.

3. The Ambassador is said to have considerable reservations about the political _____ of the South Vietnam regime.

4. Picture postcards are still part of the summer travel _____.

5. But invariably his songs have noteworthy lyrics and _____ melodies.

## III.  And the Others

(a) arcane           (h) hubris
(b) bellwether       (i) opted
(c) charisma(tic)    (j) ploy
(d) -cum-            (k) serendipity
(e) enclave          (l) spectrum
(f) epiphany         (m) tendentious
(g) escalation       (n) value judgments

1. The Army did not realize that it was the victim of a Communist _____.

2. Washington, D. C., is a voteless Federal _____.

3. The income _____ swung all the way from the millions of H. D. Hunt to the pennies of Dallas janitors.

4. The Board of Education announced that 25 per cent of the children have _____ to go to desegregated schools.

5. The figures on off-track betting put out by reformers are intended as propaganda and are thus _____.

6. John Chancellor, head of the Voice of America: It is my intent that we "swing" a little. Under my stewardship, the Voice of America will not drift into _____ intellectualism or academic pedantry.

7. One of the most difficult things in the theater is to make convincing a _____ figure like Dylan Thomas, for whom all women seem to be putty and all men willing slaves.

8. Are the two policies in Vietnam _____ of the war or neutralization the only possibilities?

9. Literary research is always that way—a blind alley today, a feat of _____ tomorrow.

10. The steel and automobile industries, two _____s of the economy, have been encouraged by a continuing pickup in their business.

## IV.  Ubiquitous Words

These are not exactly vogue words but, like the word *ubiquitous*, you see them around everywhere. (*Ubi* is Latin for "where." An alibi is really a proof that you were "elsewhere" [*alius + ubi*] when the "thing" occurred.)

Since you must have seen them around, we're going to test you on them. Several have appeared on previous tests.

1. ambivalence    (a) walking around (b) hostility (c) simultaneous attraction and repulsion (d) infatuation

2. boggles    (a) shies away from (b) trips up (c) locks out (d) stares at with wide eyes

3. castigated    (a) purified (b) tongue-lashed (c) classified (d) singled out

4. clandestine    (a) fatal (b) unknown (c) obscure (d) illegally secret

5. ephemeral    (a) lasting forever (b) fleeting (c) uncertain (d) funereal

6. euphemism    (a) a more pleasant expression (b) determination (c) fanciful speech (d) optimism

7. exacerbate    (a) punish (b) throw out (c) intensify (d) outsmart

8. intransigent     (a) aggressive (b) unyielding (c) hostile (d) unconscious

9. minuscule     (a) underrated (b) temporary (c) tiny (d) extremely simple

10. nostalgic     (a) sickly (b) painfully bored (c) worrisome (d) wistfully sentimental

11. paradoxical     (a) pleasurable (b) heavenly (c) seemingly contradictory (d) exactly opposite

12. peripheral     (a) lasting a short time (b) crucial (c) roundabout (d) fringe

13. polemics     (a) amenities (b) heated argument (c) legalities (d) strife

14. schism     (a) rift (b) confusion (c) denial (d) misunderstanding

15. ubiquitous     [just to find out whether you're paying attention] (a) clumsy (b) punctual (c) elsewhere (d) all around

## A Few Explanations

It might be a good idea to fix a few of these words by looking into their derivations or associations.

**ambivalent** has *ambi*, around, both, equal + *val*, from Latin *valere*, to be strong or well, as in *valiant, valid, valor*. Hence, *ambivalent* means having equally strong pulls in both (or opposite) directions. In words like *convalescent, invalid* (the noun), and *valetudinarian*, the idea of health is strong, the last word meaning one who thinks constantly and anxiously about his health. The health idea is prevalent in *Vale*, "Be well," the Latin word for farewell; a *valedictory* is a speech of farewell. The Latin expression *Ave atque vale* means "Hail and farewell."

**ephemeral** means literally "lasting a day" (Greek *epi* + *hemera*, a day). Ephemerids are mayflies, delicate short-lived insects, "creatures of a day."

**euphemism,** from Greek *eu*, well (adverb), and root *phem*, to speak, means a genteel or pleasant substitution for words once thought unacceptable in polite society or for words associated with unpleasant ideas such as death (*he passed away, he went to his reward*). The *eu* appears in *euphoric*, feeling exhilarated, and in *eulogy*, speaking well (i.e., in praise) of someone.

**exacerbate** has the word *acerb*, sharp (from Latin *acerbus*), in it, with the prefix *ex* acting as an intensive. *To exacerbate* a situation is to make it much worse. *Aggravate* (*ad*, to + *grav*, heavy) is a weaker word with much the same meaning.

**minuscule, miniscule** One can see the word *minus* in the first spelling. The suffix *cule* makes it even smaller.

**nostalgia,** "a longing for a return," suggests the pain (Greek *algos*), albeit a pleasant sentimental one experienced on returning (*nostos*) in memory or in actuality to former times or haunts. The pain is real in *neuralgia* and is soothed by an analgesic. The unusual word *algolagnic* (deriving pleasure from inflicting pain on oneself and others) suggests in one word both *masochistic* and *sadistic*. (See entries for these two words in Chapter 14.)

**polemic,** coming from the Greek *polemos*, war, either describes or is a controversial argument that is fiery, highly charged. *Polemics* is also used in this sense.

**schism** The Greek combining form for *cut* or *split* is *schizo*. From it we get three words in which the *sch* is pronounced in three different ways! We get *schism* via Latin, *schist* via French, and *schizophrenia* from modern medical Latin.

| | |
|---|---|
| **schism** (pronounced siz'm) | a split; a rift; a division. |
| **schist** (pronounced shist) | a type of rock that splits easily into slabs or sheets. |
| **schizophrenia** (pronounced skitso- or skizofreenia) | the name of a mental condition popularly referred to as a split personality. |

## V.  Put the Ubiquitous Words Where They Belong

So that you don't have to look back at the list of fifteen, we present them again, but in two sets, first of eight and then of seven. Here are the first eight:

(a) ambivalence  (e) ephemeral
(b) boggles  (f) euphemism
(c) castigated  (g) exacerbate
(d) clandestine  (h) intransigent

Complete each of the following sentences with a word from the above that best fits the sense.

1. Colonel Fontenele is _____ at ladies' bridge parties, because he has hauled away limousines—chauffeurs and all—for parking violations.

2. Mr. Albee said yesterday that he was looking forward to it with a kind of _____. "It's fascinating and frightening at the same time."

3. The imagination, brooding about population explosion, _____ at the possibilities.

4. There is still some _____ sale of fireworks but it doesn't bring in much profit.

5. Peace in the Middle East is threatened by the _____ insistence of Syria and the other Arab states that they are at war with Israel.

6. For nearly a half century Americans have been accustomed to "free" radio and television, a ——————— for letting advertisers pay the bill.

7. However, recent events have tended to ——————— feelings and it would be surprising if some of this were not reflected in campaign oratory.

8. It will also prove again the old saying that man is _____, the church eternal.

And now find room for each one of the second group in its appropriate sentence below the list.

    (i) minuscule, *or* miniscule      (l) peripheral
    (j) nostalgic                    (m) polemics
    (k) paradox                   (n) schism
               (o) ubiquitous

9. Each side sought to put the blame for the present _____ upon its opponent.

10. The _____ antique shops in New England had him wondering whether he should make his grandchildren millionaires by accumulating piles of junk for them.

11. Zach Wheat, Brooklyn's No. 1 idol, remarked with _____ wistfulness how nice it was to be back in a familiar setting with familiar faces.

12. But needed also is the humility to admit that there are vast areas of human need which cannot be solved by _____ and aimless militancy.

13. Up to now, the impossibility of accords, except on _____ issues, has stemmed primarily from the irreconcilability of Soviet and Western views on a solution for the central problem of Germany.

14. The Koma Stadium in Japan has no balcony and row upon row of seats stretch upward. From the rear the performers seem _____.

15. This involves the basic _____ of the nuclear age. Power has never been greater; it has also never been less useful.

## "OCCASIONAL" WORDS

> *MacArthur's body was in a room off a flag-draped hallway. The room had parquet floors and shiny oak walls. The plain gray steel coffin was on a black catafalque. This is a word you learned in November.*

> NEW YORK HERALD TRIBUNE, APRIL 8, 1964

These are words we can learn from momentous occasions in current world affairs: a weekend of national mourning, a papal convocation of cardinals. As we sit in front of our television screens, or listen to the radio, or scan the headlines of our newspapers, certain words that we hear and see over and over again are etched into our minds.

Can you still identify them? For each of the six "occasional" words given below in bold face, select from among those words and expressions listed directly below the group of six the one that comes closest in meaning.

### A.

WASHINGTON, D.C.: November 22–25, 1963
LONDON, ENGLAND: January 30, 1965

**caisson, catafalque, cortege, eulogy, plenipotentiaries, protocol.**

1. cannon
2. dignitaries
3. diplomatic etiquette
4. draped ladder
5. encomium
6. funeral coach
7. funeral procession
8. gun carriage
9. gun salute
10. official mourners
11. platform for coffin
12. solemnity

Make the proper selection also for this set of six:

### B.

ROME, ITALY: WORLDWIDE ECCLESIASTICAL CONVOCATION

**aggiornamento, ecumenical, liturgy, schema, schism, vernacular.**

1. Church Latin
2. cooperative
3. division
4. modernization, updating
5. native tongue
6. offering
7. plan
8. public worship
9. secret prayer
10. universal

## "FLASH" WORDS

Finally, here are words that suddenly leap into prominence —because of some newsworthy discovery, development, innovation, or exploit. *Astronaut, antibiotics, penicillin* came in overnight—painlessly. Some words are imported, like *pizza* and *espresso*. The word *bagel* has a mystique of its own!

Here are some less obvious words. Only a few are new; most of them are old words that suddenly came to life—but all have flashed into wide popularity. How many of them can you assign properly to the innovation, discovery, exploit, or development that gave them prominence?

Match each word on the left with the proper term on the right.

1. automation
2. boutique
3. carcinogenic
4. demographic
5. discothèque
6. geriatrics
7. isometrics
8. megalopolis
9. perigee
10. projection

a. spread of city communities
b. longevity
c. forecast of election results
d. a form of exercise
e. electronics
f. population explosion
g. ladies' specialty luxury shop
h. orbiting the earth
i. dancing
j. cigarette smoking and/or insecticide spraying, etc.

And, on June 7, 1965, as Major McDivitt and Major White of Gemini 4 fame came down safely into the Atlantic Ocean, another new word flashed across the TV screen and was heard all day on radio: SPLASHDOWN!

As Gemini flights continue, *splashdown* is repeatedly heard and seen; actually, it is more vivid and exact than the term "a landing in the sea." On December 19, 1965, a *New York Times* writer used the word as an adjective:

> In fact, the Gemini 7 astronauts had bet the Gemini 6 astronauts that they would come closer to the splashdown target.

## Again a Few Explanations

**demographic** comes from the Greek combining form *demo* (*demos*, the people) and *graph*, the root of a verb meaning to write. *Demographic*, therefore, refers to the statistical study of growth and distribution of people. One can see how—with the population explosion—this word has come into prominence.

The root of *demos* gives us the words *democracy*, *demagogue*, *endemic* (peculiar to a people, hence, native, indigenous), *epidemic* ("upon the people," therefore, widespread). *Graph*, which is used as an English word, and which is easily recognizable in *telegraph* (writing at a distance, *tele*), appears in words too many to enumerate. It is one of those dependable roots that do not change in spelling, for it remains *graph* except when the word comes to us from Italian, as *graffiti*, writings or scribblings, especially on walls and posters.

**discothèque**, a coined French word, which literally means a repository for records (compare *bibliothèque*, a repository for books, a library), is comparable, in the words of Sam Zolotow, writing in *The New York Times* of March 6, 1965, "to a glorified jukebox operation, a behind-the-scenes hi-fi system that sounds bigger than life." The fad of dancing to records began in France, swept across the Channel to England and now is more or less firmly entrenched here.

> Local 802 of the American Federation of Musicians is cracking down on discotheques, the nightclubs using recorded music, that refuse to employ its members.
>
> *     *     *
>
> From a closet-like room with three turntables, he views the dance floor through a pillbox slit. It is his function to gauge the mood of the dancers and, by his selection of disks, to keep them dancing.
> The common denominator of a discotheque is darkness, a small dance floor and the beat.

**isometrics**, from Greek *iso*, equal + Greek *metron*, measure, refers to any exercises involving the muscles in equal pressures. *Facial Isometrics* is a book described as "a systematic exercise plan to diminish wrinkles, flabbiness, double chin and improve muscle tone of the face in less than five minutes a day."

**megalopolis,** from Greek combining form *megalo,* large, of giant size + *polis,* city, describes "the coalescing of metropolitan areas in a giant urban sprawl." *Conurbation,* from Latin *con,* together, and *urbs,* city, is also used to refer to a network of urban communities.

**perigee,** from Greek prefix *peri,* around + *ge,* earth, describes the closest point of earth reached by an orbiting object, whereas *apogee* (*apo,* away from) describes the farthest point. Geometry originally meant "measuring the earth."

### DO-IT-YOURSELF DEPARTMENT

It will prove a rewarding experience to look up any unexplained words in a large dictionary, especially noting their derivations. It may become an exercise in serendipity.

### *VOCABAGRAMS*

Here are twenty-five words, some of which you have seen in this or a previous chapter; the others you will hear or see around.

For detailed instructions, see the introduction to "Vocabagrams" on the last pages of Chapters 3 and 4.

| | | |
|---|---|---|
| 1. undated | | = intimidated |
| 2. aged | + c | = beg |
| 3. alum | + q | = a scruple |
| 4. amble | + d | = scene of noisy confusion |
| 5. analgesic | + t | = stepping up |
| 6. braid | + l | = vulgar |
| 7. brush | + i | = overweening arrogance |
| 8. canape | + h | = heroic flourish |
| 9. chase | + m | = tribal chief |
| 10. course | + g | = whip |
| 11. crane | + a | = secret |
| 12. daunt | + r | = northern treeless plain |
| 13. domain | + c | = constantly on the move |
| 14. enticer | + t | = reserved in speech |
| 15. ghoul | + s | = marsh |
| 16. incite | + k | = relating to motion |
| 17. manger | + e | = pertinent |
| 18. reseat | + u | = stern |
| 19. severer | + p | = stubbornly contrary |

20. sheer    + y = unorthodox belief
21. teach    + c = seal of approval
22. tented    + e = relaxation of tension
23. vial    + c = find fault with
24. ducks    − k = skim along
25. pursue    − e = seize power

Here are the first letters: 1. d, 2. c, 3. q, 4. b, 5. e, 6. r, 7. h, 8. p, 9. s, 10. s, 11. a, 12. t, 13. n, 14. r, 15. s, 16. k, 17. g, 18. a, 19. p, 20. h, 21. c, 22. d, 23. c, 24. s, 25. u.

# 9. English: A Distillation of Many Languages

> It is, of course, a distinction *and a strength of the Anglo-Saxon vocabulary that although it may strike the French as a sort of linguistic* poubelle [garbage pail] *it is nevertheless a language of enormous precision and subtlety because it derives and distills from many tongues. No word or sound except perhaps the Oriental, is really ultimately out of place in English, or denied a use for reasons of* pureté.
>
> DON COOK, NEW YORK HERALD TRIBUNE

This epigraph is part of an article (February 27, 1964) in which Don Cook discusses the fear of some French scholars that the French language is losing its *pureté* because it is allegedly being contaminated by the intrusion of a large number of English words such as *breakfast, best seller, chewing gum, cocktail, hot dog, supermarket, teens, westerns,* etc., etc. Mr. Cook refers specifically to a book of 371 pages entitled *Parlez-vous franglais?* (1964), in which the author, René Etiemble, protests, often humorously and almost always vehemently, against the injection of English words and expressions not only into the films, radio, and television but also into the speech and writing of the French people.*

* The campaign "to protect the French language against alien incursion" (New York *Herald Tribune*, December 3, 1965) has resulted in the establishment, with Cabinet approval, of a high commission for "the defense and expansion of the French language," headed by Premier Georges Pompidou.

Mr. Cook assures Monsieur Etiemble that the latter is fighting a losing battle:

> What announcer at a French football match is going to shout "coup de pied réparation" when he can say "penalty"? I heard the other day that the French Air Force . . . has adopted the word "operational" with a French-style spelling, *"opérationel,"* because no other word quite works.

Mr. Cook has here given two reasons why foreign words are used in another language, whether French in English, or English in French. The word taken from the other language may be a shorter way of expressing a many-worded idea or it may express an idea as no word in the native language can. That is why, says Mr. Cook in another part of his article, " 'les Anglo-Saxons' have been speaking *'Franglais'* for years. Vive la France! Vive Franglais!"

## PARLEZ-VOUS FRANÇAIS?

M. Etiemble may use the term *franglais* to disparage and discourage the entry of English words into French, but the English language, into which so many French words entered before and after 1066, is hospitable to the inclusion of additional French words. Indeed, some of them are being used so often that we have given them the status of vogue words, which you have read about in the preceding chapter.

You are speaking a little French every day when you say words like these:

*action, à la carte, avenue, ballet, bonbon, boulevard, chapeau, chaperon, charade, chauffeur, chic, connoisseur, corsage, costume, encore, façade, flair, foyer, garage, maitre d', matinée, menu, palisades, personnel, promenade, rendezvous, repertoire, sabotage, souvenir, vogue*—et beaucoup d'autres.

Before you read our own selection of French words current in English speech, try the pretest below. The words on the left are a simple hors d'oeuvre, or appetizer. Match them with the English words on the right.

| | | |
|---|---|---|
| 1. débâcle | a. | composure |
| 2. élan | b. | a kind |
| 3. gaffe | c. | short descriptive sketch |
| 4. gauche | d. | connection |
| 5. genre | e. | downfall |

| | |
|---|---|
| 6. ingénue | f. blunder |
| 7. largesse | g. generosity |
| 8. liaison | h. sharp retort |
| 9. macabre | i. clumsy |
| 10. riposte | j. verve, dash |
| 11. sangfroid | k. gruesome |
| 12. vignette | l. actress in role of innocent young woman |

We have kept the accent marks but so thoroughly are these and other French words at home in the English language that they are often printed without these marks in the columns of our newspapers. Even the *cedilla*, the mark that calls for the pronunciation of a *c* like an *s*, as in the word *français*, is often omitted! Nor are most of these words italicized when used in a newspaper.

## WORDS AND PHRASES

**aplomb**    complete confidence; self-assurance; poise; self-possession. This word consists of two words, *à* and *plomb*, the metal lead; the reference is to the plummet, or plumb line, a cord that has a weight attached at one end to test verticality. Hence, when a man has aplomb, he has figuratively been tested for his ability to stand up straight in the face of any situation and has passed the test.

> Nattily dressed in a dark blue suit, blue shirt and black tie, the 36-year-old lawyer answered all questions with the aplomb of a veteran.

**au courant**    "in the current"; well-informed; up to date; abreast of; in the know; well up in.

> Most of the items listed here are going so fast that the stores will undoubtedly run out soon, so don't procrastinate if you want to be an au courant shopper.

**avant-garde**    "vanguard"; creators of new ideas; artists and writers who are unorthodox and untraditional; as an adjective it means *offbeat*, "way out front."

**bête noir(e)**    "black beast"; a bugbear; pet aversion; person or subject that is hated and detested.

> She opened the interview by characterizing the publication as a bugbear—"my bete noire."

**brouhaha**     hubbub; hullabaloo; furor; uproar.

> A brouhaha involving alleged attempts
> to influence results of magazine circula-
> tion-promotion surveys has brought a
> warning statement from the American
> Association of Advertising Agencies.

**canard**     "duck." A canard is a hoax, a false, groundless
story, a manufactured, or fabricated, report. One explanation
of the use of *canard* in this sense is that it comes from *vendre
un canard à moitié,* "to half-sell a duck." If one only half-sells
a duck, one does not sell it at all but merely deceives the supposed buyer.

> Why did the author find it necessary
> to inject the same old worn-out, un-
> merited slurs, myths and crude jokes
> about waiters, so often refuted, in par-
> ticular the canard about the "fabulous"
> earnings?

**carte blanche**     "white paper"; blank paper containing
only a signature giving another person permission to write his
own terms; "blank check."

> He has been given virtual carte
> blanche to run the show as he sees fit.

**cause célèbre**     "celebrated case"; case that arouses wide
interest; situation arousing attention and discussion; notorious
event; "big deal"; "Federal case."

> "I don't want to make a cause célèbre
> out of this," the lawyer said, "but I can't
> stand by and let someone call me a liar."

**coup de grâce**     "blow of mercy"; name given to the blow
with which a knight despatched his vanquished opponent. It is
also applied to the final stroke with which a bullfighter ends
the bull's agony or to the final action of an executioner. Hence,
in its broadest implication a coup de grace is a final, decisive
stroke.

> It was Frank Malzone who adminis-
> tered the coup de grace that sent the
> Yankees' chances aglimmering in the first
> game.

**coup d'état**   "blow, or stroke, of state"; a sudden over-turn of a government; an unexpected action of a government, usually implying the use of force. The phrase often appears simply as *coup*.

> The civil government of South Viet-nam "surrendered unconditionally" to the leaders of a swift-moving coup d'état staged by the Vietnamese armed forces.

Another expression with *coup* in it is *coup de main*, "a blow of the hand," meaning a sudden attack in force.

**dénouement**   "act of untying." In literature the denoue-ment is the unraveling of the plot; in general usage the word means the final outcome of a situation, or simply "the way things work out."

> As the play moves toward its denoue-ment the characters recede into the back-ground.

**de rigueur**   "from strictness"; indispensable; absolutely required by fashion or custom.

> As it was a special occasion, ticket prices were raised accordingly to a $20 top, and evening dress was de rigueur.

**entente**   "understanding"; an international understand-ing or agreement, not quite so formal as an alliance. Some-times the word is strengthened by the addition of *cordiale*. The famous Entente Cordiale formed in 1904 between Great Britain and France was converted by the addition of Russia in 1908 into the Triple Entente, which came to an end with the Russian Revolution of 1917.

> Although much criticism by reviewers is usually conducted on the basis of books voluntarily submitted for public ap-praisal, *ententes* between authors and critics do not necessarily grow awfully *cordiales* thereafter.

**fait accompli**   "accomplished fact or deed"; something accomplished and irrevocable; a program decided upon and presented as a final action without warning or a chance to debate its merits.

Although our chargé d'affaires and the
American commander of United Nations
troops in South Korea opposed the coup,
the United States must now accept a fait
accompli and work with the new régime
in every constructive way possible.

(Note the use of three other French terms: *chargé d'affaires*,
a diplomatic official below the rank of ambassador, *coup*, and
*régime*, government.)

**faute de mieux**     "(for) lack of better"; for want of a
better way, thing, or person.

With his bench depleted by injuries,
the skipper sent in an untried rookie
faute de mieux, and luckily the youngster delivered.

**faux pas**     "false step"; mistake; social error; egregious
blunder; gaffe.

He cannot remember names and is forever making a faux pas.

**fin de siècle**     "end of century"; referring specifically to
the nineteenth century, whose closing years are characterized
in literature as decadent, sophisticated, world-weary, devoted
to escapism, extreme estheticism, and fashionable despair.
Here we see again why such foreign phrases are used—all
these ideas are evoked by three little words!

In the story "Paris, July 14, 1959,"
one becomes aware of an insistent repetition of such words as cloak, lover, passion, darkness, lilies, silk, and wind.
Good heavens—these words evoke the
mood of the *fin de siècle*—and not the *fin*
of this century of ours, now hitting its
downhill pace, either.

**haute couture**     "high sewing"; first-class establishments
making women's clothes; the fashions created by such firms.
**haute cuisine**     "high kitchen, or cooking"; first-class
cooking; excellent table; cordon-bleu ("blue ribbon") cooking.
**haut monde**     "high world"; high society; upper class;
upper crust; the élite.
**laissez-faire**     "let do"; doctrine that the government
should regulate as little as possible, especially in respect to

business and industry; a policy of noninterference; letting things drift without direction or planning. The expression comes from the teachings of eighteenth-century French economists who advocated "letting the people do as they wish."

> The apathetic laissez-faire attitude with which most Americans view democracy as a concept should be a matter of greater national concern than it is today.

**manqué**     "missed"; failing to achieve a desired goal; frustrated; would-be.

> The same author can switch to an atelier in the Trastevere section of Rome and write about an artist-*manqué* longing for creativity and recognition.

**noblesse oblige**     "Nobility obliges, or has its obligations." This French maxim was anticipated by Euripides in an extant fragment of *Alcmene:*

> The nobly born must nobly meet their fate.

Just as the code of chivalry prescribed honorable conduct for a knight, so noble birth imposed the obligation of noble actions. Those who consider themselves the upper level of society must act in a supposedly superior manner; or, as Emerson put it (*Progress of Culture*):

> *Noblesse oblige;* or, superior advantages bind you to larger generosity.

As used today, *noblesse oblige* implies that more is expected from certain persons in keeping with their background, office, or position.

**raison d'être**     "reason of (for) being"; reason for the existence of some action or policy; justification.

> Her recognition of these qualities in Keats is the real *raison d'être* for Aileen Ward's full-length critical biography of the poet.

**roman à clef**     "novel with a key"; a novel in which real characters and events figure under a disguise. They become recognizable if the reader has a "key" to their identity.

> There were moments in "Across the Water" when I wondered if it could be a *roman à clef*. Could that loud-mouthed painter with his habit of singing and orating in public be a potshot at a real individual?

**savoir faire**   "to know how to do"; an almost instinctive ability to act appropriately in a given situation.

> She copes with every crisis at the embassy with magnificent savoir faire.

**savoir vivre**   "to know how to live"; the art of knowing how to live well, graciously, and elegantly.

> Many an American tourist, having read a book of practical information on what to do abroad, gives an impression of having savoir vivre when he orders the right wine with the main course of his *grand dîner*.

**tour de force**   "turn of strength"; a feat of skill or strength; a dramatic or literary trick; work done to exhibit the ability of an author in a field not particularly his own—just to show he can do it.

> One of Emlyn Williams's greatest triumphs in the theatre was his portrayal of Charles Dickens reading from his works. This was no mere tour de force but a unique and moving experience.

**vis-à-vis**   "face to face"; directly opposite; facing; toward; in regard to. As a noun, *vis-à-vis* means a counterpart, "the opposite number."

> These facts came to light as principals and other supervisory personnel in the school system were showing growing dismay with their financial standing vis-à-vis the custodians.

## Bref

Here is a reference list of some more French words and expressions with the briefest of explanations.

| | |
|---|---|
| **amour-propre** | self-love; self-esteem |
| **bagatelle** | a trifle |
| **bistro(t)** | small bar or cafe |
| **bon mot** | witticism; clever saying |
| **confrère** | colleague |
| **cul-de-sac** | blind alley; dead end |
| **en masse** | in a body; all together |
| **forte** | strong point |
| **habitué** | one who frequents a certain place |
| **idée fixe** | obsession |
| **maladroit** | clumsy |
| **malaise** | vague feeling of discomfort |
| **ménage** | household |
| **métier** | trade, occupation |
| **nonchalance** | cool lack of concern |
| **parti pris** | preconceived opinion; bias; prejudice |
| **sans** | without |
| **soupçon** | suggestion; trace |
| **tête-à-tête** | private conversation between two persons |
| **volte-face** | an about-face |

## ¿HABLA USTED ESPAÑOL?

> *Other words in daily use that periodically come under attack from the linguistic purists include hamburger, sofa, hit, tee, whisky, highball and cocktail. Of course the North Americans could retort that such words as lariat, barbecue and tamales have successfully crossed the border and become part of the language of the United States.*

THE NEW YORK TIMES, DECEMBER 15, 1963

It appears that not only French scholars but also Mexican purists have been objecting to the entrance of English words into their language. We, on the other hand, have welcomed *barbecue, lariat,* and *tamales,* and we shall probably continue to welcome any other Spanish words, whether from south of the border or from across the seas.

How great has English been enriched by words such as these: *adobe, armada, arroyo, bronco, burro, canyon, cargo, castanet, corral, desperado, flotilla, fritos, guerrilla, gusto, lasso, mañana, mantilla, mosquito, mustang, padre* (also an Italian and Portuguese word), *patio, plaza, pronto* (also

Italian), *señorita, siesta, sombrero, tornado, vaquero!* These and many other words of Spanish origin are in the English language to stay. ¡Olé!

Here are a few other interesting words:

**bonanza**   "calm, fair weather," "prosperity," "a gold mine"—such are the original meanings of the Spanish word. It came into English in the days of the Forty-niners when these miners "struck it rich." A *bonanza* is a rich find, a huge profit, a source of great riches, an enormous yield.

> What brought the job seekers to Albany was a bonanza of political patronage made available to them when their party won control of the Legislature.

**incommunicado**   without means of communication; deprived of contact with the outside world; a term applied to one who is in solitary confinement.

**junta**   "joined"; a council or committee; secret council; group of plotters; closely knit group of persons; cabal; clique; faction. *Junta* is encountered more often than *junto,* an alternate form.

**peccadillo**   The Spanish word is *pecadillo,* "a small sin," derived from Latin *peccatum,* fault, error, and in ecclesiastical Latin, guilt, sin, transgression. Related English words are *peccant,* sinning, faulty; *impeccant,* sinless, free from error; *impeccable,* faultless, flawless, irreproachable.

## FALA VOSSA EXCELÊNCIA O PORTUGUÊS?

From Portuguese, sometimes with a slight change of spelling, come a number of commonly used words, among them *albino, marmalade,* and *molasses.* We stop here for two others of greater vocabulary interest:

**auto-da-fé**   "act of faith." *Auto* in this expression has nothing to do with *auto,* self, but comes from Latin *actum,* act, deed. *Auto-da-fé* is a term out of history; it refers to the ceremony accompanying the pronouncement of judgment by the Inquisition, which was followed by the execution of the condemned by the secular authorities.

**fetish**   This word comes from the Latin word *facticius,* from which we get *factitious.* A *fetish* is therefore literally something made up, false, or artificial. Actually it refers to an object, image, or idol believed, among primitive people, to have magical powers of protection. Today we generally use the word figuratively to mean something for which a person has a blind, unreasoning affection.

> Practically making a fetish of atavism, both the Dodgers and Twins reverted to type yesterday.

## PARLA LEI ITALIANO?

From the Italian language we have taken many words pertaining to the arts. Most of the musical terms on concert-hall programs are Italian. We have space for only a few of these and some other words and phrases commonly met.

**bravura** "bravery, bravado"; a show of daring or brilliancy; a showy, brilliant performance which may be rewarded by the cry "Bravo!"

**brio** "animation, spirit"; vivacity; fire; often met in the phrase *con brio*, energetically, vigorously.

**chiaroscuro** from *chiaro,* clear, light + *oscuro,* dark, shadowy; a sketch in black and white; a sharp contrast; interplay of light and shade.

**cognoscenti** "knowing"; this plural form is given because the singular, *cognoscente,* is rarely met. *Cognoscenti* (now written *conoscenti* in Italian) are those who have expert knowledge, or expertise. The French equivalent of *cognoscente* is *connoisseur,* derived from the same Latin verb, *cognoscere,* to know, from which come *cognition, cognizant,* and *recognize.*

**dilettante** "delighting"; from the Latin verb *delectare,* amuse, charm, please, from which comes *delectable,* most delightful. A dilettante is an admirer or lover of the arts who cultivates them as a pastime. Hence, the term often denotes a dabbler or an amateur.

**dolce far niente** "sweet to do nothing"; delightful idleness; carefree existence. Allied to this expression is *la dolce vita,* "the sweet, or pleasant life," made famous by its ironic use as the title of the Italian film.

**diminuendo** with gradually diminishing intensity or volume; *decrescendo* is a synonym, and *crescendo,* increasing, an antonym.

**embroglio, imbroglio** a violent and complicated quarrel; an embroilment; a very embarrassing and painful misunderstanding.

**intaglio**    "cut into"; an engraving cut into stone or other hard material; a design pressed below and hollowed out of the surface of the material.

> The short story must present a single, unified experience. It has to lie before its readers, neat and polished as an intaglio.

**lingua franca**    "the Frankish language"; name given to a mixture of Italian, French, Spanish, Greek, and Arabic spoken in Mediterranean ports; any hybrid language used by peoples of different speech to enable them to understand each other; a common language.

> India was never united until the British threw a net over it, ruled it as a nation and used English as the *lingua franca*.

**presto**    quickly; rapidly; a musical direction calling for a quick tempo; a magician's command, as in *Presto chango* ("Change quickly"). *Presto* comes from the Latin adverb *praesto*, at hand, on the spot. Via a French form of this adverb we get *prestidigitator*, a magician who is nimble-fingered (*digit*, finger). His art is *prestidigitation*, or *legerdemain*, a French word for sleight-of-hand. The related words *prestige* and *prestigious* once referred to tricks and illusions, but now refer to honor, position, and influence.

**punctilio**    This word, adapted from Italian *puntiglio* and Spanish *puntillo*, "a small point," is a diminutive form derived from Latin *punctum*, point. A punctilio is a nice point of behavior or etiquette, a nice detail of ceremonial procedure about which one is finicky. *Punctilious* means being attentive to small, fine points, fastidious, meticulous.

**verismo**    "truth"; the doctrine of reality; realism confronting the hard facts of life; naturalism; faithfulness to life. It has become practically a vogue word among critics. Thus, in one paragraph a writer refers to "the stark and passionate verismo" of Rossini's *Il Tabarro* and in another to its "cruel, yet timeless reality."

**virtuoso**    "virtuous"; the Latin word *virtus* from which this is derived means "virtue" in the sense of manliness (*vir*, man, as in *virile*), courage, strength, good quality. *Virtuoso* has a number of specialized meanings, but it is generally used to denote an expert, a performer with a master touch, especially a musician who plays an instrument with great power and a display of pyrotechnics, like Vladimir Horowitz, so often called "a virtuoso of the keyboard."

## SPRECHEN SIE DEUTSCH?

Some words borrowed from German are reminiscent of German and Austrian *gemütlichkeit,* a word suggesting gracious living, comfort, and easygoing kindness. Other words deal with the cultural arts as well as the art of living well. Finally, there are words that relate to psychology and psychiatry, war and might, power and politics. Here we shall present a few of each kind, a mixture, or *Gemisch.*

(Nouns are written with a capital first letter in German; we shall use a small initial letter, treating the borrowed German word as an English word. However, where the writer of the excerpt quoted has kept the capital, we have also retained it.)

**angst**     "anguish"; dread; a feeling of anxiety. This word has become a vogue word among the literati.

> A news magazine not long ago devoted several pages to "The Anatomy of Angst" or loosely translated, "The Anatomy of Anxiety," in which it was said, "Anxiety seems to be the dominant fact of modern life. It shouts in the headlines."

**ersatz**     "replacement"; substitute; synthetic; shoddy; inferior; applied to something that is not the real thing.

> This handpicked group was an imitation council, an ersatz legislature called together to serve the immediate needs of the engineers of the putsch.

**Götterdämmerung**     "Twilight of the Gods"; the last opera in Richard Wagner's tetralogy, *Nibelungen Ring;* a word used to denote a final breakdown amid the crash of thunder and lightning; a supremely tragic end.

> Already, as emotion dries slowly out of the air, the Goetterdaemmerung side of Hitler's story is becoming legend.

(Note: German *ä, ö,* and *ü* may be written, *ae, oe, ue,* respectively.)

**kaffee klatsch**    "coffee" + "gossip"; a coffee party; a meeting where talk is exchanged over cups of coffee. This expression, often written as one word, *kaffeeklatsch,* is becoming popular with the newsmen.

> This morning the Senator explained his views on civil rights at an informal "kaffeeklatsch" at the home of a prominent Negro attorney.

**kaput**    from the French *capot,* a term in the card game bezique, meaning that not a single trick was taken; hence, finished, totally defeated, ruined. By extension it means utterly out of date, "washed up."

> Why did they have to give him the award? He was out, finished, kaput—or so the critics thought.

**kitsch**    This increasingly popular word comes from a verb meaning to slap a work of art together, to scrape up mud from the street. In critical and literary circles, *kitsch* contemptuously characterizes sensational, slushy, slick writing or art, low-quality production designed for popular appeal.

> Some critics are genuinely concerned about a thinned-down culture, in which *kitsch* flows like ketchup, drowning art. But art still finds a better long-term market than trash.

**lebensraum**    "living space"; room needed by a group or people to satisfy economic necessities.

> The three main areas of deprivation are jobs, housing, and schools, and it is in these areas that Negro reformers and city agencies are working to satisfy the demands for Negro *lebensraum.*

**leitmotif, leitmotiv**    "leading motive, or theme"; a melodic phrase in Wagnerian operas associated with a character or idea and repeated at the entrance of the character or idea; any dominant recurring theme.

> The phrase recurs like a leitmotif in "Look Homeward," and might seem a bit affected now.

**putsch**   "thrust"; a word of German-Swiss dialect meaning a sudden secret plot and attempt to overthrow a governing body; a coup. During the unrest in Paris several years ago, it was reported that the French preferred to use *putsch* rather than their own words *attentat* or *coup* because "the very ugliness of the term conveys fear and hatred of the military group which is preparing it."

> The generals had chosen to remain loyal to the government when the putsch broke, not because they thought that the insurrection was wrong but because they were convinced it could not succeed.

**schadenfreude**   "harm" + "joy"; a feeling of enjoyment gained from the misfortunes of others; a sort of Aristotelian catharsis of the lower emotions at seeing a comedy.

> Although he had a tendency to describe his characters with a touch of irreverence and cruelty—his comedy is pure *Schadenfreude*—"the joy of damage."

**strafe**   "punish," from the German slogan of World War I, *Gott strafe England,* "God punish England." The form of punishment was man-made: raking with machine-gun bullets or missiles shot from low-flying airplanes.

> Major General Benjamin O. Davis Jr., who is known to his colleagues as a "real leader without peer," was a World War II and Korean War fighter pilot. He was awarded the Silver Star for leading hazardous low-level strafing attacks on Nazi airfields in early 1945.

**wunderkind**   "wonderchild"; a prodigy; an extremely talented youngster.

> After the family realized it had a *wunderkind* on its hands, he [Vladimir Horowitz] was clapped into the Kiev conservatory.

## WORDS FROM ALL AROUND THE GLOBE

As the English roamed all over the globe and planted colonies on every continent, they took over many words from the peoples with whom they came into contact, such words as *shampoo* from Hindi, a language of India, *sampan* from Chinese, and *tabu*, or *taboo*, from the language of the Tonga Islands in the Pacific. Today, Americans stationed in many different parts of the world are repeating the process of adding foreign words to the English language.

The greatest factor in this enlargement of the language is the rapidity of communications. Because of the coming together of the representatives of so many nations, our national interest in international affairs, and the lightning-quick means of communication through radio, telephone, telegraph, Telstar, and Early Bird satellite, foreign words come home to us and appear in our newspapers and are heard daily. Some of them may have only an ephemeral interest and become a historical curiosity, whereas others last and become part of our active vocabulary.

For example, not in Webster's Second but in Webster's Third will you find three newcomers: *enosis*, "unity," from Modern Greek, referring specifically to union between Cyprus and Greece; *hibachi*, "fire-bowl," from Japanese, referring to a type of portable grill; and *sputnik*, "travelling companion," from Russian, referring to a satellite.

Here we shall give additional examples of words that came into the English language from other tongues. Some of these words are long established, so long, indeed, that few who use them realize their foreign origin, whereas others are almost as recent as yesterday's headlines.

### Afrikaans

This language, which developed from Dutch, is also called Cape Dutch and Taal. To it we owe the well-known words *spoor*, track or trail, and *trek*, journey, migration. An Afrikaans word that has come into prominence more recently is:

**apartheid** "separateness," *apart* + *heid*, like the English suffix *hood*. The word denotes racial segregation, specifically a policy of economic and political discrimination against non-Europeans in the Union of South Africa.

> The word "apartheid" is dead as far as South Africa's officialdom is concerned. The white government now prefers the words "separate development" to describe its policy of separation.

The use of different words is merely a matter of semantics; the Government is substituting a more euphemistic expression for an unpopular and hated term. It is interesting that the last syllable of *apartheid* is pronounced *hate!* No matter what the policy is called the hate will remain, and our newspapers will continue to call apartheid by its original name.

## Arabic

During the Dark Ages of European history, the Arabs were a most cultured people, who transmitted part of Greek and Roman learning. They were especially proficient in science and mathematics; some of Archimedes' Greek writings are known to us only because of their existence in Arabic. Many scientific words are of Arabic origin. Some Arabic words that are now English came to us via other languages, notably Spanish, for the Arabs (Moors) ruled over part of Spain for many centuries. In addition, the Arabs took over a number of Graeco-Latin words which have been transmitted to English through Arabic. A not so small list but still only a sampling of the different kinds of Arabic words in English would include *albatross, alchemy, alcohol, alcove, alembic,* something that refines or purifies, *algebra, assassin, burnoose,* a long hooded cloak, *carat, cipher, elixir,* a cure-all, *fakir,* a member of a Moslem sect that lives by begging, also an ascetic, *gazelle, ghoul, lute, magazine, mattress, minaret, mohair, myrrh, nadir, saffron, salaam* (like Hebrew *shalom*), *sheik, sherbet, sirocco, sirup* or *syrup, sultan, talcum, talisman, tarboosh,* a kind of cap worn by Moslem men, *tariff, vizier, zenith,* and *zero.*

And here are two more:

**hegira**    "flight." As a proper noun *Hegira* refers specifically to the flight of Mohammed from Mecca in A.D. 622, where his teachings were unpopular at first. As a common noun *hegira* means an exodus, a mass migration, a trek.

**safari**    "of a trip or journey." It is not generally known that this word is of Arabic origin, for it refers to hunting expeditions, especially in East Africa. Its meaning has been extended so that it means any expedition, especially one filled with adventure, or a long trip, usually of a political nature.

## Chinese

The few words that have been taken from Chinese are fairly familiar words, like *kowtow, mandarin,* and, of course, *tea.*

We list here one expression that has appeared in the press several times:

**gung-ho** "Everybody work together"; cooperation; teamwork. This was a nickname given to Lt. Col. Evans F. Carlson, leader of the famed guerrillas, "Carlson's Raiders," in the Pacific theater of World War II. As used by the press today it characterizes the spirit of derring-do ("daring to do"), the urge to do even better, the striving to march onward and reach upward.

> Even the new breed of astronauts cannot help but be infected with the gung-ho spirit of space adventure, and they must be strong men indeed not to use the pre-eminence which the hoopla following each flight confers.

## Hebrew

Many Hebrew words will be treated extensively in Chapter 14 as words that came into English out of the Bible. (See also *shibboleth* in Chapter 15.) In addition, words like *camel, cinnamon,* and *sapphire* may be traced back to Hebrew. More direct borrowings are *cherub, hallelujah, rabbi,* "a teacher," *Sabbath,* from a word meaning to rest, and *seraph,* an angel guarding God's throne. Finally, there are Hebrew words that have come into prominence more recently, such as:

**kibbutz** "a gathering"; specifically a collective farm under communal ownership and management. The plural is *kibbutzim.*

> Here on Mount Carmel there is a prospering kibbutz of mostly German, Austrian and Czechoslovak refugees.

**sabra** Actually, this word is of Aramaic and Arabic origin. It is the name of an edible cactus growing in Israel that is hard and tough on the outside but soft and sweet inside, like the Indian fig or prickly pear. *Sabra* is a descriptive name affectionately applied to native-born Israelis.

> Those in line represented a cross section of Israel. They included concentration-camp survivors, young Sabras (native-born Israelis), people from Oriental countries.

**shalom, sholom** "peace"; used as a greeting both for "Hello" and "Goodbye."

## Hindustani and Other Languages of India

Hindustani is the name of a group of languages spoken in India, which includes Hindi, the literary language that is also the official language of many states. Another important language is Tamil, spoken around Madras and in parts of Ceylon. From the numerous Indian tongues come such words as *bandanna, bungalow, cashmere, chintz, chutney, curry, jungle, loot, polo, pukka* ("crooked, ripe," complete or genuine), *rajah, sahib,* and *thug.*

**Brahman, Brahmin** The literal meaning of *Brahmin* is "having to do with prayer." It comes from Sanskrit, a very ancient language to which modern Indo-European languages are related. The Brahmins were a priestly caste, the highest among the Hindus. Their task was to take care of certain religious writings and rituals. The word is used in this country to denote a member of the upper class, an exclusive person who deems himself intellectually and socially superior. It is often applied disparagingly to certain New England families, especially in Boston.

**juggernaut** This word is taken from *Jaganath,* "lord of the world," the name of a leading Hindu god, a Hindi word that goes back to Sanskrit. Because of a story that frantic devotees allowed themselves to be crushed by the idol as it was being moved in a procession, the word *juggernaut* has come to mean an irresistible, ruthless force that destroys everything in its path, an engine or machine of destruction.

> The Nazi legions crashed into Poland, now helpless and caught between two fires. So was set in ugly motion a juggernaut that, before it finally rolled to a stop, cost the world at least 20 million lives.

**nirvana** from Sanskrit, "a blowing out"; freedom from pain and passion; complete inner peace; complete freedom from worldliness; paradise.

**pariah** from Tamil, "drummer," a member of the lowest caste of Hindu society serving as a laborer or farm worker; hence, an outcast, a person rejected by society.

**suttee**    from *sati*, "a good and faithful woman"; a term from Sanskrit applied to a woman who showed her devotion by cremating herself on the funeral pyre of her husband; the name was applied also to the act or custom of such self-sacrifice, now outlawed in India.

> In the old Indian practice of *suttee*, a widow, fortified by the expected recompense of thirty-five million years of connubial bliss in the hereafter, immolated herself on the funeral pyre of her deceased husband.

### Japanese

From Japanese come such words as *hara-kiri*, or *hari-kari* (*hara*, belly + *kiri*, a cutting), a form of suicide; *ju-jitsu*, or *jiu-jitsu* (literally "weakness, gentleness"!), *judo* (*ju*, "soft" + *do*, "art"!), and *karate* ("empty hand"), all names of forms of self-defense without weapons; *soy* (in *soybean*), and many other interesting ones, from which we have selected the following:

**banzai**    "ten thousand years"; a cheer of enthusiasm and triumph.

**haiku**    I sympathize with the author's wisecrack about the typographical trance of the West—he is good at such phrases; maybe he should have written his book in verse, some brief and elliptical form like the Japanese *haiku*.

A haiku is a delicate form of Japanese lyric poetry consisting of a single stanza of seventeen syllables in three lines: five in the first and third lines, and seven in the second. There is no rhyme; the subject matter is directly or indirectly concerned with the seasons; the effect is extremely delicate and suggestive. The haiku is a development of an early poetic form called *hokku*, which means "beginning," or "beginning verse."

So popular is the haiku that according to Harold G. Henderson, an authority on this kind of literary composition, hundreds of thousands of new haiku are published every year in

Japanese newspapers and magazines. And here is one made in America:

> Crickets are chirping
> And people are chattering.
> What a noisy world!

**Nisei**   "second generation," from *ni*, second, and *sei*, generation; a term applied to children of Japanese immigrants born in the United States or in other parts of America.

**samurai**   originally a retainer of a *daimyo*, a feudal baron. The samurai had the power of life and death over their own vassals and practiced the chivalrous code known as *bushido*. Today the name *samurai* is applied to the military aristocracy or to professional soldiers.

**tycoon**   a term adopted from the Chinese and meaning "great ruler." At one time it was synonymous with *shogun*, hereditary commander in chief of the Japanese army. As we use the term, *tycoon* means a business man of tremendous influence and wealth, or any powerful leader of an activity. A synonym of *tycoon* is *nabob*, a word of Hindi and Arabic origin, originally meaning a governor of a state or a vice-regent, and used also to denote a rich, powerful, or influential person. Other terms used in a similar way are *bigwig, mogul, pasha* (or *bashaw*).

**zaibatsu**   *zai*, property + *batsu*, family; name given to the small number of families controlling Japanese industries; monopolies and interlocking directorates.

## Malay

From the Malay language come the words *batik, gingham, gong, gutta-percha, sarong, teak*, and:

**amok,** or **amuck**   furious attack," "charge"; in a violent manner; frenzied; out of control; undisciplined; berserk.

> The 150,000,000 Malays in Southeast Asia have enriched the English language with priceless words such as "amok"—a word which has been in the language so long ("Man with Axe Runs Amok, Slays Six"), that its Asian origin is hardly suspected.

## Persian (Iranian)

Persian is an Indo-European language of great antiquity; many of the Persian words in English were transmitted through Greek, Latin, and French—lovely words, which in the words of Logan Pearsall Smith (in *More Trivia*) "glitter like jewels in our northern speech." Such words as *azure* and *taffeta*, *jasmin(e)* and *lilac*, *orange* and *paradise* can be traced back to Persian. Not so poetic, but interesting nevertheless are these two:

**baksheesh**    from a verb meaning to give; a tip; a gift; gratuity; by extension, money given as a bribe. Three other foreign words for a tip specifically tell what is to be done with it: French *pourboire*, "in order to drink"; Spanish *propina*, from a Latin verb meaning to drink to one's health; and German *trinkgelt*, "drink money."

**satrap**    "protector of the kingdom"; a word known to readers of Greek history, where it appears as the title of a Persian viceroy, or governor of a province. The ancient Greeks used it as a special name for a rich man, or for one who lived luxuriously. It is used today to designate either a person with final authority, or else, in a derogatory sense, a henchman.

> Almost to a man, the chairmen of the powerful Senate committees deserted Fulbright on the foreign aid bill. Most of these Senate satraps are fellow Southerners.

## Polynesian

A few words have come into English from the languages spoken on the South Sea islands and the islands close to southeastern Asia, like the word *tattoo*, which comes from Tahitian. A word worth stopping over for is:

**atoll**    This comes from the name given in the Maldive Islands to a small ring-shaped coral reef that appears as an islet, or to a chain of such small islands around a lagoon.

## Yiddish

Among the Jewish contributions to American life are some expressive words used, especially by comedians on television, because these words have an implication and vividness that their English translations lack. Moreover, the very sounds of the words often produce a humorous effect, especially those beginning with *sch,* like *schlepp,* to pull, drag.

Yiddish, from the German word for *Jewish,* is a language of High German origin which was spoken by the Jews of Eastern Europe. Into the language have entered many Hebrew words as well as other words picked up in various countries where the Jews settled. In our brief list we shall consider such adopted words as Yiddish.

**chutzpa(h)**     from Hebrew word for "gall." The word is not yet in our dictionaries but it is being used rather frequently as a synonym for *arrogance, conceit, nerve, pride,* and even *hubris.*

> But I prefer remembering this hairy customer at the height of his chutzpah, when his intolerable but undeniable conceit was coolly sneering in the face of his mockers.

**kibitzer**     Card players, especially those playing bridge or pinochle, are familiar with this term applied to the non-participating onlooker who is sure that he can play better than the active players and who always knows what should have been done. The word is therefore applied to one who watches, or kibitzes, from the sidelines and who does not hesitate to give advice during the course of the action. It is also applied to a jokester and prankster.

*Kibitzer* and its verb, *kibitz,* are derived from the German word *kiebitz,* an imitative name of the pewit, sometimes called the laughing gull; the German word also means a meddler, a busybody.

**kosher**     from Hebrew *kashir,* pure, proper. In its original sense *kosher* means sanctioned by ritual, as in the preparation of food according to prescribed ritual; in its extended meaning it is synonymous with *fit, genuine, legitimate, proper.*

> An investigation was ordered at once because the circumstances surrounding the deal did not seem at all kosher.

**luftmensch**     German *luft,* air + *mensch,* man, human being, plural *menschen.* This word does not describe one who "lives in the air," like an aviator, but a dreamy, impractical person who "lives on air," and often has no apparent occupation or means of earning a living. The term is also applied to drifters in a trade or profession.

> The vestiges of a week-end of "weddings, confirmations and banquets" were present in the converted dining halls that are rented out to theatrical and television *luftmenschen* during the week.

**megillah**     from a Hebrew word for *scroll*, especially the scroll of the Book of Esther read at the festival of Purim. In colloquial usage *megillah* means a long and detailed story, usually with the implication that it is a boring tale.

> He read off the list of offenses as if he were reciting the megillah.

**mensch**     As used in Yiddish, *mensch* means "stout fella"; stalwart person; the quintessence of man; a man endowed with character and moral fiber; "a real human being."

> But as one looks at the prodigious amount of work done, there is no sense of failure; only the exhilarating sight of men fighting windmills which have in fact, turned out to be Philistine giants. Mr. Goodman is a *mensch*. The species is getting rare.

**nebich, ne(b)bish**     This word came into vogue a few years ago when an enterprising artist and gagman used it on comic cards and souvenir plates. A nebich is a poor, insignificant chap who almost but never quite makes it, upon whom fortune never seems to smile, and who excites your pity. He becomes all the more pathetic when he is characterized by the diminutive, as in *a poor nebbishel*.

> "The sun is also rising," Newley said one afternoon, as the stage first took on a rosy hue, then brightened into blue. "What's that? It's a nebbish blue. You know what I mean, it's neither one thing or the other. Bring it up."

**schlemazel, schlimazel**     "bad luck," a combination of German *schlimm*, bad, and Hebrew-Yiddish *mazel*, luck. That's the name given to another type of unlucky person, not quite so pathetic as a nebbish. Plagued by injuries, Sandy Koufax, the star pitcher of the Los Angeles Dodgers, was reported to have called himself one early in 1965:

> Last year when he was injured, he referred to himself as a "schlemazel," an unfortunate to whom things seem to happen.

**schlemiel, schlemihl, shlemiel, shlemihl**    Yiddish has borrowed many words from German, but this is one word that German borrowed from Yiddish, although it does not appear by itself in standard German dictionaries. *Schlemihl* is found in the expression *a Peter Schlemihl* taken from Adelbert von Chamisso's novel (1814) *Peter Schlemihls wunderbare Geschichte* ("Peter Schlemihl's Wonderful Story"), in which the hero gives up his shadow in return for a never-failing purse, a cornucopia. Hence, to the Germans, *a Peter Schlemihl* is a person who makes a foolish bargain without thinking of the consequences. By itself, as we use the word, *schlemiel* characterizes an unlucky, foolish bungler, a person who allows others to take advantage of him, or, by a very broad extension, simply a fool who doesn't think things out properly.

> "What does that schlemiel of a director do but ask me to play the heavy when he knows that I am at my best in comedy roles!"

**schmaltz, schmalz**    "rendered fat," "lard or dripping." The *t* does not appear in the original German word; it seems to be a Yiddish accretion. The German adjective *schmalzig* means sentimental; *schmaltz* means something sentimental, especially in music and writing; "molasses"; "tear-jerker." So at home is this word that the adjective *schmaltzy* has been formed from it. In *The Musical Life* (1958) the critic Irving Kolodin includes a delightful and informative chapter, "Essay on Schmalz," in which he uses *schmalzing,* a verb form, and *deschmalz,* presumably a coinage!

> The author and his colleagues have found in the making of this film the perfect formula for the high-class schmaltz that even the most ascetic among us

likes on occasion—even though you hate yourself in the morning.

---

**For Good Measure**

**lagniappe**        At both the dinner and supper shows Tony Martin sings between eighteen and twenty-two songs, and, as a lagniappe, tosses in three or four request numbers.

For good measure we are tossing in the word *lagniappe* (pronounced lănyăp′), which comes from the Creole speech of Louisiana. The first part (*la*) is from the Spanish word for *the*, the second from Quechua (Peruvian Indian) *yápa*, an addition. A lagniappe is therefore something additional tossed in for good measure, like the extra dainty in a baker's dozen.

---

## I. ALL FRENCH IN CONTEXT

From the group after each sentence select the word or words most closely defining the italicized word or phrase. (In these exercises we have omitted accents, unless absolutely necessary, to show that the French words are thoroughly Anglicized.)

1. In seeking the governorship he may have delivered his own *coup de grace* when he punched a reporter in the eye.
    (a) retort (b) argument (c) credentials (d) death blow

2. The police chief said that the *denouement*—the voluntary surrender of a suspect who gave information about the case—"negates any justification for the way we were excluded from the case."
    (a) unexpected development (b) final outcome (c) lucky accident (d) result of brilliant police action

3. Although the greatest *gaffe* a child can make is to use dated slang, some of the current crop is pre-World War II vintage.
    (a) social blunder (b) bit of nonsense (c) act of sophistication (d) insult to his listeners' intelligence

4. He has no affection for the kind of *laissez-faire* system which in this country masquerades as conservatism.
    (a) disguised liberal (b) bureaucratic (c) permissive (d) utterly reactionary

5. From time to time Mary McCarthy has written acid *roman à clef* novels and short stories drawing heavily on aspects of her own life.

    (a) impressionistic (b) romantic (c) avant-garde
       (d) containing real persons presented in disguise

## II. REPLACEMENTS

Replace each of the italicized words or phrases in the sentences by a French equivalent chosen from this list.

    (a) avant-garde      (e) detente
    (b) bagatelle        (f) en masse
    (c) cul-de-sac      (g) idee fixe
    (d) de rigueur      (h) macabre

1. Another group of newspapers were hopeful that a general settlement might emerge from this momentary *easing of tension.*
2. The composer has not forgotten the kind of songs that were *absolutely required* when the musical theater was simple and undemanding.
3. This *grim* study of a group of marooned English schoolboys on a South Sea Island has been pressing J. D. Salinger's work in popularity, particularly among students.
4. His money bailed the ball club out of an impossible *dead end.*
5. The new poetry had its beginnings in a sudden efflorescence after World War II of *way-out-front* little magazines.

## III. COMPLETIONS: STILL FRENCH

Complete each of the following sentences to make it a true statement by selecting one of the words or phrases at the end of each sentence.

1. A person granted unlimited permission to act in a certain matter has been given
    (a) malaise (b) carte blanche (d) faute de mieux
       (d) entente.
2. Self-assurance in a trying situation known as
    (a) tour de force (b) piece de resistance
       (c) amour-propre (d) aplomb.
3. Justification for the existence of a policy is called its
    (a) raison d'etre (b) dernier cri (c) esprit de corps
       (d) fait accompli.
4. A sudden overthrow of a government by a show of force is called
    (a) fin de siecle (b) entente (c) coup d'etat (d) volte-face.

5. A subject that one dislikes and dreads is a
   (a) brouhaha (b) bete noire (c) coup de main (d) metier.

## IV.  TRÈS FACILE

In the left-hand column are ten French words that have
been accepted as English words. You have probably met
them in your reading. Match each one with the appropriate
term in the right-hand column.

|     |              |     |                |
| --- | ------------ | --- | -------------- |
| 1.  | abattoir     | a.  | disguise       |
| 2.  | atelier      | b.  | corpulence     |
| 3.  | badinage     | c.  | housekeeper    |
| 4.  | bruit        | d.  | workshop       |
| 5.  | camouflage   | e.  | playful talk   |
| 6.  | concierge    | f.  | picture        |
| 7.  | divertissement | g. | weariness      |
| 8.  | embonpoint   | h.  | slaughterhouse |
| 9.  | ennui        | i.  | amusement      |
| 10. | tableau      | j.  | to noise about |

## V.  ENCORE! BIS!!

Here are a dozen more to work on.

|     |              |     |                           |
| --- | ------------ | --- | ------------------------- |
| 1.  | claque       | a.  | banter                    |
| 2.  | dossier      | b.  | strong inclination        |
| 3.  | entrepreneur | c.  | specter                   |
| 4.  | milieu       | d.  | file                      |
| 5.  | penchant     | e.  | group of hired applauders |
| 6.  | persiflage   | f.  | environment               |
| 7.  | raconteur    | g.  | nickname                  |
| 8.  | rapport      | h.  | publicity                 |
| 9.  | rationale    | i.  | harmonious relationship   |
| 10. | reclame      | j.  | skilled storyteller       |
| 11. | revenant     | k.  | explanation of principles |
| 12. | so(u)briquet | l.  | promoter                  |

## VI.  LIKE AND UNLIKE IN DIVERSE LANGUAGES

You have met some of the words in the pairs below in this
chapter; others you have probably encountered in your reading. Tell which pairs are of like, or similar, meaning, and
which are unlike, or opposite.

| 1. amok ——————— out of control | (Malay) |
| 2. angst ——————— mental ease | (German) |
| 3. baksheesh ——————— gratuity | (Persian) |
| 4. blasé ——————— bored | (French) |

| | | | |
|---|---|---|---|
| 5. | bonanza ——————— rich find | (Spanish) |
| 6. | canard ——————— true story | (French) |
| 7. | chutzpah ——————— modesty | (Yiddish) |
| 8. | diminuendo ——————— crescendo | (Italian) |
| 9. | echt ——————— genuine | (German) |
| 10. | entourage ——————— retinue | (French) |
| 11. | faux pas ——————— savoir faire | (French) |
| 12. | kitsch ——————— trash | (German) |
| 13. | maladroit ——————— expert | (French) |
| 14. | manqué ——————— successful | (French) |
| 15. | megillah ——————— concise story | (Hebrew-Yiddish) |
| 16. | pariah ——————— outcast | (Tamil) |
| 17. | tycoon ——————— "big shot" | (Chinese-Japanese) |
| 18. | vendetta ——————— blood feud | (Italian) |
| 19. | verismo ——————— romanticism | (Italian) |
| 20. | weltschmerz ——————— sentimental sadness | (German) |

## VII. POLYGLOT

Match each word on the left with the correct word or phrase on the right.

| | | | |
|---|---|---|---|
| 1. conquistador | (Spanish) | a. | subservient follower |
| 2. fortissimo | (Italian) | b. | ritual suicide |
| 3. fracas | (French-Italian) | c. | stockaded village |
| 4. hacienda | (Spanish) | d. | greenish crust on metal |
| 5. hari-kari | (Japanese) | e. | ghost |
| 6. incognito | (Italian) | f. | noisy dispute |
| 7. insouciance | (French) | g. | reproduction |
| 8. janissary | (Turkish) | h. | very loud |
| 9. judo | (Japanese) | i. | large country house |
| 10. kraal | (Afrikaans) | j. | cloth worn like a skirt |
| 11. patina | (Italian) | k. | conqueror |
| 12. poltergeist | (German) | l. | learned man |
| 13. replica | (Italian) | m. | under an assumed name |
| 14. sarong | (Malay) | n. | freedom from care |
| 15. savant | (French) | o. | type of wrestling |

## VIII. MUSIC FROM ITALY

On the left are five Italian terms you will find on programs of concerts. Match each one with the proper definition on the right.

| | | |
|---|---|---|
| 1. allegro | (a) | singable |
| 2. andante | (b) | moderately slow |
| 3. cadenza | (c) | in a brisk, lively manner |

4. cantabile   (d) sprightly and humorous, usually in triple time
5. scherzo    (e) technically brilliant solo passage, sometimes improvised

## IX. ANALOGIES

Select the term from the five given choices which follow the letters so that the analogy is correctly completed. For detailed instructions see pages 329–332; 335.

EXAMPLE:   PEACE : SHALOM :: LEBENSRAUM : (a) debacle (b) living space (c) kibbutz (d) malaise (e) rumor
ANSWER:    (b), for *peace* is a translation of *shalom*, and *living space* is a translation of *lebensraum*.

1. ATOLL : CORAL :: LAVA : (a) volcano (b) melted rock (c) ruined city (d) fire (e) ashes
2. COGNOSCENTI : LUFTMENSCHEN :: CONNOISSEURS : (a) confreres (b) couturiers (c) nabobs (d) idlers (e) samurai
3. IMBROGLIO : QUIET :: KOSHER : (a) kaput (b) fetish (c) de rigueur (d) native-born (e) illegitimate
4. SATRAP : PROVINCE :: (a) citizen (b) revenue (c) governor (d) sabra (e) putsch : STATE
5. ANIMAL : SPOOR :: STROLLERS ON THE BEACH : (a) sandwiches (b) footprints (c) shelters (d) noise (e) crowds

## X. THE CONTEXT FURNISHES THE CLUE

In each of the following passages a foreign word or expression has been omitted. It is explained, however, by the context. We have italicized the words that give the explanation. You are asked to supply the missing foreign terms from the choices after each passage.

1. We did not hear about it until it was a _____. Then we were told nothing could be done because *the deal had been made*.
    (a) denouement (b) verismo (c) fait accompli (d) tour de force

2. The U.N. Cyprus mediator proposed that the question of _____ (*union of Cyprus with Greece*) should be shelved by the Greek Cypriot regime at Nicosia if peace was to be restored on the island.
    (a) entente (b) status quo (c) force majeure (d) enosis

3. Let us say simply that there has been too much *awkwardness*, too many _____, and an unbearable amount of *stupidity* on both sides.
    (a) gaucheries (b) imbroglios (c) liaisons (d) ripostes

4. The objective is a _____, a *relaxation of tensions* between East and West to avert the recurrent crises between them.

(a) volte-face (b) detente (c) leitmotiv (d) weltanschauung

5. Originally Newsom's *nickname* was Buck. He *renicknamed* himself, referring to himself as Bobo and graciously bestowing the same _____ on everyone he talked to.

(a) rapport (b) poltergeist (c) incognito (d) soubriquet

## DO-IT-YOURSELF DEPARTMENT

Learn the meanings of any of these that are unfamiliar to you.

Just in case you are going to look these up in a French dictionary we have retained the accents, although when used as English words, many of these words are written without them.

agent provocateur
aide-mémoire
arrière-pensée
arriviste
billet-doux
causerie
chanteuse
clique
comme il faut
coterie
déjà vue
démarche
démodé
dernier cri
déshabillé
de trop
double entendre
eminence grise

enfant terrible
esprit de corps
fanfare
farouche
femme fatale
force majeure
frisson
grande dame
hors de combat
impasse
je ne sais quoi
joie de vivre
le mot juste
lèse majesté
macédoine
midinette
mise-en-scène
modiste

né(e)
nouveau riche
papier-mâché
par excellence
parvenu
petit bourgeois
pièce de résistance
précis
rapportage
recherché
résumé
soigné(e)
succès d'estime
succès fou
tant pis
touché
trompe l'oeil
venue

GERMAN

blitzkrieg
flak
gestalt
hinterland

lieder
machtpolitik
realpolitik
verboten

Walpurgisnacht
wanderlust
weltanschauung
zeitgeist

HINDI

guru

mahatma

yogi

### ITALIAN

| | | |
|---|---|---|
| a cap(p)ella | fiasco | risorgimento |
| al fresco | impresario | rotunda |
| arpeggio | irredenta | segue |
| cupola | largo | sotto voce |
| extravaganza | lento | staccato |
| falsetto | pianissimo | terra cotta |

### PERSIAN

| | |
|---|---|
| checkmate (adapted spelling) | purdah |

### RUSSIAN

| | | |
|---|---|---|
| droshky | kaftan | ukase |

### SPANISH

| | | |
|---|---|---|
| aficionado | bolero | duenna |

### YIDDISH

| | | |
|---|---|---|
| meshugga | nosh(erei) | schmooze |
| schnorrer | schnozzle | shamus |

## *VOCABAGRAMS*

Every answer must be a word borrowed from French. Don't worry about the accents, we'll supply them in the answers.

| | | | |
|---|---|---|---|
| 1. chicle | | = | platitude |
| 2. coupons | | = | a dash of |
| 3. credo | | = | stage set |
| 4. funeral | | = | idler |
| 5. prices | | = | summary |
| 6. raced | | = | core group |
| 7. grime | + e | = | a rule |
| 8. irate | + d | = | a harangue |
| 9. nine | + u | = | boredom |
| 10. remit | + b | = | quality of sound |
| 11. salami | + e | = | uneasiness |
| 12. steel | + v | = | slim |
| 13. triad | + o | = | skillful |
| 14. true | + o | = | "way out front" |
| 15. vase | + u | = | smooth |
| 16. version | + n | = | surroundings |
| 17. checker | − k | = | a crib |
| 18. costing | − g | = | alarm bell |
| 19. germane | − r | = | household |

20. grimace − c = optical illusion
21. outer − t = a rake
22. pancake − k = appetizer
23. reaching − e = humiliation
24. soldiers − l = documented file

This time, answer in Spanish.

1. abode = baked clay
2. open = common laborer
3. seam = tableland
4. coral + r = animal enclosure
5. door + e = cowboys' contest
6. drama + a = fleet
7. oust + g = zest
8. pears + e or a = blanket
9. roach + n = Western farm
10. soda + i = goodbye
11. trail + a = a lasso
12. troop + n = at once

Finally, Italian will supply the answers.

1. avid = prima donna
2. poster = rapidly
3. riot = group of three
4. roost = human trunk
5. also + v = volley
6. odor + n = a movement in music
7. elfin + a = conclusion
8. mace + o = gem carved in relief
9. paint + a = color change in bronze
10. poem + t = time
11. score + f = mural painting
12. toiling + a = engraving below the surface
13. tore + f = loudly
14. vast + i = view
15. enamor − n = love
16. loose − e = unaccompanied

*He who is ignorant of foreign languages knows not his own.*

JOHANN WOLFGANG VON GOETHE, *Kunst und Alterthum*

# 10. A Miscellany of Words

> *Mr. Screvane found the report "a hodge-podge of what everybody knows, of what others have said, and what some people have been whispering back of the hand."*
>
> *Mayor Wagner said of the report, "It is a kind of chop suey containing ingredients . . . which surely represent no solid contribution to the extensive study which has been done."*

THE NEW YORK TIMES, DECEMBER 31, 1964

Messrs. Screvane and Wagner might also have used the words *bouillabaisse, farrago, gallimaufry, goulash, mishmash, olio, omnium-gatherum, pastiche, potpourri, ragout, salmagundi, smorgasbord*, for they all mean a mixture, a medley, a melange, a miscellany, an everything, *including* the kitchen sink.

Appropriately enough, almost all of these words have something to do with cooking or food.

**hodgepodge** (also *hotchpotch*, which reveals the relationship to the word *pot*), a stew of barley, peas, meat, etc.

**potpourri** (French translation of Spanish *olla podrida*, literally "rotten pot"), a highly spiced stew.

**olio** (from *olla* above), a word generally reserved for literary or musical mixtures, as is *potpourri*.

**farrago** (from Latin word for mixed fodder for cattle), related to *farina* and *farinaceous*, is used like the word *olio*.

**gallimaufry,** French *galimafrée,* a stew of leftovers, food badly prepared.

**goulash,** from Hungarian word meaning a herdsman's stew.

**mishmash** is—it may come as something of a shock— a good old English word with a long history of use dating back to 1450!

**salmagundi,** another old English word, of obscure origin, dating back to the fifteenth century, according to the Oxford English Dictionary, which, after defining *salmagundi* as "a dish composed of chopped meat, anchovies, eggs, onion with oil and condiments," has this charming entry for its figurative use: "**1764** FOOTE; By your account I must be an absolute olio, a perfect salamongundy of charms."

**pastiche** (French, from Italian *pasticcio,* "a pasty, a meat pie," a hodgepodge), an imitative literary work as well as a patchwork mixture.

**bouillabaisse,** a fish stew, of course, a specialty of Marseilles.

**ragout** (French, from Latin *re + ad + gustus,* "taste," hence something to revive the taste), a spicy stew of meat or fish and vegetables.

**smorgasbord,** "sandwich table." The Swedish words *smör, gas,* and *bord* are akin to our words *smear* (*smör* means butter in Swedish), *goose* (because of the resemblance of pats of butter to a goose), and *board,* "a groaning board," because a smorgasbord is a meal offering an abundance—buffet style—of a great variety of dishes, hot and cold.

**omnium gatherum,** "a catch-all," itself a hodgepodge, being made up of a Latin word and an English word with a Latin ending, first appeared in print in 1530!

All of these are now often used to mean an incongruous mixture, a medley, and are themselves a curious melange of many languages. Generally, too, they are used in an uncomplimentary way.

And that's the kind of word we're going to take up first.

## PEJORATIVES

Most of the words that follow—like the word *egregious*, discussed in Chapter 1—once had a favorable meaning but almost all are now used in an uncomplimentary, derogatory, pejorative sense.

Before we discuss them, try to match up a half dozen of them.

| | |
|---|---|
| 1. *doctrinaire* views | (a) immature |
| 2. *fulsome* praise | (b) nauseatingly excessive |
| 3. *gratuitous* remarks | (c) stubbornly held |
| 4. *ominous* silence | (d) stuffy |
| 5. *pedantic* manner | (e) threatening |
| 6. *puerile* behavior | (f) uncalled for |

You can check your answers as you read along.

**curt,** although a synonym for *concise, laconic, pithy, succinct,* and *terse,* now is most often used to mean brusque, discourteously short (as in *a curt reply* or *refusal*). *To curtail* means to shorten.

**diatribe,** from the Greek *diatribe,* a short ethical discourse, now means only a long abusive or bitter speech.

**didactic** (coming from a Greek word meaning taught) means teaching a lesson or pointing a moral. However, it is often used, especially in literary criticism, to mean overburdened with moral emphasis, therefore dull, pompous. An *autodidact* is a self-taught person.

**doctrinaire** (related to Latin *doctrina,* learning) has come to characterize one who maintains a stubborn, intransigent attitude toward his own views. The word *docile,* on the other hand, means easily taught, submissive, obedient, amenable.

**epithet,** though still used as a descriptive term, a name added (like Homer's "rosy-fingered dawn," "wine-dark sea"), is more often used as an abusive characterization. When we wish to be abusive, we hurl an epithet.

**erudite, erudition** are used in both a favorable and unfavorable way. A learned man, a scholar can be praised for his erudition, his great knowledge. However, *erudite* may be used in a derogatory way to mean bookish, devoted to very specialized learning, knowing more and more about less and less. *Erudite* comes from Latin *rudis,* untutored, ignorant—rude in the sense used by Gray when he refers to the "rude forefathers" who sleep in the village cemetery. The prefix *e* removes the ignorance. Rudiments are the elementary, basic principles or skills; *rudimentary* means elementary, basic, fundamental.

**factitious,** made (Latin *factus*) by human skill or art, has therefore come to mean artificial, made up, which last meaning appears in the Oxford English Dictionary entry under the word *chortle*, "a factitious word introduced by the author of *Through the Looking-Glass* and jocularly used by others after him, apparently with some suggestion of chuckle and snort."

**fulsome,** once meaning abundant, is now used only—or should be—with the meaning of excessive—nauseatingly so.

**gratuitous,** once meaning (like gratis) "given freely," is only occasionally so used today. The more frequent meaning is meddlesome, unnecessarily intrusive, uncalled for; a who-asked-you-to word (as in *a gratuitous insult*).

**impute,** the derivation helps us here—Latin *im,* in + putare, to think, thus to put thoughts into someone else's mind, to attribute views or motives to someone else—generally bad ones, blameworthy ones. We quote again from Gray's "Elegy":

> Nor you, ye Proud, impute to these the
>     fault,
> If Memory o'er their tombs no trophies
>     raise.

Other useful words coming from the root *put* are *putative,* thought to be, assumed, *reputed, disputatious,* given to thinking in opposition, hence argumentative, and *disputant,* a wrangler, one who engages in controversy.

**indoctrinate** comes from the same root as *doctrinaire* above. So suspicious is human nature that indoctrination has become equated with "brainwashing." We assume that one indoctrinates only partisan or subversive ideas.

**ineffable,** though in religious context always meaning unspeakable, inexpressible in an awesome sense (Latin *fari,* to speak, from which we get *fable, fabulous,* and Spanish *hablar,* to speak), is in a general sense sometimes used with a strong, derogatory meaning as though there were no words vile or low enough to express one's loathing.

**innuendo,** coming from Latin *innuere,* to nod, is occasionally used to mean a hint, suggestion, a nuance. But again the hinting has been perverted so that it generally refers to a sly insinuation, something thrown in with malice aforethought, a veiled remark. We have come across this neutral sense of the word, however:

> But Chopin's B Minor Sonata remained inundated with light: the needed shadowy contrasts, the half-lit innuendos were all missing.

Or maybe the writer really meant *nuances!*

**invidious,** coming from a Latin word meaning envy, has had only bad meanings: jealous, hateful, defamatory, obnoxious.

**notorious** has moved in meaning from "well known," still so used especially in a scientific sense, to the very unpleasant meaning of widely but unfavorably known.

**obsequious** once meant prompt, obedient, dutiful but, having acquired a surfeit of these qualities, is now used to mean fawning, sycophantic, servile, subservient.

**ominous,** the adjective form of the word *omen,* which may mean either a good or bad sign, is itself always used in the bad sense as are *abominate,* "to draw back from an ill omen," hence to detest, and *abominable.*

**pedantic,** coming from *pedant,* a teacher, is always used in a derogatory sense to mean formalistic, narrow, pompously learned.

**poetaster,** ending with the suffix *aster,* which is always pejorative, virtually meaning "fake," means a writer of inferior verses. A pilaster is a false pillar.

**puerile,** from Latin word *puer,* boy, can mean boyish, but now almost exclusively means childish, immature, unworthy of an adult.

**pundit,** teacher again—this time from Hindi, an official language of India. Like the other words for *teacher* (except when it is used as the title for a learned man of India) it has taken on the rather depreciatory meaning, especially in literary criticism, of one who makes pronouncements authoritatively and pompously. *Punditry* usually has this connotation.

**sanctimonious,** from Latin *sanctus,* holy, now describes one who is hypocritically so. A *sanctuary* is a holy place, as well as a place of asylum or refuge. Something *sacrosanct* is doubly holy.

**sciolist,** from Latin root *sci,* know, has always had a pejorative meaning. A sciolist is one who pretends to scholarship or knowledge. The root *sci* also gives us *omniscient*, "all-knowing," *nescient*, "not knowing," ignorant, agnostic, *prescient*, "knowing beforehand," *science*, "knowledge," all the *conscious* words, and *conscience*, an awareness of right and wrong. *Unconscionable* means not guided or restrained by conscience, hence unreasonable, unscrupulous, outrageous.

**sententious,** meaning full of maxims and sayings even to the extent of being terse and pithy, has degenerated so that it often means the opposite—wordy, verbose, ponderously trite, excessively moralizing.

**sophistry,** from Greek *sophos*, wise. The Sophists or Wise Men were a group of teachers who achieved great fame in Greece during the fifth century B.C. Although they had many good educational ideas, they got a bad reputation because they accepted pay and because they used subtle methods of argumentation. Some of them were also accused of making the weaker or worse reason appear to be the stronger or better reason.

Hence the word *sophistry* has an unfavorable connotation and means arguing deceitfully, attempting to turn a poor case into a good one by means of clever but specious reasoning. And so the word *sophistry*, that contains the root for *wise* in it, has come to be a synonym for evasion, fallacious reasoning, quibbling, and casuistry.

**specious,** once meaning pleasing in appearance, is now almost always used to mean deceptively so, as in *specious reasoning*.

**stricture,** once meaning only an incidental remark or comment, now is always used for adverse criticism. We have, however, recently noticed its use with the meaning of restriction, a usage marked rare in the Oxford English Dictionary!

**virago,** from Latin *vir*, man (Cf. *virile, triumvirate*), originally meaning a woman of great size, strength, and courage, an Amazon, is now almost entirely a synonym for a scold, a shrew, or a termagant.

As we look back at these words we are a little disturbed that so many of the words that have uncomplimentary connotations come from words that mean or suggest teach or teacher: *doctrinaire, indoctrinate, didactic, pedagogue, pedantry, punditry, sophistry*. (As long ago as 1605, Francis Bacon in his *Advancement of Learning* complained that scholars were disliked by ordinary citizens who "seek to disable learned men by the name of Pedants.")

We can ascribe this only to man's innate suspicion of all teaching or of his wish to strike back at a former authority. Indeed, teaching is not always a sharing of knowledge but often an inculcation of it. There's another interesting word: *to inculcate* (from Latin verb *inculcare*, to tread upon) literally means to grind in with the heel (*culc* from *calx, calcis*, heel). One who resents such treatment is called recalcitrant, because he "kicks back" in rebellion.

To inculcate the meanings of the words we have listed, we must see them used in sentences.

## I. PEJORATIVES

### A

In the sentences below, insert one of the following usually uncomplimentary words where it will do the most good:

> (a) diatribe      (e) gratuitous
> (b) didactic      (f) impute
> (c) doctrinaire    (g) invidious
> (d) epithet      (h) sanctimonious

1. He merely did some wishful thinking and he didn't care one bit who got that winning run. For him to indicate otherwise is outrageously unfair, a(n) _____ slap at a pillar of probity.

2. He wanted to defend the loyal convention delegates who had been given the _____ "kooks" by some journalistic and political critics.

3. Not only is he unyielding but he often seems to _____ sinister motives to those who disagree with him.

4. T. S. Eliot had a strong dislike for most teaching of poetry, and he once recalled that he had been turned against Shakespeare by _____ instructors.

5. _____ has too often ruled out an objective weighing of the arguments for and against fluoridation.

6. Mr. O'Sullivan acts the part of Tartuffe with such _____ distaste that one begins to get an idea of the man.

7. He accused his political opponent of using the word liberal in a(n) _____ sense.

8. Our magazine takes no _____ positions. It points out alternatives.

(For this exercise and the next the answers give the letter first and then the number, thus: (a) 1, or 2, or 3, etc.)

**B**

| | |
|---|---|
| (a) curt | (e) pundit |
| (b) fulsome | (f) sophistry |
| (c) pedantic | (g) specious |
| (d) polemics | (h) strictures |

1. His knowledge of literature was prodigious, but he never paraded it; he was the least _____ of men.

2. As a new impasse threatens the city's school integration controversy, the real issues—not the slogans and _____ —must be put before the people.

3. He was rather _____ in discussing the President, implying that the President's recent economy pronouncements were bogus.

4. He was _____ly praised in an editorial today in *Pravda* for his "half century of struggle for Socialism."

5. To be dramatic, "a slice of life" demands thoughtful exploration of the human predicament rather than mere documentation.

6. To argue that to cheer or jeer a bull-fighter at his deadly business is no worse than gathering in multitudes to watch two boxers knock one another senseless is sheer _____.

7. No aspect of the program—housing, roads or school construction—escapes the _____ of the investigators in assigning the blame.

8. Winston Churchill touched no theme in discourse without lifting it beyond the _____'s horizon.

## JANUS-FACED WORDS

Some words look in two directions, sometimes having equally favorable and unfavorable meanings, sometimes seemingly unrelated meanings. (For *Janus,* see entry in Chapter 13.)

**academic** Plato's school was called the Academy. It took its name from a grove called Akademia, situated in a suburb of Athens. John Milton refers to it in *Paradise Lost* as "The olive grove of Academe, Plato's retirement." The word *academic,* therefore, began its career with scholastic connotations which it still retains. Academies are places of learning. Academic degrees are sought; academic subjects are taught. However, since what goes on in academic circles is sometimes considered remote from life or reality, *academic* has also come to mean theoretical. A discussion is academic when it no longer serves a useful purpose, is too late to be a prelude to action and is being argued merely for the sake of argument.

> It is academic to talk of any other expedient. And the time for academic theorizing is past.

**cant**   This word is presumably related to Latin *cantare*, to sing. It, too, has opposed meanings. *Cant* can mean the "in" words that make up the special language of any special group in trade (legitimate or otherwise) or any special group in the professions. In this sense it is a synonym of *jargon* and *argot*.

> The pages of the current book are so interlarded with the cant terms of Freudianism that we are prompted to ask to see the writer's diplomas in medicine and psychiatry.

*Cant*, however, is more often used as a short, sharp word characterizing the language of hypocrisy, especially insincere pious talk.

> Of all the hypocrisies met with daily, none so affronts the spirit as the pious cant from high places in the government.

**cavalier**   (from Latin word *caballus*, horse). A cavalier (noun) was originally a horseman, at a time when owning a horse was the hallmark of a knight and courtier. A cavalier is therefore a gay, courtly gentleman, one from whom we expect chivalrous (French *chevalier*, horseman, knight, from *cheval*, horse) conduct.

But when is a cavalier not a cavalier? When he acts in a cavalier manner, or cavalierly. How did this paradox come about? For the answer we turn to history, to the time of the Civil War (1642–49) between Charles I and the Parliamentary forces led by Cromwell. The opponents of the King called his supporters Cavaliers, a term used derisively and reproachfully. Almost immediately the adjective *cavalier* took on the meaning of haughty, "uppity," curt, and brusque. To act cavalierly is to give someone a supercilious "brush-off."

> Justice Levy held that the Legislature had shown "obvious cavalier disregard" for the constitutional requirement that the Assembly be composed of 150 members.

**parochial** comes from the Greek *oikos,* house, which gives us such words as *economy,* originally house management, *ecumenical,* universal, all in one house, so to speak, *ecology,* the study of the effect of environment on living things. *Parochial* may refer to a denominational parish (same derivation) school or to someone whose tastes are narrow, limited, restricted. The noun form is *parochialism.*

> This view that states should rise above parochialism undoubtedly has much to recommend it in our interrelated economy.

**provincial**    Although *provincial* may be the adjective for *province,* it has also, like *parochial,* come to mean narrow, sectional, countrified, unsophisticated. Its noun form is *provincialism.*

> A second major fact about Communist China's leaders is their provincialism: they have seen extraordinarily little of the outside world.

**precious** also looks in two directions. When we speak of precious gems, we are emphasizing their value, their price (from Latin *pretium,* price). When we apply the word to someone's manner of speaking or to an author's style we are questioning the speaker's or the writer's sincerity. We are accusing him of having preciosity; of being affected, overrefined, even hypocritical! Molière's play *Les Précieuses ridicules* (1659) satirizes the affected women of his day and the salons they frequented.

> The dangers inherent in writing for a small carefully selected group have long been well known: Coterie art tends to become effete and precious.

**qualified** means competent—without reservations—(*a qualified technician*) or with some reservations (*a qualified success*). A producer would rather have an unqualified success—with no ifs or buts—than a qualified one.

> Britain is the only NATO ally to offer unqualified support for the Administration's effort.

Obviously, the other allies placed some limitations on their support—gave only qualified backing.

## TIP-OF-TONGUE WORDS

Sometimes a face looks familiar but you can't quite place it. This is sometimes true of a word. It looks familiar. As a matter of fact, you just looked it up in the dictionary last week, but somehow. . . .

That's the kind of word we deal with here—elusive, slippery, right on the tip of your tongue. We'll try to make it stick with the help of association, derivation, a story, a mnemonic, any ploy we think will work. We're going to try to help you file these words away safely inside your mind. Whenever we can, we'll put flesh and blood on the bare bones of a word by citing a newspaper or literary use.

**anomalous,** from Greek *a(n)*, not, and *homalos*, even, which comes from *homos*, same, as in *homogenized*, means not conforming to the normal, irregular, freakish. The noun is *anomaly*.

> Only in the Middle East does the U.N. confront the anomalous task of seeking to maintain the peace between a nation that seeks peace and its neighbors who refuse to talk peace.

**apocalyptic,** from Greek word *apocalypsis,* an uncovering, means prophetic, revelatory, often in terms of the final destiny or doom of the world. The noun *Apocalypse* refers to the last book of the New Testament and to the revelation of the future granted to St. John on the isle of Patmos.

> This is the unresolved and perhaps unresolvable question of risking the apocalyptic horror of nuclear war or avoiding the risk at the expense of other people and our own promises and principles.

**atavistic,** from a Latin word for an ancestor, means reverting to primitive forms or behavior.

> Hampered by extreme poverty, illiteracy, absence of adequate food or industry, some parts of that continent are atavistically engrossed in racial savagery.

**avatar,** a word coming to us from India, where it refers specifically to the reincarnation or embodiment of a god as a person on earth. Today it often means the embodiment of some idea or concept.

> He is not merely a conservative, but the very archetype, the avatar of conservatism.

**captious,** from Latin *cap, capt,* meaning to seize or catch, hence eager to catch others at mistakes. A captious critic is fault-finding to a fault, carping, caviling. This word is not to be confused with *capricious,* the adjective from *caprice,* a whim. *Capricious* means unpredictable, erratic, given to whim.

> Still, when "Boheme" has as gaily busy a Second Act and as gently touching a Third Act as this did, it is captious to complain about anything.

> \*        \*        \*

> The Almighty Nile, whose capricious fall floods have for thousands of years meant either salvation or death for the lowlands of Egypt, is now bulging dangerously with its highest flood of the century.

**contumacious,** from Latin *tumere,* to swell, means stubbornly disobedient, "swollen" with one's own importance. From the root *tum,* also come *tumor, tumid* (often used to characterize a "swollen," pretentious style, as is the word *turgid*), *tumescence,* swelling, and *tumult.* Also related is the word *contumely,* which means insolence (swollen with pride). In his famous soliloquy, Hamlet asks:

> For who would bear the whips and scorns of time,
> The oppressor's wrong, the proud man's contumely?

**dissemble** (via French, from Latin *dis,* not, and *similis,* similar, like), to pretend, to feign, to deceptively conceal one's true feelings.

> It is all very well for the writer to dissemble her love of pomposities. But why, they may ask, as they try to pick themselves up again, does she kick them downstairs?

The excerpt is an echo of the famous lines,

> Perhaps it was right to dissemble your
> love,
> But—why did you kick me downstairs?

variously attributed to Isaac Bickerstaffe, *An Expostulation*, and John Philip Kemble, *The Panel*.

**dissimulate** (also from Latin *dissimilis*) is a synonym of *dissemble* in the sense of deceptively concealing.

**eschatology,** science dealing with the ultimate destiny of mankind—what the apocalyptic vision is about—comes from a Greek word that means last, farthest. Not to be confused with *scatological*, exhibiting an interest in things filthy or obscene.

**feckless,** whose meaning can be remembered by thinking of it as effectless, hence ineffective, incompetent, helpless.

> The Scottish Queen handled her affairs of state and religion better than she handled the affairs of her heart. She married a spoiled and feckless youth, Lord Darnley.

**flagitious,** disgracefully wicked, scandalous.

> "That," he shouted, "is a cowardly, dastardly, contemptuous, and flagitious insinuation."

**fractious,** from Latin *fractus,* broken, from *frangere,* to break, means breaking the rules, refractory, unruly, tending to cause trouble, unmanageable. Also from the same root *frangible*, breakable, and *fragment, fracture, fragile*. There is a plant called *saxifrage*, which grows in crevices and therefore breaks the rocks it is embedded in. *Irrefragable*, however, comes from a different root. Although it means indestructible, it comes from Latin *refragari*, to resist, oppose. Such are the vagaries of etymology!

> The 80-year-old Premier of Turkey barely manages to keep the fractious Parliament in hand while pacifying the army overlords.

**glabrous,** smooth, hairless—from a Latin word for bald.

**glaucous,** sea-green. In Greek mythology Glaucus was a fisherman who became a sea-god.

**grisly** "causing to shudder" (from an Anglo-Saxon word meaning shudder), causing fear and horror; terrifying; ghastly; gruesome.

> Will someone drown in the pool or at
> least be heaved into it? Wait and see.
> The waiting and seeing is one of the
> grisly charms of Miss Murdoch's antic
> novels.

*Antic,* though it comes from the Latin word *antiquus,* which gives us our word *antique,* means strange or grotesque. After learning of the murder of his father, Hamlet tells Horatio that he may at times "put an antic disposition on."

**grizzled** means streaked with gray (French *gris*), as in *a grizzled beard.*

**harridan,** a haggard old woman (French *haridel,* an old horse, a gawky woman).

**jejune,** empty, barren, dull, flat, inane, vapid, and therefore, by extension, immature, juvenile, puerile. The *jejunum* (Latin) is part of the small intestine between the duodenum and the ileum and is so called from a belief that it is empty after death (a grisly thought!). You can remember the meaning of *jejune* by associating it with the French word *déjeuner,* literally "to break one's hunger" or, as we say, "to break fast." Also compare our slang expression "from hunger" for something empty, inane.

> Many corporate leaders demand to be
> told when their notions are contradictory,
> insupportable, outmoded, or jejune.

**lissome,** slender, supple, lithe (since *lissome* is just another form of *lithesome*).

**nettled,** annoyed, vexed, irritated, piqued—as if scratched by nettles.

> For this reason, he made it clear, he
> was nettled by statements of others in the
> civil rights field.

**otiose,** idle, unemployed, sterile. *Otiose* is derived from the Latin word *otium,* meaning leisure, ease. *To negotiate* is not (*neg*) to be at leisure, to be busy doing something. When something in a piece of writing is said to be otiose, the implication is that it serves no purpose, performs no useful function.

**penury,** in modern usage is generally restricted to the meaning of extreme poverty, but its adjective, *penurious,* impoverished, may also be used to mean stingy, parsimonious, or niggardly.

> Oswald was penurious to the point of neglecting the health of his family.

> \*          \*          \*

> The school system opened today and ended four years of academic penury for 1,700 Negro children in Prince Edward Township.

**putative,** thought to be; reputed to be; assumed; supposed. (See *impute* under "Pejoratives.")

**redress,** remedy (for a wrong or injustice).

> President Johnson warned that the end does not justify the means and that the proper redress of grievances is that of peaceful petition and of recourse to remedies provided by law.

**restive,** rebellious; restless for cause; "champing at the bit."

> The Rumanians may be restive under Soviet direction—but they are tied to Moscow by ideological and military links.

**tenebrous** (from a Latin word meaning dark), gloomy; mysterious; dark. *Tenebrism* is a style of painting specifically associated with Caravaggio (1565–1609) and his followers, who hid most of the figures in shadow while strikingly illuminating others. In Italian these painters are referred to as *Tenebrosi,* "the somber ones."

**tutelary,** "watching over or guarding"; protecting; watching over as guardian. From the Latin root that gives us this word, come also *tuition, tutor,* and *tutelage,* words dealing with teaching (a form of guardianship, as it were) and instruction. In *The Mikado,* the three little maids from school sing:

> Three little maids who, all unwary,
> Come from a ladies' seminary
> Freed from its genius tutelary.

*Genius* here is the same word as the Latin word for a tutelary deity, a spirit watching over a person from his birth (*gen*).

## II. DOUBLE MATCHING

Working with one word at a time in Column A, select from Column B the word that is most nearly its antonym, or opposite, and then select another word from Column C that is most nearly synonymous, or most nearly the same in meaning with the word in Column A.

| A | B (Antonyms) | C (Synonyms) |
|---|---|---|
| 1. anomalous | (a) appreciative | (1) carping |
| 2. atavistic | (b) busy | (2) gruesome |
| 3. captious | (c) competent | (3) hypothetical |
| 4. contumacious | (d) established | (4) idle |
| 5. feckless | (e) hirsute | (5) ineffective |
| 6. glabrous | (f) mature | (6) abnormal |
| 7. grisly | (g) modern | (7) primitive |
| 8. jejune | (h) normal | (8) refractory |
| 9. otiose | (i) obedient | (9) smooth |
| 10. putative | (j) reassuring | (10) juvenile |

## III. THEY DON'T LOOK IT

These words don't mean what their appearance or sound would have the unwary believe they do. So, be wary as you choose from among the choices given.

1. *bemused*  (a) entertained (b) deceived (c) befuddled (d) deranged
2. *contentious*  (a) capacious (b) argumentative (c) pleasantly happy (d) diligent
3. *demiurge*  (a) a subordinate god (b) frustrated desire (c) half-hearted effort (d) shadowy world
4. *descant*  (a) pour out (b) tip (c) make allowances for (d) expatiate on
5. *effete*  (a) festive (b) effeminate (c) worn-out (d) relaxed
6. *empirical*  (a) expansionist (b) inductive (c) arbitrary (d) domineering

7. *enervated*    (a) overstimulated (b) unnerved (c) weakened (d) aroused

8. *enjoin*    (a) restrain (b) associate with (c) delight in (d) salvage

9. *friable*    able to be: (a) panbroiled (b) tender (c) simmered (d) easily crumbled

10. *inchoate*    (a) completely disorganized (b) well arranged (c) not crowded (d) just begun

11. *indict*    (a) formally accuse (b) convict (c) tentatively condemn (d) write down

12. *interdict*    (a) meddle in (b) understate (c) settle officially (d) forbid

13. *macaronic*    referring to: (a) wheat paste product (b) mixture of languages (c) almond cookie (d) radio development

14. *mephitic*    (a) evil (b) foul-smelling (c) devilish (d) frenzied

15. *meretricious*    (a) praiseworthy (b) artificial (c) costly (d) trashy

16. *momentous*    (a) temporary (b) secondary (c) very important (d) memorable

17. *noisome*    (a) unusually loud (b) cacophonous (c) sensitively irritable (d) malodorous

18. *officious*    (a) bureaucratic (b) meddlesome (c) domineering (d) fault-finding

19. *opprobrium*    (a) disgrace (b) praise (c) investigation (d) agreement

20. *parlous*    (a) talkative (b) dangerous (c) entertaining (d) controversial

21. *piebald*    (a) almost hairless (b) open pastry (c) motley (d) bagpipe tune

22. *prosody*    study dealing with: (a) drama (b) versification (c) prose (d) music

23. *queasy*    (a) narrow (b) curious (c) slimy (d) nauseated

24. *scarify*    (a) frighten off (b) bewilder (c) criticize sharply (d) destroy

25. *testy*    (a) irritable (b) suspicious (c) nervous (d) critical

## Some Explanations

We'll try to fix the meaning of most of these in the usual way.

**bemused** can mean anything from befuddled to hypnotized, from dazed to preoccupied. It is, therefore, seen around a great deal, most of the time in the sense of *befuddled* or *bewildered*. To Lorenz Hart's "bewitched, bothered, and be-wildered" from *Pal Joey*, we add "bemused."

**contentious** is related to the verb *contend*, to struggle, to fight against; therefore *contentious* means full of struggle, pugnacious, argumentative.

**demiurge** has no connection with *demi*, half, or with our word *urge*. The *dem* in *demiurge* is from Greek *demos*, people, as in *democracy*, *demagogue*, and *demotic*, "popular." The last element in *demiurge* is related to the Greek word *ergon*, work, as in *erg*, "a unit of work," in *energy*, and in *synergy*, "a working together." *Demiurge*, therefore, literally means "a worker for the people." It actually means a secondary deity, a blind force that created the world, one that lacks nous (see *nous*, a supreme intelligence, under the word *paranoia*). Other words containing the second element of *demiurge*, besides *dramaturgy* and *metallurgy*, are:

> **liturgy**    which comes from a Greek word meaning public service, "work (*urg*, from *ergon*) by the people" (from *laos*, people, from which we get also the words *lay*, as in *layman*, and *laity*, the people as distinguished from the clergy).

> **thaumaturgist**    "one who works miracles," hence a magician.

**descant** is a musical term (Latin *dis + cantare*, sing) applied to a counter-melody sung above the solo song. In its more general use it means to discuss a subject at length, dilate upon, expatiate upon. To *decant* is to tip a vessel so that the liquid can pour out.

**effete** (related to the word *foetus*), coming from Latin *e*, out, plus *fetus*, pregnant, means no longer able to bear young, hence exhausted, worn out, spent, enervated.

**empirical** (from a Greek word for *experience*), describes a practical method that relies on experience, observation, experimentation for drawing of conclusions—not on theory or logic alone. The method is inductive. From the body of ascertainable facts a conclusion is drawn; it is not deduced from some general theory. When one arrives at something empirically, he does it through experience and observation, from collected data.

**enervated**, literally out of (*e*) nervous energy, hence weakened, enfeebled, debilitated.

**enjoin** has as its noun form *injunction*, a restraining order; *enjoin* means to restrain, forbid.

**friable,** from the Latin verb, *fricare,* to rub, to crumble, means easily crumbled. The word *friction* is related to it, as well as *dentifrice,* something to rub or clean teeth with.

**inchoate** (pronounced inкон'*ate* or inкон'it) is not to be confused with *chaotic* (adjective of *chaos*). *Inchoate* comes from a Latin verb meaning to begin, and hence means incomplete, incipient, imperfected, amorphous. It means disordered only in the sense of not yet being in order. This meaning is well illustrated in a review of a novel which is characterized as "an almost inchoate mass of unorganized and irrelevant material."

**indict** means only to bring formal charges against someone. It does not mean to condemn or to convict.

**interdict** means to prohibit, forbid. The French word for forbidden is *interdit;* the German *verboten* is cognate with *forbidden.*

**macaronic** refers to verse or prose in which a mixture of languages is used for humorous effect. Here are two stanzas of macaronic verse (Latin-English mixture):

| | |
|---|---|
| Puer ex Jersey | (A boy from Jersey |
| Iens ad school. | Going to school. |
| Vidit in meadow | Saw in a meadow |
| Infestum mule. | A hostile mule. |
| | |
| Ille approaches. | (It approaches. |
| O magnus sorrow! | O great sorrow! |
| Puer it skyward. | Boy goes skyward. |
| Funus ad morrow. | Funeral tomorrow.) |

**mephitic** has nothing to do with Mephistopheles; the word describing him is *Mephistophelian. Mephitic* means offensive to the sense of smell and harmful as well.

**meretricious,** although coming from the same Latin word as *meritorious* (*meritum,* earned) is not a synonym. Quite the contrary. Coming from *meretrix,* a Latin word for harlot, literally "a woman who earns," *meretricious* means tawdry, flashy, cheaply gaudy. The film industry likes the story of the young press assistant who was working on a very bad picture. When *The New York Times* came in with Bosley Crowther's review, he grabbed the paper and began to read. Suddenly, he caroled triumphantly, "We're in, fellas—he says it's meretricious."

**momentous** does come from the word *moment,* not in its meaning of time as in *momentary,* but in its meaning of weight or importance as in the phrase *of great moment* and in the line "And enterprises of great pith and moment," near the end of Hamlet's "To be, or not to be" soliloquy.

**noisome** has nothing to do with noise. The word is made up of a shortened form of *annoy* + the suffix *some*, having the quality of. It is sometimes used to mean harmful or disagreeable, but most frequently it is used to describe an offensive odor, "annoying" to the point of being nauseating.

**officious** is sometimes equated by the unwary with domineering, "bossy" (a meaning not yet recorded in Webster's Third), but its specific meaning is meddlesome, intrusive, volunteering one's services where they are neither asked nor needed, as when Robert Browning has the Duke of Ferrara complain that his last Duchess found pleasure in:

> The bough of cherries some officious fool
> Broke in the orchard for her. . . .

**opprobrium** is a Latin word meaning disgrace, infamy, reproach. The adjective is *opprobrious*, infamous, despicable, scurrilous.

**prosody** looks as if it had something to do with prose, a word of Latin origin, but it breaks down into Greek *pros*, near, and *ode*, song. Prosody is the study of versification, accents, meters, rhythms. *Pros* appears in the words *proselyte* and *proselytize*, to convert or literally to "come near to." *Ody* sings its song in *melody*, *parody*, *rhapsody*, and *threnody*, a song of lamentation for someone dead.

**queasy** has many meanings but it is most often used in the sense of *nauseated*. A mnemonic that may help is to think of *queasy* as meaning "un*easy* in the stomach" or to associate it with an interesting synonym, *squeamish*.

**scarify** is related to the word *scar*, coming from a Greek word meaning to scratch an outline. It is used both literally to scratch or cut into (*to scarify the earth*) and figuratively to make a cutting criticism, to flay, to excoriate.

To use *scarify* in the sense of frighten (from *scare* + *ify*) is according to Webster's Third to use a localism and is one of the few words in Webster's Third marked *dial.* (i.e., not acceptable as standard English usage).

**testy** comes from a Latin word *testa*, literally an earthenware jug, then, figuratively as slang, a skull or head. *Testy* means headstrong, irritable, waspish, quicktempered. The French word *tête* (as in *tête-à-tête*) also comes from *testa*.

*Test,* an easy word, has an interesting history. It is related to *testa,* and once designated a vessel that the alchemists used for refining or testing gold.

## IN WHICH WE MAKE A FUTILE GESTURE

We mourn the loss of the distinction such words as *deprecate, disinterested, enormity,* and *infer* once proudly wore.

Just for the record and for those who'd rather be discriminating users of words, here are the distinctions these words once had.

### Deprecate, Depreciate

To *deprecate* an action is to disapprove of it, to frown upon it. The idea of regret that the action has occurred is implied.

To *depreciate* an action is to belittle it, to lessen it in value. But today *depreciate* is used almost solely to mean a decrease of values in currency, stocks, real estate, etc., while *deprecate* and *deprecatory* have taken over the duties formerly assumed by *depreciate* and *depreciatory.*

There are two different Latin roots that have the same form in English—*prec.* One of them means price or value and is seen in the words *precious* (from *pretiosus,* "of great value," root *pret* changing to *prec* in Medieval Latin) and *appreciate,* "to attach a price to (*ad*)," to value properly. As an antonym of *depreciate,* the word *appreciate* means to rise in value.

The other *prec* comes from the Latin *precari,* to pray. You "pray down (*de*)" or disapprove when you deprecate. An imprecation, "a praying against," is a curse. A precarious situation is a dangerous one in which prayer is of the essence. A pilot in trouble comes "down on a wing and a prayer."

### Disinterested, Uninterested

To be *disinterested* is to be without selfish motives or interest, therefore objective or impartial. But it is often used to mean *uninterested,* bored, indifferent, apathetic.

> During a trial a judge should be a *disinterested* but not an *uninterested* listener.

*Disinterested, depreciate,* and *depreciatory* are lost causes, and it is advisable to use *impartial* rather than *disinterested,* and *belittle* rather than *depreciate,* if one doesn't want to run the risk of being misunderstood.

**Enormity, Enormousness**

*Enormity* emphasizes the abnormality, the outrageousness rather than the size (as in *the enormity of his crime*).

*Enormousness* refers to size only, but *enormity* has taken over the functions of *enormousness* as well and is used as a synonym for hugeness, vastness, immensity—with no pejorative connotation.

**Imply, Infer**

*To imply* is to suggest indirectly, to hint, to insinuate.

*To infer* is to draw a conclusion, to deduce.

But again one of the words—this time *infer*—has taken over both functions.

**We'd Like to Draw a Line**

But we would like to take a stand against the approval given to the use of *flaunt* for *flout*, and *fortuitous* for *fortunate*. Permissive linguisticians approve of this interchange; Webster's Third records it.

**Flaunt, Flout**

*To flaunt* means to make a show of, display ostentatiously.

*To flout* means to disregard contemptuously, to pay no attention to, to defy. *Flout* comes from the Anglo-Saxon verb *flouten*, meaning to play the flute, an instrument which, when used for obbligatos, seems to mock the coloratura singer's cadenzas—*mock* being one of the early meanings of *flout*. *Flout* generally has a much stronger meaning today, almost becoming a synonym for *defy*.

> A group of international quarantine experts charged today that diplomats flouted world health regulations by failing to obtain vaccination certificates.

**Fortuitous, Fortunate**

*Fortuitous* until recently meant only one thing—happening by chance, accidental. Now it is sometimes—carelessly, we think, and fortuitously, we hope—used to mean fortunate or lucky.

Sometimes when we feel nasty, we ask ourselves (or each other), "Do certain lexicographers and linguisticians, themselves, ever use *flaunt* for *flout*, *fortuitous* for *fortunate*—or even *disinterested*, *deprecate*, *enormity*, and *infer* for *unin-*

*terested, depreciate, enormousness,* and *imply?* Or are these usages just considered good enough for hoi polloi?"

However, we don't feel nasty and so we break only a feeble lance. Though we have often been bewildered by the pronunciation key in Webster's Third and sometimes dismayed by the pronunciations recorded, nevertheless we can go along with the editors' recording of disputed usages that they believe may *in the years ahead* develop into a sizable tidal wave. But we do question their ready and apparent acceptance of these usages on an equal footing with long-established ones. We agree, of course, that the function of a dictionary is to hold the glass up to current usage, but does it have to be a magnifying glass?

## IV. WHAT'S THE GOOD WORD? OR, BUCKING THE TIDE

In the following sentences, taken from newspapers, the writer used the "less good" word. (We've included some other words not treated above that are sometimes interchanged fortuitously or intentionally.) Show that you are a discriminating user of words by choosing the "good" word.

1. In a penetrating study CBS-TV focuses on these people without hope, whose bodies are cared for by welfare aid, but whose spirit is often neglected by a(n) (disinterested, uninterested) society.

2. His arrest made it virtually impossible for scholars to do (disinterested, uninterested) research in the Soviet Union.

3. Only now are we beginning to realize the (enormity, immensity) and importance of the musical production of Poulenc.

4. *Regina* was (adopted, adapted) from Lillian Hellman's play *The Little Foxes,* which provided Mr. Blitzstein with a particularly strong libretto.

5. The Senator himself has (deprecated, depreciated) the significance of party platforms, claiming that they are "a packet of misinformation and lies."

6. I agree with his goals, yet his attitude is to be (deprecated, depreciated) as much as that of the recalcitrant white supremacist.

7. Mr. Scott's performance as Shylock is brilliant and exciting but the cast around him is less (fortuitously, fortunately) chosen.

8. Is the Senator representing the people of his state or is he (flaunting, flouting) their wishes?

9. It is unfair to suggest, if only by (implication, inference), that architects who designed some of the school buildings were endangering the lives of school children.

10. In the film based on Allen Drury's Pulitzer Prize novel, Dr. Martin Luther King was to have played a Senator in a (climactic, climatic) scene on a vote concerning approval of a new Secretary of State.

11. Many of its episodes take place during psychoanalytic treatment with Miss Stanley (prone, supine) on a couch, looking at the ceiling.

12. King Carlos of Spain was "utterly uneducated, without will or understanding, a weak puppet in the hands of a scheming woman, (venal, venial) courtiers, lying diplomats, fanatical confessors."

## THESE WORDS DON'T REALLY EXIST

But we've seen them around—or heard them.

**presumptious** (obsolete!)

Today the word is *presumptuous* with the "choo" sound clearly heard, not *presumptious*. It means impertinently bold or forward, taking too much for granted.

The verb *presume*, from which it comes, is another Janus-faced word having two meanings (*suppose* and *take liberties*), as this anecdote about Sir James M. Barrie aptly illustrates. One day, he opened the door on a reporter he didn't want to see.

"Mr. Barrie, I presume," said the reporter.

"Yes!" snapped back the usually calm Mr. Barrie and slammed the door closed.

**prophesize** (*sic*)

The word is *prophesy* (last syllable pronounced like *sigh*), to make a prediction. The noun is *prophecy* (last syllable pronounced like *see*), a prediction.

*Sic* is a Latin word meaning *thus* or *so*. In English it always comes wrapped in parentheses or brackets when tossed into a quoted passage. The (*sic*) points an accusing finger at the word immediately before it and says for the writer who has put it into the quotation or excerpt, "This is the way it appeared in the original. Don't hold me responsible for this misspelling or misusage. I know better." When a writer really wants to rub it in, he adds an exclamation mark after *sic*, thus (*sic!*).

The word *sic* appears in two familiar Latin quotations:

*Sic semper tyrannis!*     Thus always to tyrants!
*Sic transit gloria mundi.*     So passes away the glory of the world.

**portentious**

The word is *portentous*, coming from the noun *portent* (strange portents, signs or omens). It means ominous, threatening, presaging something extraordinary and solemn.

It is probably confused with *pretentious*, a word meaning showy.

**unctious**

Though *unctious* can be found in Webster's Second and Third, the more acceptable form of the word is *unctuous* with the "choo" sound clearly heard. It generally means oily in a suave, insincere, and gushing manner—the way we sometimes use the word "dripping."

The words *unctuous*, *ointment*, and *anoint* (notice the one *n*) come from the same Latin verb. For the different spellings, compare the words *punctual* and *point*, from Latin *punctum*, "a point, a puncture."

**unequivocably** (*Unequivocally wrong!*)

The word is *unequivocally*, without any qualifications, absolutely, clearly, unambiguously.

A similar mistake is made by those who use *undoubtably*. The word they undoubtedly want is **undoubtedly**.

## VOCABAGRAMS

Here is a melange of words of all kinds as befits this chapter.

| | | |
|---|---|---|
| 1. choir | | = blood of the gods |
| 2. deliver | | = attacked with abusive language |
| 3. unsex | | = a link |
| 4. festoons | | = forthwith (Anglo-Saxon) |
| 5. grouse | | = wrinkled |
| 6. acrid | + n | = not fresh |
| 7. coding | + n | = deserved |
| 8. inroads | + c | = sarcastic |
| 9. meanest | + l | = prospective jurymen |
| 10. mingle | + m | = arctic rodent |
| 11. morale | + n | = distributor of charity |
| 12. muse | + p | = foam |
| 13. nacre | + e | = to lurch |
| 14. paid | + v | = empty |
| 15. quays | + e | = squeamish |
| 16. rapture | + e | = an opening |
| 17. recant | + u | = mythological creature |
| 18. remand | + u | = talk foolishly |

| 19. orders | + e | = ornamental screen behind an altar |
| 20. theirs | + u | = hairy |
| 21. tumble | + a | = inconstant |
| 22. whistler | + e | = former (Anglo-Saxon) |
| 23. chanted | − h | = pour |
| 24. monstrous | − o | = quack medicines |
| 25. pertinent | − p | = persistently opposed |

If you're having trouble with some of these, here are the first letters: 1. i, 2. r, 3. n, 4. e, 5. r, 6. r, 7. c, 8. s, 9. t, 10. l, 11. a, 12. s, 13. c, 14. v, 15. q, 16. a, 17. c, 18. m, 19. r, 20. h, 21. m, 22. e, 23. d, 24. n, 25. r.

*WORDS: Some Appellate Division judges discussed the late flamboyant Magistrate J. Roland Sala, who'd faced censure for not having been candid in court. "There was no mendacity," Sala told them. "I equivocated, yes. The judge misconstrued, yes. But there was no lie. There was sophistry, a lot of paralogism and double-talk. But mendacity? None at all."*

LEONARD LYONS, "The Lyons Den," NEW YORK POST
NOVEMBER 19, 1963

*Once I remember I used the words* sarcasm *and* irony *in an English essay. Mr. H. read them out and asked me what I meant by them and told the class he bet I didn't know. I replied that sarcasm was making fun of people, as he was making fun of me, but that irony was when the truth was funny, because it was quite different from what people pretended. It would be irony if he punished me. I was a horrid little prig. But it is a bad schoolmaster who tells small boys to stick to words they understand and holds precocity up to ridicule.*

DAVID GARNETT, *The Golden Echo*

*[After dipping] to the depths in exploring the John Wayne mystique via* The Sons of Katie Elder *and the Jerry Lewis charisma in* The Family Jewels, *one plunges into the festival frenzy, an orgy of 25 films to be swallowed with countless shorts, panel discussions and glimpses of and probably meetings with film folk in a tidy 12 days.*

*One prepares. One anticipates. Did you watch that "mystique" and "charisma" bit above? That's vocabulary building.*

JUDITH CHRIST, NEW YORK HERALD TRIBUNE
SEPTEMBER 12, 1965

# 11. From Native and Kindred Roots

> *Loveliest of trees, the cherry now*
> *Is hung with bloom along the bough,*
> *And stands about the woodland ride*
> *Wearing white for Eastertide.*
>
> *Now, of my threescore years and ten,*
> *Twenty will not come again,*
> *And take from seventy springs a score,*
> *It only leaves me fifty more.*
>
> *And since to look at things in bloom*
> *Fifty springs are little room,*
> *About the woodlands I will go*
> *To see the cherry hung with snow.*
>
> A. E. HOUSMAN, *A Shropshire Lad*

Except for the word *cherry* every word in this poem is of Anglo-Saxon* origin. Although A. E. Housman was a renowned scholar and teacher of Latin and Greek and wrote Latin fluently, nevertheless in his poems he used with telling effect words that are derived mainly from Anglo-Saxon.

The words in this poem are simple; only two call for comment: *ride* and *Eastertide*. Here *ride* means a road used for riding or a lane cut through a forest, and *tide* in *Eastertide*

---

* Historically, the English language is divided into three periods: Anglo-Saxon or Old English, from about 450 to 1100; Middle English, 1100–1500; and Modern English, 1500 to date. Anglo-Saxon, a Germanic, or Teutonic, language, into which entered some Danish words as well as a few Celtic and Latin words, is referred to as the native language. Middle English, into which it developed, borrowed more freely from other Germanic languages and from Latin and French. For the sake of convenience we occasionally list a Middle English word under the heading *Anglo-Saxon*, but only when that word is of Germanic origin.

means time, as in *Yuletide,* another name for Christmas, and in *eventide,* which is found in the line "Fast falls the eventide," the opening words of the hymn "Abide with Me," by Henry Francis Lyte.

In the proverbial expression "Time and tide wait for no man," *tide* originally was merely a duplication of *time* but today it refers to the tide of the sea. *Tide* also means a happening, as in the verb *betide* meaning befall, happen. Other meanings of *to betide* are betoken, forebode, presage.

To impart an archaic flavor, to achieve a simple and beautiful effect, a writer may often resort to an Anglo-Saxon word. However, Anglo-Saxon roots do not spread very far for anyone who is seeking to enlarge his store of words. Of 20,000 words in common, everyday use, not more than about 20 per cent are of Anglo-Saxon descent.* Since most of them deal with everyday things and simple ideas they do not present vocabulary difficulties, nor do Anglo-Saxon roots produce large clusters, especially of difficult words. For example, you can draw up a long list of English words derived from the roots of the Latin verb *ferre* and the Greek verb *pherein,* both meaning to bear or carry, but from their Anglo-Saxon cognate ** *beran,* you will obtain only a few simple words like *bairn,* a child, *barrow,* a cart, as in *handbarrow* and *wheelbarrow, berth, bier, birth,* and *burden.*

Hence, instead of listing a few roots that may be productive, we shall treat at length some interesting words coming from

* From the count made by Roland G. Kent (see note at beginning of Chapter 4). The percentage varies with the number of words counted. According to a study made by Edward L. Thorndike of one thousand most frequently used English words, about 62 per cent are of Anglo-Saxon origin. When only five-hundred such words were counted, the percentage of those of Anglo-Saxon origin rose to 72 per cent. Conversely, as the number of words counted is increased, the percentage of words of Anglo-Saxon origin steadily decreases.

** Cognates (from Latin *cognatus,* "born together,") are etymological cousins, words in different languages that bear the resemblance of kinship because they are descended from the same root or word in a common parent or ancestral language. Thus, *ami* (French), *amico* (Italian), *amigo* (Portuguese and Spanish), and *amic* (Romanian) are recognizable as cognates, for all of them are derived from the Latin word *amicus,* friend. In like manner our word *friend* and the German word *Freund* are cognates, both coming from a common Teutonic ancestor.

French, Italian, Portuguese, Spanish, and Romanian—the Romance languages—are cognate languages, for all of them have a common parent—Latin. Almost all the European languages are cognate languages, descendants of a common ancestor known as Indo-European, whose existence can be deduced.

Anglo-Saxon and kindred languages. But first, here's a simple pretest. Each word on the left is of Latin origin; next to each is the first letter of an Anglo-Saxon word of similar meaning. Complete the words on the right; each bar represents a letter.

EXAMPLE:    beverage    d _ _ _ _    ANSWER:    drink

1. announce    t _ _ _
2. assistance    h _ _ _
3. deprived    b _ _ _ _ _
4. estimable    w _ _ _ _ _
5. important    w _ _ _ _ _ _
6. (to) judge    d _ _ _
7. onerous    b _ _ _ _ _ _ _ _
8. realm    k _ _ _ _ _ _
9. relatives    k _ _
10. residence    a _ _ _ _
11. (to) retreat    w _ _ _ _ _ _ _
12. suspend    h _ _ _

## A GARLAND OF WORDS

**awry**    This word, pronounced awry', is derived from the verb *wrigian,* to turn, from which we also get *wriggle.* *Awry* means turned to one side, askew, aslant, amiss. When plans go awry or amiss, they have definitely gone wrong. The Anglo-Saxon prefix *a* means on; at one time *awry* was written *on wry.* Compare the expression *on a bias,* meaning on a diagonal, obliquely.

A Scottish equivalent of *awry* is *aglee,* which comes from a verb meaning to squint. Hence, *aglee,* or *agley,* means "squintingly"; as used by Robert Burns in "To a Mouse," it means wrong, contrary to expectations:

> The best-laid schemes o' mice an' men
>     Gang aft agley.

**baleful**    This word goes back to a root meaning malice, evil. A baleful influence is one that is harmful, malicious, even deadly. Even stronger is the word *baneful;* the word *bane* once referred to a deadly poison.

> From their folded mates they wander far,
>     Their ways seem harsh and wild;
> They follow the beck of a baleful star,
>     Their paths are dream-beguiled.

RICHARD EUGENE BURTON, "Black Sheep"

**beguile**    We quoted an entire stanza of Burton's poem for two reasons: (1) every word in it is of Anglo-Saxon origin; (2) its last word leads into this entry.

*Beguile* comes from a verb meaning to deceive, a meaning that it still has. It also means to mislead, to hoodwink, to divert or lead away from the matter at hand, often through deceit. On the most pleasant side, it means to charm, to while away the hours.

When we behead the verb *beguile* by removing the prefix *be*, we get the noun *guile*, meaning trickery, stratagem (in a bad sense). *Guileful* means tricky, and *guileless* means innocent. *Wile*, a trick, is virtually a doublet of *guile*.

> His words, replete with guile,
> Into her heart too easy entrance won.
>
>                              JOHN MILTON, *Paradise Lost*

**bode**    This word goes back to Germanic words meaning both messenger and proclaim, command. In the same family are the words *bid*, *forbid*, and *beadle*, the name given to a herald or messenger of a law court, a bailiff. A beadle may also be a church usher.

*To bode* means to be an omen, to indicate a future event through signs and portents. Longer words containing *bode* are *forebode*, to foretell, and *foreboding*, a premonition, a prediction, an apprehension.

The *bode* family is not large but you can enlarge your vocabulary by learning the numerous synonyms of *bode* and *forebode*.

**Synonyms:** augur; forecast; portend; predict; presage; prognosticate; prophesy.

**boor**    Under the entry **boor**, Webster's Third lists as synonyms: CHURL, LOUT, CLOWN, BUMPKIN, CLODHOPPER, HICK, YOKEL, RUBE—all these words have the connotation of dull, insensitive, rude. Coming from the Dutch word *boer*, which is related to an Old English root meaning to dwell, *boor* once denoted a small farmer (like German *Bauer*) or peasant. Capitalized, the Dutch form *Boer* names a descendant of the original Dutch settlers of South Africa. Related to the word *boor* are the words *neighbor*, "one who dwells near (*neigh = nigh*)," *bower*, a rustic cottage or dwelling and also a sheltered place in a garden, and *bowery*, from the name given to a Dutch farm in New York when it was New Amsterdam, from which the Bowery, the famous street in New York City, received its name.

Once a respectable word, *boor* is now an antonym of *gentleman; boorish,* its adjective, has the connotation of rude, ill-mannered, uncultured, crude, awkward, gauche, and unpolished. The modern meanings of *boor* and *boorish* are notable examples of the downgrading of words, a linguistic phenomenon which often has social and snobbish overtones. The words themselves may not have denoted anything bad originally, but society has given them such meanings.

On the other hand, other words may go up in the world, a process known as amelioration. Thus, *urbane,* from Latin *urbanus,* "city-dweller or pertaining to a city," means polished, cultured, civilized; even the Romans gave such implications to their word! (*Urban,* another word from *urbanus,* means simply having to do with a city.)

**boot** This boot, no relation to the article of footwear, comes from *bot,* compensation, remedy. It survives in the phrase *to boot,* meaning in addition. At one time, *boot,* used both as a noun and a verb, had the meaning of avail, help, profit. These meanings appear in the adjective *bootless,* meaning of no avail, fruitless, futile.

> And trouble deaf heaven with my boot-
> less cries.
>
> SHAKESPEARE, Sonnet 29

**dole** This word (no relation to *doleful,* sad) is related to *deal;* both words come from a root meaning a division, a share. As a noun *dole* means a distribution of food, clothes, or money to the poor or unemployed. It also means a mere pittance, something handed out in driblets. As a verb *dole* means to measure out, or mete. Tennyson coupled *mete* and *dole* in *Ulysses:*

> It little profits that an idle king,
> By this still hearth, among these barren
> crags,
> Match'd with an aged wife, I mete and
> dole
> Unequal laws unto a savage race.

*Ordeal* is derived from the same root. From the idea of a division or distribution, *ordeal* came to mean the amount to be allotted, hence a judgment or verdict. In early society *ordeal* had a special meaning—a trial by combat, fire, or water to which an alleged wrongdoer was subjected. If he escaped injury or death, his innocence was established. Today an ordeal means a severe test, a trying experience, a period of great suffering.

**gainsay**     The first part of *gainsay* is nothing more than *against* in a shorter version; hence, *to gainsay* is to contradict, to deny.

> You are too great to be by me gainsaid.
> > SHAKESPEARE, *II Henry IV*

**harbinger**

> Now the bright morning star, day's har-
> binger
> Comes dancing from the East.
> > JOHN MILTON, "Song: On May Morning"

A harbinger is a forerunner or herald, a person or thing that announces something beforehand. This word developed from *herberge* (*here*, army, and *bergan*, protect), which meant an army encampment. The harbinger was the person who went ahead of the army to obtain food and lodging for the men. Today, of course, the word is used in its figurative sense only.

> That harbinger of the holiday season, Handel's "Messiah," was performed last night by the exemplary Masterwork Chorus and Orchestra, under David Randolph's directi n.

*Harbinger* is one of the many words taken over into Middle English from French but it goes back to Germanic, from which the French borrowed it. The root *here*, meaning army, has given us the names Herbert, "army-famous," Hereward, "army-defense," a name made famous by Charles Kingsley's novel *Hereward the Wake*, and the words *harbor, herald*, and *harry*, the last meaning to ravage, to attack constantly, to worry somebody. Not so *harass*, a synonym of *harry*. This is derived from a word meaning to incite dogs, to set them on.

In the *harbinger* word family may be put the word *harangue*, forms of which are found in Medieval Latin and early Italian, but which is ultimately related to Germanic words for army, host, or crowd, and ring, or circle. Originally, a harangue was either a place of assembly or the speech made to the host assembled there. Then the word degenerated into the meaning of a violent speech, a scolding and ranting address!

> Half an hour later Cassius was back from his dressing room haranguing what was left of the crowd through a loudspeaker.

**soothsayer**     *Sooth,* meaning truth, is found in the phrase *in sooth,* meaning truly, in fact, and in the words *forsooth,* truly, verily, and *soothsayer,* "one who speaks the truth." *Soothsayer* is still used today to refer to a person who makes predictions; the best-known soothsayer in literature is the one in Shakespeare's *Julius Caesar* who warns Caesar to "beware the Ides of March."

**underling**     In the same play Cassius thus advises Brutus:

> The fault, dear Brutus, is not in our stars,
> But in ourselves, that we are underlings.

An underling is "one whose quality it is to be under, or inferior." In other words, he is a subordinate.

In its earliest uses the Anglo-Saxon suffix *ling* indicated a quality, a characteristic, or an association or concern with something. Thus, *darling* means somebody who has the quality of being dear, or loved, and *worldling* indicates a person who is concerned with things of the world rather than with spiritual matters.

A few more examples follow:

**changeling**     a child that has been changed; a child left as a substitute for another child that has been stolen away.

**fingerling**     "that which is like a finger"; a fish no longer than a finger; a young fish up to the age of a year.

**firstling**     "that which is first"; the first of a kind; first product; first offering.

> The very firstlings of my heart shall be
> The firstlings of my hand. And even now,
> To crown my thoughts with acts, be it
>       thought and done.
>                                   SHAKESPEARE, *Macbeth*

**fledg(e)ling**     A fledgling is a bird that has fledged, that is, it has acquired the feathers necessary for it to fly. Naturally, it is a young bird; hence, the word *fledgling* is applied to somebody who is inexperienced, a mere beginner, as in the expression *a fledgling author*.

**hireling**   "one who is hired." Originally meaning simply somebody doing work for pay, a hired hand (as in the Bible), the word *hireling* took on a pejorative sense. It is used as a synonym of *mercenary* and denotes somebody who will do anything questionable, as long as he is paid for the job.

**inkling**   "a small hint"; a slight indication. This word has nothing to do with *ink*, which comes from the same source as *caustic*, "burning," biting, and *encaustic*, "burned in."

**sibling**   This goes back to an adjective meaning related; the noun *sib* means a blood relation or a group descended from a common ancestor. *Consanguinity* (*con*, together + *sanguin*, blood) is a word of Latin origin referring to such a relationship. The word *sibling*, in its most general use, refers to brothers and sisters.

**yearling**   Strictly speaking, this term refers to a child, animal, or plant a year old. However, some latitude is allowed. For example, an animal may be called a yearling when it is in its second year.

An interesting observation about the words ending in *ling* that we have commented on above is that almost all of them refer to something or somebody young or small, or, as in the case of *hireling*, somebody contemptible. The words themselves have that connotation; the suffix did not bring such a meaning to the word. For example, a nursling is not a small or young nurse, but a child that is being nursed.

However, a later use of the suffix *ling* did impart a diminutive force to words formed with it. There are at least two different implications in a suffix used as a diminutive. It may indicate that which is physically little or it may belittle. When used to indicate actual smallness or shortness, the suffix *ling* terminates words that refer to the young animals, like *duckling* and *gosling*, a young goose. In words that are applied to persons, the suffix *ling* may show contempt, say something derogatory. Thus, a princeling is not a young prince but a petty, insignificant one. The word *stripling* means a mere youth, with no offense implicit in the word itself, but when we call somebody a stripling, we may unconsciously be showing a degree of condescension!

An interesting word that contains both implications of the suffix *ling* flashed by in the news on June 3, 1965. This is the word *groundling,* known especially to students of Shakespeare. In Elizabethan days, the ground, or pit, of a theater, the location corresponding to our orchestra, was the cheapest place in which to see the play. Those who occupied it—standing— were called the groundlings. So, as to other words, like *boor,* society gave a pejorative connotation to *groundling.* It came to mean a person of simple, low, and uninformed taste and judgment. This particular meaning of *groundling* was fixed for all time by Shakespeare in Hamlet's speech to the players:

> O! it offends me to the soul to hear a robustious periwig-pated fellow tear a passion to tatters, to very rags, to split the ears of the groundlings, who for the most part are capable of nothing but in- explicable dumb-shows and noise.

Etymologically, *groundling* means nothing more than a per- son who lives and works on the ground, as against those who spend a great part of their time on the sea or up in the air. The word has come back into use in its original meaning be- cause of man's activities in the air, as in the news report of June 3, 1965, appearing in the New York *Herald Tribune:*

> And for the men on the ground there is the test of operating the most complex flight ever attempted by this nation. Seated at consoles around the world, the groundlings will monitor both men and machine to pick up adumbrations of a catastrophic nature.

*Airman* and *spaceman* already exist as names for those who earn their living in the air or are occupied with conquering outer space; perhaps we groundlings, or earthlings, or ter- restrials, may someday speak of them as *airlings* and *space- lings.*

There is still another suffix *ling,* which comes from a dif- ferent root. This suffix shows direction and originally it was used to form adverbs. Incidentally, the *long* in *headlong* was originally the suffix; we can now see how *headlong* means head first, "in the direction of the head."

This suffix *ling* also formed adverbs showing manner or a condition. Some of these adverbs were used later as adjectives. Of this kind of word the most interesting is *darkling,* noteworthy because it appears in two great passages in English poetry.

> Darkling I listen; and, for many a time
> I have been half in love with easeful
>     Death.
>
> JOHN KEATS, *Ode to a Nightingale*

> And we are here as on a darkling plain
> Swept with confused alarms of struggle
>     and flight,
> Where ignorant armies clash by night.
>
> MATTHEW ARNOLD, *Dover Beach*

**whit**

> Is life a thorn?
>     Then count it not a whit!
> Man is well done with it.
>
> W. S. GILBERT, *The Yeoman of the Guard*

*Whit* is a variant of *wight* (*wiht*), a creature, thing, a bit. *Not a whit* means not a jot, a bit, a tittle, or an iota. Two simple words from the original root are *naught*, or *nought*, where the *n* stands for *no*, and *naughty*, which originally meant good for nothing. A *dreadnaught*, or *dreadnought* ("Fear nothing"), a certain kind of warship, received its name from a British vessel audaciously named the *Dreadnaught*.

**wizen**     Pronounce the *i* like the *i* in *with* or like the *e* in *we*. *Wizen* has nothing to do with *wizard*, a magician, which is related to the word *wise*. *Wizen* means to dry up, to shrivel, to wither; the form *wizened*, meaning withered, appears more often than *wizen* itself.

**wrought**     This is the past participle of the Anglo-Saxon verb *worken*, to work. We still use it in the meanings of created, worked into shape, fashioned. In the sense of *created*, the word *wrought* was forever commemorated by the first message sent by telegraph, when on May 24, 1844, Samuel F. B. Morse flashed the message "What hath God wrought!"

*Wrought* refers to a special type of manufacture in *wrought iron* and to special methods of hammering or working in *wrought iron* and *wrought silver*.

*Overwrought* and *wrought up* mean "all worked up," very tense and agitated, overexcited, highly stimulated.

From the same root as *wrought* comes the noun *wright*, a worker, a craftsman. It was attached as a combining form to show a specific trade or occupation in words like *boatwright, cartwright, plowright, wainwright,* a person who makes and repairs wagons, and *wheelwright.* These words and *wright* by itself are used now chiefly as surnames, for when Englishmen had to "take unto them a surname" by order of Edward IV in 1465, among the choices were last names coming from "some Arte or Science, as Smyth or Carpenter, or some office as Cooke or Butler." However, one word with *wright* in it is still viable, very much so. This is *playwright*, "one who makes, or creates, plays."

## I.  REVIEW: MULTIPLE CHOICE

Select the proper term from the words after the letters.

1. baleful      (a) careful (b) harmful (c) crammed (d) sad
2. baneful      (a) deadly (b) serious (c) bland (e) ineffectual
3. beguile      (a) to direct (b) pass the time pleasantly (c) countermand (d) understate
4. fingerling   (a) small finger (b) fidgety person (c) miniature cameo (d) tiny fish
5. fledgling    (a) young ram (b) first harvest (c) early planting (d) rank beginner
6. groundling   (a) stickler for fundamentals (b) small mound (c) person of low tastes (d) novice
7. guileless    without: (a) craft (b) wisdom (c) resources (d) innocence
8. harangue     (a) rain (b) eulogy (c) provender (d) tirade
9. hireling     (a) mercenary (b) hypocrite (c) petty employer (d) small fee
10. wizened      (a) sagacious (b) dried up (c) entranced (d) bewildered

## II.  ELIMINATE THE IMPOSTOR

In each group of five words below, one is not related to the other four in meaning. Cast out the one that does not belong.

1. (a) agog (b) askew (c) awry (d) amiss (e) abash
2. (a) loutish (b) uncouth (c) boorish (d) crude (e) thrifty
3. (a) test (b) severe trial (c) trying experience (d) guilt (e) tribulation
4. (a) deny (b) affirm (c) oppose (d) controvert (g) gainsay
5. (a) harbinger (b) messenger (c) haven (d) herald (e) portent

6. (a) dole (b) grieve (c) give (d) measure out (e) mete
7. (a) title (b) iota (c) jot (d) whit (e) bit
8. (a) soothsayer (b) prophet (c) deceiver (d) prognosticator
     (e) truthteller
9. (a) bootless (b) fruitless (c) unshod (d) useless (e) futile
10. (a) wrought up (b) embellished (c) deeply stirred
     (d) overstimulated (e) excessively excited

## III.  TWO-TONGUED MATCHING

The words on the left are of Anglo-Saxon (including later English) origin; those on the right are of Latin (classical or later) origin. Match the words in the two columns.

| | |
|---|---|
| 1. belittle | a. ablution |
| 2. bypass | b. inebriate |
| 3. drunkard | c. circumvent |
| 4. enthrall | d. verbose |
| 5. a forebear | e. torment |
| 6. forebode | f. depreciate |
| 7. forerunner | g. enslave |
| 8. harry | h. ramify |
| 9. spread | i. oppose |
| 10. a washing | j. precursor |
| 11. withstand | k. presage |
| 12. wordy | l. progenitor |

## IV.  MORE MATCHING FROM TWO LANGUAGES

Match as before; this time the words on the left are of Latin origin.

| | |
|---|---|
| 1. abjure | a. abid? |
| 2. consanguineous | b. amazement |
| 3. debilitate | c. a bent |
| 4. impediment | d. sleep-bringing |
| 5. iniquity | e. weaken |
| 6. predestined | f. forbearance |
| 7. propensity | g. foredoomed |
| 8. remain | h. forswear |
| 9. restraint | i. overcome |
| 10. somniferous | j. unrighteousness |
| 11. stupefaction | k. hindrance |
| 12. surmount | l. sibling |

## V.  COMPLETING WORDS

The words on the left are of Latin origin. On the right, corresponding to each one we have given you the first letter of a word of Anglo-Saxon origin that means the same thing. Complete the words; each bar represents a letter.

EXAMPLE:   insensate   u _ _ _ _ _ _ _ _
ANSWER:     unfeeling

1. condign          w _ _ _ _ _
2. confuse          b _ _ _ _ _
3. delude           m _ _ _ _ _
4. discursive       w _ _ _ _ _ _ _
5. edify            u _ _ _ _ _
6. incredible       u _ _ _ _ _ _ _ _ _
7. legacy           b _ _ _ _ _ _
8. malfeasance      w _ _ _ _ _ _ _ _
9. minatory         t _ _ _ _ _ _ _ _ _
10. precipitate (adj.)  h _ _ _ _
11. prohibit        f _ _ _ _ _
12. sanguinary      b _ _ _ _

## VI.  ONCE MORE, A TRIPLE THREAT

Once more, as in Chapter 4, Exercise VIII, we are asking you to complete the missing word in the following sets or triplets.

EXAMPLE:   book   volume   t _ _ _    ANSWER:  tome

| Anglo-Saxon | Latin | Greek |
|---|---|---|
| 1. beginner | n _ _ _ _ _ _ | neophyte |
| 2. old | antique | a _ _ _ _ _ _ _ |
| 3. w _ _ _ _ _ _ _ | venerate | idolize |
| 4. angry | i _ _ _ _ | choleric |
| 5. many-tongued | multilingual | p _ _ _ _ _ _ _ |
| 6. f _ _ _ _ _ _ _ | preface | proem |
| 7. fleeting | t _ _ _ _ _ _ _ _ | ephemeral |
| 8. fellow-feeling | compassion | s _ _ _ _ _ _ |
| 9. h _ _ _ _ _ | occult | cryptic |
| 10. forsaker | d _ _ _ _ _ _ _ | apostate |
| 11. token | sign | s _ _ _ _ |
| 12. sorrowful | d _ _ _ _ _ _ _ | melancholy |

## VII.  MORE OF THE SAME

| | | |
|---|---|---|
| 1. rift | d _ _ _ _ _ _ _ | schism |
| 2. m _ _ _ _ _ | potent | dynamic |
| 3. foe | adversary | a _ _ _ _ _ _ _ _ _ |
| 4. b _ _ _ _ _ | proverb | aphorism |
| 5. thrifty | f _ _ _ _ _ | economical |
| 6. healthful | sanitary | h _ _ _ _ _ _ _ |

7. "firebug"          i＿＿＿＿＿＿＿          pyromaniac
8. s＿＿＿＿＿＿＿＿     dispersion              diaspora
9. talk                conversation            d＿＿＿＿＿＿
10. wrangler          d＿＿＿＿＿＿＿          polemicist

## DO-IT-YOURSELF DEPARTMENT

### Assorted Questions

1. *Benighted, betoken,* and *betrothal* come from Anglo-Saxon. Give a synonym for each, using words of Latin origin.

2. In the following group, five words are related in meaning, two are not. Cast out the two interlopers.

  (a) sorcerer (b) warlock (c) contractor (d) conjurer
  (e) wizard (f) warrior (g) magician

3. What is an *aftermath?* What does *math* in this word mean?

4. *Gossamer* is a lovely word. What does it mean and what is its origin?

5. Give a synonym for these two words: *albeit* and *anent.*

6. What is a synonym of Latin origin for the word *beholden?* We shall help you by giving the first letter and a bar for each missing letter: i ＿ ＿ ＿ ＿ ＿ ＿ ＿.

7. These two words come from the Latin word for *meat: carnival* and *charnel.* What is the meaning of each word, and what does the meaning have to do with meat?

8. The Latin verb *crescere* means to grow, to increase. From it are derived words like *increase* itself, *increment,* an increase, and *decrease.* In "Elaine," one of the *Idylls of the King,* Alfred, Lord Tennyson beautifully used a word of Latin origin (from *crescere*) near two short, simple words of Anglo-Saxon origin—in these lines spoken by Lancelot to Guinevere:

> Queen, if I grant the jealousy as of love,
> May not your crescent fear for name and fame
> Speak, as it waxes, of a love that wanes?

a. Give two synonyms, one of Anglo-Saxon and one of Latin origin for *crescent.* (Do not use any word in the poem as answers to these questions.)

b. Give one synonym of Anglo-Saxon origin and one of Latin origin for *waxes.*

c. Give one synonym of Anglo-Saxon and two of Latin origin (all three beginning with the letter *d*) for the word *wanes.*

(You will have to check your answers in a dictionary. None are given for this exercise.)

## VOCABAGRAMS

Every one of the answers must be a word of Anglo-Saxon origin.

| | | | |
|---|---|---|---|
| 1. beat | | = aid | |
| 2. dole | | = ore deposit | |
| 3. door | | = a cross | |
| 4. file | | = gladly | |
| 5. hotel | | = oar pin | |
| 6. lurch | | = boor | |
| 7. ocher | | = task | |
| 8. role | | = knowledge | |
| 9. thaws | | = a strip | |
| 10. throw | | = angry | |
| 11. town | | = custom | |
| 12. den | + w | = go | |
| 13. foal | + f | = garbage | |
| 14. gnome | + r | = dealer | |
| 15. leader | + t | = foot lever | |
| 16. neat | + n | = about | |
| 17. rustle | + b | = swagger | |
| 18. their | + w | = squirm | |
| 19. there | + n | = lower (adj.) | |
| 20. tins | + t | = to be sparing | |
| 21. wrath | + i | = a spirit | |
| 22. mothers | − m | = agony | |
| 23. servile | − e | = thin piece | |
| 24. stuffy | − f | = moldy | |
| 25. theme | − h | = fitting | |

# 12. Much Latin, Less Greek

Carpe Canem
or Was It Cave Diem? *

*Non sequiturs*
*Ad nauseam*
*I suffer through*
*In toto.*
*(I once wrote down*
*An author's name*
*As Auturo Ignoto.)*

*Per se, ad hoc,*
*The status quo . . .*
*You simply cannot*
*Beat 'em.*
*For saying much with*
*Pithy punch, e.g. ad*
*Infinitum.*

*But heu mihi*
*Ipso facto*
*Mirabile oh*
*Dictu . . .*
*Methinks the tongue unlatinized*
*And clear is what I'll*
*Stick to.*

SISTER ROSE ALICE, S.S.J.

With the exception of *Auturo Ignoto*, written in jest for
*auctor ignotus*, "author unknown," or *ab auctore ignoto*, "by
an unknown author," and *heu mihi* (a similar variation of
*hue me*, or *hei mihi*, "Ah me," or "Alas, woe is me!"), you
will probably encounter all the other Latin expressions in the

* From Martin Levin's "Phoenix Nest," *Saturday Review*, June 1, 1963.

poem in not too long a period of reading. Even the expressions humorously scrambled in the title *Carpe diem,* "Seize the day," meaning that we should enjoy the present moment, a quotation from Horace, and *Cave canem,* "Beware of the Dog," a warning found on a Roman mosaic, are fairly familiar.

See how familiar you are with the other ten Latin expressions appearing in this poem by matching each one with its English equivalent:

| | |
|---|---|
| 1. non sequitur | a. to the point of disgust |
| 2. ad nauseam | b. by itself |
| 3. in toto | c. existing state of affairs |
| 4. per se | d. endlessly |
| 5. ad hoc | e. wonderful to relate |
| 6. status quo | f. for example |
| 7. e.g. (exempli gratia) | g. entirely |
| 8. ad infinitum | h. specifically for this occasion |
| 9. ipso facto | i. by the very fact |
| 10. mirabile dictu | j. conclusion that does not follow from the evidence |

Some speakers and writers, it is true, use Latin expressions to evoke memories of passages studied in school or college, others may use them to display erudition, but in general those who utter Latin phrases do it because these expressions are often more vivid than their English equivalents. Even Sister Rose Alice and others who declare that they want to stick to "the tongue unlatinized" will, we dare say, nevertheless insert Latin words in their speech and writing because these words often do say so much "with pithy punch," to quote her, or, to use another Latin phrase, they offer *multum in parvo,* "much in little." How much shorter is *non sequitur* than the lengthy definition given in the test above! And—this many-worded definition is an abridgment of what you will find under *non sequitur* even in an abridged dictionary!

Whatever, therefore, may be the reason for their use in English, Latin phrases have been with us for centuries and they will undoubtedly remain in circulation. From our own file of several hundred that we have met in our reading during the last few years we are presenting a selection of useful and interesting ones.

(Once more, we call attention to the fact that quotation marks around a definition indicate a literal translation. See Chapter 4, section called "Fixed Roots.")

## NOT SO "SMALL LATIN"

**ad hoc**      "for this (purpose)"; for the present matter or situation; temporary. An ad hoc committee is one whose existence is limited to the time it takes to dispose of the matter at hand.

> But our various programs in the field, Senator Fulbright notes, have been "limping along under severe restraints," largely because "they have grown up in an ad hoc, piecemeal" way over the years.

**ad libitum**      "at pleasure, at will." This is generally shortened to *ad lib*. *Ad lib* is used both as a verb and as a noun. As used in the entertainment world, to *ad lib* means to improvise, to add something extemporaneously to a script. As a noun, an ad lib is an "off-the-cuff" remark.

> If they were permitted to automate *ad libitum*, the more prosperous papers could easily afford to pay even higher wages.

**bona fide; bona fides**      "in good faith," "good faith," sincere, genuine; sincerity. The first expression is used to modify some other word, as in *bona fide intentions;* the second is generally used as the subject or object of a verb, as in "His bona fides is above reproach," and "We do not question his bona fides." *Bona fides* is a singular noun.

> Nothing could be more pathetic than the efforts of this group of self-styled "liberals" to maintain the fiction of a bona fide political party.

**cui bono**      "for whose good?" This is what William Forsyth wrote about this expression in his *Life of Marcus Tullius Cicero* (1863):

> *Cui bono?* These two words have perhaps been oftener misapplied than any in the Latin language. They are constantly translated or used in the sense of "What good is it? To what end does it serve?" Their real meaning is "Who gains by it?" "To whom is it an advantage?" And the origin of the expression

was this:—When L. Cassius, who is said to have been a man of stern severity, sat as *quaesitor judicii* [judge] in a trial for murder, he used to advise the *judices* [jurors] to inquire, when there was a doubt as to the guilty party, who had a motive for the crime, who would gain by the death: in other words, *cui bono fuerit?* This maxim passed into a proverb. The great scholar Gronovius protested against the mistranslation as a vulgar error two centuries ago.

Vulgar or popular, the error has persisted, and you will find *cui bono* still used in the sense of *usefulness* or *utility*.

**de facto; de jure**     The first phrase means functioning, existing in fact, in reality; the second means legal, legally, right, rightly. A de facto government is one that has been set up and is carrying on the functions of an established government, although it has not yet come into existence in accordance with legal procedure and is not yet recognized as existing de jure, or legally.

The terms are applied to things other than government, and are very much in the news in connection with segregation and desegregation. Both terms occur in the following:

> Since segregation is de facto and not
> de jure it goes without saying that the
> evils of segregation will not be corrected
> by laws which may be passed by the City
> Council, or the State Legislature, or by
> the Congress of the United States.

**deus ex machina**     "god from the machine." A god or goddess (*dea*) appearing in a Greek tragedy was brought into view by a crane or derrick. The special duty of the divinity appearing at the end of the play was to ordain the ritual or to bring the action to a quiet ending. However, the appearance, or epiphany, of the god or goddess was interpreted by some critics, notably the Roman poet Horace, as proof that the dramatist, especially Euripides, had so piled up the complications that he needed divine intervention to untangle the situation. Hence, a person or thing that solves a difficulty artificially and abruptly is called a deus (or dea) ex machina.

> To provide the story's well-chopped
> ending, a deus ex machina from the
> Internal Revenue Department is rolled on
> the scene to claim so much in back taxes
> and penalties that the contestants for the

> estate have nothing to do but kiss and
> make up.

\* \* \*

> As nearly as we can remember, she
> wasn't even in "Peyton Place." Now she
> is the dea ex machina and leading
> troublemaker in the film.

**ex post facto**      after the fact or event; retroactive.

> They were punished under a law passed
> after the commission of their crimes—in
> other words, it was ex-post-facto punish-
> ment.

**ignis fatuus**      "foolish fire"; a light that misleads; name
given to a light that sometimes appears at night, usually over
marshes, probably because of the combustion of marsh gas.
Other terms for it are *jack-o'-lantern* and *will-o'-the-wisp*. The
expression refers to a false hope, an illusion, a vain hope.

> The treaty must be followed by
> further and more decisive steps, or it
> will turn out to be the mortal *ignis fatuus*
> of our era.

**in extremis**      "in extreme circumstances"; in desperate
straits; near death.

> Then comes the quest for Mr. X, that
> always possible outside figure to whom,
> in extremis, American political parties
> have been known to turn when all other
> leadership bids have failed.

**in loco parentis**      "in place of a parent"; acting as
guardian.

> The schools legally act *in loco paren-
> tis,* and supervision of their pupils' read-
> ing is only a part of the supervision that
> is assumed necessary as youngsters ap-
> proach the magical age of 21.

**in vacuo**      "in emptiness"; "in a vacuum, or void"; without reference to surroundings; without regard for reality.

> Every writer portrays himself in his
> writing. A writer does not write *in vacuo,*

he writes from his own experiences and
what he knows about.

**magnum opus**      "a great work"; a crowning achievement;
a masterpiece, like the French *chef d'oeuvre*. By itself *opus*,
often abbreviated to *op.*, is used to identify a composer's
works, as Beethoven, *Quintet for Piano and Winds*, Op. 16.

> "Exactly, Watson. Here is the fruit of
> my leisured ease, the magnum opus of my
> latter years." He picked up the volume
> from the table and read out the whole
> title, *Practical Handbook of Bee Culture,
> with Some Observations upon the Segre-
> gation of the Queen.*
>
>                    Sir Arthur Conan Doyle, "His Last Bow"

**mea culpa**      "my fault"; an expression used as a personal
acknowledgment of guilt. From the root of *culpa* come
*culpable*, deserving blame, *culprit*, an accused person, a wrongdoer, a guilty person, *inculpate*, to incriminate, and *exculpate*,
to free from blame, to prove somebody innocent.

### A German's 'Mea Culpa' in Israel

> The president of the West German
> Bundestag last night told an Israeli audi-
> ence that nothing his generation of Ger-
> mans can do will enable them to escape
> from the burden of guilt and shame for
> Nazism and its crimes.

**modus operandi**      "manner of operating"; a working
method; a working arrangement; characteristic manner of procedure.

> Then he offered: "I don't think at this
> time I have found an MO [modus
> operandi] for myself." He was referring
> to the way he would involve himself in
> programming.

**modus vivendi**      "manner of living"; a way of life; temporary arrangement. This phrase, much used in this era of
talking about peaceful coexistence, refers to a way of getting
along with another person or nation in spite of basic differences.

The leaders of the two countries realize that a modus vivendi, some workable
compromise, must be attained if a nuclear holocaust is to be avoided.

**obiter dictum**     "said by the way"; plural, *obiter dicta;* an
incidental remark or opinion by a judge that is not binding
on the final decision; a side remark; a digression; a casually
interjected comment or reflection.

No one will argue that the Soviet
Union is unchanged from what it was in
Stalin's time, but Mr. Kennan's *obiter
dictum* on this point, which is independent of the supporting material in the
book, does not help the reader to judge
how much if any of his foregoing analysis
Mr. Kennan considers relevant to the
present.

**persona grata; persona non grata**     "an acceptable person"; "an unacceptable person." A person who is named as an
ambassador or other kind of representative by one country to
another must be acceptable to the country to which he is being
sent. If acceptable, he is considered persona grata, if not, he
is persona non grata. The terms are used in a more general
sense, also, to mean welcome and unwelcome.

The coach had vowed that if the Jets
signed Sauer, any representative of the
American Football League would be
persona non grata at the University of
Texas.

**prima facie**     "on first appearance"; at first glance; ade-
quate at first view; apparent; self-evident. Applied to evidence,
it means sufficient, unless refuted, to establish a fact.

By that time we had enough evidence
to establish a prima facie case of conspiracy.

**quid pro quo**     "something for something"; something
given for something received; a fair exchange; tit for tat.

Conrad Aiken's limerick book is dedicated to Mr. Sobiloff with the line "a very
small quid for a very large quo."

**sine qua non**      "without which, not"; an indispensable condition; a prerequisite; an essential.

> The New York stamp of approval is
> the sine qua non of a musical career.

**status quo**      "the condition in which"; present condition; the state of affairs up to now. An upholder of the status quo wants to keep things as they are. A related phrase is *in statu quo*, "in the condition in which things are." Purists contend that the word *ante*, "before," should end both phrases, that the condition referred to is a previous one that is to be restored. However, in general usage the present is referred to. Because of its brevity, *status quo* is popular with headline writers to indicate the idea of preserving without change:

> **Englewood Poll**
> **Backs Status Quo**

**sui generis**      "of his, hers, its, their own kind"; unique; nonpareil; in a class by himself, herself, etc.

> In contrast to the glass slab of today,
> which was already on drafting boards in
> the Europe of the 20's, the "topless
> tower" of New York is sui generis.

**vade mecum**      "Go with me." Everyman's Library books, a series of small hardbacks which appeared long before the surge of the paperbacks, bear this legend on the inside cover:

> Everyman,
> I will go with thee
> & be THY GUIDE
> IN THY MOST NEED
> TO GO BY THY SIDE.

In other words, the publishers wanted the book to be a literal vade mecum, a guide and constant companion.

The term *vade mecum* first appeared in print in 1629 as the title of a reference work. As used today *vade mecum* designates a special kind of reference work, a handbook, or manual (from Latin *manus*, hand), something ready and close at hand, like a guidebook.

> But a vade mecum for beginners is al-
> ways useful. Here is a sampling of Asian
> English which should help you to face

the linguistic hazards of attending a high-powered Asian conference with equanimity and even fortitude.

However, the meaning of *vade mecum* has been extended. We have seen it used to mean a stock in trade, a ready tool, or simply something that accompanies a reader's mind.

Indeed, we are required to exercise a considerable amount of that novel readers' vade mecum—the willing suspension of disbelief.

## LOQUERISNE LATINE?

In addition to these phrases, there are in the English language a large number of words that have been taken over without any change of spelling. Although the meaning has sometimes been changed to fit new times and culture, these words have been accepted without complaint and are good verbal citizens. They are so thoroughly naturalized that they are pronounced as English words. To a certain degree you are speaking Latin as well as English when you use any of a multitude of words ending in *or*, a Latin suffix meaning one who: words like *actor, agitator, auditor, benefactor, curator, dictator, editor, educator, janitor, monitor, orator, sculptor, sponsor, victor,* etc. (from Latin *et cetera,* "and others," "and the rest"). Still others of a different kind are *album, alumna, alumnus, animal, appendix, bonus, color, elevator, honor, humor, index, inferior, junior, minor, minus, miser, plus, senior, terror, tumor, tutor, vacuum, vapor, veto,* et al. (*et alia,* "and others").

The meanings of these are undoubtedly obvious to you. Here are ten others whose meanings may present a small amount, or modicum (another of those Latin-English words), of difficulty. Match each one with the correct term on the right.

| | |
|---|---|
| 1. compendium | a. continuing hatred |
| 2. consensus | b. driving force |
| 3. furor | c. burden |
| 4. gratis | d. filth |
| 5. impetus | e. summary |
| 6. nucleus | f. lack of color |
| 7. onus | g. wild enthusiasm |

8. pallor               h. core
9. rancor               i. free of charge
10. squalor             j. general opinion

Here are some additional words of this kind:

**aura**      "breeze"; a subtle feeling; aroma; flavor; radiant atmosphere; sensation. (From Greek via Latin.)

> In the course of my explorations, I came to rest in Geneva; a city with a considerable aura of internationalism.

**condominium**      "control together"; a New Latin word, that is, one made up of Latin elements in the Medieval Age and later. *Condominium* means joint rule or tenancy; today it has a special meaning and appears frequently in print because it is applied to a type of apartment ownership that is spreading:

> Under condominium ownership a resident has title to his apartment, like a homeowner to his house. However, he shares with his neighbors the management of communal facilities.

**congeries**      a heap; a pile; a collection or mass of objects, forces, or individuals; an aggregation; an agglomeration.

> It is being carried on by a congeries of organizations, not one of which was designed to cope with the mass flareup which rose suddenly out of long-smoldering repression.

**consortium**      "a sharing together." The Latin word means also a community of goods, a fellowship, a society. As used today, it means a group working together; an international banking agreement like a cartel.

> The ailing publishing company worked out a $35 million refinancing deal with a consortium of banks headed by the First National of Boston.

**crux**      "cross." The crux of the matter is the point that must be decided or resolved in order to clear up the situation —hence the crucial or critical point. *Nub* is a synonym.

> The President put his finger on the
> crux of the whole problem of our inabil-
> ity to have ourselves followed, often in-
> deed listened to, in so many parts of the
> world.

The cross as a religious symbol appears in the words
*crucifix, crusade, crucifer,* one who carries the cross at the
head of a religious procession, and *crucible,* originally a hanging lamp, the eternal light hanging before the cross of Christ,
now meaning a heat-resistant container for melting metals, and
figuratively, a severe test. *Cruciform* means cross-shaped. An
altered form of the root *cruc* appears in *cruise,* which comes
to us via Dutch, originally meaning to sail or move cross-
wise. Because the Romans used the cross as an instrument of
torture and capital punishment, we get the idea of agony in
the word *excruciating.*

**emeritus**     "having earned"; having served one's time.
After he had completed his term of service a Roman soldier
was called *emeritus,* for after he served, he deserved his dis-
charge and whatever stipend went with it. Nowadays, the title
*emeritus* is bestowed upon a person, especially in the academic
world, who has served with distinction. The feminine is
*emerita;* the plural forms are respectively *emeriti* and *emeritae.*

> Dr. James Bryant Conant, president
> emeritus of Harvard University, gave
> public lectures and seminars in seven
> Japanese cities in five weeks.

**ergo**     therefore; hence; and so; accordingly. It appears
in the famous dictum of Descartes, *Cogito, ergo sum* ("I
think, therefore I am").

**fiat**     "Let it be done"; "Let it be made"; a Latin verb
form that has become a noun meaning an order; an arbitrary
edict; a ukase; a command that is to go into effect without
further ado. *Fiat lux* is the Latin for the biblical "Let there be
light."

> Can the theater's ills be cured by fiat?
> Will the three bills proposed accomplish
> their admirable objectives?

**gravamen**     "heaviness"; the burden, or weight, of a
charge; the esssential point; a formal charge.

> Nor do the authors face up to the real gravamen of my criticism. It is not the attempt at a general synthesis that I object to, but to the soft-mindedness of their approach.

**hiatus**     "a gaping"; a gap; an interval; an interruption; a lapse of time.

> Winter used to be a time of waiting, the hiatus before the spring time, a time when the only things that moved were fleeting gray clouds and swirling snowflakes.

**ibidem**     "in the same place," generally shortened to *ibid*. In books and articles annotated copiously, a writer may make many references on the same page to the same source. To avoid the constant repetition of the name of the author and the title of the work quoted or cited, the writer saves space by using *ibid.,* a shortcut for saying "in the same book listed above." *Ibid*. has been humorously termed an admission of legalized plagiarism, an allegation that prompted this anonymous limerick:

> A wonderful bird is the Ibid.
> His color is pale and insipid.
>     He stands like a sage
>     At the foot of the page
> To tell where the passage was cribbèd.

**imprimatur**     "Let it be pressed upon"; New Latin, "Let it be printed"; approval; sanction. *Imprimatur* found on books written by members of the Catholic clergy indicates that permission to have the book printed was granted by a superior. The term is used also in the general sense of *imprint;* the words *press* and *print* come from the same root as *imprimatur*.

> First came the seemingly routine request of the Central Intelligence Agency to publish disparaging statistics about the Soviet Union under its own imprimatur.

**incubus**     "something lying upon"; a nightmare; an oppressive burden.

> Although France was quite willing to be freed of the incubus of the Indo-

Chinese war, French pride was deeply
wounded by the circumstances under
which that freedom was obtained.

**mores**    "customs"; fixed customs of a community; moral
attitudes; moral code; manners and habits of a group.

Spain is, in fact, in the throes of a
revolution in mores.

**nostrum**    "ours"; a secret remedy or medicine recom-
mended by its maker or seller. This word, plural *nostrums,*
has a bad connotation and is used disparagingly to indicate
a supposed cure-all, a panacea of doubtful effectiveness; an
illusory cure; a quack medicine.

The American Medical Association
said that Americans wasted a lot of time
and money on pills, nostrums, and treatment for common colds.

**qua**    "on which (side)"; as; in the capacity of.

But Newman's essential concern is the
scientist qua scientist—a man who expresses his humanity by seeking to im-
pose order on the chaos of fact.

**simulacrum**    "likeness"; something having the semblance
but not the substance; unsubstantial likeness; image; imitation.

The group held that the enactment of
universal military training would create
a simulacrum of power without the reality.

## Breviter

In brief capsule form here are some additional Latin words
and phrases for quick reference.

**ad infinitum**    endlessly; incessantly; forever.
**alter ego**    "the other I"; a second self; bosom friend;
boon companion.
**ante bellum**    before the war, especially the Civil War.
**Caveat emptor.**    "Let the buyer beware"; a caveat is
a warning.
**corpus delicti**    "body of the crime"; evidence that a

crime has been committed. *Corpus* by itself refers to the complete works of an author.

**cum laude**      "with praise"; with honor; *magna cum laude,* with high honor(s); *summa cum laude,* with highest honor(s).

**dramatis personae**      "persons of the drama"; cast of characters; participants.

**exemplar**      example; model; copy.

**ex officio**      by virtue of or because of one's office or position.

**facsimile**      "Make like"; an exact copy.

**factotum**      "Do everything"; person hired to do all kinds of work; general handyman; jack-of-all-trades.

**homo sapiens**      "wise man"; member of the human race; thinking man.

**id est**      "that is," generally abbreviated to *i.e.,* a term introducing an explanation of what has just been written or said.

**in extenso**      at full length; in detail.

**infra dignitatem**      "beneath dignity," usually shortened to *infra dig.;* unworthy of one's rank or position.

**in medias res**      "into the middle of things"; starting in the middle of a story or play and going back; without preliminaries.

**inter alia**      "among other things"; *inter alios,* among other persons, among others.

**interim**      "meanwhile"; in the meantime; provisional; temporary; an interval.

**in toto**      "in all"; in full; entirely.

**ipso facto**      "by the fact (act) itself"; by the very act or fact; by the nature of the thing, situation, or case; automatically.

**lapsus linguae**      "slip of the tongue"; *lapsus calami,* "slip of the pen." A *calamus* was a reed used as a pen.

**laudator temporis acti**      "praiser of time gone by"; one who thinks "the good old days" were better than the present.

**literati**      "lettered"; men of letters; learned men; connoisseurs; intelligentsia.

**ne plus ultra**      "not more beyond"; acme; pinnacle; peak of perfection.

**non compos mentis**      "not in control of the mind"; of unsound mind.

**pace**    "with peace"; with apologies to; with all due respect to.

**passim**    "everywhere, throughout."

**per se**    "by himself, herself, themselves, itself"; of its own accord; independently.

**post bellum**    "after the war"; see *ante bellum*.

**pro forma**    "for the sake of the form"; as a matter of form; perfunctory; for the record.

**pro tempore**    "for the time (being)," often shortened to *pro tem*; temporary.

**quidnunc**    "What now?"; a bore; busybody; a gossip; newsmonger.

**rara avis**    "a rare bird"; unusual person; unusual specimen.

**re; in re**    "in respect to the thing"; concerning; in the matter of.

**sanctum sanctorum**    "holy of holies"; sacred place; inner sanctum; private office.

**seriatim**    "serially"; in a series; in order; one by one.

**sub rosa**    "under the rose"; privately; secretly.

**summum bonum**    "the highest good."

**Tempus fugit.**    "Time flies."

**terra firma**    "solid ground"; dry land.

**verbatim**    "word for word"; exactly as said or written.

**viva voce**    "with the living voice"; orally; aloud.

**vox populi**    "the people's voice"; part of the expression *Vox populi, vox Dei,* "the voice of the people is the voice of God."

## GREEK, THE LANGUAGE OF WISDOM

That is what George Bernard Shaw called Greek, and fittingly so, since from the Greek language come many words having to do with philosophy, a word from Greek meaning "love of wisdom." Thousands of words used in the sciences, especially in medicine, have also been borrowed or formed from Greek—and the process is still going on. Many of these words, like *asthma* and *neuralgia, derma* and *eczema,* are too well-known to be treated here, and others are too technical.

Instead, we shall present ten words or phrases of a less specialized nature that are more useful for building your vocabulary. These have been taken over from Greek with an occasional change of spelling. Thus, the Greek diphthong *ai* appears here as *ae,* as in *aeon; k,* called *kappa,* becomes *c,* as in *acme;* Greek *u,* called *upsilon,* is written *y,* as in *apocrypha;* and Greek *x,* known as *chi,* is transcribed as *ch,* as in *chaos.*

Incidentally, if you are wondering why *Christmas* is so often written *Xmas,* the fact that Greek *X = Ch* solves the mystery for you. In Greek, *Christos,* our way of transliterating the Greek name for Christ, begins with *X,* or *Chi;* medieval scribes used the *X* as a short way of writing *Christ.* Therefore, those who write *X* for the *Christ* in *Christmas* are, knowingly or not, continuing a very old practice.

And now for a decade (a word treated under *ten* in Chapter 6) of useful words or phrases:

**aeon**     "an age"; an indefinitely long period of time.

**agon**     "a struggle"; a conflict. In ancient Greece *agon* referred to any kind of contest—athletic, literary, dance. "Agon" is a ballet with music by Stravinsky. The word appears in *agony, antagonist, antagonize,* and *protagonist.*

**alpha and omega**     Since *alpha* is the first and *omega* the last letter of the Greek alphabet the expression obviously means the beginning and the end, that is from *A* to *Z* (or *A* to *Zed* in England and Canada), the all-in-all. The expression gains awe and majesty from its appearance in the Book of Revelation 22:13:

> I am Alpha and Omega, the begin-
> ning and the end, the first and the last.

**anathema**     This is a Late Latin coinage from Greek. Literally, it means "something set up." Its early specific meaning was "something devoted to evil." If a person was called "anathema," he was being condemned as an evildoer. An anathema means something accursed, something detested.

**antipodes**     "with the feet opposite." This term was applied to dwellers at an opposite point in the world, and it is so used today. Australia and lands near it are the Antipodes to those who live in the Northern Hemisphere. The adjective *antipodal* is applied to something diametrically opposed.

> Thou art as opposite to every good
> As the Antipodes are unto us,
> Or as the south to the septentrion.
>                         SHAKESPEARE, *III Henry VI*

(You will recall *septentrional,* northern, from the words under *seven* in Chapter 6.)

**apotheosis**   Formed from the Greek word *theos*, a god, and coming into English via Late Latin, this word means deification (Latin *deus*, a god, and *fic*, make). In its religious sense it means the ascension from earthly existence to heavenly glory; in its general sense it means an exalted position, highest development, quintessential or ultimate form.

**ethos**   This is a term with a wide meaning: character; disposition; fundamental outlook; the spirit that animates the customs and moral values of a people. Aristotle used it to mean the character of man in the struggle between passion and moderation; in Greek tragedy it refers to an element of character that determines what a man does in contrast with what he thinks.

The word *ethical* is, of course, derived from *ethos*. The Romans had the word *mores* for the same idea as *ethos*, but *ethos* is a much stronger word than *mores*, and has deeper implications.

**eureka**   "I have found it!" The scientist Archimedes is supposed to have run through the streets of Syracuse in Sicily shouting "Eureka!" after he had discovered a method of finding the exact weight of the gold in a crown while he was in his bath. His discovery led to the formulation of the principles of flotation known as Archimedes' principle. *Eureka* is a cry of triumph after a great accomplishment. Appropriately, it is the motto of the state of California, where gold was discovered about twenty centuries after Archimedes' discovery.

**hoi polloi**   "the many"; a term applied to the masses, the common, ordinary people, of whom there are so many. *The* is not needed in front of *hoi polloi*, because *hoi* means *the*. Incidentally, this phrase has derogatory overtones, often being equated with *the rabble, tag rag and bobtail,* and worst of all, *the great unwashed*.

**kudos**   "glory, renown"; fame; honor; prestige. Like *accolade*, the word *kudos* has become a vogue word. Some writers forget that it is a singular form, and by a process known as back formation they erroneously drop the *s* and come up with *kudo*, which sounds like the name of a Japanese style of wrestling.

## I. TRANSLATION, PLEASE

We shall not give you cause to complain about the use of Latin expressions, for we are giving you the translation of each italicized Latin phrase in the passages below. Select the correct translation from the group below each passage.

1. The results of the games this coming weekend will identify *bona fide* contenders and help determine if there are to be races rather than runaways.
    (a) genuine (b) spurious (c) upstart (d) hopeful

2. Integration in a city with deep areas of *de facto* segregated slum housing cannot be brought about by magic wands, political oratory or extremist tactics.
    (a) compulsory (b) existing in name (c) broken down
       (d) existing in fact

3. In the long history of promotion this has been the most botched job on record and only a *deus ex machina* can save the game now.
    (a) superhuman promotion (b) unexpected helper to save
       the situation (c) popular demand (d) feat of leger-
       demain

4. Since a few years after World War II, when the cold war began in earnest and was coupled with the nuclear race, the U.S. military, and particularly the Air Force, have pursued the *ignis fatuus* of nuclear security.
    (a) fatal fire (b) destructive notion (c) will-o'-the-wisp
       (d) shortsighted policy

5, 6. Surely Auschwitz (or Warsaw) has taught us that men, especially men (5) *in extremis,* cannot be rendered justly when reduced to the (6) *dramatis personae* of a pretentious (or portentous) novel.
    *in extremis* (a) at the utmost (b) in their last hours
       (c) during their suffering (d) in prison
    *dramatis personae* (a) ranting puppets (b) lurid proportions
       (c) sad figures (d) characters

7. About all that can be done is to encourage fresh discussions that might lead to a *modus vivendi* more satisfactory than the present embittered situation.
    (a) slackening of tension (b) settlement of frontier disputes
       (c) diplomatic exchange (d) temporary workable com-
       promise

8. Some officials derided the proposal that a sixth-grade education should be *prima-facie* evidence of literacy for voting purposes.
    (a) adequate on first view (b) incontrovertible (c) setting a
       precedent (d) breaking with tradition

9. You can't argue with success, but simply *pro forma,* I must set down my opinion that this is a silly and tedious novel.

(a) as a protest (b) as a matter of form (c) in accordance with conscience (d) on account of its format

10. More surprising, indeed, is the gratifying number of times the name of F. Scott Fitzgerald is invoked in this admirable *vade mecum* to American thought.

(a) addition (b) contribution (c) handbook (d) tribute

## II. LATIN VERBS THAT BECAME ENGLISH NOUNS

You have already met some examples of Latin verbs, single words that could form a sentence all by themselves, which have become English nouns: *caveat*, *fiat*, and *imprimatur*. Other examples are *credo*, "I believe," which, as an English word, means a creed, a belief, and *veto*, "I forbid," which is both a noun and a verb in English, and *stet*, "let it stand," a proofreader's instruction to a printer that deleted copy is to be restored.

Here are twelve more such words; match each one with the correct meaning on the extreme right. As a guide we have given the literal translation of each Latin verb.

| | | | |
|---|---|---|---|
| 1. **affidavit** | "He has stated on faith." | a. | souvenir |
| 2. **caret** | "It is lacking." | b. | direction in cooking |
| 3. **deficit** | "It is wanting." | c. | writ requiring something to be done |
| 4. **dele** | "Destroy." | d. | doctrine |
| 5. **habitat** | "He (it) dwells." | e. | sworn statement |
| 6. **ignoramus** | "We do not know." | f. | prayer for mercy |
| 7. **mandamus** | "We order." | g. | native environment |
| 8. **memento** | "Remember." | h. | medicine given to humor patient |
| 9. **miserere** | "Have pity." | i. | dunce |
| 10. **placebo** | "I shall please." | j. | amount by which a sum is less than expected or due |
| 11. **recipe** | "Take." | k. | proofreader's sign indicating something is to be added |
| 12. **tenet** | "He holds." | l. | proofreader's sign showing something is to be taken out |

## III. THE PHRASE IS FAMILIAR

The expressions on the left are among the Latin phrases most frequently used in English. Some of these you have already met in this chapter, the others you may have encountered in your reading elsewhere. Match each Latin expression with the appropriate term on the right.

| | | | |
|---|---|---|---|
| 1. ad nauseam | a. without setting a day for meeting again |
| 2. alma mater | b. an absolute essential |
| 3. a priori | c. unique |
| 4. casus belli | d. "from the chair"; by authority of one's position |
| 5. de jure | e. "without the crime blazing"; in the very act |
| 6. ex cathedra | f. "to seasickness"; to a sickening degree |
| 7. flagrante delicto | g. legally |
| 8. per capita | h. based on theory rather than on experience |
| 9. post factum | i. "by heads"; for each one |
| 10. sine die | j. an event used as a pretext for war |
| 11. sine qua non | k. "after the deed" |
| 12. sui generis | l. "fostering mother"; one's school or college |

## IV. THE WORD IS FAMILIAR

And here are a dozen words that should not be too difficult —all of them taken from Latin. Match each one with the appropriate definition on the right.

| | | | |
|---|---|---|---|
| 1. decorum | a. "rest"; a dirge |
| 2. folio | b. speaker's platform |
| 3. impromptu | c. system for keeping healthy |
| 4. item | d. "under penalty"; legal order summoning a person to appear in court |
| 5. locus | e. finery; emblems and insignia |
| 6. nimbus | f. "at length"; one behind another |
| 7. regalia | g. "likewise"; a separate unit |
| 8. regimen | h. good taste |
| 9. requiem | i. halo |
| 10. rostrum | j. "in readiness"; on the spur of the moment |
| 11. subpoena | k. large sheet of paper folded once; very large book. |
| 12. tandem | l. a place |

## V. A LATIN-ENGLISH WORD LIST

Select the proper definition from the choices following the letters.

1. acumen — (a) bitterness (b) mental keenness (c) argumentative disposition (d) exactness

2. animus — (a) ill will (b) memory (c) kindness (d) exception

3. cadaver — (a) poisonous plant (b) corpse (c) fall (d) excavator

4. colloquium — (a) drama (b) concurrence (c) conference (d) insult

5. conspectus — (a) brief survey (b) optical instrument (c) search (d) handbook

6. desideratum — (a) unfailing remedy (b) firm decision (c) regard for others (d) something needed

7. errata — (a) angry acts (b) deviations (c) errors (d) commissions

8. genus — (a) talent (b) class (c) charity (d) naiveté

9. impedimenta — (a) obstacles (b) articles of furniture (c) early printed books (d) speech patterns

10. impetigo — (a) dizziness (b) violence (c) volatile temper (d) skin disease

11. interregnum — (a) tyranny (b) dynasty (c) rule during a temporary vacancy (d) royal decision

12. juvenilia — (a) period of early manhood (b) children's home (c) acts of delinquency (d) youthful productions

13. lacuna — (a) yearning (b) gap (c) inland body of water (d) small animal

14. nonplus — (a) debar (b) limit (c) fail (d) baffle

15. odium — (a) hatred (b) rest (c) excess (d) fragrance

16. optimum — (a) final (b) hopeful (c) chosen (d) most favorable

17. propaganda — (a) spreading of ideas (b) subtlety (c) unquestioned faith (d) misinformation

18. quondam — (a) boring (b) former (c) quibbling (d) hidden

19. redivivus — (a) twice-told (b) prepared (c) reborn (d) rampant

20. scintilla — (a) intelligence (b) very slight trace (c) cutting edge (d) venial fault

## VI. FROM ALPHA TO OMEGA

There are twenty-four letters in the ancient Greek alphabet. We are presenting to you the same number of words, which, except for the necessary transliterations of some letters, have been taken over intact as English words. Match each one with its correct definition or synonym on the right.

| | | |
|---|---|---|
| 1. alpha | a. | the beginning |
| 2. antithesis | b. | dictionary |
| 3. apotheosis | c. | reason, The Word |
| 4. chaos | d. | doctrine |
| 5. climax | e. | summary |
| 6. cosmos | f. | utter confusion |
| 7. dogma | g. | deification |
| 8. ellipsis | h. | universe |
| 9. enigma | i. | culmination |
| 10. epitome | j. | exact opposite |
| 11. lexicon | k. | riddle |
| 12. logos | l. | omission of words |

\*            \*            \*

| | | |
|---|---|---|
| 13. acme | o. | close formation |
| 14. aeon | p. | soul |
| 15. agon | q. | gravestone |
| 16. apocrypha | r. | highest point |
| 17. canon | s. | elephant's trunk |
| 18. diapason | t. | writings of doubtful authenticity |
| 19. phalanx | u. | very long period of time |
| 20. proboscis | v. | mark of disgrace |
| 21. psyche | w. | a struggle |
| 22. stele | x. | body of laws |
| 23. stigma | y. | full range of voice or instrument |
| 24. omega | z. | the end |

## VII.  ANALOGIES

From the words after the letters select the one that best completes the analogy. See instructions on pages 329–332; 335.

EXAMPLE: EPITOME : SUMMARY :: TREMOR : (a) fear (b) earth (c) shaking (d) seismograph (e) chill

ANSWER:   (c) since *epitome* and *summary* mean the same thing, and a tremor is the same as a shaking.

1. FACSIMILE : REPLICA :: SIMULACRUM: (a) duplicate (b) imitation (c) treachery (d) metaphor (e) light
2. MAGNUM OPUS : CHEF D'OEUVRE :: OBITER DICTUM: (a) obstacle (b) clever saying (c) wonderful story (d) final decision (e) side remark

3. A GROUP OF BUILDINGS : CONGERIES :: NUMBER OF POEMS:
   (a) literati (b) poetasters (c) critic (d) anthology
   (e) consortium
4. CONTIGUOUS : ANTIPODAL :: PRO TEMPORE: (a) permanent
   (b) contrary (c) adjacent (d) impromptu (e) dilatory
5. ANTE BELLUM : POST BELLUM :: SUB ROSA: (a) laughingly
   (b) secretly (c) openly (d) maliciously (e) ornately

## DO-IT-YOURSELF DEPARTMENT

Look up the meanings of the following Latin expressions:

| | |
|---|---|
| ad valorem | Morituri te salutamus. |
| a fortiori | nolle prosequi |
| amicus curiae | Nolo contendere. |
| a posteriori | Nota bene. |
| arbiter elegantiarum | nunc pro tunc |
| argumentum ad hominem | panem et circenses |
| cum grano salis | pro bono publico |
| disjecta membra | pro rata |
| ex parte | Quis custodiet ipsos custodes? |
| habeas corpus | reductio ad absurdum |
| hic jacet | rigor mortis |
| in camera | scribendi cacoëthes |
| in situ |    *or* cacoëthes scribendi |
| Ipse dixit. | sub judice |
| Jacta alea est. | sub specie aeternitatis |
| Lares et Penates | tabula rasa |
| mare nostrum | terra incognita |

### *VOCABAGRAMS*

A Latin word used as an English word will supply the answer every time.

| | | | |
|---|---|---|---|
| 1. imputes | | = | moving force |
| 2. insister | | = | evil |
| 3. poses | | = | sheriff's helpers |
| 4. retain | | = | part of the eye |
| 5. sprout | | = | mental numbness |
| 6. visa | | = | bird |
| 7. barter | + i | = | mediator |
| 8. boil | + m | = | place of oblivion |
| 9. carved | + a | = | corpse |
| 10. entire | + g | = | whole number |
| 11. near | + a | = | place for contests |
| 12. overt | + x | = | whirlpool |

13. scamp   + u = college grounds
14. scare   + i = tooth decay
15. score   + n = overseer of morals
16. start   + a = levels of society
17. troop   + r = sluggishness
18. varies  + c = internal organs
19. about   − o = trumpet
20. amnesty − y = part of a flower
21. avid    − d = by way of
22. bruise  − i = a type of puzzle
23. correct − c = parish or college official
24. sound   − d = a burden

This time a Greek word will supply the answer.

1. coin              = image
2. those             = moral nature
3. cash     + o = utter confusion
4. dusk     + o = renown
5. game     + o = the end
6. amateur  − e = injury
7. atone    − t = long period of time
8. chore    − r = a repeating of sound
9. elated   − e = sand deposit at mouth of river
10. imagine − i = riddle
11. ratio   − r = an extremely small quantity
12. top + hats − t = what arouses pity

*And though thou hadst small Latin, and less Greek,*

> BEN JONSON, *To the Memory of My Beloved,*
> *the Author, William Shakespeare*

---

### A Galaxy of Latin Quotations

Here is a cluster of six favorite Latin quotations together with a literal translation of each and similar or equivalent English sayings.

\*        \*        \*        \*

**De gustibus non est disputandum** \*\*\* "There must be no disputing about tastes" \* There is no accounting for tastes.

\*        \*        \*        \*

**Errare humanum est** \*\*\* "To err is human."

\*        \*        \*        \*

**Homo sum; humani nihil a me alienum puto** (Terence) \*\*\* "I am a man and I consider nothing that has to do with a human being foreign to me" \* As a human being I am touched by everything that affects mankind \* "No man is an island."

\*        \*        \*        \*

**Mens sana in corpore sano** (Juvenal) \*\*\* "A sound mind in a sound body."

\*        \*        \*        \*

**Quot homines, tot sententiae** (Terence) \*\*\* "As many men, so many opinions" \* Everybody has his own idea \* No two men think alike.

\*        \*        \*        \*

**In labore quies** \*\*\* "In work, (there is) peace of mind."

# 13.  The Old Myths Are Still Alive

> *Sleepy Jim never was at a loss for words. In one game the referee kept making call after call against Notre Dame. At the final gun the official turned to Crowley with a snarl.*
>
> *"You fellows sure were lucky to win this game," he said.*
>
> *"Yes, Cyclops," agreed Sleepy Jim, "judging from the way you officiated we were mighty lucky to win."*
>
> ARTHUR DALEY, THE NEW YORK TIMES,
> JANUARY 6, 1964

The reader of this epigraph cannot fully appreciate the retort of Jim Crowley, one of the backs of Notre Dame's legendary, almost mythical Four Horsemen, unless he is familiar with a character out of mythology, the Cyclops, a giant having only one eye. Very often the word we need in order to point up a story, to make an apt reference or comparison, to enrich a spoken or written passage comes straight out of the myths of the Greeks and the Romans.

Here are ten such words often met in our daily reading; match them with the definitions on the right.

| | | | |
|---|---|---|---|
| 1. | aegis | a. | very changeable |
| 2. | chimerical | b. | tremendous |
| 3. | cornucopia | c. | visionary |
| 4. | hector | d. | gloomy |
| 5. | lethargic | e. | sponsorship |
| 6. | protean | f. | pertaining to dancing |
| 7. | stentorian | g. | very loud |
| 8. | stygian | h. | abundance |
| 9. | terpsichorean | i. | sluggish |
| 10. | titanic | j. | bully |

The old myths have never died; they live on in hundreds of words. Through the use of such words, allusions to the myths are made daily in the press and over the air. Here we shall give you a comprehensive sampling of the more useful words of this nature, together with the story behind them.

### aegis

> The firm belief in this corner is that all umpires should be under the aegis of the commissioner, working interchangeably in both leagues.

The aegis (also written *egis*) was the mantle and shield of Zeus,* for even the king of the gods needed protection in his war with the Titans. Zeus lent the aegis to his daughter Athena (Athene) when she fought on the side of the Greeks in the Trojan War. Homer describes it as a kind of cloak. Whether it was a cloak or a shield, it undoubtedly had protective powers, since on it were serpents and the head of a Gorgon, which turned those who looked at it into stone.

In modern usage, *aegis* has become a vogue word to mean sponsorship, auspices, guidance. In the above excerpt, it has the implication of *control* or *direction*.

### antaean, Antaeus

> That Navy football team apparently is not unlike Antaeus, who grew in strength every time he was knocked down. Being the son of Terra, the earth, he was invincible because every time he was felled Mother Earth imparted new powers to his sinews.

Very often the mythological allusion is explained by the writer, in this case Arthur Daley, sports columnist of *The New York Times,* to whom we credit also the excerpt under *aegis.*

The name *Antaeus* is used as a symbol of renewed vigor and invincibility; the adjective *antaean* means invincible, possessing superhuman strength.

Like *antaean,* many other words formed from names out of mythology are written with either a small or a capital initial

---

* For the Greek and Roman names of some of the important gods and goddesses, see "Twelve on Olympian Heights" after the end of the text of this chapter.

letter; others, like *Cassandra*, are always capitalized; and still others, like *mentor*, meaning a teacher, are always written with a small first letter.

## Cassandra

> I know from my newspaper experience how risky it is to be optimistic, and I know that the prudent man who wishes to play it safe will always lean to Cassandra, never to Pollyanna. For if Cassandra is right, which I am sorry to say is all too frequently, the man becomes without any trouble at all a true prophet. If, on the other hand, Cassandra is wrong, everyone is too well pleased to remember what he said.
>
> WALTER LIPPMANN (speech), MAY 25, 1962

Cassandra, daughter of Priam and Hecuba, was loved by Apollo, who gave her the gift of prophecy. However, when she failed to carry out her promise to love him, the god decreed that, although she spoke the truth, nobody would believe her. As she appears in Greek tragedies and Vergil's *Aeneid*, Cassandra prophesied calamity and woe. Hence, a person who is called a Cassandra is a pessimistic prophet. The name is applied to anybody who utters warnings of trouble—whether the prophecy is believed or not.

### Dire Prophet Knighted
### by British Queen

> Queen Elizabeth II today [January 1, 1966] bestowed a knighthood on one of her most irreverent subjects, the newspaper columnist Cassandra.

*Cassandra* is the pseudonym of the "dire prophet" William Neil Connor, noted for his caustic attacks on authority and privilege.

## chimera, chimerical

> The nub of the matter is that the notion of exterminating pests by chemical means is quite chimerical; a remnant will always escape.

The Chimera, or Chimaera, was a monster that breathed fire, had the head of a lion, the body of a goat, and the tail of a serpent. The name of such an incongruous and fantastic combination is used to denote a wild dream, an illusion; the adjective *chimerical* means unreal, visionary, extremely fanciful.

### cornucopia

> The statisticians of *Fortune* calculated the percentage of increase and drew predictions of an industrial cornucopia in the years to come.

*Cornucopia* is formed from two Latin words, *cornu*, horn, and *copia*, supply, wealth. According to one version, the infant Zeus was nursed by a nymph named Amalthea. Later, to show his gratitude, the god broke off a goat's horn and presented it to her. This horn, "The Horn of Plenty," would miraculously be replenished with all the fruits that the nymph desired. Hence, a cornucopia is a never-ending supply.

### hector, hectoring

> Right out in the sky-vaulted open and on the decks of a sturdy square-rigged ship, is played the better part of this drama of the hectoring of the innocent young tar by his monstrously warped superior.

Who, on reading the *Iliad*, is not moved by the death of Hector, the Trojan hero? Who is not more sympathetic to him than to Achilles, the Greek hero? Hector was certainly superior to Achilles as a human being and his equal as a fighter. Yet the gods played a cruel trick on the Trojan so that he was overcome by Achilles, and history, the history of words, played still another cruel trick on his name.

Although at one time the name *Hector* was synonymous with *hero*, and in medieval lore he was listed among the Nine Worthies, superior beings including King David, Alexander the Great, and Charlemagne, nevertheless, at about the end of the sixteenth century the word *hector* came to mean a bully or braggart, and the verb *to hector*, to act the bully or braggart, to swagger, to badger, to intimidate.

**hydra-headed**

> The military authorities who have so
> far testified on the Army-Navy merger
> have made plain the peril of a hydra-
> headed national defense policy.

One of the Twelve Labors of Hercules was the killing of the
Hydra, a water monster with nine heads. To get rid of this
monstrosity was truly a herculean task, for as soon as one
head was cut off, two new ones replaced it. However, the
severed head could not grow back if fire could be applied at
once to the amputated part. Hercules accomplished the labor
through the aid of an assistant who cauterized the necks as
fast as Hercules cut off the heads!

*Hydra-headed* means hard to eliminate or destroy. The term
is applied to a condition or an evil, which, apparently put
down in one place, springs up in another. Or else, as in the
excerpt, the word may mean having many centers or branches,
multifarious.

**Janus, Janus-faced, Januslike**

> The face of the Comédie Française is
> a reversible face, as recent visitors to the
> City Center can testify. When comedy
> palls, it can turn Januslike, serious and
> even tragic.

The clue to the meaning of *Januslike* is the use of the words
"reversible face." Janus (after whom the month of January
was named), the Roman god of beginnings and also of portals,
gateways, and doors (hence, *janitor*), was represented with
two faces, looking in opposite directions, to illustrate his power
of seeing both past and future at the same time. On the seal
of the City College of New York a third face has been added
to give Janus an additional power, that of looking at the present also; the motto on the seal reads *Respice, Adspice,
Prospice,* "Look back upon the past, look at the present, look
to the future."

The words *Janus, Janus-faced,* and *Januslike* may be noncommittal, meaning simply looking in two directions, or they
may be complimentary, meaning versatile, having contrasting
abilities, as in the excerpt above, or finally, *two-faced* in the
sense of deceitful:

> Russia's larger and more beguiling aim
> is to create an international chorus line
> of what may be called Janus-States, who,
> as they dance, smile west and look east.

## Pandora's box

> But even if there is not the slightest
> doubt that fluoridation is beneficial to all
> segments of New York's population, I
> shudder at the future that this Pandora's
> box opens up for my children.

According to Greek mythology, Pandora was the first woman. In *Paradise Lost* Milton tells how she received her name:

> Pandora, whom the gods
> Endowed with all their gifts.

*Pan* means all, and *dora* means gifts.

Every god and goddess had contributed some gift to make Pandora a perfect being. However, Zeus, angered at mankind, sent her down to be a curse to man. She was given a box which she was warned not to open, but unable to curb her curiosity, she did open it. Whereupon, all the evils that plague mankind were let loose—only hope remained.

A Pandora's box is a source of evil, a seething cauldron on which a lid must be kept. The expression is much used in today's troubled world; in fact, our files show more instances of its use than of any other expression from mythology.

## Scylla and Charybdis

> Emphasizing that "we're entering a
> difficult period," he said the teacher must
> steer a "precarious course between the
> Scylla of overemphasis on mastery of
> fundamentals and the Charybdis of ex-
> cessive permissiveness."

Geographically, Scylla has been identified as a headland projecting into the Strait of Messina from the Italian side, and Charybdis as a whirlpool on the Sicilian side opposite to Scylla. Mythologically, Scylla and Charybdis were monsters that preyed upon ships and their crews attempting to pass through the strait. Either Scylla pulled them up with her twelve lower limbs, or else Charybdis sucked them in. If the sailors gave one of these horrors a wide berth, they were almost sure to come too close to the other. Even the wily Odysseus (Ulysses) had to sacrifice six of his men to Scylla to get himself and the rest of his men through.

Scylla and Charybdis therefore denote destructive dangers, most often unescapable ones. Their names are generally met in the expression "to be between Scylla and Charybdis," meaning to fall between two dangers where escape from one brings on destruction by the other. In nonmythological language, we fall "out of the frying pan into the fire" or we are "between the devil and the deep blue sea."

### Sisyphean, Sisyphian, Sisyphus

> Whatever the city does not give to the Shakespeare Festival Company, a fund-raising committee appointed by the Mayor must coax and wheedle out of citizens and private foundations. Every year Mr. Papp has to face this Sisyphian labor.

Sisyphus, a cruel king of Corinth in Greece, was punished for his misdeeds by being forced to roll a huge boulder uphill in Tartarus, a section of Hades (the Lower World, or Infernal Regions) reserved for wrongdoers. No sooner had he pushed the rock to the top of the hill than it slipped down again.

So, a never-ending labor is described as Sisyphean, or Sisyphian, a term often applied to the attempts of wage earners to keep up with the rising cost of living, or of a government to keep its budget balanced.

### Stygian

> In the next few minutes, the Cornell stands changed from wild elation to Stygian gloom. In five plays after recovering on their 12-yard line, the Elis went 88 yards to tie the score.

The Styx was the chief river of the Lower World. Ferried across by Charon, the spirits of the dead crossed this river to enter Hades. The scene is beautifully described by Vergil in the sixth book of the *Aeneid*.

*Stygian* refers to the nether world; it implies gloom and darkness.

Lethe was another river of the Lower World. Souls that were to return to earth as new beings drank from this stream, whose waters had the property of inducing forgetfulness. The Greek word *lethe* means forgetfulness, oblivion. The poetic adjective *lethean*, or *lethaean*, means relating to or causing forgetfulness:

> We have drunken of things Lethean, and
> fed on the fullness of death.

ALGERNON CHARLES SWINBURNE, "Hymn to Proserpine"

The noun *lethargy*, meaning apathy, lassitude, and the adjective *lethargic*, meaning apathetic, listless, come from the same root. Not so *lethal*, meaning deadly, causing death, which comes from the Latin noun *letum*, death. Even in Roman days, the *h* was inserted because of the relationship of ideas between the River Lethe and death.

**titan(ic)**

> The autobahn exit leads to the charming city of Weimar, the home of Goethe, Schiller and other titans of eighteenth-century culture.

The Titans, children of Heaven and Earth, were deities of tremendous strength, who fought with Zeus but were vanquished. A titan is a giant in any field of endeavor, a person of outstanding ability who towers above all others in his field. Appropriately enough, the name *Titan* has been given to the most powerful intercontinental missile produced by the United States of America—up to 1966.

### The Magic Word That Winged Wonder Starts*

Pegasus, the winged horse, and Mercury, Titan and Apollo, Atlas and Jupiter—these are only a few of the names met in mythology to which men turn when they want to give names to gigantic modern inventions, missiles and rockets, satellites and space machines. They are truly magic words for the figuratively winged wonders that surpass in reality the imaginative creations of the mythographers of ancient Greece. The

* From a poem by Roscoe C. E. Brown on the façade of the Brooklyn Public Library.

names of Daedalus and Icarus, first humans to fly, of Castor and Pollux, the *Gemini*, or Twins, who were placed in the heavens as a constellation, are evoked whenever a new tremendous aerial feat is accomplished. So, the New York *Herald Tribune* paid tribute both to the mythological heroes of antiquity and to the almost mythical heroes of the present—first (March 19, 1965) to Lieutenant Colonel Alexi Leonov and second (June 5, 1965) to Major James Alton McDivitt and Major Edward White. Parts of each editorial follow; they show how aptly the ancient myths can be used.

### Long Stride Into Space

Many an early aeronaut gave his life as did Icarus. But what was so often overlooked in the myth was that Daedalus, who made the wings on which Icarus flew to his death, fled Crete safely by the same means—observing the rules that his unhappy son ignored.

\*        \*        \*

### "The Great Twin Brethren"

When Jove, their father, set Castor and Pollux in the heavens (where they were to be known as the Gemini, the twins), he little reckoned that presumptuous mortals would dare to do the same. But first the Russians, then the Americans, launched themselves in pairs in space. . . . And both a Russian and an American have now walked in space, speeding weightlessly beside their vehicles, moving with giant strides across whole continents and seas. . . .

## PROTEAN POSSIBILITIES AND INEXHAUSTIBLE QUARRY

Closer to the immediate subject of this book is another excerpt from a newspaper, this quotation coming from *The Times Literary Supplement*, London, November 23, 1962:

The protean possibilities of the Greek myths being what they are, and Troy-

town having certain advantages over
Toytown as a spur to the imagination, it
is surprising that more frequent use has
not been made of so inexhaustible a
quarry for children's stories.

The myths are a rich quarry not only for children's stories,
plays, musical compositions, ballets, themes of paintings, but
also for our field of inquiry: etymology, word stories, and the
meaning of words. Here are some additional words and
phrases out of mythology, most of them flashing by and covering space more rapidly than the ones that appeared earlier in
this chapter:

**Achilles, heel of**     By dipping the infant Achilles into the
River Styx, his mother, Thetis, made him invulnerable, except
in the heel by which she held him. Therefore, *an Achilles heel*
means a weak spot, and so it proved in his case, for he was
killed by a poisoned arrow shot by Paris into the heel that
had not been rendered "wound-free."

**Adonis**     This young shepherd, beloved by Aphrodite
(Venus) was extremely handsome; hence, his name is used to
describe a very handsome man.

**Amazon**     The Amazons were female warriors; hence,
*amazon* means a strong woman, a female warrior.

**ambrosia**     Ambrosia, meaning deathless, was the food of
the gods. It is usually coupled with *nectar*, the name of the
divine drink; hence, the expression *ambrosia and nectar*, or
*nectar and ambrosia*, meaning "a dish fit for the gods."

**Argus-eyed**     Argus was a monster with a hundred eyes,
some of which never closed. Quite naturally, he served at
times as a watchman. Hence, *argus-eyed* means vigilant, ever
awake, all-observant.

**Augean stables**     One of the labors of Hercules was the
cleaning of the stables of King Augeas of Elis, who had a herd
of three thousand oxen. Their stalls had not been cleansed for
thirty years. Hercules accomplished the task by diverting the
course of two rivers and letting the streams run like a hose
through the filthy stalls. "To clean the Augean stables" means
to clear up a mess. It is often applied to the efforts of a reform
government to undo the efforts of the corruption left by its
predecessors.

**bacchanalian**     Bacchus was the god of wine (among
other things). Wild celebrations held in his honor were called

... *bacchalia* (compare *saturnalia*). Bacchanalian celebrations ... characterized by revelry or ecstatic frenzy.

**Cerberus** Cerberus was the three-headed dog that guarded the entrance to the Lower World. Hence, his name is sometimes used to mean a watchdog, a conscientious guardian.

Aeneas, the Trojan hero who was granted permission to visit his father in Hades, got by Cerberus when his guide, the Sibyl, threw a drugged honey cake that put the dog to sleep. "Throwing a sop to Cerberus" therefore means to appease somebody by an offering or a conciliatory gesture.

**Cyclopean** The Cyclopes were giants with a single round (*cycl*) eye (*ops*) in the middle of the forehead. *Cyclops* is the singular: one Cyclops, two CYCLŌ'pēs (pēz). One of the most memorable stories in the *Odyssey* recounts the adventure of Odysseus in the cave of a Cyclops named Polyphemus.

*Cyclopean* means huge, massive; the term is used in architecture for a type of construction in which huge irregular blocks of stone are placed on each other without cement.

**Elysium** This was the region of the Lower World where the spirits of those who had led an upright life on earth spent a happy existence. *Elysium* signifies a state of extreme happiness, a paradise. A paradise for the living is that beautiful avenue in Paris named Les Champs Elysées, "The Elysian Fields."

**Harpy** The Harpies were flying monsters with the heads of women and the bodies and claws of vultures. Their name comes from a Greek verb meaning to snatch. As told in the story of Jason and the Golden Fleece, the Harpies swooped down upon their victims and snatched away their food. Today the word *harpy* is sometimes used to denote a shrewish woman, but more often it means a greedy, grasping person.

> The harpies of the shore shall pluck
> The eagle of the sea!
>
> OLIVER WENDELL HOLMES, "Old Ironsides"

**hermetic, hermetically** Hermes, better known by his Roman name Mercury, was the patron god of magic. In the Middle Ages, alchemy, the predecessor of chemistry, was known as a hermetic art. To put the seal of Hermes, or the hermetic seal, on a bottle in a laboratory meant to twist the neck with flame and thereby seal it airtight. *Hermetic* and *hermetically sealed* refer, therefore, to an impenetrable barrier, particularly to ideas; the words imply that a person's mind is shut, willingly or unwillingly, against the infiltration of ideas or news from the outside.

**jovial**   The Latin adjective *Jovialis* means "belonging to Jupiter"; *Jovis* means "Jupiter's." From *Jovis* comes *Jove*, another name for Jupiter.

The ancient sculptors and poets often represented Jupiter, father of gods and men, as smiling upon mankind. However, we owe the present meaning of *jovial*, like that of *saturnine*, to astrology, since persons born under the planet Jupiter are supposed to be joyful. Hence, the word *jovial* means merry, inspiring mirth. *Jovian*, however, means detached and aloof, or powerful, as befits the ruler of gods and men.

**lotos-eater, lotus-eater**   In the *Odyssey*, Odysseus and his men reach the land of the Lotus-eaters, who gave to some of the visitors the plant called the lotus. When eaten, this plant induced a state of dreamy content, together with forgetfulness of home and friends. A lotus-eater is therefore one who gives himself up to daydreaming and complete indolence.

**Myrmidons**   They were the faithful followers of Achilles, who obeyed him implicitly. Today the word *myrmidons* is used synonymously with *hirelings*—the appellation denotes not only loyal attendants but also those who execute orders unquestioningly and pitilessly.

**Narcissus**   He was a handsome youth who fell in love with his own reflection. Therefore, a person who is very vain of his beauty or of his accomplishments may be referred to by that name. Words related to *Narcissus* are:

*narcissist, narcist:* a person in love with himself; self-admirer. *narcissan, narcissistic, narcistic:* self-admiring; vain about one's own accomplishments.

**Nemesis**   Nemesis was the goddess of retribution and punishment who humbled the proud and arrogant. Hence, a successful person feared to offend her, for if he became too haughty, his downfall might follow. Today, the word is used to denote an avenger or punisher and also the punishment itself, usually a just one. In the sports pages *nemesis* is applied to an athlete who consistently beats an opponent.

**paean**   The Homeric name for Apollo, as physician of the gods, was Paean (*Paian*, or *Paion*, healer or deliverer). Hymns of thanksgiving to Apollo for deliverance from evil began with the invocation *Io Paean*. The song itself came to be called a *paean*, a name which was extended to songs of triumph after victory addressed to Apollo and other gods. Today, a paean means a song of thanksgiving or praise, a shout or song of great exultation or triumph.

**palladium**    The image of Pallas Athene (Minerva) was called the *palladium*, meaning belonging to Pallas. As long as it stood within the city walls, Troy could not be taken by the Greeks. Hence, a safeguard, something on which the safety of an individual, a people, or an institution depends is called a palladium.

> The liberty of the press is the palladium of all the civil, political, and religious rights of an Englishman.
>
> LETTERS OF JUNIUS (1769–1772)

**phoenix**    Among the tall stories brought back from Egypt by Herodotus, "Father of History" and a wonderful teller of tales, was the one about a sacred bird called the phoenix, which appeared only once every five hundred years. After being consumed in fire, it arose fresh and youthful from its own ashes. It was compared to the sun, which sets, or dies, then rises, or is born anew. The story of the phoenix was readily adopted by the Greeks and the Romans, was taken over later by the Arabs (originally, the bird was supposed to have come to Egypt from Arabia), and its symbolism is explained in the Talmud, the works of early Christian writers, Petrarch's writings, and medieval bestiaries. The phoenix symbolizes resurrection and immortality; the word *phoenix* is used to refer to a person or an institution that is supposed to have died or to have passed into oblivion, but rises again, fresh, youthful, and vigorous.

**Procrustean**    Procrustes, "the Stretcher," was an innkeeper-cum-highwayman who had an ingenious method of accommodating his guests. He insisted that each one must fit exactly the one iron bed in his inn. He stretched a guest who was too short and shortened the legs of one who was too tall. According to another version Procrustes had two beds, one very long, the other very short. He made the tall traveler fit the small bed by lopping off his limbs, and stretched the short traveler to fit the large bed. Hence, a system, especially a political or educational one, in which the individual must fit a uniform pattern and conform to it arbitrarily, without allow-ance for individual differences, is characterized as *procrustean*.

**protean**    Proteus was a sea god who could assume all manners of shapes and forms. Hence, the adjective *protean* means varying, changing. It is often used when *versatile* would do as well.

**saturnine**    Saturn, father of Jupiter, was a jovial god; the Romans looked upon the era of his rule as a golden age. The feasts celebrating his worship were wild and unrestrained like our festivities on New Year's Eve. The name *Saturnalia* (a plural noun) was given to the festival of Saturn; used as a singular noun today, it means unrestrained revelry, a wild, tumultuous celebration, or just a happy time.

Nevertheless, astrology has had the last word, for *saturnine* means gloomy, serious, because persons born under the influ-ence of the planet Saturn are supposedly somber, sad, and morose.

**stentorian**    Stentor, the Greek herald in the Trojan War, was the original loudspeaker, for his voice could be heard all over the Grecian camp. Hence, *stentorian* means bellowing, loud-voiced.

**terpsichorean**    Since Terpsichore was the Muse of choral dance, *terpsichorean* means relating to the dance.

**Trojan Horse**    In the tenth year of the Trojan War, hav-ing been unable to capture Troy by siege, the Greeks resorted to stratagem. They constructed a colossal wooden horse, filled it with armed men, and managed by trickery to have the unsuspecting Trojans break down part of their walls and draw the horse inside the city. The capture of Troy followed.

Although the wooden horse was a Greek subterfuge, it is generally called the Trojan Horse, an expression which has become a symbol of treacherous infiltration, "a fifth col-umn."

The expression "Greeks bearing gifts" comes from the same episode. The only Trojan who thought that the horse was a ruse was Laocoön, priest of Poseidon (Neptune), who uttered a warning that has become a byword advising caution against enemies who suddenly seem to be generous: *Timeo Danaos et dona ferentis* (Vergil's *Aeneid*, Book II), "I fear the Greeks even though they bear gifts."

"To work like a Trojan" and "to fight like a Trojan" are ex-pressions that pay honor to the perseverance and bravery of the Trojans.

## TWELVE ON OLYMPIAN HEIGHTS

For most of the Greek gods there are corresponding ones in Roman mythology. Thus, the Greek Eros was Cupido (Cupid) to the Romans. We have dedicated the column on the left to the names of the twelve major Greek gods who dwelled on Mount Olympus; the center column contains the names of their Roman counterparts. In order that you may easily identify them we have given an important attribute of each deity.

However, on each line, one of the names is incomplete, only the first letter being given. Complete each name; each bar represents a letter.

| | | |
|---|---|---|
| 1. Zeus | J _ _ _ _ _ | King of the gods |
| 2. H _ _ _ | Juno | Queen of the gods |
| 3. Aphrodite | V _ _ _ _ | Goddess of love |
| 4. P _ _ _ _ _ _ Apollo | Apollo | God of sun, music, medicine |
| 5. A _ _ _ | Mars | God of war |
| 6. Artemis | D _ _ _ _ | Goddess of the hunt |
| 7. P _ _ _ _ _ Athena | Minerva | Goddess of wisdom |
| 8. Demeter | C _ _ _ _ | Goddess of agriculture |
| 9. Hephaestus | V _ _ _ _ _ | God of fire |
| 10. Hestia | V _ _ _ _ | Goddess of the hearth and home |
| 11. H _ _ _ _ _ | Mercury | Messenger of the gods |
| 12. P _ _ _ _ _ _ _ | Neptune | God of the sea |

## I.  WORDS IN REVIEW

The words on the left have been defined in this chapter. Their number is twelve to suggest the Twelve Labors of Hercules, but it should not be difficult to match them with the terms on the right.

| | |
|---|---|
| 1. ambrosia | a. hireling |
| 2. cyclopean | b. grim |
| 3. harpy | c. never-ending |
| 4. hydra-headed | d. two-faced |
| 5. Januslike | e. safeguard |
| 6. lethean | f. very loud |
| 7. myrmidon | g. pertaining to death |

|  |  |  |  |
|---|---|---|---|
| 8. palladium | | h. | grasping person |
| 9. phoenix | | i. | having many branches |
| 10. saturnine | | j. | divine food |
| 11. sisyphean | | k. | gigantic |
| 12. stentorian | | l. | something that rises again |

## II. NONHERCULEAN LABORS

Which pairs are like, or similar, and which pairs are unlike or opposite?

| | | |
|---|---|---|
| 1. Adonis | ———— | handsome man |
| 2. antaean | ———— | almost always invincible |
| 3. argus-eyed | ———— | vigilant |
| 4. bacchanalia | ———— | quiet celebration |
| 5. Cerberus | ———— | watchdog |
| 6. Elysium | ———— | paradise |
| 7. jovial | ———— | gloomy |
| 8. lethal | ———— | immortal |
| 9. lotus-eate. | ———— | realist |
| 10. nectar | ———— | divine drink |
| 11. procrustean | ———— | flexible |
| 12. saturnalia | ———— | joyous feast |

## III. WORDS IN CONTEXT

The sentences below contain words or phrases arising from the myths. From the group after each sentence make the choice that is closest in meaning to the italicized word or expression.

1. This coach's prime probing plot is to spot a lax defender. He immediately sets up a screening play to explore that weakness, but he is capable of detecting any other *Achilles heel*.
    (a) weak spot (b) false move (c) shifting pattern
      (d) deceptive alignment

2. Forget what the Broadway *Cassandras* are saying about the imminent demise of the theatre.
    (a) commentators (b) prophets of disaster (c) cognoscenti
      (d) discouraged investors

3. Despite frequent reorganizations and dismissals, and countless *hectoring* addresses to farmers throughout the country, this year's cereal harvest is slated to be at a very high level.
    (a) encouraging (b) repetitious (c) badgering
      (d) threatening

4. Mayor Willy Brandt asserted that morale was on the upgrade after the serious decline caused by the wall which *her-*

*metically* sealed off East Berlin from the western sector of the city.
    (a) tightly (b) illegally (c) immorally (d) cruelly

5. *Pandora's box* is open, thanks to the brilliance of modern scientists, and thanks to the lack of brilliance among modern statesmen nobody has yet conceived a way to slam it shut.
    something containing: (a) the key to the mystery of nature
                (b) future troubles (c) the way to outer space
                (d) enmity among large nations

6. San Francisco is the *Narcissus* of the Pacific; it can stare at itself for hours.
    (a) metropolis (b) beauty spot (c) self-admirer
      (d) melting pot

7. Devils' Island was the former *Nemesis* of France's hardened criminals.
    place of: (a) refuge (b) exile (c) penance (d) just
      punishment

8. The last chapter is a straight chamber of commerce *paean* which manages to ignore all negative factors in the future development of the Southwest.
    (a) song of praise (b) objective report (c) sharp analysis
      (d) advertisement

9. Tammany Hall, we are told, has changed. It is always changing, having a *Protean* ability to adapt itself to new situations.
    (a) capable of assuming different shapes (b) cynically
      opportunistic (c) tested through the years (d) generally
      successful

10. Eighty acres of subterranean rooms and corridors spread like so many fingers beneath the hills, and workers fitted with lamps roam the *stygian* silence loading their 15 tons a day.
    (a) protective (b) gloomy (c) unbroken (d) menacing

## DO-IT-YOURSELF DEPARTMENT

See how many of the questions in all of the following exercises you can answer without the aid of a reference work; then find the answers to the others in a large dictionary or a book on mythology.

### Names That Fit

The names on the left have a special significance; they are used as a shortcut to denote the character or role of a person. Match each of the twelve with the correct term on the right.

| | |
|---|---|
| 1. Apollo | a. wise counselor |
| 2. Atalanta | b. lovesick swain |
| 3. Circe | c. patient, devoted woman |
| 4. Diana | d. sad and tearful woman |
| 5. Ganymede | e. cruel, passionate woman |
| 6. Hebe | f. handsome man |
| 7. Helen | g. woman who lures by her charms |
| 8. Leander | h. swift female racer |
| 9. Medea | i. huntress |
| 10. Nestor | j. young man who serves drinks |
| 11. Niobe | k. very beautiful woman |
| 12. Penelope | l. young female attendant |

## Men and Women, Gods and Goddesses

Every one of the following words contains an element related to the name of a mythological character, human or divine. Name the character, then tell how the name has contributed to the meaning of the word.

| | | |
|---|---|---|
| 1. aeolian | 9. flora | 17. panic |
| 2. aphrodisiac | 10. herm | 18. plutonian |
| 3. arachnid | 11. hymeneal | 19. sibyl, sibil |
| 4. aurora borealis | 12. junoesque | 20. siren |
| 5. calliope | 13. martial | 21. tantalize |
| 6. cereal | 14. mentor | 22. uranium |
| 7. erotic | 15. mercurial | 23. vulcanize |
| 8. fauna | 16. odyssey | 24. zephyr |

## A Small Herculean Labor

Here are twelve more words and names stemming from the myths. Trace the meaning of each according to its origin in mythology.

| | |
|---|---|
| 1. Acheron | 7. morphine |
| 2. atlas | 8. nymph |
| 3. caduceus | 9. phaëton |
| 4. chaos | 10. Philomel |
| 5. iridescent | 11. Rhadamanthine |
| 6. labyrinthine | 12. satyr |

## Another Set of Twelve

| | |
|---|---|
| 1. to carry water in a sieve | 7. to climb Parnassus |
| 2. clue or thread of Ariadne | 8. to mount (ride) Pegasus |
| 3. faithful Achates | 9. Promethean fire |
| 4. Jupiter Pluvius | 10. riddle of the Sphinx |
| 5. Olympian detachment | 11. sowing the dragon's teeth |
| 6. to pile Ossa on Pelion | 12. triton among the minnows |

### Information, Please

1. Why is the term *a sulking Achilles* sometimes applied to somebody who withdraws from an action because his feelings have been hurt?

2. Why is provoking a quarrel known as *throwing the apple of discord?*

3. What is the meaning of the suffix *naut* in the words like *aeronaut, aquanaut, astronaut,* and *cosmonaut?* Relate these words to the story of Jason and the Argonauts.

4. Why is a society of learned men sometimes called an *Athen(a)eum?*

5. What is the significance of the name *Dedalus* as used by the novelist James Joyce in *A Portrait of the Artist as a Young Man* and *Ulysses?* Also, what is the significance of the name *Ulysses* used as the title of his major novel?

6. Why are calm or prosperous days, heydays, referred to as *halcyon days?*

7. What do the words *mosaic, museum,* and *music* have in common?

8. Why are some recital halls and theaters named *Orpheum?*

9. Why is a decision at a beauty contest sometimes called *the judgment of Paris?*

10. Why did George Bernard Shaw give the name *Pygmalion* to the play from which *My Fair Lady* was created?

11. Which day of the week was named after a Roman god? Also, which names of days in French, or Spanish, or Italian were named after Roman gods?

12. Which of our months were named after Roman deities?

### F.  Finale

Words and expressions derived from mythology other than Greek and Roman have also come into the English language.

1. Give the meaning of the following taken from Teutonic mythology:
> (a) Götterdämmerung (b) Lorelei (c) The Three Norns
> (compare *The Three Fates*) (d) Valhalla (e) Valkyrie.

2. Name the Teutonic deity whose name is contained in the following:
> (a) Tuesday (b) Wednesday (c) Thursday (d) Friday.

3. Give the meaning of the following taken from Celtic mythology:
> (a) banshee (b) leprechaun.

## VOCABAGRAMS

The answer will be the name of somebody or something mythological or a word formed from such a name.

EXAMPLE:  rose = Greek god of love    ANSWER:  Eros

| | | | |
|---|---|---|---|
| 1. adore | | = mountain nymph |
| 2. amused | | = best-known Gorgon |
| 3. Diana | | = fresh-water nymph |
| 4. stave | | = goddess of the hearth |
| 5. reined | | = ocean nymph |
| 6. crate | + n | = drink of the gods |
| 7. dray | + h | = nine-headed monster |
| 8. entrap | + o | = changeable |
| 9. heel | + t | = river of forgetfulness |
| 10. lout | + p | = god of the Lower World |
| 11. ravine | + m | = goddess of wisdom |
| 12. rice | + c | = enchantress |
| 13. sage | + i | = shield, protection |
| 14. said | + m | = king with the golden touch |
| 15. sir | + i | = goddess of the rainbow |
| 16. store | + n | = wise counselor |
| 17. tenors | + t | = loud-voiced announcer |
| 18. tool | + s | = plant inducing forgetfulness |
| 19. torch | + e | = Trojan hero |
| 20. yard | + d | = tree nymph |
| 21. monarch | − m | = ferryman over the River Styx |
| 22. imagine | − a | = a pair of spacemen |
| 23. torment | − t | = teacher |
| 24. wroth | − w | = Teutonic god of war |

Here are the first letters of the more difficult ones: 1. o, 2. M, 3. n, 4. V, 5. n, 10. P, 20. d, 21. C.

*That there are different versions of mythological tales and various interpretations which may be put upon them is a tribute to the compelling power which they exert upon us. The true myth is not so much an invented story as a kind of flexible mould into which a story can be poured; a container which, while retaining its basic archetypal shape, will adapt itself to the particular nature and circumstances of the artist who uses it; and this is why it has a significance which is both timeless and impersonal.*

THE TIMES LITERARY SUPPLEMENT (LONDON),
NOVEMBER 2, 1962

# 14. Persons, Places, and Books

> *The daily repasts of Lucullus were such as the newly rich affect. Not only with his dyed coverlets, and beakers set with precious stones, and choruses and dramatic recitations, but also with his arrays of all sorts of meats and daintily prepared dishes, did he make himself the envy of the vulgar. . . .*
>
> *And once, when he was dining alone, and a modest repast of one course had been prepared for him, he was angry, and summoned the servant who had the matter in charge. The servant said that he did not suppose, since there were no guests, that he wanted anything very costly. "What sayest thou?" said the master, "dost thou not know that today Lucullus dines with Lucullus?"*
>
> PLUTARCH, "Life of Lucullus"

## I. NAMES THAT MEN REMEMBER

This fondness of Lucullus, a distinguished Roman general, for rich food and extravagant living is commemorated in the English word *Lucullan,* meaning lavish, luxurious, sumptuous. In like manner, the names of many other men and women have been turned into words because of a trait of character, their position in the world, or some action associated with them. Often the man is not so well known as Lucullus, but he has achieved a certain kind of immortality in the word that bears his name, although he himself may now be known only to students of words who take the trouble to look up the history of the word.

For example, how many have heard of General Jean Marti-

net, who was a strict drillmaster in the army of Louis XIV?
Yet, his name lives on in the word *martinet*, which is applied
to a rigid disciplinarian, a stern taskmaster, a stickler for details.

The meaning of many name-words is so obvious that knowledge of their origin is a mere verbal or historical point of interest. Everybody knows what a sandwich is, but not everyone
knows that this culinary tidbit was named after John Mon-
tagu, fourth Earl of Sandwich (1718–1792), a renowned gam-
bler who once was too busy to take time out for a meal, so
that he contented himself with slices of cold roast beef between slices of toast. We shall eschew words of that kind, but
will take up only some of the more useful name-words that
may present a vocabulary difficulty.

First we shall list ten such words or expressions. See how
many you already know by selecting from the words after each
the one that is closest in meaning.

1. Annie Oakley    (a) type of bonnet (b) free ticket (c) domineering woman (d) charmer
2. bowdlerize    (a) annihilate (b) tyrannize (c) set in order (d) expurgate
3. cicerone    (a) weakling (b) statesman (c) guide (d) buffoon
4. draconian    (a) very harsh (b) reptilian (c) poisonous (d) demanding
5. Fabian policy    one characterized by: (a) rapidity (b) duplicity (c) weakness (d) caution
6. Machiavellian    characterized by: (a) gentle persuasion (b) political cunning (c) nepotism (d) ambition
7. masochist    a person addicted to: (a) self-punishment (b) self-admiration (c) self-pity (d) self-hypnosis
8. maverick    (a) skillful deceiver (b) long-winded speaker (c) nonconformist (d) pretender
9. pinchbeck    (a) sham (b) constrained (c) obedient (d) corrugated
10. Pyrrhic victory    one that is: (a) complete (b) renowned (c) won by attrition (d) too costly

## A Roster of Name-Words

**Annie Oakley**    Her real name was Phoebe Anne Oakley
Mozee; she starred as a markswoman in Buffalo Bill's Wild

West Show from 1885 to 1902. She is the subject of the musical *Annie Get Your Gun,* in which she was portrayed by Ethel Merman. Because of the real Annie Oakley's skill at shooting holes through the spots of a playing card, a free ticket or pass which is punched with many holes is called an Annie Oakley.

### bowdlerize

> His biography of Horatio Alger is bowdlerized, fictionized, and especially superficial.

In 1818 Dr. Thomas Bowdler, an English editor, published *The Family Shakespeare,* an edition in which "those words and expressions are omitted which cannot with propriety be read aloud in a family." *To bowdlerize,* therefore, means to expurgate a book by leaving out or changing words and passages considered (by the editor) indelicate or offensive. An extended meaning of *to bowdlerize* is to render weak by omitting forceful parts.

### cicerone

> Norris Houghton has the background and equipment to be a sound cicerone for a tour of the Soviet Union's theatres.

Because of the traditional talkativeness of most guides, they are sometimes referred to by an Italian word formed from the name of Rome's greatest orator, Marcus Tullius Cicero (106 B.C.–43 B.C.). The term *cicerone* is also a tribute to their eloquence and knowledge.

### draconian

> Draconian measures are being undertaken in the battle against such economic crimes as speculation and bribery as well as a variety of criminal offenses described as hooliganism.

In about 621 B.C. Draco (or Dracon) compiled the first written code of laws in ancient Athens. Death was the punishment he assigned to almost all crimes, even petty ones, so that the saying arose that his laws were written in blood, not in ink. Hence *draconian* means very rigorous and severe.

**Synonyms:** cruel, drastic; harsh; immitigable; rigid; stern; stringent.

## Fabian

> They meant that socialism would be achieved in all reasonable societies by gradually doing one thing after another, each in its proper turn. This faith became the cornerstone of the Fabian Society, of which the Webbs, George Bernard Shaw and Edward R. Pease were founding members.

Quintus Fabius Maximus, appointed dictator in 217 B.C. to lead the Roman army against Hannibal, decided that cautious delaying tactics would be more successful than engaging the enemy in pitched battles. He therefore harassed Hannibal's army, cut off its supplies, and raided its lines. Fabius earned the appellation of *Cunctator,* or, "The Delayer"; today, such a policy, in any field, is described as *Fabian.* In politics, *Fabianism* means gradualism, a slow step-by-step evolutionary change.

## gerrymander

### Gerrymandering, Modern Style

> The spirit of that revolutionary patriot, Elbridge Gerry of Massachusetts, must have walked by night in Albany when the Legislature approved the realignment by which New York State's Congressional districts were reduced from 43 to 41. It was Mr. Gerry and his Jeffersonian friends, it must be remembered, who redistricted Massachusetts in forms that suggested real and mythical animals and which were intended to make every Jeffersonian vote count for all that it was worth.

The excerpt from an editorial in the New York *Herald Tribune* (November 12, 1961) gives the gist of the story of the event (in 1812) which led to the introduction of the word *gerrymander* into the language. Benjamin Russell, editor of a paper in a county that had been drastically altered, had hung

PERSONS, PLACES, AND BOOKS

a map of the redistricted county in his office. Seeing this map, the eminent painter Gilbert Stuart remarked that the shape of the county suggested a monstrous animal. Drawing a few strokes on it, he said, "That will do for a salamander." "Call it a gerrymander," Russell retorted.

## Machiavellian

> The grandeur is real enough, but the grandeur also conceals the Machiavellian talents de Gaulle has shown in the tragic, intricate Algerian affair.

Niccolò Machiavelli (1469–1527), a Florentine, wrote a famous book called *The Prince* as a handbook of government, in which he set down the principles of taking and holding power. This work and his correspondence are often referred to; for example, Arthur Krock, in his column of January 28, 1965, in *The New York Times,* quotes a typical Machiavellian remark:

> "Princes," wrote Machiavelli to Lorenzo the Magnificent, "should delegate to others the enactment of unpopular measures."

(It's what we call "passing the buck.")

Although originally the book merely reduced to a science what is now called power politics, *Machiavellian,* as used today, means crafty, cunning, and deceitful, basically because Machiavelli promulgated the doctrine that any means could be used by a ruler to maintain power. Machiavellianism is characterized by shiftiness, bad faith, duplicity, and cunning.

## masochist(ic)

> Football coaches seem to get a masochistic kick talking about the stars their team will run up against every week.

The novelist Leopold von Sacher-Masoch (1835–1895) described an abnormal mental condition in which a person derives pleasure from being abused and punished by someone he loves. A masochist may also direct destructive impulses against his own ego; he is a self-tormentor, one who takes pleasure in extreme self-denial and self-punishment. The adjective for him is *masochistic;* the noun for his condition is *masochism*.

### maverick

> A decade ago, Bill Veeck, a maverick in the Finley mold but a sounder operative, was doublecrossed by the American League when he sought to move the moribund St. Louis Browns franchise to Baltimore.

Samuel A. Maverick was a Texan rancher of the 1840's who did not bother to brand his calves. At first the word *maverick* was applied only to unbranded calves, but later, since such animals were different from the ordinary run of animals, the meaning of *maverick* was extended to apply to anybody who does not follow the common herd. A person of independent turn of mind, an individualist who does not conform, an unpredictable politician who does not always follow the dictates of his party may be termed a *maverick*. The word is also used as an adjective.

**Synonyms** for the adjective: recalcitrant; refractory; unorthodox.

### mesmerize

> Constant repetition of the fiscal formula for super-prosperity for all has mesmerized a considerable number of influential Americans.

Friedrich A. Mesmer (1734–1815) created a sensation in Vienna and Paris by his assertion that there existed a power which he termed animal magnetism. Quickly, the name *mesmerism* was given to this power, which now goes under the name of *hypnotism*. However, the verb *mesmerize* is used today in the sense of to fascinate, to spellbind.

### pasquinade

> The white walls of the barracks were covered with epigrams and pasquinades leveled at Cortez.

WILLIAM H. PRESCOTT, *History of the Conquest of Mexico*

In the Piazza Navona in Rome the mutilated remains of an ancient statue were set up in 1501. Once a year the fragment was dressed up to represent some mythological or historical personage; professors and students paid their respects in Latin verses which were generally placed on this statue. According to some accounts, there lived opposite the old statue a tailor or shoemaker or schoolmaster, his occupation varying according to which version you choose to accept. At any rate, all agree that his name was *Pasquino*. This was the nickname given to the statue, and the verses posted on it were called *pasquinatas*, from which comes the French and English word *pasquinade*.

Soon the style of the learned verses changed. Anonymous writers, among whom, some say, were the scholarly clientele of Pasquino's shop and even Pasquino himself, began to place satirical poems dealing with politics on the statue, short epigrams biting in tone and with a lash in their tails. The most famous one is the one-line epigram directed against the Barberini family, one of whose members had torn down or despoiled ancient monuments to build palaces and churches:

*Quod non fecerunt barbari, fecerunt Barberini.* ("What the barbarians have not done, the Barberini have done.")

The name *pasquinade* was applied not only to such poems composed in Rome but to similar satirical compositions in other parts of Europe.

**Synonyms:** lampoon; libel; satire; squib.

### stormy petrel

> "A very commonplace little murder," said he. "You've got something better, I fancy. You are the stormy petrel of crime, Watson."
>
> SIR ARTHUR CONAN DOYLE, "The Naval Treaty"

The petrel, a sea bird, may have received its name from a diminutive form of *Peter*, from the biblical account of St. Peter's walking on the waves. Because of an old belief that petrels are very active before a storm, the term *stormy petrel* is applied to a person who is a harbinger or warning of trouble. A person who is fond of fighting or stirring up strife may also be referred to as a stormy petrel.

### pinchbeck

> The greater part of what I once took
> on trust is really paste and pinchbeck.

JAMES RUSSELL LOWELL, *The Old English Dramatists*

The surname of Christopher Pinchbeck, a London toy-maker and watchmaker, lives on because he invented an alloy of copper and zinc that looked like gold. He and his son, who carried on the business after the father's death in 1732, did not attempt to deceive the public but plainly declared in their advertisements that their cheap toys, clocks, and watches were made of "a curious metal." However, the word *pinchbeck* by which this metal was popularly known degenerated in meaning until it has become synonymous with something shoddy and spurious. The word is also used as an adjective.

### Pyrrhic victory

> This is the beginning of a disaster
> which will be all the greater because it
> is taking the initial form of a victory. The
> price for this Pyrrhic victory will be paid
> later.

A Pyrrhic victory costs more than it gains. This kind of hollow triumph is named after Pyrrhus, King of Epirus in Greece, who invaded Italy in 280 B.C. and defeated the Romans in a number of battles. However, he himself was wounded and he lost so many soldiers that he was unable to follow up his victories. Pyrrhus won the battles but lost the war and had to return to his homeland. According to Plutarch, Pyrrhus remarked, "Another such victory and we are undone."

### sadism, sadist(ic)

> Natural goodwill, intelligence, religion,
> and love can sustain the human spirit
> against the forces of savagery and sadism;
> not permanently perhaps, and not flaw-
> lessly, but at least longer than without
> them.

Count Donatien de Sade (1740–1814), a French soldier who was infamous for his misdeeds and his writings, described a situation in which a person derives pleasure from tormenting someone he loves. Hence, a person who directs his destructive impulses outward, who takes pleasure in inflicting pain, is called a sadist. In their broader meanings, *sadism* means excessive cruelty and *sadistic* means abnormally cruel. *Masochist* is the opposite of *sadist*.

## II.  A LOCAL HABITATION AND A NAME

Behind the arras I'll convey myself.

SHAKESPEARE, *Hamlet*

An arras is a type of curtain so named because its material was a kind of tapestry originally made in Arras, France. Many other materials, articles, and products are named after places associated with their origin or sale. Often the name is used unchanged, as in the case of *arras* and *tulle,* a fine netting originally made in Tulle, France; sometimes the name is slightly altered as in the case of *cambric, lisle,* and *denim* (from *serge de Nîmes*), materials named after the French cities of Cambrai, Lille, and Nîmes, respectively. Going from textiles and clothing to food and drink, we can offer a cup of coffee, or java, with which you can have a frankfort, or frankfurter, named after a German city, or a hamburger, named after another German city (*er* is the true suffix in this word).

Whether the name of the place in such words is transparent or slightly concealed, the meanings of most words coming from place-names are easily discernible. We are presenting only a few that are a little more difficult or unusual.

### billingsgate

> The Chinese themselves have not yet got around to denouncing Kosygin and company by name; but that will come soon, no doubt, since the Albanians are already publishing billingsgate attacks on "the Brezhnev-Kosygin-Mikoyan troika."

Billingsgate (presumably from the personal name Billings) is an old gate and fishmarket of London. References made to it in the seventeenth century indicate that the language heard there was most abusive. Hence, *billingsgate* means foul, scurrilous, and abusive language.

**forensic**

> In six weeks of stumping as his party's forensic virtuoso, the candidate has gained a firm hold on the Golden Fleece sought by orators down the ages: the ability to trigger instant applause.

In the ancient Roman world the name *forum* was applied to the marketplace and civic center of a city. Since public business was transacted and orators declaimed there, the word *forum* itself means not only a public meeting place but also a program involving discussions of a problem. The adjective *forensic*, "pertaining to a forum," has two meanings. Technically, it means related to judicial procedure, or to the law, as in *forensic medicine, pathology, psychiatry,* etc. More generally, it refers to the ability to speak in public.

The root of the word *forum* means outdoors; in ancient Greece the outdoor meeting place corresponding to the forum was the *agora*, from a Greek root meaning to gather together. From *agora* comes the English word *agoraphobia,* fear of open spaces.

The Greek word *agora* gave rise to a verb meaning to address an assembly, and from this verb have come a number of English words such as:

| | |
|---|---|
| *category* | universal concept; class; group. |
| *panegyric* | eulogy; praise. The word literally means "relating to something said before a full (*pan*, all) assembly." |
| *paregoric* | an anodyne; a soothing medicine. The original idea is that of words of cheer and encouragement spoken to, or alongside (*para*), a person. The doctor's "bedside manner" comes to mind. |

**laconic, laconism**

> Tape recordings of his voice as reportedly broadcast from the ship indicated that his comments had been laconic and that he had given little detailed description of what he had seen or felt during his flight.

The Spartans, inhabitants of that part of Greece known as Lacedaemonia or Laconia, were noted for saying the most in the smallest possible number of words. For example, when the Persian invader Xerxes demanded that the Spartan leader Leonidas surrender his weapons, the latter replied, "Come and take them!" King Archelaus of Macedonia must have had Spartan training, for when a barber asked him how he wanted to have his hair trimmed, he laconically answered, "In silence." Such economy of words is called a laconism after the name of the Spartans' homeland; the adjective is *laconic*.

**Synonyms:** concise; pithy; succinct; terse.

**meander**

> The purpose of the trip, an informal survey of the mighty river and some of the denizens of its valley, seemed merely to meander down the 2,500-mile course, stopping where whim and curiosity dictated.

The Menderes River in Asia Minor has been noted since ancient times for its winding course. From *Maiandros*, its Greek name, or *Maeander*, its Latin name, comes the English verb *meander*, meaning to go off course, to drift, to twist and turn.

**solecism**

> But she used the word "less" in a construction in which Fowler, the Grand Panjandrum of English usage, prefers "fewer." To judge from the spate of letters, that solecism gave a number of Americans a heady feeling of upmanship.

The inhabitants of Soloi in Asia Minor spoke a corrupt form of Attic, the Greek dialect of the Athenians. Hence, a solecism means a mistake in the idiom of a language, incorrect grammatical usage. In its broader implications a solecism refers to a deviation from the accepted order or norm, something illogical, incongruous, or absurd, or even to an impropriety, such as a breach of etiquette. (Incidentally, you'll find an explanation of "Grand Panjandrum" in the next section of this chapter.)

**stoic(al), stoicism**

> On a team such as the Mets of 1965,
> the pitchers had to learn to view the lack
> of scoring by their team and the abun-
> dance of run making by their opponents
> with stoic fortitude.

*Stoic* is derived from the name of a place still in existence as
a reconstructed site, the *Stoa,* a colonnade, or portico, in
Athens, where the philosopher Zeno founded a school in
308 B.C. One of the principles of Stoicism is that the wise
man should be free from passion, untouched by joy or grief,
and submissive to natural law. The modern use of the words
*stoic, stoical,* and *stoicism* as common nouns and adjectives
commemorates only one aspect of Stoic doctrine. A person who
controls his emotions under stress, who endures the hardships
of life without complaining, is said to possess stoic, or stoical,
resignation.

**Synonyms** of *stoicism:* fortitude; impassivity; pluck; stolidity.

In the ancient world a doctrine considered to be in opposition to Stoicism was known as Epicureanism, named after its
founder, Epicurus (342–270 B.C.). Although he taught that
intellectual pleasures were superior to sensual pleasures and
advocated renunciation of temporary pleasures for more permanent ones, nevertheless, today the word *epicureanism*
stresses the hedonistic or "pleasure" aspect of his teachings.
Hence, an *epicure* is a person who is fond of choice food and
drink or has delicate, fastidious tastes.

**Synonyms:** connoisseur; bon vivant; gastronome; gourmet;
gourmand.

**sybarite, sybaritic**

> Or take the Ritz in Lisbon, one of the
> world's finest hotels. There are ankle-
> deep carpets, mahogany walk-in cabinets,
> sybaritic bathrooms with sophisticated
> showers, white telephones on marble
> walls, and stuccoed ceilings.

A sybarite is a stronger version of an epicure. He gets his
name from Sybaris, a Greek city in southern Italy, which was
noted in the sixth century B.C. for its wealth and luxury. A
sybarite is, therefore, a lover of luxury and pleasure, a voluptu-

ary; the adjective *sybaritic* means luxurious to a high degree, "super de luxe," as well as sensuous and voluptuous.

## III.   EX LIBRIS

> Dr. Bush knows very well that many of the greatest scientific discoveries were made by what is known as "serendipity," a word meaning "the finding of valuable or agreeable things not sought for"—in other words, by chance. The discovery of America is an outstanding example of serendipity. Other examples are the chance discovery of penicillin and of nuclear fission.
>
> THE NEW YORK TIMES, Editorial, "Space and Serendipity," MAY 24, 1961

Happily and felicitously, the word *serendipity* links this section with the preceding one on place-names, for it comes from the old Arabic name of the island of Ceylon, and it was coined from that place-name as it appears in a Persian fairy tale called "The Three Princes of Serendip." * In a letter written on January 28, 1754, Horace Walpole tells how he coined the word *serendipity* from the title of that story, whose heroes "were always making discoveries, by accidents or sagacity, of things they were not in quest of." Hence, *serendipity* means the ability to make lucky finds, or the gift or faculty of making unexpected and happy discoveries by chance or accident.

*Serendipity* is only one of a long list of words and phrases from names of characters and places in books. Such words serve as a shortcut or impart vividness; the allusion is worth many words of description or explanation. For example, if someone were to say of a detective, "He's no Sherlock Holmes," there are few among us who would not understand the speaker's implication. Moreover, the creations of some authors are more real than living beings, and the final mark of immortality is put upon them when words containing their

---

* Even children will get to know the word *serendipity*, for in 1964 Elizabeth Jamison Hodges retold the story for them in a book bearing the same title. And, for scholarly readers, in the same year, there appeared *Serendipity and the Princes*, from the *Peregrinaggio* of 1557, edited by Theodore C. Remer, "the tale from which Walpole coined his word 'serendipity,' accompanied by a discussion of its use and misuse."

names are written with small initial letters! Here is a selection
of such words.

### chauvinism, chauvinist

> As Mr. Moross, a native Lower East
> Sider, says, without self-consciousness:
> "Not that I'm an ardent chauvinist, but I
> do have a love affair with this country."

Nicolas Chauvin was a legendary soldier in Napoleon's
army, extremely devoted to his employer. After Napoleon's
downfall, Chauvin is supposed to have displayed such exaggerated patriotism that he was held up to ridicule. In 1831 the
Brothers Cogniard wrote a play called *La Cocarde tricolore,* in
which a young man named Chauvin sang couplets expressing
enthusiasm for national supremacy and military glory. *Chau-
vinism* therefore means exaggerated patriotism; a person holding such views is called a chauvinist.

*Chauvinist* is sometimes equated with *jingoist,* a word with
an interesting history of its own. *By jingo* was originally a
conjurer's expression which was taken over in popular English
speech to show strong affirmation. It became famous through
its use in a music-hall song of 1878, the year in which Disraeli,
the British prime minister, sent a fleet into Turkish waters to
hold back the Russians. Disraeli's strong nationalistic policy of
"brinkmanship" was supported in these lines of a song of the
day:

> We don't want to fight, but by jingo, if
>     we do,
> We've got the ships, we've got the men,
>     we've got the money too.

A jingoist is an arrogant nationalist, a supporter of a
belligerent policy against other nations, a "war hawk," a term
that has recently been revived. "War hawk" was first used—
about 1812—against a group of Congressmen who clamored
for war against England in order to annex Canada.

*Jingoism* is the noun for what the jingoist advocates.

> To be sure, when nationalism de-
> generates into jingoism it becomes a dan-
> ger to the peace of the world and must
> be resisted.

**gargantuan**

> There are those who say musicals
> should stop becoming so gargantuan;
> that it's absurd to spend $600,000 for a
> musical; that musicals are becoming too
> overblown, too ponderous, too expensive.

Gargantua, the eponymous hero of the novel *Gargantua*
(1535) by François Rabelais, is a gigantic, loudmouthed king,
with an appetite to match his size. Anything on an extremely
large scale or of tremendous proportions may therefore be
termed *gargantuan*.

**Synonyms:** huge; colossal; brobdi(n)gnagian.

This last word designates the inhabitants of Brobdingnag, an
imaginary country inhabited by giants in Dean Jonathan Swift's
*Gulliver's Travels*, who were as "tall as church steeples." Its
opposite is *lilliputian*, after the inhabitants of Lilliput, another
imaginary country in the same book; these people were only
about six inches tall—or short.

Gargantua had a son named Pantagruel, to whom Rabelais
devoted another novel. Pantagruel was coarsely humorous; the
word *pantagruelism* refers to coarse, satirical humor.

**malapropism**

> I would by no means wish a daughter
> of mine to be a progeny of learning.
>
> RICHARD BRINSLEY SHERIDAN, *The Rivals*

Audiences still laugh at the mishandling of words by Mrs.
Malaprop in *The Rivals*, just as did playgoers of the 1770's,
when the play was first produced. From her name, we get the
word *malapropism*, which describes what countless comedians
may do to get a laugh. A malapropism is a blundering use of a
word that sounds like the one intended; in general it is con-
trived for humorous effect, but often it is made unintentionally,
as when somebody says that she is throwing things down the
insinuator. The name of Mrs. Malaprop comes from the
French *mal à propos*, not apropos, inappropriate.

**panjandrum**

> So she went into the garden to cut a
> cabbage leaf to make an appie pie, and
> at the same time a great she-bear came

> running up the street and popped its head
> into the shop. "What! no soap?" So he
> died, and she—very imprudently—mar-
> ried the barber. And there were present
> the Joblillies, the Garyulies, and the
> Grand Panjandrum himself.

This bit of nonsense was written by the eighteenth-century actor and playwright Samuel Foote to test the vaunted memory of the actor Charles Macklin. The latter refused the challenge! The incident and text might have been forgotten except for the fact that from it has been extracted a lasting and sturdy word —*panjandrum*, which was coined from the Greek *pan*, all, and a mock Latin ending. *Panjandrum*, with or without *grand*, refers mockingly and humorously to an exalted or powerful person or a pretentious official. Sometimes its force is weakened so that a panjandrum means "a high priest," a leading figure, an authority, as in the reference to Fowler under *solecism* in Section II of this chapter.

### pecksniffery, pecksniffian

> Among the words outlawed in Parlia-
> mentary talk are blackguard, cad, gross
> calumny, hypocrite, Pecksniffian cant,
> Pharisees, slanderer, vicious and vulgar,
> villains. . . .

These are only a few of the terms not to be used in the House of Commons of the British Parliament by any member to refer to other members. From the company in which *Pecksniffian* finds itself in the incomplete listing above, it is obvious that it is not a complimentary term. The word *Pecksniffian* (the noun is *Pecksniffery*) comes from *Seth Pecksniff*, the name of a character in *Martin Chuzzlewit* (1843–1844) by Charles Dickens. Pecksniff is a hypocrite who conceals his selfishness behind a display of feigned benevolence.

**Synonyms:** hypocritical; pharisaical; pietistic; sanctimonious.

### quixotic

> Quixotic is his enterprise, and hopeless his
>     adventure is,
> Who seeks for jocularities that haven't
>     yet been said.
>
>            W. S. GILBERT, *His Excellency*

The word *quixotic* comes from the name of the eponymous hero of Cervantes' immortal satire (1605–1615) of a once-flowering knighthood that was going to seed. Don Quixote de la Mancha was a would-be knight who believed that it was his mission to correct the wrongs of the world and whose excited imagination led him to turn lonely inns into castles and windmills into fearsome giants. One who entertains idealistic, romantic, impractical and unattainable notions is called quixotic. His quixotism impels him to "tilt at windmills," to fight imaginary enemies.

**Synonyms:** chimerical; fanciful; fantastic; visionary.

*Utopian* and *utopianism*, also words from literature, are almost synonymous with *quixotic* and *quixotism*. They come from the title of the book on an ideal state written by Sir Thomas More in 1516. Book and place are both called *Utopia*, meaning "No Place," from Greek *ou*, not, and *topos*, place, as in *topic* and *topography*. As the title indicates, this state can be found nowhere; it is an impracticable and unfeasible ideal.

**robot**

> The errant behavior of the robots at inauguration headquarters has made this long holiday weekend a weekend of work for the humans there.

In 1923 the Czech playwright Karel Čapek wrote a celebrated and terrifying play, *R. U. R.* ("Rossum's Universal Robots"); *robot* is from the Czech word *robota*, work. In this play the robots ("workers") are mechanical monsters in human form who turn upon their masters; in the excerpt above they are computers, which in this case, went astray and duplicated invitations. In this age of automation, the prophecy of *R. U. R.* has come true in part! The word *robot* is often applied, in reverse, to human beings who have become automatons, mechanical men who have lost their souls.

**rodomontade**

> These assertions are not the rodomontade of a crackpot.

Rodomonte, a Saracen king in Ludovico Ariosto's epic, *Orlando Furioso* (1515–1533), is brave but exceedingly boast-

ful. From his name comes the word *rodomontade*, used both as
an adjective and a noun.

**Synonyms:** boasting; blustering; bragging; braggadocio.

This last synonym is also from a literary source, Spenser's
*Faërie Queene* (1590–1611), in which it is the name of a
character. Still another boaster in literature is Thraso, in a
play by Terence, the Roman writer of comedies. From his
name is derived the word *thrasonical*, which is used by Rosa-
lind in Shakespeare's *As You Like It:* Caesar's thrasonical brag
of "I came, I saw, I overcame" (*Veni, vidi, vici*).

## yahoo

> There is a good deal of the yahoo in
> every gang of adolescents that goes ber-
> serk, whatever their color.

In Dean Swift's *Gulliver's Travels* (1726), the Yahoos are
a tribe of brutes having human form and embodying all the
vices of mankind. A yahoo is consequently a lout, a ruffian, or
a rowdy.

## A Brief Appendix

Here is an additional list with brief identifications:

**babbitt**      a worshiper of material success; a despiser of
intellectual values—from the name of the leading character in
Sinclair Lewis's *Babbitt* (1922).

**bumbledom**      actions and mannerisms of petty officials—
from the name of the beadle (Mr. Bumble) in Charles Dickens's *Oliver Twist* (1838).

**micawberism**      a habitually optimistic point of view—
from the name of Wilkins Micawber, an optimistic, shiftless,
but likable character in Dickens's *David Copperfield* (1849–
1850).

**panglossian**      very optimistic—from the name of Dr.
Pangloss in Voltaire's *Candide* (1759), who believed that "all
is for the best in this best of all possible worlds."

**Pickwickian**      taken in a special sense to suit the occasion
—from the name of the leading character in Dickens's *Pick-
wick Papers* (1836–1837).

**poo(h)-bah**      a pretentious official; a person holding many
offices at the same time—from the name of the official in the
Gilbert and Sullivan operetta *The Mikado* (1885) who as-

sumed virtually every office in the town of Titipu, and called himself "The Lord-High-Everything-Else."

**scrooge**    a mean, miserly person—from the name of the miser in Charles Dickens's *Christmas Carol* (1843).

**simon-pure**    genuine; unadulterated—from the phrase "the real Simon-pure," referring to a character impersonated by another in the play *A Bold Stroke for a Wife* (1718) by Susanna Centlivre.

**tartuffery, tartuffism**    hypocrisy; sanctimoniousness—from the character with these qualities in Molière's *Tartuffe* (1669).

## Good Words from The Good Book

Many biblical references have become part of our everyday speech, like *babel* for a din, a confusion of sounds, *Eden* for a paradise, *Goliath* for a giant, *Methusaleh* for an old man, and *Samson* for a strong man. Here are some others, not so obvious, together with the text that is the source of the word.

### Armageddon

> And he gathered them together into a place called in the Hebrew tongue Armageddon. . . .
> And there were voices, and thunders, and lightnings; and there was a great earthquake, such as was not since men were upon the earth, so mighty an earthquake, and so great.
>
> REVELATION 16:16, 18

The forces of good and evil are ultimately to meet at Armageddon to fight the last decisive battle. The term is symbolic of a battle or war marked by overwhelming slaughter and destruction making further combat impossible. The term is often applied to the vision of an all-out nuclear war, as in the phrase *an atomic Armageddon.*

### behemoth

> Behold now behemoth, which I made with thee; he eateth grass as an ox. . . .
> Behold, he drinketh up a river and hasteth not: he trusteth that he can draw up Jordan into his mouth.
>
> JOB 40:15, 23

Some authorities think that the hippopotamus is meant by this colossal creature; at any rate *behemoth* is used to denote a large massive animal, the size of a mammoth or mastodon. Figuratively, the term is used to describe anything huge:

> Some of us who have never heard Koussevitzky play the bass fiddle could never guess from his conducting alone that he was an incomparable artist on this behemoth of instruments.

## Gadarene

> So the devils besought him, saying, If thou cast us out, suffer us to go away into the herd of swine.
> And he said unto them, Go. And when they were come out, they went into the herd of swine: and behold, the whole swine ran violently down a steep place into the sea, and perished in the waters.

> MATTHEW 8:31, 32

At Gadara, near the sea of Galilee, Jesus drove out the devils that had entered two men. The demons then entered into the swine, which rushed headlong into the waters. Hence, *gadarene* means rushing into headlong, or precipitate, flight; usually the word is met in the phrase *Gadarene swine* to characterize persons carried along and swept up by a mass movement, as in this excerpt from a review by Alan Pryce-Jones of *The Men Who Tried to Kill Hitler* by Roger Manvell and Heinrich Fraenkel:

> Already it seems impossible that someone so uncommonly like an *ersatz* Chaplin could have come so near to treating the populations of an entire continent like the Gadarene swine of the Bible.

## jeremiad

> How doth the city sit solitary, that was full of people! hcw is she become as a widow! she that was great among the nations, and princess among the provinces, how is she become tributary.

> LAMENTATIONS OF JEREMIAH 1:1

So begins the book of the Lamentations of Jeremiah, the prophet who wept for Jerusalem and Zion. The book of Jeremiah, especially Chapter 9, contains similar lamentations. Hence, a jeremiad is a sorrowful tirade, a continued lament, and often a bitter denunciation and complaint.

> A stimulating discussion of all that troubles us is presented in Edgar Ansel Mowrer's book, "An End to Make-Believe." It is a controversial jeremiad from start to finish.

## leviathan

> In that day the Lord with his sore and great and strong sword shall punish leviathan the piercing servant, even leviathan that crooked servant.
>
> ISAIAH 27:1

Leviathan is a monstrous beast referred to many times in the Bible, often as a symbol of evil. In modern usage a leviathan is anything monstrous, the largest and most immense thing of its kind. Thomas Hobbes used this concept in *The Leviathan* (1651), which refers to the state, so that the term *leviathan state* denotes an all-powerful, bureaucratic, and oppressive state.

## mammon

> No man can serve two masters. . . .
> Ye cannot serve God and mammon.
>
> MATTHEW 6:24

*Mammon* goes back via Latin and Greek to an Aramaic word for riches. As used in the New Testament, it conveys the idea that too much value is attached to material wealth as against spiritual concern. Its general meaning is simply material possessions or a greed for them; personified, *Mammon* means the evil demon of covetousness.

## maudlin

> There were also women looking on afar off; among them was Mary Magdalene. . . .
>
> MARK 15:40

Mary of Magdala, known as Maria Magdalena in ecclesiastical Latin, was one of the mourners at the sepulchre of Christ. *Maudlin* is the vernacular form of *Magdalena* through Middle English *Maudeleyn* and old French *Madelaine*. The names of *Magdalene* College at Cambridge and of *Magdalen* at Oxford are pronounced as if written *maudlin*.

Because medieval and later painters depicted Mary Magdalene as weeping, the word *maudlin* came to mean tearfully sentimental.

**Synonyms:** mawkish; oversentimental; weakly emotional.

### Pharisee, pharisaic(al)

> Woe unto you, scribes and Pharisees, hypocrites! for ye are like unto whited sepulchres, which indeed appear beautiful outward, but are within full of dead men's bones, and of all uncleanness.
>
> MATTHEW 23:27

The Pharisees were a sect (the name comes from a Hebrew word meaning apart) that was extremely devout and scrupulously exact in their religious observances. They were accused of adhering to the letter rather than to the spirit of the law. In modern usage, *pharisaical* describes persons of rigid adherence to the outward forms and rituals rather than to the true spirit. Incidentally, *Pharisees* is one of the terms, like *Pecksniffian* mentioned earlier, which are forbidden on the floor of the British House of Commons.

**Synonyms** of *pharisaical:* censorious; formal; rigid; sanctimonious; self-righteous.

### Philistine

> Then the lord of the Philistines gathered them together for to offer a great sacrifice unto Dagon their god, and to rejoice: for they said, Our god hath delivered Samson our enemy into our hand.
>
> JUDGES 16:23

The Philistines, so well-known not only from the story of Samson but also from that of David and Goliath, engaged in many wars with the Hebrews. Since they were an alien, non-Semitic people, and worshiped strange gods, their name became a term for a foreigner. Centuries later, German university students called a person who was not educated and who preferred material gains to intellectual pursuits a *Philister*, "Philistine," which was picked up in that sense by English writers. Its vogue is due in great measure to Thomas Carlyle and especially to Matthew Arnold, who wrote in *Culture and Anarchy* (1869):

> The people who believe most that our greatness and welfare are proved by our being very rich, and who most give up their lives and thoughts to becoming rich are just the very people we call the Philistines.

A Philistine is one who looks down upon intellectual and cultural activities:

> Those who fear we have become a nation of Philistines, so lost in material pursuits that we trample on culture, may take some comfort from the report of the book publishing industry that this will be their biggest year.

When a writer or an artist accuses his critics of being Philistines, he implies that the critics lack aesthetic sense, knowledge, appreciation, and sensitivity.

## I.  WORDS IN CONTEXT

Select the word or phrase that is closest in meaning to that of the italicized word in the passage.

1. The speech writer behind the *arras* has become an essential functionary in politics and government during the past thirty years.
    (a) throne (b) curtain (c) desk (d) façade

2. We have learned, painfully, that a city needs buildings of a human scale along with new *behemoths*.
    (a) tunnels (b) means of transportation (c) waterfront improvements (d) gigantic structures

3. The method he chooses is *draconian*—self-sacrificial, indeed —and so utterly obvious and romantic it amounts to a big, fat cliché.
    (a) unselfish (b) superficial (c) drastic (d) visionary

4. He attracted attention with his ostentatious display of diamonds, his *gargantuan* appetite, and his lavish spending.
    (a) tremendous (b) delicate (c) epicurean (d) fastidious

5. Ocean tides and weather cause a ship to *meander* during a voyage.
    (a) accelerate (b) pitch and roll (c) slow down (d) drift

6. But in truth *serendipity* is rare in the stock market, and selectivity always has been one of the important secrets of success.
    (a) lucky find (b) avoidable risk (c) infallibility
        (d) absolute patience

## II.  MATCHING

Match each word on the left with the word on the right that is closest in meaning.

| | | |
|---|---|---|
| 1. bumbledom | a. | grammatical error |
| 2. chauvinistic | b. | mawkish |
| 3. forensic | c. | hypocrisy |
| 4. laconic | d. | sumptuous |
| 5. Lucullan | e. | intensely optimistic about the world |
| 6. maudlin | f. | pertaining to public debate |
| 7. panglossian | g. | miser |
| 8. scrooge | h. | pompous official actions |
| 9. solecism | i. | rabidly patriotic |
| 10. tartuffism | j. | terse |

## III.  MULTIPLE CHOICE

In each group select the word that is a synonym of the italicized word.

1. *bowdlerized* text        (a) enlarged (b) annotated (c) vulgarized (d) expurgated

2. improvised *malapropism*        (a) scheme (b) remedy (c) misuse of words (d) mischief

3. *mesmerized* audience        (a) bored (b) entranced (c) elite (d) apathetic

4. *quixotic* behavior        (a) foolishly impractical (b) completely charming (c) utterly devoted (d) insufferably boring

5. *sadistic* tendencies        (a) very arrogant (b) hypocritical (c) pessimistic (d) extremely cruel

6. worshiping *mammon*        (a) romance (b) wealth (c) food (d) idealism

## IV.  ELIMINATE THE IMPOSTOR

Three of the words in each group are related in meaning; select the remaining word that is unrelated to the others.

1. (a) robot (b) magnate (c) machine (d) automaton
2. (a) boastful (b) rodomontade (c) thrasonical (d) billingsgate
3. (a) lament (b) scurrility (c) denunciatory complaint (d) jeremiad
4. (a) babbitt (b) bourgeois (c) pinchbeck (d) philistine
5. (a) sanctimonious (b) self-righteous (c) pharisaical (d) conciliatory
6. (a) simon-pure (b) visionary (c) chimerical (d) utopian
7. (a) panjandrum (b) brobdingnagian (c) poo-bah (d) high muck-a-muck
8. (a) stoicism (b) fortitude (c) empiricism (d) stolidity
9. (a) pasquinade (b) pastiche (c) lampoon (d) squib
10. (a) sentimental (b) luxurious (c) epicurean (d) sybaritic

## V.  SYNONYM WORD GAME

To the right of each numbered word or phrase there is a letter followed by blanks. Each blank represents a letter. Using the first letter given, complete the word which is a synonym of the word or phrase on the left. The completed word has been taken up in this chapter.

EXAMPLE:  a ruffian   y _ _ _ _        ANSWER: yahoo

1. final conflict            A _ _ _ _ _ _ _ _ _
2. soothing medicine         p _ _ _ _ _ _ _ _
3. war hawk                  j _ _ _ _ _ _ _
4. eulogy                    p _ _ _ _ _ _ _ _
5. sanctimoniousness         P _ _ _ _ _ _ _ _ _ _

## DO-IT-YOURSELF DEPARTMENT

### Twenty Questions

In each of the following questions there is an italicized word formed from a name. Look up the origin of those words you do not know offhand. In addition to a good dictionary a student of words should have at hand such valuable reference works as a Bible dictionary, a dictionary of word origins, and a literary handbook. Answers to these are not given in this book.

1. How did a noisy, confused situation come to be called *bedlam?*

2. Why do we give the name *blarney* to smooth, coaxing talk?

3. Why is empty, insincere talk called *buncombe*, or *bunkum?*

4. How did a battle in which one side envelops and virtually destroys the other come to be called a *Cannae?*

5. To what historical event does a *Canossa* as a symbol of abject humiliation refer?

6. Why is a shrewd trader sometimes called a *David Harum?*

7. Why is a rough, rowdy fight called a *Donnybrook?*

8. Why is a chivalrous person renowned for the nobility and purity of his life sometimes called a *Galahad?*

9. How did *galvanize* come to mean arouse, stimulate?

10. How did *hackneyed* get the meaning of commonplace through overuse?

11. Why is a patron of the arts often called a *Mæcenas?*

12. Why is a large and stately tomb called a *mausoleum?*

13. What is the difference between a book bound in Morocco and one bound in *morocco?* When can they be the same?

14. Why is a persistently optimistic person called a *Pollyanna?*

15. What kind of test is a *Rorschach?*

16. Why are legislators often called *solons?*

17. Why is a person who stumblingly says, "I'll sew you to a sheet," when he means "I'll show you to a seat," said to be guilty of committing a *spoonerism?*

18. What is the origin of the word *thespian*, an overworked term for an actor?

19. Why is a certain shade of reddish yellow or auburn called *titian?*

20. Why are destructive acts called *vandalism?*

## Words from Names of Persons

Give the meaning and origin of the following words or names used as words (no answers given for such exercises):

| | | |
|---|---|---|
| boycott | Dr. Jekyll and Mr. Hyde | simony |
| daguerreotype | Lothario | solander |
| damask | Malthusian | Svengali |
| euphuism | namby-pamby | Tommy Atkins |
| Frank Merriwell | neanderthalic | Trimalchio |
| gasconade | silhouette | Walter Mitty |

## Names in Phrases

Do the same for the following:

| | |
|---|---|
| Aesopian language | cutting the Gordian knot |
| like Caesar's wife | What will Mrs. Grundy say? |
| King Charles's head | Hobson's choice |
| rich as Croesus | Homeric laughter |
| sword of Damocles | crossing the Rubicon |
| Frankenstein('s) monster | 'twixt Tweedledum and Tweedledee |

## From the Bible

Give the meaning and origin of the following:

| | |
|---|---|
| Ananias | walls of Jericho |
| Belshazzar's feast | Jezebel |
| from Dan to Beersheba | Job's comforter(s) |
| a Daniel come to judgment | Laodicean |
| Four Horsemen of the Apocalypse | Lazarus |
| Gideon's army | Macedonian cry |
| Golgotha | nimrod |
| Jacob's ladder | jesting Pilate |
| jehu | Sodom and Gomorrah |

## Bible Supplement

The following do not come from names but we have entered them because they are used so often. What do they mean, and what is the story behind each one?

| | |
|---|---|
| handwriting on the wall | mess of pottage |
| manna from heaven | scapegoat |

## Finale

Here is an additional miscellany for those of you who wish to do further research in the interesting field of name-words. Once again, look for the meaning and origin.

| | | |
|---|---|---|
| argosy | Jimmy Valentine | Rip van Winkle |
| benedict | laws of the Medes and | Robin Hood |
| brummagem | the Persians | romance |
| Damon and Pythias | mansard (roof) | Ruritania |
| Enoch Arden | Mr. Chips | shanghai |
| Falstaffian | nankeen | Shangri-La |
| Girl Friday | Nostradamus | Simon Legree |
| Graustarkian | Portia | slough of despond |
| hawkshaw | Raffles | Socratic method |

# 15. Discovering the Old, Inventing the New

> *Philologists who chase*
> *A panting syllable through time and space,*
> *Start it at home, and hunt it in the dark*
> *To Gaul, to Greece, and into Noah's ark.*
>
> WILLIAM COWPER, "Retirement"

Words come to us from out of the past, sometimes encrusted with a bright patina, sometimes eroded by time and use. Often the original meaning has been obscured and is brought to light only after we scrape off the corrosion of the ages and go back to the time when the word acquired its meaning.

Such a journey into the past may give us interesting glimpses into other times, other customs, send us back to the pages of history or the Bible, tell us how ancient peoples thought or felt.

Before we dip into the past, here is a pretest of words that have stories to tell. As you have done in the past, match the words in the two columns.

1. auspicious        a. banish from society
2. cynosure          b. speech of denunciation
3. dirge             c. criterion
4. gamut             d. favorable
5. immolate          e. range or scope
6. ostracize         f. song of grief
7. philippic         g. heading or motto
8. rubric            h. kill as a sacrifice
9. sycophant         i. center of attraction
10. touchstone       j. servile flatterer

## WE DIP INTO THE PAST

If we turn to the word *shibboleth* in a dictionary, we discover that it comes from a Hebrew word meaning either an ear of corn or a stream. How then has *shibboleth* come to mean a password and, as most often used today, a catchword, or slogan?

If we turn to Judges 12:5, 6 in the Old Testament, and read the account of the defeat of the Ephraimites by the Gileadites, we find an answer.

> And the Gileadites took the passages of Jordan before the Ephraimites: and it was so, that when those Ephraimites which were escaped said, Let me go over; that the men of Gilead said unto him, Art thou an Ephraimite? If he said, Nay;
> Then said they unto him, Say now Shibboleth; and he said Sibboleth: for he could not frame to pronounce it right. Then they took him, and slew him at the passages of Jordan and there fell at that time of the Ephraimites forty and two thousand.

*Shibboleth* was the test word chosen to separate friend from foe. Unable to pronounce the sound *sh,* the Ephraimites failed the test and were slain.

Thousands of years later, on the peninsula at Bataan in the Philippines, history repeated itself. The Japanese were successfully infiltrating our lines by learning the password of the day and posing as friendly Filipinos.

An American officer, remembering that the Japanese are notoriously unable to pronounce the letter *l* (the closest they get to *hotel* is *hoteru* and to *slogan, surogan*), hit on the device of using only passwords that had *l*'s in them. On January 20, 1942, *lallapaloosa* was used as the password and sentries were ordered to fire upon anyone who could not say the word. The closest the Japanese got to our lines was "rarraparoosa."

Such tests based on differences of language and speech are true shibboleths, but today the word *shibboleth* has many extended meanings. It may mean a repeated saying (platitude, cliché), a word or phrase used by adherents of a party or sect (catchword, slogan). All these various meanings are aptly illustrated in the following:

> What the world needs today are not the shibboleths of democracy but its dynamic practice.

*Ostracize*, the dictionary tells us, comes from a Greek word *ostrakon*, a shell, a broken piece of pottery. How did a word that means a fragment of pottery give us a word that means to banish from one's society? We find part of the answer in Plutarch's "Life of Aristides." There we read:

> The method of procedure—to give a general outline—was as follows. Each voter took an ostrakon, or potsherd, wrote on it the name of that citizen he wished to remove from the city, and brought it to a place in the agora [marketplace] which was all fenced about with railings. The archons [chief magistrates] first counted the total number of *ostraka* cast. For if the voters were less than 6,000 the ostracism was void. Then they separated the names, and the man who had received the most votes they proclaimed banished for ten years with the right to enjoy the income from his property.

Because the Athenians wrote the name of a citizen they wished to banish on a shell or on a potsherd (*sherd* or *shard*, a piece of broken pottery), we have the words *ostracize* and *ostracism*. Today, however, ostracism is a social rather than a political act. When we ostracize somebody, we avoid his company or bar him from our society. The instrument or method implicit in the root is no longer used, but the purpose and result are the same.

The name Philip means "a lover of horses" (*phil*, love + *hippos*, horse). How did a name with love in it come to give us a word which means so violent a denunciation that a *philippic* is hurled rather than uttered?

Again we look to history for the answer. In the fourth century B.C., in a series of celebrated speeches, Demosthenes of Athens, the greatest orator of ancient times, thundered against King Philip of Macedon, who was bent on conquering all of

Greece. His fiery invectives were called *Philippics;* later, Cicero, the Roman counterpart of Demosthenes, gave the name *Philippics* to a set of speeches he delivered or wrote against a man named not Philip, but Mark Antony. Hence, any speech of denunciation may be termed a *philippic,* no matter who is on the receiving end.

The word has some interesting synonyms: *tirade* (which comes from a French word meaning to shoot), *invective,* which will be dealt with later in this chapter, *excoriation,* literally "ripping the hide off," and *vituperation,* literally "act of finding fault," from *vitium,* fault, and *parare,* to prepare.

## SOME MORE QUESTIONS—AND ANSWERS

How does a word like *sycophant,* which breaks up into Greek *syco,* fig, and *phant,* show or reveal, come to mean a fawning self-seeker? In ancient Athens informers were called *sycophantes.* Many explanations, ancient and modern, have been given for the use of the word in this sense. Here is what Plutarch says on the subject in his "Life of Solon":

> One cannot, therefore, wholly disbe-
> lieve those who say that the exportation
> of figs also was anciently forbidden, and
> that the one who *showed* up, or pointed
> out, such exporters was called a "syco-
> phant," or *fig-shower.*

Originally meaning an informer or defamer, *sycophant* took on the meanings of servile self-seeker, base flatterer. Nouns for the action of a sycophant are *sycophantism* and *sycophancy:* the adjective is *sycophantic.*

A toady is perhaps a more repulsive kind of sycophant—a cringing, servile menial, a parasite and hanger-on. He fawns upon those above him, shows obsequious deference to the rich and powerful in the hope of furthering his self-interest.

If you think the word *toady* comes from the word *toad,* you are right. Actually, *toady* is short for *toad-eater.* For the origin of these words we must go back to the fairs of long ago to which quacks came to sell their remedies. To build up interest and to increase sales, the quack, or charlatan, employed a young attendant who would pretend to eat toads, which were then considered poisonous. Soon, the lad, who would be called a "shill" today, writhed as if in pain. Thereupon, the master would try out his bottle of medicine on his "toad-eater," or "toady." The remedy, of course, worked like magic, and the toady was soon smiling gratefully. Anyone performing such service work for a superior (toadying to him) came to be called a toady.

Because the quacks and salesmen often displayed their wares and gave their sales talks from a platform, they were called *mountebanks*, from the Italian phrase *montare in banco*, "to get up on a bench." Today we apply the term *mountebank* to a buffoon or to a person who uses cheap tricks to gain attention or sell his wares—a quack, a pitchman, a charlatan.

*Truckle* is another interesting word applied to a toady. A toady defers obsequiously, or truckles, to the person he is subserviently flattering. A truckle, or trundle, bed is a smaller bed that is put under a bed of standard size and that can be rolled out. The picture then is, whether figurative or actual, one in which the toady sleeps on the bed beneath the master's bed. He is truly subservient (*sub*, under, beneath)!

## FOR BIRD WATCHERS AND DOG FANCIERS

### auspicious

> The Celtics, having won a dozen games in a row, have made an auspicious start toward winning, as usual, the Eastern Division crown [1964–65].

In ancient Rome certain priests called augurs were delegated to interpret omens, especially through watching the flight of birds. If the signs appeared favorable to them, public business could begin, or be inaugurated. *Auspices*, *auspicious*, and its opposite, *inauspicious*, are derived from Latin *avis*, a bird, and the root *spic*, look. Taking the auspices was, one might say, a form of bird-watching. *Auspices* means signs or portents looking to the future; the expression *under the auspices of* means under the guidance or sponsorship of.

From *augur*, which may have the same root as the word *author*, comes, in addition to *inaugurate*, the word *augury*, omen. Used as a verb, *augur* means to foretell, presage, betoken. *To augur well* means to be of good omen, to have favorable prospects.

**cynic, cynical, cynicism**

> Launched amid the derision of those who characteristically turn a cynical eye on any effort suggesting man has a higher as well as a baser nature, the Peace Corps has become an accepted instrument of national defense.

A certain school of Greek philosophers taught the principles of self-control and independence. Some of their disciples mistrusted humanity and assigned only selfish motives to man's actions. Diogenes, the man who with a lantern in broad daylight went searching for an honest man or, more cynically, for *a man,* is cited as the classic example. The founder of the school of Cynics taught at Kynosarges; playing on the first part of his name, which is similar to the Greek word for dog, and disliking the snarling manner some members of the sect used, the Athenians referred to them as Cynics.

> Cynics have suggested that commencement speakers tend to make daring appeals, largely because they feel that nobody is listening.

*Cynicism* indicates distrust and disbelief in man's sincerity, and questions human values. The adjective *cynical* has many interesting synonyms, some strong, some weak: captious, carping, caviling, censorious, misanthropic, pessimistic, sarcastic.

**cynosure**

> Where perhaps some beauty lies,
> The cynosure of neighboring eyes.
>
> JOHN MILTON, *L'Allegro*

*Cynosure* is another "dog" word, being derived from the Greek word for a dog's tail. One of the ancient names of the constellation Ursa Minor, the Little Bear, or the Little Dipper, was *Kynosoura,* Greek, or *Cynosura,* Latinized form. Since this constellation contains Polaris, the North Star, the eyes of mariners were naturally directed to it. Hence, *cynosure,* from the ancient name of the constellation, means something that attracts, a center of attention.

## RELIGIOUS DEVOTIONS

**dirge**

> Thus, like a dying swan, to a sad tune,
> I sing my own dirge.
>
> PHILIP MASSINGER, "Emperor of the East"

*Dirge,* a funeral song, is a contraction of *dirige,* the second singular imperative of the verb *dirigere,* to direct, to guide, with which a chant in the Latin funeral service opens:

> *Dirige, Domine, Deus meus, in conspectu tuo viam.*
> ("O Lord, my God, direct my way in thy sight.")

The Latin text is based on Psalms 5:8, ". . . make Thy way straight before my face."

By extension *dirge* means any mournful music, any literary composition expressing sorrow.

**gamut**

> When asked to name some of his prominent customers, he replied that the gamut ran from George Abbott, the director, to Darryl Zanuck, the Green producer.

The monks illuminated manuscripts not only of sacred books and secular literature but also of musical compositions used in the church services, such as masses and hymns. Guido d'Arezzo, a Benedictine monk of the eleventh century, a teacher of singing, invented a Great Scale which is the basis of our modern musical notation. He used letters to indicate the notes, and corresponding to each letter he used a syllable which can be sung, since it is impossible to sing single consonants. He started his scale with the Greek letter *Gamma,* which is G, and called his corresponding note Ut.

Guido d'Arezzo took the syllables *ut, re, mi, fa, sol, la* from a hymn to St. John the Baptist:

> UT queant laxis REsonare fibris
> MIra gestorum FAmuli tuorum
> SOLve pollutis LAbiis reatum
> Sancte Johannes (Iohannes).

("That thy servants may sing out thy wondrous acts strongly and freely, remove the guilt from their polluted lips, St. John.")

Later *ut* was changed to *do,* which is easier to sing since it ends in a vowel, and *si* was added, probably from the initial letters of *Sancte Johannes* (St. John).

The entire scale was known as the *gamma-ut* or *gamut* from the first note and its equivalent syllable, just as *alphabet* is derived from the first two Greek letters, *alpha* and *beta.* *Gamut,* the complete scale of notes, is applied to fields other than music and means the entire range or compass of any activity.

### immolation

> Thich Quang Duc was a Buddhist priest who immolated himself publicly in protest against the Government's religious policies.

*Immolate* and *immolation* come from the Latin word *mola,* a millstone; *molars,* the name of the grinding teeth, is derived from the same word. The Latin word *mola* came to mean the thing ground, a kind of grain or meal. In accordance with prescribed ritual, Roman priests sprinkled this finely ground grain, with a portion of salt added, over a sacrificial animal's head. By another transfer of meaning, the word *immolatio,* literally "the act of spreading the ground grain," was applied to the sacrifice itself. Its English derivative, *immolation,* meaning a sacrifice, has appeared in print many times to describe the self-sacrifice of Buddhist monks and nuns in South Vietnam.

### rubric

> The play adverts to a large assortment of Big Themes that belong properly under the general rubric of Playing the Game. Religion, hunger, work, love, the ladder of success, death, the Negro, and rebellion are among the major topics touched upon.

Before the invention of printing, the monks who copied by hand the works of ancient authors or set down the services and holy books of the Church adorned their own manuscripts with beautiful decorations. Following the practice of the Roman scribes, the monks used red ink for headings and parts of chapters. Such a special heading or initial letter in red was called a rubric, from *ruber,* Latin for red. Since the heading often gave instructions, the word *rubric* came to mean an ecclesiastical canon, a directive or rule of conduct, as well as a heading.

The meaning of the word has been extended still further so that we meet it today in the sense of a special motto, a pet phrase, a category, classification, settled custom, and even a shibboleth.

The history of the word *rubric,* which began as a simple name for a red letter, illustrates how a word takes on new meanings through the centuries while the original idea behind the word, in this case that of redness, is practically forgotten.

## TWO ODD ONES

**lampoon**

> The late-night satirical program, which created a sensation last year lampooning sacred institutions, nevertheless received scores of complaints.

The origin of this word is attributed to French slang of the seventeenth century. It is presumed to come from *lampons* ("Let us drink"), with which satirical poems and songs of that period often ended. A lampoon may be either a light, mocking satire or a bitter, scurrilous one. The verb lampoon means to ridicule or satirize. An interesting synonym is *pasquinade,* treated in the previous chapter.

**touchstone**

> Calamity is man's true touchstone.
>
> BEAUMONT and FLETCHER, *The Triumph of Honor*

The touchstone was a black stone related to flint, with which the purity of gold and silver was tested by the streak left when the stone was rubbed over the metals. Hence, a touchstone is a test or criterion by which the genuineness of anything is measured. A more modern method, in which nitric acid is used to test the gold content, is called the acid test. This phrase denotes a severe or crucial test of authenticity, effectiveness, and value.

## FINAL WORDS

**vernacular**    The word that begins this closing section not only contains a story but also, quite appropriately, has to do with words. *Vernacular* is derived from *verna*, a Latin word meaning a homeborn slave, one born in the master's house. In the English word, the idea of slave has been lost, but the idea of *homeborn* has been kept. *Vernacular* refers to a native, indigenous, domestic language. Thus, centuries ago, when the Romance languages were developing from Latin, *vernacular* designated French, Spanish, and Italian as contrasted with Latin which, though still used by learned groups, was being used less and less by the people.

Here are six more words dealing with language.

**argot**    a word of French origin meaning the slang of the underworld, a type of "occupational language."

**cant**    presumably from Latin verb *cantare*, to sing; "the same old song"; similar to *argot*, a kind of talk that is deliberately secret; any special language of a group. (See the discussion of *cant* in Chapter 10.)

**dialect**    language of a region having its own special words and grammatical usage; local language.

**jargon**    jumble or mixture of languages; gibberish; special vocabulary of a group.

**patois**    a French word meaning a provincial dialect but sometimes used in English to mean a language of a special group.

**gobbledegook, gobbledygook**    pretentious high-sounding language; unintelligible inflated language. In his column of May 26, 1965, James Reston of *The New York Times* cited the following as "one of the most remarkable examples of bureaucratic gobbledegook in recent history":

> It was that telegram which was emergent, which was what we call a critic telegram—that is, it's the fastest and most emergent kind we have. That is, [it was] that telegram that indicated that there was a most immediate problem on the scene.

## FOSSILIZED METAPHORS

There's another kind of word that needs no knowledge of historical events or ancient customs to reveal its meaning. All we need to do is to dig a little deeper to find imbedded in the word a revealing metaphor, a vivid comparison that sometimes shows startling parallels with our own picturesque language, whether colloquial or slang.

. Many English words were formed with elements that once presented such vivid comparisons. A metaphor, as we already know, is a figure of speech, or a trope, that conveys an implied comparison. Thus, figuratively, metaphorically, and trōpically, Hamlet speaks of the world as "an unweeded garden/That grows to seed."

The Latin word for seed is *semen*. From *semin*, its root, comes the word *disseminate*, literally "to scatter seed." In a phrase like "disseminating information," the idea of scattering seeds has been lost sight of but it becomes a more vivid expression to one who sees the word *seed* planted in it. The same figure is imbedded in *seminar* and *seminary*, where "the seeds of knowledge" are sown.

Such forgotten comparisons are called fossilized, or fossil, metaphors; they were once alive and though now extinct, they have left traces of their existence. The very term *fossilized metaphor* is in itself an example of what it names, for *fossil* comes from the Latin verb *fodere,* dig. You figuratively dig it up.

## SLANG AND OTHER PICTURESQUE METAPHORS

Gilbert K. Chesterton once wrote that "All slang is metaphor, and all metaphor is poetry." To a certain extent that is true. But there are two kinds of slang—good and bad. The bad becomes feverishly popular for a while and soon dies. "So's your old man" and "twenty-three skiddoo" had their brief run, but they were neither metaphorical nor poetic. Today they are museum pieces, tags to identify a bygone age. But the best slang lasts a long time because it has roots in the imagination and because it takes a vivid shortcut to our thoughts. Even our statesmen find it hard to get along without such colloquial or slang expressions as "going out on a limb," "left holding the bag," "throwing mud on," "passing the buck," "talking turkey," and "flash in the pan."

However, we are not going to deal here with slang as a special form of language. We are interested in the relationship between slang and metaphor only because it may give us insight into words. We will discover that some words that are completely dignified and respectable may, when dissected, reveal a picturesque metaphor, a striking image, or a literal interpretation which is akin to one of our own slang or colloquial expressions.

For example, a person who is easily annoyed or irritated may be said "to fly off the handle." This slang expression has its counterpart in the word *volatile*, from a Latin verb meaning to fly. A volatile situation is one that is explosive, one that may erupt and break loose, "fly out of control," so to speak.

"To tell the world" is a colloquialism. (See entry for colloquial(ism) on page 56). When information is divulged, the world is also told about it, for *divulge* is formed from the Latin word *vulgus*, people, the crowd. From *vulgus* comes the adverb *vulgo* (once used also as an English word), meaning before all the world, everywhere—exactly the idea contained in "to tell the world."

*Invective* is another metaphorical word dealing with speech and language. The basic element of this word comes from the Latin verb *vehere*, to carry, from which come the easy words *convey*, *vehicle*, and *vehicular*. In the passive, the Latin verb means to be transported, that is, to ride, to sail. Hence, the English verb *inveigh*, which comes from *vehere*, means "to sail into somebody." More elegantly, to *inveigh* means to rail against somebody, to complain bitterly; and *invective*, its noun, means violent abuse, vituperation, bitter denunciation, philippic.

So strong is an invective, that an orator thunders, or fulminates, when he delivers it. Here another metaphor comes into play, for *fulminate* comes from a Latin verb that means both to strike with lightning and to hurl a thunderbolt.

## CAN YOU DIG THESE?

We have done the preliminary digging for you, unearthing the Latin roots. We are giving you modern lively and picturesque expressions—metaphors, slang, colloquialisms, formal

English—that are related to the meanings of the roots. As lagniappe we've thrown in synonyms.

What you are asked to do is to give the dignified word, which, according to its parts, is a "translation" of the picturesque expression. Each bar stands for a letter.

The word ahead of Number 1 is given as an example.

| RELATED EXPRESSION | LATIN ROOT | SYNONYM | DIGNIFIED WORD |
|---|---|---|---|
| "play along with" | *lus*, play | fraudulent, secret agreement | collusion |
| 1. "like a dog wagging its tail" | *adulat*, wag the tail | effusive praise | ——————— |
| 2. "catch on" | *prehend*, grasp | understand | ——————— |
| 3. "cook up" | *coct*, cooked | put together | ——————— |
| 4. "wink at," "shut one's eyes to" | *niv*, blink | cooperate secretly | ——————— |
| 5. "take a cut" | *falc*, scythe | misappropriation | ——————— |
| 6. "off one's trolley" | *lira*, furrow | wildly excited | ——————— |
| 7. "ill-starred" | *astr*, star | calamitous | ——————— |
| 8. "sitting it out" | *sid*, sit | disagreeing | ——————— |
| 9. "cheek" | *front*, forehead | impudence | ——————— |
| 10. "double talk" | *aequ*, equal + *voc*, call | ambiguity | ——————— |
| 11. "piling it on" | *agger*, mound | overstatement | ——————— |
| 12. "strip the hide off" | *cori*, hide, leather | denounce strongly | ——————— |
| 13. "burnt up" | *cens*, set on fire | enraged | ——————— |
| 14. "moon-struck" | *luna*, moon | insane | ——————— |
| 15. "tied up in knots" | *plex*, entangled; intricate | puzzled | ——————— |
| 16. "straddle the fence"; "with a foot in both camps" | *varic*, straddle | equivocate, lie | ——————— |
| 17. "on the dot" | *punct*, point | prompt | ——————— |
| 18. "step into his shoes" | *plant*, sole of the foot | replace | ——————— |
| 19. "sing a different tune" | *cant*, sing | take back publicly | ——————— |
| 20. "a cover up" | *text*, covered | excuse | ——————— |

## INVENTING THE NEW

As new discoveries in science are made, as new inventions are created by the ingenuity of man, as new situations arise—man must find words to name them. Sometimes we take an old word and assign new duties to it (we have already mentioned *escalate* and *escalation*); sometimes we use Latin or Greek roots and create neologisms, new words (the word *telephone*, Greek *phone*, sound + *tele*, afar, obviously did not exist in Shakespeare's time); sometimes we telescope words, as we ourselves did, when we took *vocabulary* and *anagram* and coined the word *vocabagram;* sometimes we take the initial letters of a process described in several words and produce a word like *radar* (**r**adio **d**etecting **a**nd **r**anging).

## BLENDS, PORTMANTEAU WORDS

When in *Through the Looking-Glass* Lewis Carroll invented the word *chortle* by blending the sounds and meanings of *chuckle* and *snort*, he was not inventing a new process, for words like *splatter*, probably from *splash* and *spatter*, existed before his time. But he did give the name *portmanteau* to such formations, as can be seen from his explanation of *slithy:* "Well, 'slithy' means 'lithe and slimy.' . . . You see it's like a portmanteau—there are two meanings packed into one word."

Some of the words we have packed into a portmanteau (French word for traveling bag) are *brunch* (breakfast and lunch), *motel* (motor and hotel), and *smog* (smoke and fog).

## WORDS IN SCIENCE AND MEDICINE

As new discoveries are made, especially in science and medicine, new words are formed to give them a name. Latin and Greek elements are generally used, with the emphasis on Greek. Sometimes the two are mixed, giving what is called a hybrid, or a hybridized word, like *terramycin*, from Latin *terra*, earth, and Greek, *myke*. Incidentally, *mycology* is the study (*logy*) of fungi (*myco*), more popularly the study of mushrooms.

**cybernetics**

> Norbert Wiener was an exceptional hu-
> man being—he graduated from Tufts at
> 14 and was a Doctor of Philosophy at 19.
> And that is why he was a leader in as-
> similating man to the machine, in draw-
> ing, under the name of cybernetics,
> parallels between human thinking and
> mechanical methods of control and com-
> munication.

Dr. Norbert Wiener, who died in 1964, coined the word
*cybernetics\** from the Greek *kybernetes,* "helmsman, steers-
man"; it is cognate with the Latin *gubernator,* from which
come *governor* and *gubernatorial.* An explanation of cybernetics is given in the excerpt above; Webster's Third defines it
as "the comparative study of the automatic control system
formed by the nervous system and brain and by mechano-
electrical communications systems and devices (as computing
machines, thermostats, photoelectric sorters)." That's a long
way of saying IBM and all its works!

**cyborg**

> If we are ever to transform ourselves
> into high-grade cyborgs, something will
> have to be done about the most complex
> organ of all [the mind].

The above is from a review in *The New York Times Book
Review* of May 23, 1965, of a book titled *Cyborg* by D. S.
Halacy, Jr. The advertisement tells us that "cyborg is a word
coined to mean 'augmented man,'" a computer-designed
superman! *Cyborg* is, of course, an acronymic portmanteau
word, telescoping the words *cyber*netics and *org*anism.

**hypokinesia**    FIGHT HYPOKINESIA is the slogan of the
President's Council on Physical Fitness. On its placard hypokinesia is defined as "soft, flabby muscles caused by lack of
activity or exercise." The word *hypokinesia* is made up of the

* Such is the interest in words and their origin that *The New York
Times Book Review* of May 30, 1965, in its Queries and Answers section, printed a long letter discussing Norbert Wiener's "re-invention" of
the word *cybernetics,* tracing it back to *kybernetike,* "the art of steers-
manship, or governing," used by Plato, and to the French *cybernétique.*

Greek elements *hypo*, below, under + *kines*, motion + *ia*, condition, thus literally "a condition of insufficient motion." The root word *kine* (sometimes *cine*) is easily recognized in *cinema* (the Greek word *kinema*, meaning movement), *kinoscope*, *kinetic*, relating to motion, and *kinetics*, scientific study dealing chiefly with motion.

**googol**     Scientists can sometimes be playful, too. *Googol* may seem like a nonsense word to those who do not know it, but it is a word in good standing in the dictionaries. This excerpt from an article by Harold C. Schonberg in *The New York Times* of March 22, 1964, shows that it means a very large number:

> Shakespeare's 400th anniversary is hard upon us, and the occasion is sure to foster another googol of commentary about the greatest virtuoso with words any language has produced.

*Googol* was introduced by the eminent mathematician Edward Kasner, co-author of *Mathematics and the Imagination*, where he wrote:

> The definition of a googol is: 1 followed by a hundred zeros. It was decided after careful mathematical researches in the kindergarten that the number of raindrops falling on New York in 20 hours, or even a year, or a century, is much less than a googol.

Actually, the word *googol* was coined by Dr. Kasner's nine-year-old nephew, who thought that a number like that ought to have a name to match what it represented.

## AFTERWORD

Advertisers love to coin new words. For example, there is the word *periodromphilist*, whose meaning breaks up into one who (*ist*) loves (*phil*) to run (*drom*) around (*peri*)—a long way of saying "a tourist." The same advertisers used an unusual word, *deltiologist*, which looks as if they had made it up, too, but it is found in Webster's Third and means one whose hobby is collecting postcards.

## ACRONYMS

Acronyms (Greek *acro*, tip, beginning + *onym*, name) have become increasingly popular in this country. They offer a useful shortcut when one has to give the names of the ever increasing many-worded agencies, bureaus, organizations—and even scientific discoveries. NATO and SEATO are convenient and pronounceable shortcuts. However, the present tendency is not only to produce a pronounceable combination but to make it a significant word as well. CARE is a good example, though many may have forgotten that it stands for Cooperative for American Relief in Europe. ZIP in *Zip Code* stands for Zone Improvement Plan and gives promise of speedier mail deliveries. But CARE, ZIP, and acronyms CORE (Congress of Racial Equality), PLATO (Programmed Logic for Automatic Teaching Operation), and ACTION (American Council to Improve Our Neighborhoods) are not really new words—though they have been given new meanings.

Besides *radar* already noted, some new words have been formed in this way.

**laser**   In a news item in *The New York Times* of April 30, 1965, we read:

> A beam of light has been used to produce sound waves more than a million times higher in pitch than those audible to the human ear.
> Dr. Charles H. Townes, provost of Massachusetts Institute of Technology, who recently shared a Nobel Prize in physics for his role in the invention of the maser and laser, reported the development today.

*Laser* is an acronym for Light Amplification by Stimulated Emission of Radiation.

One can imagine the length and complexity of a single word made up of Greek or Latin words or roots to describe this process fully. The German "Licht-verstärkung durch Strahlungsanregung unter Verwendung einer fremden Strahlungsquelle" was too staggering even for the Germans. They also use the word *laser*.

On July 6, 1965, astronauts Frank Borman and James

Lovell said that they would attempt to communicate with a ground station via laser beam during their planned fourteen-day earth orbit—completed on December 17, 1965.

**maser** stands for **M**icrowave **A**mplification by **S**timulated **E**mission of **R**adiation.

**scuba** **S**elf-**C**ontained **U**nderwater **B**reathing **A**pparatus; the word has become an adjective to describe a popular aquatic sport, as in *scuba diving*.

**snafu** A most viable acronym, originally military slang, standing for "Situation Normal, All Fouled Up." Webster's Third labels *snafu* slang, but the word has been steadily gaining respectability through repeated use in headlines, news items, and even editorials.

*Snafu* is used to describe a resulting mess or a chaotic situation that is not altogether unexpected.

## I. MULTIPLE CHOICE

From the group after each word select the word or words closest in meaning to the listed word.

1. disseminate    (a) deceive (b) discourse (c) spread widely (d) defer (e) disappear

2. divulge    (a) deviate (b) destroy (c) lower (d) grow (e) make known

3. invective    (a) denunciation (b) long haul (c) defeat (d) inexperience (e) byword

4. mountebank    (a) card game (b) charlatan (c) long ascent (d) versatile comedian (e) mountain climber

5. mycology    study of: (a) sound (b) rodents (c) fungi (d) microscopic marine life (e) parasitic insects

6. neologism    (a) theory (b) nasal disease (c) logical fallacy (d) new word (e) ancient language

7. philippic    a speech of: (a) praise (b) farewell (c) excoriation (d) welcome (e) nomination

8. shibboleth    (a) catchword (b) exotic plant (c) Syrian dish (d) long speech (e) stern refusal

9. truckle    (a) move slowly (b) laugh heartily (c) act as a toady (d) deliver quickly (e) praise sincerely

10. volatile    (a) unstable (b) willing (c) lengthy (d) even-tempered (e) unfeeling

## II.  LIKE AND UNLIKE

Tell which pairs are of like or similar meaning, and which
are of unlike or opposite meaning.

1. augur ___ presage
2. auspicious ___ ill-starred
3. cynical ___ optimistic
4. immolation ___ slaughter
5. jargon ___ elegant language

6. pasquinade — satire
7. platitude — original remark
8. recant ___ repudiate
9. rubric ___ canon
10. snafu ___ orderly condition

## III.  FILLING IN

Fill in the blanks on the right so that the complete word
will correspond to the brief definition or the synonym on the
left. The first letter of each word to be completed is given;
each blank represents a letter.

EXAMPLE:  to indicate  b _ _ _ _ _ _     ANSWER:  betoken

1. word formed from initial letters        a _ _ _ _ _ _
2. to thunder at                           f _ _ _ _ _ _ _
3. pretentious language                    g _ _ _ _ _ _ _ _ _ _
4. to make a formal beginning              i _ _ _ _ _ _ _ _
5. to attack, "sail into"                  i _ _ _ _ _ _ _ _
6. a squib                                 l _ _ _ _ _ _
7. provincial dialect                      p _ _ _ _ _
8. base flatterer                          s _ _ _ _ _ _ _
9. figure of speech                        t _ _ _ _
10. violent abuse                          v _ _ _ _ _ _ _ _ _ _

## IV.  PAIRS OF SYNONYMS AND ANTONYMS

In each group two words have similar meaning, and two
others have unlike meaning. Select first the pair of synonyms,
and then the pair of antonyms.

EXAMPLE:  (a) jargon (b) quack (c) censorious (d) argot
              (e) praising (f) irksome
ANSWER:   Synonyms—(a) and (d); Antonyms—(c) and (e)

1. (a) balance (b) spread widely (c) disseminate (d) seminary
       (e) welcome (f) ostracize
2. (a) carping (b) gamut (c) pasquinade (d) augury
       (e) prophecy (f) constructive

3. (a) subservient (b) independent (c) catchword (d) scuba
   (e) lexicon (f) underwater apparatus
4. (a) cynosure (b) dirge (c) vituperation (d) joyous song
   (e) disease (f) attraction
5. (a) philippic (b) auspicious (c) touchstone (d) unfavorable
   (e) well-intentioned (f) test

## V. FITTING AN ADJECTIVE TO ITS NOUN

After each noun there is a group of five adjectives. Select
the adjective that best describes the noun.

EXAMPLE: excoriation   (a) smooth (b) glistening (c) ebullient
                                    (d) bitter (e) faded

ANSWER:   (d)

1. cynic        (a) appreciative (b) caviling (c) clearminded
                    (d) capricious (e) deceitful
2. fossil       (a) clever (b) redoubtable (c) silly (d) imbedded
                    (e) remarkable
3. googol       (a) very large (b) nonsensical (c) agape
                    (d) infinitesimal (e) astrological
4. platitude    (a) erudite (b) convenient (c) polished
                    (d) euphemistic (e) trite
5. scurrility   (a) clownish (b) rapid (c) abusive (d) clean
                    (e) overbearing

## VI. LET THE CONTEXT HELP YOU

In each of the following passages one word has been
omitted, a word that you have come across in this chapter. In
each group select the word needed to complete the sentence
correctly.

1. A Buddhist monk drenched himself with gasoline and died a
flaming death in protest. Scores of strollers witnessed his self-
_____.
        (a) subservience (b) immolation (c) denunciation
        (d) deification
2. He contended that a boycott had been imposed against him
and that he had been socially _____.
        (a) vituperated (b) censured (c) ostracized (d) lampooned
3. As far as I can see the true _____ for his book
should be *Vive la Différence.*
        (a) accolade (b) tirade (c) gamut (d) rubric
4. The declaration _____ against paternalism and
calls for a tight defense against nondefense spending.
        (a) inveighs (b) augurs (c) divulges (d) disseminates

5. It's amazing what _____ they think up: MIDAS for Missile Detection Alarm System; VISTA for Volunteers in Service to America! What will they think of next?
(a) acronyms (b) ideas (c) organizations (d) lasers

## VII.  ANALOGIES

Complete the following analogies (see pages 329–332; 335):

1. SHARD : OSTRACIZE :: (a) aegis : protection (b) ballot : elect (c) immolate : ground grain (d) prophesy : augur
2. GOOGOL : NUMBER :: (a) nonsense : reality (b) gigantic : dwarf (c) infinity : eternity (d) megaton : weight
3. SHIBBOLETH : HEBREW :: (a) cinema : Greek (b) cliché : Spanish (c) lallapaloosa : Japanese (d) platitude : German
4. SNAFU : LASER :: (a) quasar : ZIP (b) confusion : chaos (c) CARE : NATO (d) scuba : radar
5. GAMUT : SPECTRUM :: (a) burgeon : wither (b) scope : trope (c) scale : colorful (d) invective : tirade
6. EXCORIATION : ADULATION :: (a) caviling : carping (b) imitation : sincerity (c) insult : flattery (d) ingratiating : scurrilous
7. PHILIPPIC : SPEECH :: (a) Mansard : roof (b) fulminate : raillery (c) bowdlerize : literature (d) chauvinistic : theater
8. CYNICAL : AUSPICIOUS :: (a) sneer : cheer (b) dog : bird (c) Machiavellianism : diplomacy (d) philosopher : wisdom
9. FOSSIL : FULMINATE :: (a) lightning : trace (b) dig : abuse (c) antediluvian : avant-garde (d) vestige : thunder
10. FAWN : SYCOPHANT :: (a) mountebank : pitch (b) augur : omen (c) truckle : today (d) deer : hunter

## VIII.  THE ROOT THAT TELLS A STORY

This is different from the other types of matching you've had to do before. The words on the right do not define the words on the left but they do give a meaning of the root which tells the story hidden in the word. Match each word on the left with the proper choice on the right.

EXAMPLE: If *auspicious* were in the left-hand column and *bird* on the right, you would choose *bird* because *auspicious,* as you remember from the story in the chapter, means "bird-watching."

| | |
|---|---|
| 1. cybernetics | a. notes in the scale |
| 2. dirge | b. a man's name |
| 3. fossil | c. a seed |
| 4. gamut | d. flint |
| 5. immolate | e. govern |

| | |
|---|---|
| 6. philippic | f. first word in a Latin chant |
| 7. rubric | g. homeborn slave |
| 8. seminary | h. to dig |
| 9. sycophant | i. a red letter |
| 10. tirade | j. ground meal |
| 11. touchstone | k. to shoot |
| 12. vernacular | l. to show figs |

## DO-IT-YOURSELF DEPARTMENT

Some of these are easy as vocabulary words but every word in this list contains an interesting story which you can hunt down in the pages of an unabridged dictionary, an etymological dictionary, or any other reference work on word origins.

| | | |
|---|---|---|
| accost | eliminate | puny |
| ambition | extenuating | quinsy |
| ancillary | fiasco | reverberate |
| anthology | fiscal | rival |
| cadence | genuflection | sabotage |
| calculate | hypocrite | scrupulous |
| candidate | inveigle | scrutiny |
| concatenation | meticulous | scurrilous |
| contrite | nave | shambles |
| cretin | ogle | subjugate |
| dilapidated | pandemonium | suborn |
| dismal | pedigree | tawdry |
| divest | profane | viscous |

## VOCABAGRAMS

As a grand finale, since this is the last chapter, we have made a special arrangement of this word game. There are fifteen words, corresponding to the number of chapters. The word asked for after each number is related, as closely as possible, to the subject matter of the chapter bearing the same number. In addition, as lagniappe and a reward for all the work you've done, we have added a sixteenth word that is most appropriate to its position.

For detailed instructions see "Vocabagrams," last pages of Chapters 3, 4, 6.

1. enmities      + a = everyday civilities, not necessarily religious

2. their pens        + s  = where we found most of our sentences
                             (3 words)
3. thistle           + m  = what you should do with new words
                             you meet in your reading (2 words)
4. miscrs            + u  = take a guess; a conjecture
5. ample             + i  = to pierce
6. ceded             + a  = anything by tens
7. truce             + a  = a clergyman in a lower echelon
8. spot                   = chooses
9. cant + bleacher        = full authority in French (2 words)
10. mangle           + e  = a French mixture
11. bestial          − s  = although—with an archaic flavor
12. commune          + i  = praise, the Graeco-Roman way
                             (a noun)
13. shade                 = place where Pluto ruled
14. dismays          − y  = extreme cruelty
15. groat                 = specialized vocabulary—from French

*            *            *

LAGNIAPPE

16. undergo               = a reward, poetically speaking


I love bright words, words up and singing early;
Words that are luminous in the dark, and sing;
Warm lazy words, white cattle under trees;
I love words opalescent, cool, and pearly,
Like midsummer moths, and honied words like bees,
Gilded and sticky, with a little sting.

ELINOR WYLIE, "Pretty Words"

# Our Own Battery of Tests

> *When work started on Kentucky Dam, the Tennessee Valley Authority devised a series of questions to pick the best workmen for the project. One applicant was thrown for a loss by the first question: "What does hydrodynamics mean?" The man thought for a while, then wrote, "It means I don't get a job."*
>
> AP DISPATCH

For those who are preparing for a test these sections are for immediate use; for those who are interested in building their vocabularies in a leisurely way these sections are a long-term project.

If a position comes under civil service and a test is given, that test is sure to contain a considerable number of vocabulary questions. Job-placement and personnel tests, aptitude and intelligence tests, scholarship and comprehensive examinations in English—all include an important section on vocabulary.

There are many types of vocabulary questions. In this book you have come across practically every type—occasionally in the body of a chapter—but most often at the end of each chapter.

Here we are concentrating on:

1. Sentence Completions (one- and two-word)
2. Analogies (one- and two-word)
3. Multiple Choices

because they are most frequently met in high-echelon scholastic and civil service examinations. As usual, answers will be found at the end of the book.

## I. ONE-WORD COMPLETIONS

In this type of test you are asked to complete a sentence by choosing—of the four (or five) words offered—the one that will make the statement true or complete it most satisfactorily. The first group requires very little more than a knowledge of the definition of the word to be supplied.

### A.

1. The science of words and language is known as (a) philology (b) paleontology (c) bibliography (d) entomology.

2. One of the time-tested ways of remembering a series of items is known as a(n) (a) recollection (b) schematizing (c) mnemonic (d) ingenuity.

3. Nations that do not trust each other look upon each other (a) calmly (b) hopefully (c) askance (d) retrospectively.

4. If a person cannot be easily handled or dealt with, he will not be complimented for his (a) domesticity (b) knowledge (c) tractability (d) eulogy.

5. A person who constantly thinks he is sick is a (a) hypochondriac (b) misogynist (c) misanthrope (d) hyperpituitary.

6. But a person who is really sickly and is unduly solicitous about his health is a (a) valedictorian (b) vegetarian (c) valetudinarian (d) dialectician.

7. The order to stay in one's own bailiwick means that a person should remain in his own (a) room (b) district (c) country (d) bed

8. Because the orator's speech was high-flown and pretentious, the reporters termed it (a) bombastic (b) austere (c) untruthful (d) vituperative.

9. When the courtier had advanced to the highest position attainable, he was said to have reached the (a) vigil (b) precipice (c) threshold (d) pinnacle.

10. Accepting his fate with calmness, the camel driver said, "It is (a) growing late (b) kismet (c) kiosk (d) suttee."

### B.

This group offers more of a challenge because you will have to fit in the word that makes the sense intended by the writer. Let the context be your guide.

EXAMPLE:
To the average _____, golf is not a game that humbles but one that frustrates, tortures, and ruins.

(a) aficionado (b) sadist (c) masochist (d) individualist

ANSWER is (c), because the context emphasizes the torture and frustration of some golf players.

1. The primary purpose of modern weapons is _____: to prevent a particular course of action by a specific threat.

    (a) prognostic (b) deterrent (c) minatory (d) hegemony

2. As for the free world, trade with Cuba has been taking place on a modest scale despite the _____ opposition of the United States.

    (a) overt (b) independent (c) clandestine (d) casual

3. The basic structure of the living cell is a problem whose _____ can be judged by reference to the difficult exploration of the structure of the atom.

    (a) importance (b) universality (c) antiquity
       (d) complexity

4. The endless battle to modernize the _____ structure of work rules on the nation's railroads appears destined to reach the showdown stage with a strike at one minute after midnight tonight.

    (a) anemic (b) impracticable (c) archaic (d) streamlined

5. Cyprus is still not economically viable, and though _____ important, it is militarily weak in its own right.

    (a) necessarily (b) strategically (c) scarcely
       (d) independently

6. He's gone through a _____. He is not at all the man he was when he was a combat officer.

    (a) metamorphosis (b) crisis (c) frustration
       (d) surveillance

7. It was Jacob Grimm who transformed philology from an _____ study into an exact science.

    (a) abstruse (b) alleged (c) esoteric (d) errant

8. As the waves rose and the ship tossed, many of the passengers felt _____.

    (a) lethargic (b) subdued (c) tremulous (d) queasy

9. Although advertising men often complain that their industry is hemmed in by government regulations, the fact remains that a(n) _____ attitude toward Madison Avenue continues to exist in this country.

    (a) laissez faire (b) savoir faire (c) bête noire (d) idée fixe

10. The knockout wallop traveled only seven or eight inches and, admittedly, did not look like much. But boxing experts, and _____ scientists, will attest that punches that travel more than a foot lose much of their initial force.

    (a) nuclear (b) biological (c) electronic (d) kinetic

11. Are not the youngsters, viewing such war films, hypnotized by _____ thrills and the oldsters, especially the veterans, deluded into identifying themselves with the hero breed?

    (a) sensational (b) specious (c) auspicious (d) vicarious

12. It is fascinating to note how many travelers return from their gastronomic tours of Europe with a _____ of la grande cuisine and a haunting hunger for the simplicity of local dishes.

    (a) memory (b) suspicion (c) surfeit (d) superfluity

13. To avoid any outside influences, the judge has wisely decided to _____ the jury.

    (a) admonish (b) sequester (c) preclude (d) dismiss

14. The remarkable thing about *Spoon River Anthology* is the way its _____ little autobiographies merge into a unity.

    (a) concatenated (b) undeveloped (c) superficial
        (d) disparate

15. The general scientific assumption is that any amount of radiation, however small, will cause genetic damage that will appear as _____ in the future.

    (a) diseases (b) disabilities (c) mutations (d) handicaps

## II.  TWO-WORD COMPLETIONS

### A.

Each question in this group consists of a sentence from which two words have been omitted. Below each incomplete sentence are five pairs of words. You must choose one of these groups to complete the sentence and make it a true statement. Try each pair and choose the one that makes the most sense.

EXAMPLE:

    A _____ response is one that is made with _____.
    (a) stupid, fear (b) speedy, alacrity (c) sure, slowness
        (d) harmful, grimaces (e) pleasant, surmise
    The correct answer is (b).

  1. A _____ is a _____.
    (a) norm, standard (b) criterion, mistake (c) disciple,
        school (d) doctrine, follower (e) thesis, superstition

  2. A _____ shade of distinction is a _____.
    (a) fine, vindication (b) crass, profanity (c) subtle, nuance
        (d) thorough, prejudice (e) complete, paradox

  3. _____ flattery is known as _____.
    (a) continuous, maturity (b) indiscriminate, encomium
        (c) servile, adulation (d) unasked for, gratitude
        (e) cowardly, temerity

  4. At some private schools pupils are under the _____ of a
_____.
    (a) guidance, palladium (b) tutelage, preceptor (c) coach-
        ing, verity (d) assiduity, library (e) consensus, mentor

  5. A large _____ center is a(n) _____.

(a) district, affliction (b) transport, automobile (c) civic,
    utarchy (d) shopping, emporium (e) educationa⎯,
    indignity

6. _____ persons are inclined to _____.
    (a) obese, corpulence (b) generous, leanness (c) domineer-
    ing, temperance (d) vacillating, determination
    (e) cowering, effrontery

7. A _____ is a temporary _____.
    (a) deviation, rest (b) shambles, journey (c) respite, relief
    (d) paradox, enchantment (e) feint, spell

8. _____ language may also be termed _____.
    (a) eloquent, exiguous (b) frenzied, placid (c) abusive,
    scurrilous (d) contumelious, flattering (e) denunciatory,
    peripatetic

9. A _____ of small stones is called a _____.
    (a) collection, numismatist (b) collar, tiara (c) seller,
    connoisseur (d) mound, lithograph (e) pattern, mosaic

10. Suzerainty is _____ control over a _____ state.
    (a) complete, democratic (b) native, backward (c) central,
    unified (d) political, dependent, (e) economic, federated

# B.

These two-word completion exercises are designed to find
out:
    (1) whether you can comprehend through clue words the
meaning of a sentence still incomplete
    (2) whether your vocabulary is not only precise but also
discriminating
    (3) whether you possess some sense of style.

1. Athletes have so perfected their techniques in track and field
events that the _____ becomes _____ before record books can be
published.
    (a) announcement, public (b) meet, official (c) time,
    authentic (d) fantastic, commonplace (e) result,
    universal

2. Like the _____ part of an iceberg, much of what is really
interesting in the capital is not _____.
    (a) inner, known (b) submerged, visible (c) greater,
    dangerous (d) upper, viable (e) lower, penetrable

3. Such stalling tactics are _____ to all fans and cannot be
_____.
    (a) repugnant, condoned (b) anathema, ascertained
    (c) injurious, explained (d) unfair, superseded
    (e) understandable, countenanced

4. The _____ of democratic freedom is dialogue and the _____ interchange of diverse ideas.
   (a) debasement, untrammeled (b) pinnacle, restrained
     (c) essence, unhampered (d) alienation, compulsory
     (e) epitome, discriminating

5. Although there were _____ circumstances in this particular violation of the law, the judge ruled that there had to be strict _____ or there would be no law at all.
   (a) extraordinary, complaisance (b) specific, obedience
     (c) tantalizing, adherence (d) extenuating, compliance
     (e) questionable, observation

6. In spite of all _____, in spite of penalties for examinees when cheaters were caught, there is evidence of the _____ of the rigid rules of external help on civil service tests.
   (a) threats, encompassment (b) surveillance, vulnerability
     (c) temptation, flouting (d) precautions, circumvention
     (e) discouragement, acceptance

7. Hungarians may grumble about the difficulty of acquiring cars, but they point quickly to a compensation: the _____ look of their tree-lined avenues and the absence of _____ exhaust fumes.
   (a) placid, superfluous (b) otiose, poisonous (c) unclut-
     tered, noxious (d) anomalous, fetid (e) tranquil,
     copious.

8. Even as _____ machines free men from drudgery, they _____ displace men from jobs.
   (a) automated, simultaneously (b) robotlike, unwillingly
     (c) animated, ineluctably (d) accelerated, seemingly
     (e) antiquated, understandably

9. To cross the Rubicon means to take a final _____ step which may have dangerous _____.
   (a) hazardous, antecedents (b) unnecessary, potentialities
     (c) inconsequential, concomitants (d) well-considered,
     implications (e) irrevocable, consequences

10. Though the Oxford English Dictionary is undoubtedly the greatest dictionary ever _____, it is designed for scholars and research workers rather than for the _____ dictionary user.
   (a) projected, omniscient (b) compiled, casual (c) assem-
     bled, assiduous (d) published, professional (e) demon-
     strated, amateur

11. Into the limited space given him a headline writer must compress the _____ of the news and he must do it without _____.
   (a) synopsis, reservations (b) bias, apology (c) magnitude,
     distortion (d) totality, hedging (e) gist, ambiguity

12. If it were true that enduring lessons are learned from _____ errors, Broadway would be the repository of _____ theatrical wisdom.

(a) stupid, attenuated (b) egregious, sublime (c) dubious,
profound (d) dramatic, lasting (e) accidental,
occult

13. It is a well-known _____ that the lover of the sea craves
for dry land—the age-old _____ to be where we are not.

(a) aphorism, antipathy (b) anomaly, demiurge (c) credo,
inspiration (d) paradox, yearning (e) contention,
duplicity

14. Why should a university _____ the values which are supposedly basic to its functioning and give an honorary doctorate to
one who has not distinguished himself in a(n) _____ manner?

(a) inflate, scholarly (b) forestall, worldly (c) vilify,
collegiate (d) abuse, doctrinaire (e) debase, academic

15. To encourage colonial peoples in their aspirations to attain
independence before it is _____ proved that a _____ state will
evolve instead of anarchy is unforgivable.

(a) inevitably, formidable (b) definitively, sympathetic
(c) succinctly, redoubtable (d) incontrovertibly, viable
(e) unequivocally, mobile

16. Human memory is not _____, especially on ancient hap-
penings that smack of the _____.

(a) infallible, mythological (b) dependable, ordinary
(c) trustworthy, credulous (d) reliable, inventive
(d) noteworthy, fanciful

17. Hence the word sophistry has an unfavorable _____ and
means arguing deceitfully, attempting to turn a poor case into a
good one by means of clever but _____ reasoning.

(a) denotation, ingenuous (b) meaning, ingenious (c) connotation, specious (d) significance, vague (e) impact,
cogent

18. He warned the workers against supporting these antisocial
policies, which he declared would _____ rather than _____ the
plight of the common people.

(a) rescue, destroy (b) encourage, defy (c) aggravate, alleviate (d) empower, improve (e) protract, inhibit

19. The defense proposes to show that the incident that the
prosecution so _____ rejects as _____ did indeed take place, is indeed historical fact.

(a) blithely, undesirable (b) cavalierly, apocryphal
(c) cautiously, factual (d) persuasively, ignorance
(e) positively, inevitable

20. We have criticized our university students for preferring the
security of political silence and the safety of _____ to the excitement of social _____ and humanitarian action.

(a) acquiescence, dissent (b) college, adventure (c) concealment, revolution (d) tolerance, antagonism
(e) security, insecurity

21. The practice of painting slogans on rock faces, once a thriving industry in Britain, has fallen into ——, but there has recently been a(n) —— in County Antrim.

  (a) oblivion, demand (b) misuse, artisan (c) disfavor, upheaval (d) mediocrity, surfeit (e) disuse, recrudescence

22. Curiously enough the very passages which set out to clarify only ——; the details are served up in —— three-page paragraphs which stupefy the reader.

  (a) adumbrate, excessive (b) obscure, succinct (c) mystify, stimulating (d) disturb, compact (e) obfuscate, monolithic

23. Oddly enough —— the prestige of the United States in such countries as Britain, France, and Italy is considered important here, Congress has been —— about supplying funds to the U.S. Information Agency in these countries.

  (a) although, niggardly (b) since, dilatory (c) when, generous (d) whereas, wasteful (e) inasmuch as, chary

24. The increasing revival of dramatic classics is, to one critic, ——; it seems to him a sign of the —— of the modern theater.

  (a) understandable, revival (b) deplorable, anemia
  (c) suspicious, resurgence (d) astounding, futility
  (e) incomprehensible, fatuousness

25. For some years past, French governments had been —— and divided, and French parliaments had been incoherent and ——.

  (a) inarticulate, responsive (b) unstable, domineering
  (c) weak, inchoate (d) many, few (e) vacillating, irresponsible

26. Scientific imagination is a specific intellectual power that is —— in every population that has learned to be —— about the mechanisms governing the physical world.

  (a) encouraged, wary (b) evoked, self-deprecatory
  (c) latent, curious (d) growing, self-possessed
  (e) teeming, diffident

27. In diplomatic —— the —— sought by one government from another to the name of a proposed ambassador is known as an "agreement."

  (a) dealings, understandings (b) parlance, assent
  (c) circles, permission (d) channels, condition
  (e) language, interpretation

28. Camille Pissarro, eldest of France's great impressionist —— that included Monet, Manet, Renoir, and Degas, was both the movement's —— and its saint.

  (a) brotherhood, demon (b) entity, defector (c) sodality, gadfly (d) hierarchy, patriarch (e) cabal, doyen

29. The westerlies normally cross the United States at altitudes from 10,000 to 50,000 feet along the Canadian border, acting as a

———— to Arctic winds and giving the Middle Atlantic States relatively ———— winters.

> (a) deterrent, cold (b) propellant, mild (c) catalyst, unsettled (d) buffer, temperate (e) counterpart, unsettled

30. But even Mr. Moses, one of the most ———— public servants of our time, is at a loss to convey in words the size, the imaginative engineering ———— that built this contribution to the welfare of family and industry.

> (a) articulate, ingenuity (b) dedicated, appositeness
> (c) unappreciated, technique (d) public-spirited, skill
> (e) tongue-tied, miracle

31. Among the younger people there are complaints that the sight of ex-Nazis flourishing recommends ———— to youth, that it instills, instead of needed moral values, the dubious precept that ———— is the best policy.

> (a) precepts, intolerance (b) cynicism, expediency
> (c) emulation, honesty (d) selfishness, indifference
> (e) desperation, dishonesty

32. In architecture, much more than in any of the other fine arts, there is a marked time lag between the ———— of ideas and their ———— in the shape of completed buildings.

> (a) settlement, fruition (b) creation, welcoming (c) tradition, modernization (d) dawn, practicability
> (e) emergence, application

33. In analyzing the ———— teen-age population, Madison Avenue has decided that it is eminently receptive to the ———— of advertising.

> (a) proliferating, buncombe (b) ubiquitous, mystique
> (c) diminishing, fantasy (d) viable, syndrome
> (e) burgeoning, blandishments

34. No matter how ———— the Russians are or wish to appear, they, as well as we, know that to survive it is necessary to reach agreements which may ———— mutual sacrifices.

> (a) fatuous, necessitate (b) intransigent, entail
> (c) refractory, obliterate (d) indifferent, subsume
> (e) bellicose, evade

35. For nearly a century the ———— travelers check has been the nearest thing to an international currency yet devised by man, and has guided generations of Americans and other tourists through the ———— of foreign exchange.

> (a) surreptitious, complexities (b) useful, excesses
> (c) plausible, maze (d) sacrosanct, fluctuations
> (e) ubiquitous, labyrinth

36. It is panic-mongering to ———— ourselves into paroxysms of anguish and shame at the prospect of negotiating an end to our ———— in East Asia.

(a) foment, engagement (b) coerce, aggresion (c) flagellate, involvement (d) excoriate, apathy (e) depreciate, commitment

## III. ANALOGUES

### A.

This type of question involves more than merely a knowledge of the meanings of words—it tests your ability to see relationships, your power to reason, and your knowledge of subject matter and everyday affairs. Often the words themselves are very simple, but you must be careful to distinguish the fine shades of meaning.

The more usual form of questions involving analogies consists of two words or phrases (generally printed in CAPITAL letters) that are related to each other in a specific way followed by five pairs of words or phrases. Of these five pairs you are asked to select the *one* pair that *best* or *most closely* expresses a relationship *similar* to or the *same* as that expressed in the original pair. The symbols used are those used in ratio and proportion:

2 : 4 :: 3 : 6.

The sign : means *is to* or *are to*, and :: means *as*. An example of a simple verbal analogy is:

APPLE : FRUIT :: carrot : vegetable.

It is, of course, impossible to list all the relationships existing among persons, places, things, words, and ideas, but we are putting down a list of most of the types that have been used on scholarship and aptitude examinations. In each case we are giving you an example to fix the idea firmly in your mind.

Please note that the relationships may be expressed vice versa.

### Examples of Types of Analogies

1. Like is to like, such as synonyms, including similarity between persons, objects, concepts, as well as degree of similarity.
   (a) DECLARE : ASSERT :: impugn : attack verbally
   (b) APPLE : PEAR :: carrot : turnip
   (c) SADNESS : DEPRESSION :: happiness : exhilaration

2. Like is to unlike, such as antonyms, including dissimilarity between persons, objects, concepts, as well as degree of dissimilarity.

INEPT : CLEVER :: languid : active

Both for similarity as well as dissimilarity, the words in the choices may be very simple, denoting size, quantity, number, lightness and darkness, weight, etc. In making your selection you must see to it that the relationship is the same as that which exists in the original pair.

Examples: MULTITUDE : HANDFUL :: many : few
            DEMI : HEMI :: 1 : 1

3. One is to many or part is to the whole.
   (a) SOLDIER : ARMY :: sailor : navy
   (b) CHIEF : TRIBE :: governor : state
   (c) BEAD : NECKLACE :: link : chain
4. User is to object, tool, or implement that he uses.
   (a) WOODSMAN : AX :: farmer : scythe
5. Material is to its product.
   WOOL : BLANKET :: leather : shoes
6. Collector or scholar or professional man is to a specialty.
   PHILOLOGIST : WORDS :: podiatrist : feet
7. One geometric figure or body is to another.
   SPHERE : CUBE :: circle : square
8. Units of number and quantity are to other units.
   (a) TEN : DECADE :: 1,000 : millennium
   (b) PINT : QUART :: nickel : dime
9. Special article of dress is to the wearer.
   LIVERY : DOORMAN :: uniform : soldier
10. Person, animal, or object is to a characteristic activity or trait (expressed by verbs, nouns or adjectives).
   (a) HEN : CLUCKS :: goose : quacks
   (b) LAMB : MILDNESS :: leopard : ferocity
   (c) LAMB : GENTLE :: leopard : fierce
11. Noun is to its corresponding adjective.
   BULL : TAURINE :: sheep : ovine
12. Adjective is to its abstract noun.
   AMICABLE : FRIENDSHIP :: inimical : unfriendliness
13. Noun is to a verb showing what is being done to the noun.
   GRAIN : SOW :: ideas : spread
14. Thing or idea is to what it ordinarily does.
   SCISSORS : CUT :: pens : write
15. Cause is to effect.
   GRIEF : TEARS :: joy : laughter
16. Symbol is to what it stands for, including insignia and the person or group the insignia are associated with.

    (a) TRYLON AND PERISPHERE : 1939 WORLD'S FAIR :: Uni-
        sphere : 1964–1965 World's Fair
    (b) CHEVRONS : SERGEANT :: eagle : colonel

17. Young is to old.
    COLT : HORSE :: cub : lion
18. Singular is to plural.
    GOOSE : GEESE :: passerby : passersby
19. Grammatical case form is to another form.
    I : ME :: who : whom
20. Masculine is to feminine.
    BULL : COW :: fox : vixen
21. One form of a verb is to another of the same verb.
    DO : DID :: sing : sang
22. Implied relationships and comparisons, such as metaphors.
    (a) PREJUDICE : JUSTICE :: clouds : sun
    (b) IGNORANCE : DARKNESS :: knowledge : light
    (c) SKELETON : BODY :: laws : society
23. The roots of the original pair may be the same.
    COMMIT : PERMIT :: complex : perplex
24. Finally, the words in the original pair may have no relationship to each other; hence, you must choose as your answer a
pair in which the first word corresponds to the first word of the
original pair and the second to the second.
    CASTANETS : STEPPES :: guitar : tundra


## AND MANY MORE!

Before we put you on your own, we shall work out one
example together.

    HAMMER : CARPENTER :: (a) reins : horse (b) brush :
    painter (c) shaves : barber (d) anchor : sailor (e) blue-
    print : architect

FIRST STEP! Examine the relationship in the first pair from
all possible angles. Express the relationship not "as this is to
that," but in more specific terms. *Example:* "A hammer is used
by a carpenter as an essential tool."
SECOND STEP! Repeat the formula for each of the choices.
Discard those that obviously do not fit, such as (a) and (c).
THIRD STEP! Weigh the arguments for each of the choices
that appear to fit: (b), (d), ond (e), then make the final decision. Where two or more seem to fit because of general
agreement with the original pair, you must find additional
specific agreement to narrow the choice to only one pair. In
the above question, the sailor and the architect make use of

an anchor or blueprint, respectively. However, the sailor does not handle the anchor or make anything with it, as a carpenter does with a hammer. The architect constructs but does not wield a blueprint. Therefore, the remaining choice (b) is correct, because the correspondence with the original choice is the closest.

Of course, you might have made this choice at first glance, but remember that about 230 years ago, Alexander Pope wrote, "For fools rush in where angels fear to tread." Be an angel! Test all possibilities; beware of traps.

NOTE. In the example just given for analysis, the first pair of words consists of two nouns. Most frequently, the correct choice will consist of the same kinds of words as in the original pair. However, it is possible for a pair of nouns to be compared with two verbs or two adjectives. You may also find a noun and an adjective in the original pair. In such instances, the correct choice will also contain two unlike parts of speech. What you must see clearly is that the relationship of the parts of speech in the original pair must be maintained in the correct choice. Within each pair there must be exact correspondence.

Now you are ready to try the questions below.

1. WE : OUR :: (a) they : there (b) who : whose (c) you : you're (d) him : his (e) it : it's

2. SLEEK : GLOSSY :: (a) credible : believable (b) rapid : tepid (c) vapid : complete (d) dejected : jubilant (e) contrite : unrepentant

3. STRINGS : VIOLIN :: (a) wind : leaves (b) air : flute (c) pedal : organ (d) membrane : drum (e) plectrum : mandolin

4. DOUGH : BREAD :: (a) ink : pen (b) paper : writing (c) cold : ice (d) words : speech (e) sugar : cake

5. ENGINEER : CAB :: (a) shepherd : flock (b) passenger : taxi (c) sailor : cabin (d) driver : wheel (e) aviator : cockpit

6. ASTRONOMY : ASTROLOGY :: (a) symbolism : superstition (b) geology : geometry (c) magic : science (d) chemistry : alchemy (e) folklore : fable

7. SCALP : HAIR :: (a) shoe : foot (b) earth : grass (c) house : roof (d) curtain : window (e) cloth : table

8. ISTHMUS : LAND :: (a) wire : pole (b) strait : body of water (c) neck : head (d) bar : trapeze (e) opening : tunnel

9. MEMORANDUM : MEMORANDA :: (a) bacillus : bacilli (b) strata : stratum (c) alumna : alumni (d) automata : automata (e) insignia : insigne

10. PRONE : SUPINE :: (a) likely : unlikely (b) aslant : akimbo
(c) recumbent : prostrate (d) face down : face up
(e) backward : forward

11. MULE : BURDEN :: (a) scholar : books (b) animal : oppression
(c) ship : cargo (d) musician : cello (e) house : tenants

12. ALTHOUGH : NEVERTHELESS :: (a) albeit : however (b) because : therefore (c) since : yet (d) notwithstanding : if
(e) when : simultaneously

13. ZENITH : NADIR :: (a) high : higher (b) zero : cipher (c) perfection : baseness (d) slough : despair (e) pinnacle : bottom

14. SPATE : TRICKLE :: (a) much : little (b) much : more
(c) copious : abundant (d) much : many (e) small : less

15. RAM : EWE :: (a) doe : hart (b) swan : cygnet (c) marquis :
marquee (d) stallion : colt (e) testator : testatrix

16. FAÇADE : BUILDING :: (a) drawer : desk (b) dial : watch
(c) page : book (d) fence : garden (e) cork : bottle

17. PULSATE : THROB :: (a) condone : condemn (b) abate :
increase (c) disperse : gather (d) expropriate : deprive
(e) accede : disagree

18. MORASS : SWAMP :: (a) peak : mountain (b) desert : oasis
(c) sea : gulf (d) forest : tree (e) prairie : plain

19. ISLANDS : ARCHIPELAGO :: (a) stamps : philately (b) stars :
constellation (c) nickels : dollar bill (d) hors d'oeuvre :
banquet (e) birds : apiary

20. SERRATED : SAW :: (a) mountain : jagged (b) sharpness : knife
(c) dappled : horse (d) pronged : fork (e) incisor : tooth

21. FRIGHT : STAMPEDE :: (a) flow of water : erosion (b) clouds :
tornado (c) rain : snow (d) haste : crowds (e) wildness :
cattle

22. GUTTURAL : THROAT :: (a) venal : wine (b) mantle : cloak
(c) hair : hirsute (d) palmar : wrist (e) brachial : arm

23. LOBSTER : CRUSTACEAN :: (a) eagle : sparrow (b) reason : man
(c) tiger : cat (d) dolphin : whale (e) lion : man

24. ABOMINATE : MAGNATE :: (a) noun : noun (b) adjective : noun
(c) noun : adjective (d) verb : verb (e) verb : noun

25. PREDATORY : HAWK :: (a) contortion : grimace (b) voracious :
glutton (c) tawny : lion (d) speedy : cruiser (e) ugly : vul-
ture

26. MINARET : MOSQUE :: (a) cross : basilica (b) muezzin : prayer
(c) nave : cathedral (d) belfry : steeple (e) campanile :
church

27. INCONGRUOUS : HARMONIOUS :: (a) tall : short (b) fickle : rebellious (c) wearisome : tedious (d) laughable : ludicrous
(e) nonplussed : distracted

28. COGENT : CONVINCING :: (a) dubious : certain (b) nonchalant :
disturbed (c) banal : unoriginal (d) cunning : disingenuous
(e) insular : continental

29. DECANTER : CARAFE :: (a) salver : tray (b) bottle : barrel
    (c) cruet : kettle (d) cup : plate (e) crystal : glass

30. INTERMITTENTLY : INCESSANTLY :: (a) interminably : wearily
    (b) slowly : rapidly (c) strongly : weakly (d) vicariously :
    frequently (e) occasionally : continuously

31. MERCURY : CADUCEUS :: (a) Vulcan : forge (b) Pegasus :
    Muses (c) palladium : Athena (d) Jupiter : thunderbolt
    (e) Neptune : trident

32. ENERVATE : STRENGTHEN :: (a) aver : attribute (b) divert :
    turn (c) apprise : appraise (d) stultify : enliven (e) in-
    vigorate : brighten

33. DOLT : DOUR :: (a) bolt : door (b) escape : subterfuge
    (c) reticent : silence (d) numbskull : sullen (e) infant : cry

34. EXORDIUM : PERORATION :: (a) epilogue : prologue (b) in-
    cipient : inchoate (c) certain : uncertain (d) alpha : omega
    (e) exhortation : denunciation

35. MENDACITY : DISTRUST :: (a) begging : charity (b) stupidity :
    failure (c) truth : falsehood (d) untruth : doubtful
    (e) integrity : confidence

36. CARELESSNESS : JEOPARDIZE :: (a) penalty : chastise (b) fail-
    ure : discouragement (c) carefulness : security (d) neglect :
    endanger (e) crowding : discomfort

37. PERMEATE : RUEFUL :: (a) truculent : merciful (b) sadden :
    pitiful (c) evaporate : mournful (d) penetrate : sorrowful
    (e) frighten : lamentable

38. FLAMBOYANT : ROCOCO :: (a) ornate : baroque (b) inflam-
    mable : phlegmatic (c) counterfeit : invaluable (d) flagrant :
    flagitious (e) florid : fragrant

39. HYPERTENSION : HYPOTENSION :: (a) high : low (b) excessive :
    deficient (c) super : minimal (d) abnormal : normal
    (e) iso : sub

40. OAF : FRESHET :: (a) lout : novice (b) stupidity : imperti-
    nence (c) fool : flood (d) silly : brash (e) gaucherie : élan

41. IMPLICATE : COMPLICATE :: (a) vitality : inevitable (b) em-
    pathy : sympathy (c) importune : construct (d) imply : sim-
    plify (e) belligerent : embellish

42. CUPID : PSYCHE :: (a) Zeus : Aphrodite (b) Damon : Pythias
    (c) Hero : Leander (d) Apollo : Cassandra (e) Venus :
    Adonis

43. PRECEDENT : JUSTIFICATION :: (a) kindness : obedience
    (b) authority : sanction (c) usage : submission (d) tradition :
    novelty (e) orthodoxy : heresy

44. RACHITIC : RICKETS :: (a) adulatory : adoration (b) Oxford :
    Oxonian (c) scorbutic : scurvy (d) deification : deify
    (e) therapy : therapeutic

45. LAUREL : VICTOR :: (a) chevrons : army (b) Oscar : movie star

(c) power : glory (d) blue ribbon : cooking (e) rabbit's foot : luck

46. CORVINE : CROW :: (a) elephantine : dinosaur (b) lioness : lion (c) viceregal : viceroy (d) corvette : automobile (e) urbane : urban

47. ZEALOT : FANATICISM :: (a) impostor : sham (b) orator : frenzy (c) umpire : game (d) vagabond : vagrant (e) parasite : food

48. PAIN : ANODYNE :: (a) savagery : music (b) grief : solace (c) harshness : softness (d) trifle : enormity (e) accident : insurance

49. FORGERY : SIGNATURE :: (a) faked : genuine (b) proxy : delegate (c) carbon copy : original (d) embezzlement : blank check (e) multigraph : duplicate

50. PHILOLOGIST : LANGUAGE :: (a) numismatist : stamps (b) herbalist : tropical flowers (c) philatelist : charms (d) fish : ichthyologist (e) conchologist : shells

## B.

In another type of question involving analogies, you are asked to choose a single term instead of an entire pair. One complete pair and one term—all three capitalized—of another pair are given. You are to complete the second pair by choosing the correct term from a number of given choices, generally five. Apply the same principles of selection as you did in answering part A of this section.

EXAMPLE 1: SWIMMER : HANDS :: SEAL :(a) tusk (b) tentacles (c) tail (d) flippers (e) fin

ANSWER 1: (d). The seal *uses* flippers to aid its swimming as a swimmer *uses* his hands.

EXAMPLE 2: URANIUM (U-235) : FISSIONABLE :: (a) diamond (b) ideas (c) nucleus (d) atoms (e) gold : MALLEABLE

ANSWER: 2: (e). Gold *is* malleable just as uranium *is* fissionable. Figuratively, ideas may be malleable but they are not elements; gold and uranium are elements.

Note that the three fully capitalized terms do not always come at the beginning. Make your choice from the terms in small letters, and link it with the single fully capitalized term.

1. DONKEY : BRAYS :: WOLF : (a) bellows (b) howls (c) whimpers (d) roars (e) whines

2. ANXIETY : ALLAY :: GRIEF : (a) banish (b) condole
   (c) heighten (d) assuage (e) display
3. (a) colors (b) small stones (c) straw (d) papyrus (e) bricks :
   MOSAICS :: WORDS : SENTENCES
4. MINOTAUR : BULL :: CHIMERA : (a) heifer (b) lion (c) goddess
   (d) tiger (e) dog
5. BLANDISH : COAX :: ASSEVERATE : (a) affirm (b) cut
   (c) repeat (d) complain (e) twist
6. SYLVAN : WOODS :: TERRESTRIAL : (a) urban (b) fear (c) earth
   (d) planets (e) stars
7. ASTRONAUTS : SPACE :: ARGONAUTS : (a) fire (b) ship
   (c) birds (d) treasure (e) sea
8. SCION : PROGENITOR :: DESCENDANT : (a) children (b) brother
   (c) ancestor (d) progeny (e) guardian
9. PEDIATRICIAN : (a) children (b) feet (c) plants (d) philosophy
   (e) hair :: DERMATOLOGIST : SKIN
10. SLEAZY : FLIMSY :: SHODDY : (a) tenable (b) despicable
    (c) queasy (d) tenuous (e) detrimental
11. INVEIGLE : CAJOLE :: MALIGN : (a) slander (b) enlighten
    (c) acclaim (d) eulogize (e) compile
12. CYGNET : SWAN :: (a) bridle (b) hoof (c) mule (d) colt
    (e) stallion : HORSE
13. SNAKE : REPTILIAN :: LION : (a) leotard (b) vulpine
    (c) lemurine (d) tiger (e) feline
14. HERCULES : (a) trident (b) spear (c) club (d) poisoned bow
    (e) hydra :: CUPID : ARROW
15. SINECURE : CARE :: INTREPIDITY : (a) hesitation (b) entangle-
    ment (c) fear (d) support (e) forethought
16. SANCHO PANZA : DON QUIXOTE :: (a) Perry Mason (b) Don
    Ameche (c) Maigret (d) John H. Watson (e) Nero Wolfe :
    SHERLOCK HOLMES
17. OGLE : EYES :: MANEUVER : (a) fingers (b) human beings
    (c) minds (d) machines (e) hands
18. PURLOIN : STEAL :: NEBULOUS : (a) frustrating (b) scanty
    (c) dishonest (d) stormy (e) vague
19. RUBESCENT : RED :: CERULEAN : (a) sky (b) brilliant (c) pale
    (d) seagreen (e) blue
20. (a) sincere (b) simple (c) pretentious (d) thoughtless
    (e) accidental : CLAPTRAP :: PITHY : MAXIM
21. GENUINE : SIMULATED :: UNAFFECTED : (a) elevated
    (b) bombastic (c) dynamic (d) destructive (e) emulated
22. ACTOR : STAGE :: (a) pilot (b) acrobat (c) soldier (d) rider
    (e) orator : ROSTRUM
23. ANSWER : TEST :: DENOUEMENT : (a) symphony (b) horse race
    (c) mystery story (d) circus (e) complete understanding
24. (a) Lerner (b) Bellini (c) Gilbert (d) Mozart (e) Purcell :
    SULLIVAN :: HAMMERSTEIN : ROGERS

25. RECONDITE : ABSTRUSE :: BANTER : (a) delay (b) tease
   (c) bargain (d) exchange (e) deceive
26. BASILICA : CHURCH :: DORMER : (a) movie (b) chapel (c) room
   (d) window (e) servant
27. CICERONE : GUIDE :: DRAGOMAN : (a) cavalry officer (b) in-
   terpreter (c) hauler (d) turnkey (e) mythological monster
28. VILIFICATION : DEFAMATION :: (a) parody (b) garment
   (c) stripping (d) deterioration (e) journey : TRAVESTY
29. SUPPOSITITIOUS : FALSE :: SPURIOUS : (a) inciting (b) duplicate
   (c) exhilarating (d) not authentic (e) not technical
30. MULCT : DEFRAUD :: RATIOCINATION : (a) reasoning (b) bilk
   (c) detective (d) proportion (e) self-defense

## IV. WORDS, WORDS, WORDS!

> *Professor Edgeworth of All Souls' avoided
> conversational English, persistently using
> words and phrases that one expects to meet
> only in books. One evening, Lawrence [the
> famous Lawrence of Arabia] returned from
> a visit to London, and Edgeworth met him
> at the gate. "Was it very caliginous in the
> Metropolis?"*
>
> *"Somewhat caliginous, but not altogether
> inspissated," Lawrence replied gravely.*
>
> ROBERT GRAVES, *Goodbye to All That*

Since for the most part we are not including words already discussed in the body of this book or those used in
previous exercises, it would be advisable—if you are preparing for a test—to review the exercises at the end of chapters
and also those occasionally found in the body of chapters. Below are words of some difficulty, some more difficult than
others but any of them may appear on vocabulary tests.

In this type of test you are asked to select the definition
*closest* in meaning. The correct answer is not necessarily an
exact equivalent or even a very good definition. But it is the
one choice that comes *closest* in meaning to the word to be
defined.

### A.

1. abash                    (a) obliterate (b) send away (c) embar-
                            rass (d) condemn

2. abnegation        (a) indignation (b) renunciation (c) affirmation (d) abstention

3. abrade        (a) rub off (b) attach (c) scold (d) twist

4. absolution        (a) despotism (b) punishment (c) positiveness (d) forgiveness

5. abstruse        (a) stupid (b) diffuse (c) obscure (d) missing

6. abut        (a) border on (b) collide with (c) refuse (d) excuse

7. accoutrements        (a) sealed orders (b) equipment (c) adjustments (d) financial records

8. actuarial        (a) realistical (b) normal (c) by virtue of (d) relating to statistical calculations

9. adjunct        (a) solemn oath (b) addition (c) adaptation (d) decree

10. afferent        (a) diffident (b) unmoved (c) bringing toward a central point (d) removing

11. affiant        (a) affidavit signer (b) betrothed (c) opponent (d) confidential agent

12. afflatus        (a) gastric ailment (b) egoism (c) notoriety (d) inspiration

13. affront        (a) pride (b) insult (c) success (d) projection

14. agglomeration        (a) enumeration (b) vagueness (c) resplendence (d) confused mass

15. alembic        (a) drinking mug (b) chemical formula (c) rhythmic foot (d) distilling vessel

16. altercation        (a) loud explosion (b) drastic change (c) angry dispute (d) outright denial

17. altruistic        (a) unselfish (b) radical (c) egoistic (d) wastrel

18. ambergris        (a) forever oily (b) piece of costume jewelry (c) perfume base (d) healing ointment

19. ampersand        (a) the symbol & (b) figure of speech (c) material for grinding glass (d) electronic unit

20. amulet        (a) charm (b) hamlet (c) phial (c) turban

21. ana        (a) foolish act (b) collection of odd literary items (c) insect group (d) worthless bric-a-brac

22. ancillary        (a) obvious (b) auxiliary (c) pertaining to the ankle (d) feeble

23. anneal        (a) heal (b) rescind (c) patch (d) temper

24. anthropomorphic    (a) geological (b) changeable (c) primitive (d) having human form

25. aphasia    (a) loss of sight (b) shapelessness (c) loss of memory (d) loss of speech

26. apologue    (a) excuse (b) afterpiece (c) moral fable (d) farewell speech

27. apposite    (a) hostile (b) appropriate (c) antipodal (d) appointive

28. apprise    (a) reward (b) approach (c) evaluate (d) inform

29. arraign    (a) serve on jury (b) put in order (c) bring before a court (d) convict

30. arroyo    (a) ranch (b) gully (c) prairie (d) cliff

31. ascetic    (a) sterilized (b) unbiased (c) self-denying (d) haggard

32. asseveration    (a) assertion (b) anger (c) retention (d) separation

33. asteroid    (a) star-shaped body (b) canine tooth (c) flowerlike (d) disease

34. astringent    (a) attenuated (b) flexible (c) styptic (d) poignant

35. astrolabe    (a) falling star (b) astronomical instrument (c) ship's rigging (d) small space capsule

36. atrabilious    (a) shameful (b) ungrateful (c) feverish (d) melancholy

37. attrition    (a) wearing down (b) sadness (c) repentance (d) cheerfulness

38. aureole    (a) halo (b) bird (c) gold fabric (d) vestment

39. baize    (a) transparent cotton (b) curtain (c) coarse woolen cloth (d) Indian corn

40. baldric    (a) part of a castle (b) melody on a horn (c) belt for sword (d) coat of mail

41. barbate    (a) drug (b) jagged (c) bearded (d) ironical

42. barnacle    (a) shell-bearing sea animal (b) place for animals (c) small telescopic instrument (d) seafarer

43. baroque    (a) extravagantly ornamented (b) mosaic pattern (c) baronial (d) medieval

44. barouche    (a) wild dance step (b) jeweled clip (c) portico (d) carriage

45. bastion    (a) part of a fortification (b) column (c) stitching (d) great figure

46. batten        (a) pound to a pulp (b) roast lightly
                  (c) make into a paste (d) grow fat

47. beldam        (a) old woman (b) cosmetic (c) harm-
                  ful drug (d) prima donna

48. bespeak       (a) engage in advance (b) praise (c) be
                  critical of (d) promise

49. bezel         (a) kind of nut (b) embezzlement
                  (c) jewel (d) edge of a cutting tool

50. bibelot       (a) large book (b) child's garment
                  (c) trinket (d) idle chatter


# B.

1. bibulous       (a) addicted to drink (b) talkative
                  (c) well-dressed (d) frothy

2. bight          (a) pestilence (b) hoist (c) bay
                  (d) small village

3. bilboes        (a) posters (b) vegetables (c) fetters
                  (d) elbows

4. bittern        (a) condiment (b) marsh bird (c) part
                  of a harness (d) northern tree

5. blatant        (a) futile (b) depressing (c) tardy
                  (d) noisily obtrusive

6. bosky          (a) impertinent (b) stout (c) vague
                  (d) wooded

7. breviary       (a) authority (b) prayer book (c) testa-
                  ment (d) cage

8. brindled       (a) marinated (b) streaked with a darker
                  color (c) tethered (d) resembling a
                  cow

9. brummagem      (a) foul odor (b) vagrancy (c) tinsel
                  (d) sharp cheese

10. buccal        pertaining to: (a) cheek (b) nose
                  (c) bugle (d) cow

11. cabala        (a) mystical doctrine (b) conspiracy
                  (c) type of pipe (d) acrostic

12. cacchination  (a) loud laughter (b) hypocritical
                  applause (c) confused medley
                  (d) slanderous language

13. cadge         (a) hide (b) bicker (c) imprison (d) beg

14. caesura       (a) surgical operation (b) aria (c) rhyth-
                  mic break (d) ripping sound

15. caitiff       (a) defendant in a lawsuit (b) person of
                  low character (c) judicial officer
                  (d) hunting dog

16. calligraphy    (a) exact measurement (b) type of ballet (c) beautiful handwriting (d) musical instrument

17. cantilever    (a) suspension bridge (b) supporting bracket (c) instrument for prying open (d) mathematical curve

18. capillary    pertaining to: (a) chapter (b) head (c) climax (d) thin tube

19. capitulate    (a) repeat (b) execute (c) summarize (d) surrender

20. carapace    (a) sea snail (b) gaudy banner (c) animal shell (d) medieval carriage

21. careen    (a) fondle (b) lurch (c) decay (d) secure

22. carrion    (a) wild animal (b) large bell (c) dead flesh (d) mechanical belt

23. caryatid    (a) turtle shell (b) type of beetle (c) tooth decay (d) column in shape of a female figure

24. catalytic    (a) accelerating an action (b) destroying (c) ineffectual (d) nonparticipating

25. categorically    (a) relatively (b) introductorily (c) unqualifiedly (d) wilfully

26. catharsis    (a) emotional purgation (b) Chinese custom (c) inner stress (d) eternal damnation

27. celibate    (a) unmarried (b) leafy (c) heavenly (d) joyous

28. cenobite    (a) individualist (b) beginner (c) monk living communally (d) empty tomb

29. cenotaph    (a) wax engraving (b) empty tomb (c) optical illusion (d) inscription on a statue

30. centrifugal    (a) symmetrical (b) flying from the center (c) divisive (d) fearful

31. centripetal    (a) attracted to the center (b) tending to deceive (c) circular (d) leaf-shaped

32. chaffer    (a) haggle (b) vex (c) small bird (d) sip

33. chaparral    (a) thicket (b) spur (c) cowboy hat (d) cattle enclosure

34. cheetah    (a) Chinese sailing vessel (b) small prayer rug (c) catlike animal (d) multicolored bird

35. chine    (a) kiln (b) succession of bell sounds (c) part of the face (d) backbone

36. chitterling    (a) trifling expense (b) small child

                (c) part of small intestine (d) smattering

37. cicatrix     (a) chirping insect (b) female cyclist (c) scar tissue (d) sharp spur

38. cinerary     pertaining to: (a) motion (b) offal (c) chanting (d) ashes

39. cinnabar     (a) bright-red mineral (b) spice (c) tropical fruit (d) bird of bright plumage

40. coadjutor     (a) extra juror (b) assistant (c) partner (d) umpire

41. cockatrice     (a) pedigreed fowl (b) fabulous serpent (c) deep wound (d) breed of dog

42. codicil     (a) addition to a will (b) minute particle (c) legal brief (d) unwritten code

43. colander     (a) grinder (b) Oriental potentate (c) strainer (d) container

44. collop     (a) fruit pudding (b) part of harness (c) small drinking cup (d) small piece of meat

45. colophon     (a) sound-recording device (b) cabbage-like plant (c) Oriental headdress (d) publisher's ornamental device

46. comatose     (a) obstinate (b) bemused (c) unconscious (d) disheveled

47. comestibles     (a) odds and ends (b) superior products (c) food (d) companions

48. comity     (a) beauty (b) courtesy (c) council (d) association

49. commensurate     (a) acquainted with (b) certain (c) requited (d) proportionate

50. complaisant     (a) unruffled (b) obliging (c) querulous (d) moody

## C.

1. complicity     (a) large number (b) bewilderment (c) a sharing of wrongdoing (d) difficulty

2. comstockery     (a) blockhouse (b) large warehouse (c) marksmanship (d) overzealous censorship

3. conative     relating to: (a) an attempt to perform an action (b) a figure in solid geometry (c) a type of evergreen (d) symbiotic existence

4. concatenation    (a) resonance (b) smugness (c) hollow-ness (d) linking together

5. conch    (a) thick strap (b) clamp (c) heavy blow (d) spiral shell

6. concomitant    (a) half-asleep (b) superfluous (c) multi-farious (d) accompanying

7. concordat    (a) document (b) agreement (c) treaty of peace (d) indorsement

8. concupiscence    (a) brotherly love (b) secret plot (c) burning desire (d) recuperation

9. contemn    (a) struggle with (b) convict (c) mar (d) despise

10. contiguous    (a) contemporary (b) constricted (c) infectious (d) adjacent

11. convoluted    (a) accompanied (b) transformed (c) coiled (d) knotted

12. corollary    (a) part of a flower (b) consequence (c) small diadem (d) artery of the heart

13. coruscate    (a) befuddle (b) roughen (c) deprive by force (d) sparkle

14. covert    (a) hidden (b) ditch (c) lid (d) boon companion

15. cozen    (a) ridicule (b) convince (c) flatter (d) cheat

16. crapulous    (a) depending on luck (b) ill from over-drinking (c) bloated (d) long-winded

17. crass    (a) gross (b) sure (c) brittle (d) long-established

18. crepitate    (a) make a rattling sound (b) crawl (c) become weak (d) fear

19. crepuscular    pertaining to: (a) crackling noise (b) drunkenness (c) twilight (d) circulation of the blood

20. croft    (a) skill (b) small farm (c) large barn (d) piece of pottery

21. crotchety    (a) broken down (b) full of whims (c) bent (d) knitted badly

22. cruet    (a) large cake (b) small bottle (c) thick oil (d) fancy napkin

23. cubicle    (a) sailing craft (b) geometric figure (c) measure of length (d) small bed-room

24. culvert    (a) drain (b) tillage (c) crossing (d) weapon

25. curmudgeon    (a) buffoon (b) churlish fellow (c) tropi-cal fish (d) high anger

26. dado
(a) extinct bird (b) frantic caper (c) modern school of painting (d) middle section of a pedestal

27. daedal
(a) ambiguous (b) lethal (c) two-faced (d) ingenious

28. debauch
(a) cheapen (b) branch off (c) open a bottle (d) corrupt

29. debenture
(a) servitude (b) bond (c) amount due (d) stronghold

30. decadent
(a) deteriorating (b) subtle (c) occurring at ten-year periods (d) aristocratic

31. deciduous
(a) downcast (b) not evergreen (c) acidulous (d) trifling

32. decoction
(a) liquid preparation (b) stew (c) effervescent drink (d) a turning away

33. deglutition
(a) stickiness (b) cosmetic treatment (c) swallowing food (d) tearing apart

34. deleterious
(a) tardy (b) harmful (c) eliminating (d) considerate

35. demesne
(a) resignation (b) region (c) lowly conduct (d) good behavior

36. depilate
(a) unscramble (b) displease (c) remove hair (d) pillage

37. depredation
(a) decrease in value (b) warding off (c) disapproval (d) plundering

38. deracinate
(a) pull up by the roots (b) shunt off (c) slow down (d) tear to shreds

39. desuetude
(a) bluntness (b) rich style of cooking (c) disuse (d) sweetness

40. detrition
(a) wearing away (b) sudden departure (c) prevention (d) anguish

41. diaeresis
(a) dispersion (b) two dots over a vowel (c) take off of a plane (d) gastric disorder

42. dialectics
(a) kind of patois (b) socialism (c) elocution (d) logical argumentation

43. discrete
(a) separate (b) sagacious (c) broken up (d) faraway

44. disquisition
(a) formal request (b) itemized list (c) dissertation (d) uneasiness

45. distrait
(a) inconvenienced (b) afflicted (c) absentminded (d) twisted out of shape

46. diurnal
(a) everlasting (b) solar (c) daily (d) news item

47. doggerel      (a) small pet (b) pomposity (c) short slogan (d) trivial verse

48. dolorous      (a) parsimonious (b) financial (c) sorrowful (d) sacred

49. doxology      (a) study of propaganda (b) heresy (c) hymn of praise (d) obstinate belief

50. dross      (a) Chinese temple (b) worthless matter (c) thin thread (d) laziness

## D.

1. dudgeon      (a) small fish (b) resentment (c) pride (d) underground cell

2. dulcimer      (a) sweet song (b) small scimitar (c) musical instrument (d) soothing remedy

3. ecdysis      (a) migration (b) frenzy (c) partition (d) molting

4. edacious      (a) eatable (b) bold (c) haughty (d) devouring

5. edentate      (a) indented (b) saw-toothed (c) toothless (d) idyllic

6. effigy      (a) image (b) fireplace (c) scaffold (d) attachment

7. effulgent      (a) sacred (b) radiant (c) thunderous (d) sickening

8. elegiac      (a) mournful (b) select (c) desirable (d) laudatory

9. emblazon      (a) set on fire (b) adorn magnificently (c) set as an example (d) persist

10. embryonic      (a) developed (b) ingrown (c) hereditary (d) rudimentary

11. emendation      (a) praise (b) correction (c) elimination (d) legislative proposal

12. emollient      (a) milky (b) soothing (c) oily (d) adhering

13. empyrean      (a) the firmament on high (b) basis of rule (c) experience (d) tremendous conflagration

14. emulate      (a) adulate (b) overcome (c) strive to equal (d) begrudge

15. ensconced      (a) illuminated (b) immersed (c) snugly settled (d) deeply baked

16. eolithic      pertaining to: (a) harp music (b) earliest

human culture (c) modern sculpture
(d) mineral springs

17. epicene
(a) sexless (b) pertaining to the stage
(c) esthetic (d) luxurious

18. erose
(a) self-educated (b) spontaneous
(c) having irregular notched edges
(d) smooth-surfaced

19. eructate
(a) falsify (b) get rid of (c) plead
against (d) burp

20. esculent
(a) wealthy (b) hungry (c) lovable
(d) edible

21. estivate
(a) cram full (b) give incentive to (c)
procrastinate (d) spend the summer

22. esurient
(a) inaudible (b) crafty (c) voracious
(d) refractory

23. euphuism
(a) excessive elegance of language
(b) constant attention to health
(c) pleasing harmony of sound
(d) concise manner of speech

24. euthenics
(a) belief in euthanasia (b) theory of
human origin (c) science of dealing
with improvement of well-being
(d) system of ballet training

25. eviscerate
(a) disembowel (b) make less sticky
(c) bring out into view (d) extract

26. execrate
(a) develop (b) reveal (c) eliminate
(d) detest

27. exegesis
(a) crucial moment (b) strict accuracy
(c) outward show (d) critical explanation of a text

28. exiguous
(a) precarious (b) meager (c) demanding (d) inexplicable

29. exoteric
(a) essential (b) easily understood
(c) strange (d) final

30. expiate
(a) atone (b) demolish (c) succumb
(d) sanctify

31. expostulation
(a) violent threat (b) remonstrance
(c) outburst of temper (d) after-
thought

32. extant
(a) outstanding (b) valueless (c) no
longer in existence (d) still in existence

33. extrinsic
(a) not inherent (b) strange (c) romantic (d) high-priced

34. exude
(a) wither away (b) overflow (c) ooze
out (d) evaporate

35. farthingale — (a) strap (b) small British coin (c) affectionate farewell (d) hoop skirt

36. febrile — (a) nervous (b) moody (c) feverish (d) slight

37. fecundity — (a) depth (b) fertility (c) poverty (d) validity

38. fenestrated — (a) having windows (b) enclosed (c) deployed (d) mired

39. feracious — (a) fierce (b) predatory (c) fruitful (d) bearing away

40. fetid — (a) celebrated (b) heavy (c) malodorous (d) insipid

41. figment — (a) something imagined (b) romantic art (c) worthlessness (d) small part

42. fillip — (a) large dose (b) acrobatic trick (c) beverage (d) stimulus

43. flippancy — (a) levity (b) clumsiness (c) adroitness (d) lack of understanding

44. flocculent — (a) fluffy (b) pretentious (a) insipid (d) congregating

45. floe — (a) Arctic hut (b) winter sport (c) mass of floating ice (d) red caviar

46. fluted — (a) arched (b) intoned (c) fretted (d) grooved

47. foible — (a) decoration (b) animal story (c) frailty (d) deceptive scheme

48. foment — (a) cherish (b) instigate (c) whip into a froth (d) drive mad

49. foray — (a) raid (b) campaign hat (c) food for cattle (d) hullabaloo

50. frenetic — (a) psychological (b) wildly excited (c) cheering (d) exhausted

## E.

1. frieze — (a) niche (b) ornamental strip (c) top section (d) pedestal

2. frond — (a) superstructure (b) bending tree (c) leaf (d) stem

3. fruition — (a) fulfillment (b) seed dispersal (c) parsimoniousness (d) temporary use

4. fugacious — (a) fanciful (b) transitory (c) breaking loose (d) irresponsible

5. fustian — (a) antique (b) dusty (c) bombastic (d) patrician

6. garrulity — (a) cheapness (b) murmuring sound

(c) untamable nature (d) talkative-ness

7. gastronomy    (a) art of good eating (b) stomachic distress (c) study of minerals (d) fortunetelling

8. germinate    (a) inoculate (b) sprout (c) end suddenly (d) carry disease

9. gibbous    (a) talkative (b) boring (c) apelike (d) humpbacked

10. gnomon    (a) type of indicator (b) pygmy (c) logical inference (d) wise saying

11. gonfalon    (a) small predatory bird (b) Mediterranean fishing boat (c) type of flag (d) design of a coat of arms

12. guise    (a) wile (b) protection (c) malice (d) appearance

13. gustatory    (a) fitful (b) loathsome (c) pertaining to taste (d) having to do with wind currents

14. hackles    (a) open carriages (b) small bones (c) bristles on a dog's back (d) wornout horses

15. haft    (a) weapon (b) knife handle (c) scabbard (d) weight

16. heinous    (a) outrageous (b) incredible (c) insignificant (d) raucous

17. hibernal    (a) vegetative (b) wintry (c) Spanish (d) Irish

18. histrionic    (a) theatrical (b) famous (c) erudite (d) deluded

19. hobbledehoy    (a) gawky lad (b) tomboy (c) great uproar (d) child's game

20. homily    (a) scolding (b) porridge (c) sermon (d) recipe

21. hortatory    (a) leading (b) threatening (c) urging (d) arising

22. hoyden    (a) tomboy (b) old coin (c) mischievous boy (d) loud noise

23. hustings    (a) election platform (b) billboards (c) ladders (d) frenzied appeals

24. hyperborean    (a) exaggerated (b) frigid (c) tedious (d) sensitive

25. hypothecate    (a) reason (b) store away (c) conjecture (d) mortgage

26. iconoclast    (a) worshiper (b) attacker of tradition (c) painter of images (d) supporter of the status quo

27. ictus — (a) metrical foot (b) verse stress (c) small fish (d) cutting tool

28. imbrue — (a) bring about (b) fill (c) heat (d) stain

29. immanent — (a) prominent (b) departing (c) impending (d) inherent

30. impinge — (a) encroach (b) pilfer (c) paint (d) constrict

31. implacable — (a) dissatisfied (b) fuzzy (c) well hidden (d) unappeasable

32. imponderable — (a) unthinkable (b) very small (c) incapable of being weighed (d) of tremendous importance

33. inadvertence — (a) hatred (b) unwillingness (c) oversight (d) unpleasantness

34. inanition — (a) passivity (b) emptiness (c) silliness (d) beginning

35. incantation — (a) pouring liquids into casks (b) long operatic aria (c) repentance (d) magic formula

36. incarcerate — (a) burn completely (b) imprison (c) torture (d) imperil

37. incidence — (a) rate of occurrence (b) cutting into (c) uprising (d) similar event

38. incontinent — (a) unrestrained (b) unhappy (c) innumerable (d) surrounded

39. indenture — (a) written contract (b) verbal promise (c) dental plate (d) partial invasion

40. inordinate — (a) uncountable (b) excessive (c) permissive (d) not ordained

41. inscrutable — (a) tightly shut (b) malicious (c) undeniable (d) enigmatic

42. insinuate — (a) cause injury (b) liberate (c) suggest slyly (d) spy upon

43. insuperable — (a) insurmountable (b) unenviable (c) delightful (d) unwanted

44. integument — (a) covered entrance (b) large shelter (c) proclamation (d) outer covering

45. interloper — (a) intruder (b) malingerer (c) acrobat (d) slanderer

46. interstices — (a) digressions (b) small openings (c) stitches (d) internal organs

47. invidious — (a) apt (b) subtle (c) unconquerable (d) giving offense

48. iterative — (a) pertaining to travel (b) repetitious (c) haphazardly (d) problematical

49. jape — (a) yawn (b) rip (c) scream (d) trick

50. jocose            (a) useless (b) playful (c) illusory
                      (d) trite

# F.

1. jocund             (a) cheerful (b) heavenly (c) rotund
                      (d) fast-moving
2. joist              (a) tenon (b) mortise (c) timber laid
                      horizontally (d) juncture
3. jowl               (a) small jar (b) pork sausage (c) jaw
                      (d) shrieking sound
4. juxtapose          (a) pretend (b) discard (c) juggle
                      (d) put side by side
5. lanyard            (a) sail (b) short rope (c) lower deck
                      (d) open court
6. lectern            (a) literary conference (b) reference
                      work (c) storm lantern (d) reading
                      desk
7. levity             (a) frivolity (b) increase (c) fermenta-
                      tion (d) forgetfulness
8. lexicographer      (a) forger (b) shorthand expert (c) dic-
                      tionary maker (d) typesetter
9. libidinous         (a) disagreeable (b) headstrong (c) lust-
                      ful (d) discolored
10. licentious        (a) dramatic (b) sanctioned (c) wanton
                      (d) self-seeking
11. ligneous          (a) woodlike (b) carboniferous (c) re-
                      clining (d) explosive
12. lintel            (a) bitter spice (b) small vegetable
                      (c) flax thread (d) bar above a door
13. litany            (a) deep moan (b) legal battle (c) popu-
                      lar choice (d) repeated series of
                      responses
14. litotes           (a) stanza (b) making of an affirmative
                      by use of two negatives (c) exaggera-
                      tion (d) literary output
15. livid             (a) smarting (b) black and blue (c) sen-
                      sational (d) bilious
16. macerate          (a) strike (b) soften by soaking (c) cut
                      into strips (d) disfigure
17. malleable         (a) stringy (b) puncture-proof (c) per-
                      meable (d) pliant
18. mandrill          (a) baboon (b) musical instrument
                      (c) tropical fruit (d) narcotic herb
19. manifesto         (a) secret treaty (b) cargo list (c) revo-
                      lutionary plot (d) public declaration

20. marmoreal — pertaining to: (a) marble (b) tomb (c) coat-of-mail (d) lower order of monkeys

21. marmot — (a) tureen (b) rodent (c) tile (d) monkey

22. martingale — (a) warbler (b) harness strap (c) period costume (d) atmospheric disturbance

23. mastic — (a) ear trouble (b) kind of resin (c) extinct mammal (d) overlordship

24. mastodon — (a) gigantic hound (b) threat (c) extinct elephant (d) type of dinosaur

25. matutinal — (a) early (b) devotional (c) musical (d) mature

26. maunder — (a) hesitate (b) chew thoroughly (c) talk incoherently (d) weep

27. mayhem — (a) murder (b) act of chance (c) criminal mutilation (d) deep sigh

28. miasma — (a) dizzy spell (b) potent drug (c) poisonous exhalation (d) deep swamp

29. militate — (a) work against (b) pacify (c) serve a term (d) endanger

30. minion — (a) power (b) wing (c) small measure (d) hanger-on

31. misprision — (a) contempt (b) egregious error (c) illegal arrest (d) official misconduct

32. mitigate — (a) soften (b) harm (c) make more severe (d) delight

33. moiety — (a) half (b) delicacy (c) easy disposition (d) lion's share

34. mollification — (a) slight change (b) softening of ruffled feelings (c) washing with soap (d) dressing expensively

35. mordacious — (a) surly (b) deathly (c) bold (d) caustic

36. morganatic — related to: (a) marriage for wealth (b) marriage of royalty to a commoner (c) pompous ceremony (d) black magic

37. motley — (a) abundant (b) undistinguished (c) dirty (d) variegated

38. murrain — (a) plague (b) walled city (c) small mouse (a) swampy land

39. mutation — (a) variation (b) silence (d) display (d) severance

40. myopic — (a) negligent (b) obscure (c) shortsighted (d) big-hearted

41. neap (a) short hair (b) back of neck (c) dance step (d) type of tide
42. nepotism (a) misconduct (b) undue affection (c) infringement (d) favoritism to a member of the family
43. niggling (a) stingy (b) twitching (c) finicky (d) scolding
44. nirvana (a) exotic flower (b) pacifism (c) complete inner calm (d) fantasy
45. nomadic (a) wandering (b) fierce (c) equestrian (d) lawless
46. nugatory (a) sweet (b) trivial (c) negative (d) solid
47. obeisance (a) forethought (b) deference (c) conduct (d) justification
48. obsidian (a) obstruction (b) fixed idea (c) glassy rock (d) siege
49. obverse (a) face of a coin (b) stubbornness (c) retreat (d) vagary
50. odalisque (a) Oriental female slave (b) couch (c) style of painting (d) tiled floor

## G.

1. olfactory pertaining to: (a) sense of smell (b) design (c) gasoline (d) manufacture of perfume
2. oriflamme (a) display of fireworks (b) battle standard (c) detonation (d) sparkling jewel
3. orison (a) early rising (b) the east (c) distant view (d) prayer
4. ormolu (a) old clock (b) reed furniture (c) imitation gold (d) delicate filigree
5. orotund (a) gilded (b) resonant (c) stout (d) hoarse
6. overweening (a) fondling (b) outstripping (c) pampering (d) arrogant
7. pachyderm (a) skin eruption (b) heavy cloth (c) thick-skinned animal (d) leather traveling bag
8. palpable (a) excited (b) persuasive (c) subtle (d) obvious
9. palpate (a) examine by touching (b) quiver (c) shock (d) conciliate

10. pannier (a) large wicker basket (b) small pan (c) rapier (d) exquisite brooch

11. panoply (a) kaleidoscope (b) cure-all (c) dowry (d) full array

12. parturition (a) exodus (b) childbirth (c) plunder (d) division

13. peculation (a) sinning (b) gambling (c) trading in cattle (d) embezzlement

14. pelagic pertaining to: (a) the sea (b) fur (c) prehistoric life (d) mountains

15. pendulous (a) heavy (b) tawdry (c) hanging down loosely (d) contrite

16. pennate (a) winged (b) pointed (c) having a long tail (d) tooth-edged

17. percipience (a) participation (b) avarice (c) keen perception (d) realism

18. peremptory (a) abrupt (b) advisory (c) unusual (d) absolute

19. perfunctory (a) superficial (b) complete in all details (c) nobly done (d) thoroughly mastered

20. peristyle (a) decoration (b) quill pen (c) nautical instrument (d) enclosure formed by a row of columns

21. perquisite (a) art of speaking (b) fiery address (c) prerogative (d) persuasive plea

22. pertinacious (a) unabashed (b) stubbornly persistent (c) audacious (d) related

23. peruse (a) condense (b) change (c) read through (d) exhaust

24. petard (a) explosive device (b) pulley (c) stratagem (d) winch

25. picaresque relating to: (a) fish (b) rogues (c) spears (d) bullfighters

26. pilchard (a) spike (b) felt hat (c) small case (d) young herring

27. piscatorial relating to: (a) fishing (b) portraiture (c) fortunetelling (d) letter writing

28. plagiarize (a) catch in a trap (b) remodel (c) appropriate another's ideas (d) flatter

29. plangent (a) affected with great joy (b) resounding deeply (c) soft and mellow (d) headlong

30. plankton (a) thin board (b) microscopic life (c) resonant sound (d) small percussion instrument

31. plaudit        (a) expression of approval (b) pleasure (c) consent (d) appraisal
32. plinth         (a) large tomb (b) crossbeam (c) square stone base (d) kindling material
33. pluvial        (a) mighty (b) wealthy (c) deadly (d) rainy
34. polity         (a) diplomatic action (b) rules of etiquette (c) tenure of office (d) basic structure of a government
35. popinjay       (a) fop (b) gadabout (c) circus clown (d) type of magpie
36. porphyry       (a) ointment (b) velvet hanging (c) reddish purple rock (d) jade
37. posset         (a) clay bottle (b) spiced hot drink (c) group of deputies (d) drinking song
38. postprandial   (a) dilatory (b) after-dinner (c) after midnight (d) posthumous
39. pother         (a) medicinal drink (b) comforting agent (c) disturbance (d) dull story
40. predatory      (a) carnivorous (b) powerful (c) anticipatory (d) plundering
41. predicate      (a) base upon facts (b) notify in advance (c) dictate (d) assume without inquiry
42. preempt        (a) place a bet (b) establish prior claim (c) vacate (d) substitute
43. prevenience    (a) source (b) impediment (c) foregathering (d) foresighted action
44. privative      (a) plundered (b) making negative (c) secretive (d) privilege
45. privy          (a) sharing secret knowledge (b) doing without (c) depriving (d) underprivileged
46. probity        (a) investigation (b) integrity (c) disgrace (d) absolute proof
47. proclivity     (a) infirmity (b) adherence (c) sudden action (d) natural tendency
48. prodigality    (a) great fame (b) sinfulness (c) lavishness (d) negligence
49. profligacy     (a) forward motion (b) productivity (c) ability to foretell the future (d) dissoluteness
50. prognathous    (a) having projecting jaws (b) before birth (c) closely related (d) quarrelsome

## H.

1. prophylactic — (a) toxic (b) sterile (c) preventive (d) curative

2. propinquity — (a) stinginess (b) nearness (c) searching quality (d) absolute proof

3. propitiate — (a) conform (b) appease (c) influence (d) approach

4. provender — (a) dry food for animals (b) hawker (c) careful person (d) thriftiness

5. prurient — (a) impoverished (b) guiltless (c) prudish (d) lewd

6. pullulate — (a) grasp (b) swarm (c) tug (d) applaud

7. purblind — (a) dazzling (b) lacking understanding (c) incomprehensible (d) conceited

8. pylon — (a) gateway (b) synthetic fabric (c) accumulation (d) asp

9. quagmire — (a) gradual rise (b) large clam (c) bog (d) underbrush

10. quietus — (a) conservatism (b) comfort (c) soft speech (d) release from life

11. quizzical — (a) antiquated (b) puzzling (c) odd (d) ill-tempered

12. quotidian — (a) trite (b) occurring every day (c) word for word (d) apportioning

13. raucous — (a) despairing (b) pugnacious (c) immature (d) harsh-sounding

14. recrimination — (a) counter-accusation (b) double jeopardy (c) flattery (d) needless repetition

15. redaction — (a) conquest (b) submission (c) editing (d) rehearsal

16. redolent — (a) fragrant (b) needy (c) lazy (d) grieving

17. refection — (a) meditation (b) light meal (c) remedy (d) dessert

18. refulgent — (a) brilliant (b) unstable (c) capacious (d) explosive

19. relegate — (a) put in order (b) tie together (c) assign to an inferior position (d) relieve

20. reprehensible — (a) easy to grasp (b) blameworthy (c) deferential (d) returnable

21. reprobate — (a) sinner (b) deserter (c) stickler for

accuracy (d) official in charge of wills

22. reproof     (a) check (b) strengthening (c) demonstration (d) censure

23. reticulated     (a) purchased (b) in a network pattern (c) sewed together (d) drawn together

24. revulsion     (a) change of government (b) a drawing back in disgust (c) backward motion (d) degradation

25. rhapsodic     (a) ecstatic (b) fervent (c) bombastic (d) tightly knit

26. risible     (a) shimmering (b) likely (c) inducing laughter (d) climbable

27. runnel     (a) underground passage (b) race track (c) grain stalk (d) small stream

28. salacious     (a) flavored (b) briny (c) obscene (d) purchasable

29. saltatory     (a) healthy (b) leaping (c) spicy (d) attacking

30. salver     (a) tray (b) ointment (c) salute (d) rescuer

31. sartorial     (a) costly (b) flashy (c) well-dressed (d) relating to a tailor

32. scrimshaw     (a) carved decorated object (b) gimlet (c) doodling (d) gadget

33. scurf     (a) coarse linen (b) menial attendant (c) rough water (d) dandruff

34. semantics     study dealing with: (a) earthquakes (b) tides (c) changes in meanings of words (d) military signals

35. senescence     (a) process of growing old (b) belief in hereafter (c) rebirth (d) dotage

36. sequacious     (a) preceding (b) following (c) isolated (d) forever questioning

37. seraglio     (a) silk culture (b) mediation (c) fracas (d) harem

38. serried     (a) notched (b) scattered (c) pursued (d) crowded together

39. sibylline     (a) poetic (b) oracular (c) hissing (d) luxurious

40. simian     (a) foolish (b) resembling (c) apelike (d) pertaining to Malaysia

41. sirocco     (a) hot wind (b) contagious disease (c) leather binding (d) style of painting

42. skittles (a) pretzels (b) ale (c) bowling game (d) trifles

43. sleazy (a) flimsy (b) disgusting (c) asthmatic (d) slippery

44. slough (a) marsh (b) bed of coal (c) difficult journey (d) massacre

45. sluice (a) microscopic section (b) period between two wars (c) multitude (d) artificial water channel

46. sodality (a) sogginess (b) temperance (c) fellowship (d) saltiness

47. soporific (a) indiscreet (b) inducing sleep (c) adolescent (d) causing trouble

48. speleology study of: (a) caves (b) rhetoric (c) geysers (d) soil conservation

49. splenetic (a) effusive (b) gorgeous (c) spiteful (d) damaging

50. spoliation (a) marring (b) plundering (c) recession (d) embellishing

# I.

1. sporadic (a) enclosed (b) relating to plants (c) occurring at irregular intervals (d) momentary

2. spume (a) venom (b) foam (c) scorn (d) decoration

3. squalid (a) unclean (b) cramped (c) humble (d) firm

4. strepitant (a) insistent (b) boisterous (c) rapid (d) infected

5. subliminal (a) dejected (b) lofty in tone (c) highly colored (d) subconscious

6. subsume (a) reject (b) undermine (c) include (d) suffer

7. succulent (a) cringing (b) flaccid (c) withered (d) juicy

8. sudorific (a) hypnotic (b) inducing pain (c) promoting sweat (d) magnificent

9. sumptuary (a) illegal (b) regulating expenditure (c) extravagant (d) impressive

10. sunder (a) break apart (b) go off course (c) defeat (d) astound

11. supercilious (a) foolish (b) eminent (c) haughty (d) respectful

12. supervene — (a) countermand (b) precede (c) interject (d) happen in addition

13. suppurate — (a) condemn (b) breathe with difficulty (c) form pus (d) crush

14. surcease — (a) onslaught (b) end (c) survival (d) relief

15. symbiotic — (a) evolutionary (b) attacking bacteria (c) unreal (d) living in close association

16. tactile — (a) capable of being touched (b) discreet (c) attached to a wall (d) of a quiet disposition

17. talesman — (a) charm (b) juror (c) lecturer (d) informer

18. talon — (a) hunting horn (b) card game (c) buzzard (d) claw

19. tantamount — (a) superior (b) far-removed (c) equivalent (d) gigantic

20. tarn — (a) heather (b) hedge (c) small mountain lake (d) dry meadow

21. tatterdemalion — (a) mythical monster (b) maniac (c) ragamuffin (d) obstructionist

22. tautology — (a) superfluous repetition (b) fine distinction (c) tension (d) hasty judgment

23. tellurian — (a) pertaining to the earth (b) explorer of outer space (c) planetary (d) infinite

24. temerarious — (a) cowardly (b) watchful (c) delicate (d) rash

25. termagant — (a) fishy (b) shrewish (c) unreliable (d) desperate

26. terrapin — (a) canvas covering (b) small diamond (c) defensive earthwork (d) turtle

27. titivate — (a) cause laughter (b) tickle (c) attempt (d) spruce up

28. transmogrify — (a) pierce (b) change completely (c) terrify (d) haunt

29. troglodyte — (a) grotesque idol (b) figure of speech (c) prehistoric animal (d) cave dweller

30. trumpery — (a) loud blast (b) deceptive maneuver (c) easy victory (d) showy trash

31. tumbrel (tumbril) — (a) musical instrument (b) climbing vine (c) two-wheeled cart (d) juggler's trick

32. tussock (a) thick clump of grass (b) soft cushion (c) hammock (d) small hill

33. ululate (a) plead with (b) sing nonsense syllables (c) howl (d) mumble

34. unmitigated (a) downright (b) fixed (c) untouched (d) loosened

35. unwonted (a) neglected (b) unwilling (c) unpleasing (d) not habitual

36. upbraid (a) chide (b) escalate (c) bind tresses (d) cause to tremble

37. verger (a) border (b) amalgamation (c) minor church official (d) slope

38. vertiginous (a) avoidable (b) dizzy (c) upright (d) greenish

39. virulent (a) sudden (b) manly (c) venomous (d) overpowering

40. vitreous (a) sticky (b) malicious (c) lifelike (d) glassy

41. volition (a) flight (b) determination (c) demand (d) power of willing

42. votary (a) worshiper (b) legal partner (c) cavity (d) elector

43. vouchsafe (a) grant security (b) deign (c) lock up (d) accept responsibility for

44. wattle (a) awkward creature (b) slow gait (c) form of fowl (d) fleshy flap

45. welter (a) limpness (b) confusion (c) heat (d) secretion

46. whilom (a) pensive (b) temporary (c) quondam (d) quaint

47. whorl (a) confusion (b) globe (c) spiral design (d) token

48. wicket (a) stool (b) gate (c) basket (d) batsman

49. winnow (a) sort out by sifting (b) minimize (c) blow (d) tiny fish

50. zany (a) ne'er-do-well (b) beggar (c) sad fellow (d) clown

## V.  FOR WORD SPECIALISTS

> *A teacher's dedication to the subject he is teaching is generally commendable, but the newsletter of the Modern Language Association has learned of a teacher of French in Copenhagen who may have gone a bit far. He urged his class to make a special effort to learn a certain word because it was so rare that they might never see it again.*

THE NEW YORK TIMES, APRIL 26, 1964

These are, we think, the especially difficult ones, although some words may to readers with special interests appear easier than the earlier 450. We have selected these from various examinations and from words we have met in our reading. Look back at the words—Chapter 2, Section II—taken from Pamela Hansford Johnson's novel. Such are the words you are likely to find on special examinations.

### A.

1. acatalectic    (a) revelatory (b) deceptive (c) complete (d) curtailed
2. acephalous    (a) leaderless (b) formless (c) bitter (d) sterilized
3. adit    (a) ledger balance (b) publicity release (c) mine entrance (d) calculating machine
4. aleatory    (a) congratulatory (b) depending on chance (c) airtight (d) comforting
5. amaranthine    (a) everlasting (b) bittersweet (c) flowery (d) ephemeral
6. amerce    (a) trade away (b) rinse (c) pound to bits (d) punish by fine
7. amphibology    (a) ability to live on land and sea (b) study of environment (c) ambiguity (d) acrobatic ability
8. anagogic    (a) relieving pain (b) mystical (c) leading astray (d) contrary
9. analects    (a) word games (b) legal codes (c) proverbs (d) miscellaneous excerpts

10. ancipital      (a) just beginning (b) two-edged (c) expectant (d) sudden

11. anfractuous      (a) lacking polish (b) unmanageable (c) domineering (d) winding

12. antinomy      (a) rebellious spirit (b) metallic element (c) unreasonableness (d) opposition between principles

13. aphesis      (a) speechlessness (b) lack of feeling (c) initial curtailment (d) classification of insects

14. apodictic      (a) necessarily true (b) uncertain (c) opposing (d) judicial

15. apolaustic      (a) regretful (b) given to rationalizing (c) devoted to enjoyment (d) over-praising

16. aposiopesis      (a) alienation (b) slow pacification (c) foot ailment (d) sentence left unfinished

17. appanage      (a) long plume (b) pain soother (c) natural attribute (d) panoramic view

18. appetency      (a) glamour (b) craving (c) capability (d) urgent request

19. apterous      (a) related to church altar (b) most likely (c) eminently fitted (d) wingless

20. ansate      (a) crooked (b) having a handle (c) gooselike (d) always hungry

21. asthenic      (a) weak (b) cultivated (c) baseless (d) breathing heavily

22. asyndeton      (a) flowery language (b) lack of cooperation (c) omission of conjunctions (d) poetic fancy

23. auscultation      act of: (a) kissing (b) hiding (c) listening (d) vibrating

24. austral      (a) primitive (b) severe (c) eastern (d) southern

25. avuncular      (a) relating to one's ancestor (b) curvaceous (c) like an uncle (d) jewel-like

26. azygous      (a) unmusical (b) single (c) plentiful (d) without a stem

27. baleen      (a) beautiful girl (b) evil look (c) dance step (d) whalebone

28. barratry      (a) enclosure (b) a kind of fraud (c) legal discussion (d) emptiness

29. brachylogy      (a) study of ferns (b) study of bones of

prehistoric animals (c) condensed
expression (d) treatment of arm
fractures

30. brumal        (a) lighthearted (b) impeccably groomed
                  (c) harmful (d) wintry

31. calescent     (a) merging (b) beautifying (c) growing
                  warm (d) waning

32. caliginous    (a) handsome (b) misty (c) overbearing
                  (d) chalklike

33. camber        (a) curve upward (b) exchange
                  (c) curdle (d) climb rapidly

34. carious       (a) deficient (b) decayed (c) solicitous
                  (d) covered with scars

35. catatonic     relating to: (a) irregular rhythmic stress
                  (b) upheaval of nature (c) muscular
                  ailment (d) catalepsy

36. catenary      (a) type of suspended cable (b) aged
                  person (c) fit of depression
                  (d) precious pendant

37. caudle        (a) warm drink for invalids (b) birth-
                  mark (c) overfondness (d) short tail

38. chasuble      (a) incense (b) form of a mass
                  (c) Gregorian chant (d) ecclesiasti-
                  cal garment

39. chiastic      relating to: (a) Greek alphabet
                  (b) crossing of species (c) type of
                  inverted word order (d) monastic
                  life

40. chiromancy    (a) beautiful handwriting (b) care of
                  the feet (c) period of trial
                  (d) palmistry

41. claymore      (a) quagmire (b) bed of peat (c) broad
                  sword (d) shillelagh

42. coryphee      (a) herald (b) chorus girl (c) medieval
                  light sword (d) witch

43. covin(e)      (a) conspiratorial band (b) secret shelter
                  (c) crow's nest (d) exotic liqueur

44. crampon       something used by: (a) amateur radio
                  operator (b) mountain climber
                  (c) tobogganist (d) lacrosse player

45. cunctation    (a) dilatoriness (b) insecurity (c) uni-
                  versality (d) momentary blackout

46. delitescence  (a) pretended joy (b) concealment
                  (c) growing old (d) inclination to
                  argue

47. dimidiate     (a) interfering (b) very small (c) halved
                  (d) slow

48. discalced — (a) barefooted (b) severed (c) whitewashed (d) ejected

49. dithyramb — (a) gland (b) drug addict (c) poisonous insect (d) frenzied emotional poem

50. dollop — (a) outcast (b) blob (c) final touch (d) sweet mixture

## B.

1. eirenic (irenic) — (a) working for peace (b) pertaining to Irish ballads (c) related to early satire (d) diabolical

2. eldritch — (a) doddering (b) magnificent (c) long continued (d) eerie

3. embrocate — (a) pour into a flask (b) rub with a liniment (c) entangle (d) embroider

4. eristic — (a) argumentative (b) amorous (c) fortunate (d) inquiring

5. etiolated — (a) exultant (b) branching out (c) bleached (d) fan-shaped

6. etiology — (a) theory of motion (b) study of temperature (c) rules of poetic structure (d) inquiry into physical causes

7. eyas — (a) glacial crevasse (b) unfledged bird (c) aerie (d) lowest rank of yeoman

8. falchion — (a) medieval sword (b) bird of prey (c) varlet (d) strong support

9. fane — (a) strong desire (b) temple (c) maze (d) willingness

10. farrier — (a) tanner (b) carriage maker (c) blacksmith (d) tavern keeper

11. feculent — (a) falling apart (b) covered with filth (c) foolish (d) productive

12. ferial — pertaining to: (a) holidays (b) embryology (c) diplomacy (d) plenitude

13. fuliginous — (a) sooty (b) thundering (c) gleaming (d) overflowing

14. galliard (gaillard) — (a) wandering medieval scholar (b) long lance (c) prancing steed (d) lively dance

15. germination — (a) jewel setting (b) budding (c) doubling (d) incandescence

16. glair — (a) splendor (b) glen (c) slimy substance (d) mountain shelf

17. hamartiology — (a) branch of theology dealing with sin (b) study of early Egyptian art

(c) medieval hunting handbook
(d) study of coastal regions

18. hamate            (a) broad (b) hooked (c) fleshy
                      (d) of a small village

19. hatchment         (a) heraldic panel (b) opening of a
                      ship's deck (c) enclosure for fowl
                      (d) tight covering

20. helicoid          (a) asteroid (b) spiral (c) pertaining to
                      the sun (d) gaslike

21. heuristic         (a) following a formula (b) stirring up
                      strife (c) employing specious
                      reasoning (d) stimulating inquiry

22. horripilation     (a) tearing the hair (b) sudden attack
                      of fear (c) hoarding (d) standing up
                      of hair on end

23. hyaline           (a) marine (b) potent (c) glassy
                      (d) diaphanous

24. illative          (a) enthusiastic (b) unrelated (c) in-
                      ferential (d) demonstrative

25. imbricate         (a) overlap evenly (b) rain heavily
                      (c) accuse of complicity (d) become
                      entangled in thorns

26. incrassate        (a) denounce (b) thicken (c) vulgarize
                      (d) glut with food

27. inspissated       (a) made thick (b) encouraged (c) scat-
                      tered (d) leaning

28. intercalate       (a) keep records (b) warm up (c) insert
                      a day in a calendar (d) measure a
                      diet

29. labefaction       (a) rubbing (b) weakening (c) civil
                      strife (d) immorality

30. labile            (a) pertaining to the lips (b) unstable
                      (c) elapsing (d) arduous

31. laches            (a) skin disease (b) cowardice (c) con-
                      trivance to close a door (d) inex-
                      cusable delay

32. latifundia        (a) wide stripe (b) large landed estate
                      (c) molten metal (d) huge financial
                      reserve

33. machicolated      (a) having loopholes for dropping mis-
                      siles (b) impregnated with resin (c)
                      latticed (d) pounded to a pulp

34. maieutic          pertaining to: (a) elevation of words
                      (b) hyperbole (c) dialectic method
                      of Socrates (d) power of healing

35. mantic            (a) grotesque (b) entranced (c) having
                      meaning (d) prophetic

36. marasmus          (a) confusing evidence (b) poisonous exhalation (c) progressive emaciation (d) unofficial sanction

37. marcescent          (a) withering (b) increasing (c) unfolding (d) macerating

38. meiosis          (a) disease of the tissues (b) understatement (c) minor inflammation (d) indefatigability

39. melic          pertaining to: (a) honey (b) darkness (c) song (d) ancient Spartan slave

40. mescaline          (a) eyebrow pencil (b) type of lacework (c) heavy lacquer (d) drug producing hallucinations

41. midden          (a) battleground (b) unharvested hay (c) halfway house (d) refuse heap

42. muliebrity          (a) womanliness (b) intoxication (c) obstinacy (d) renown

43. necromancy          (a) magic through communication with the dead (b) divination by means of the stars (c) art of embalming (d) reincarnation

44. nepenthe          (a) geometric curve (b) poverty (c) opiate (d) penitence

45. nimiety          (a) undervaluation (b) excess (c) imitation (d) good manners

46. noetic          relating to: (a) intellectual comprehension (b) mental aberration (c) desire to wander (d) lure of the unknown

47. nuncupative          (a) secluded (b) unsophisticated (c) unwritten (d) lacking desire

48. oneiric          relating to: (a) wine (b) dreams (c) black magic (d) harmony

49. operose          (a) surgical (b) flowery (c) tuneful (d) laborious

50. opsimath          (a) autodidact (b) student of snakes (c) specialist in rare eye diseases (d) a very late learner

## C.

1. orthoepy          (a) correction of dental irregularities (b) study of pronunciation (c) care of children (d) treatment of deformities

2. pandect          (a) universal cure (b) ancient ruler

                          (c) complete digest (d) serious operation

3. paraclete      (a) sycophant (b) selfish person (c) advocate (d) eminent author

4. parale(i)psis   (a) type of paralysis (b) study of butterflies (c) symmetrical form (d) pretended omission

5. patchouli     (a) mint perfume (b) fish stew (c) mincemeat cake (d) parlor game

6. piacular      (a) requiring a sacrifice (b) most holy (c) priestly (d) revelatory

7. podagra      (a) gout (b) special shoe (c) speaker's platform (d) tropical illness

8. prolegomena  (a) compilation of laws (b) preliminary remarks (c) hereditary estate (d) mannered style of writing

9. propaedeutic  relating to: (a) introduction to a study (b) care of infants (c) early history (d) child labor

10. psittacism   (a) lisping (b) sibilance (c) parrotlike speech (d) vile manners

11. raptorial    (a) selfish (b) enamored (c) authoritative (d) predacious

12. recidivism   (a) ancestor worship (b) revival (c) habitual relapse into crime (d) suicide

13. recusant    (a) dissenting in religion (b) extremely shy (c) hardhearted (d) not meeting standards

14. reification   act of: (a) confirming (b) repeating (c) making something concrete (d) turning assets into cash

15. renitent    (a) brilliant (b) depending (c) squirming (d) constantly opposed

16. rimose     (a) covered with ice (b) full of cracks (c) possessing poetic quality (d) having a circular surface

17. rugose     (a) coldish (b) reddish (c) wrinkled (d) modest

18. sabulous    (a) furry (b) splotched (c) itching (d) sandy

19. scabrous    (a) swordlike (b) rough (c) uncooperative (d) wholesome

20. scholiast    (a) maker of marginal annotations (b) pedant (c) preparatory school headmaster (d) master of a sailing vessel

21. scutate       (a) evanescent (b) chivalrous (c) shield-shaped (d) indistinguishable

22. sericeous       (a) Chinese (b) silky (c) inducing laughter (d) liquid

23. siffilate       (a) dust off (b) whistle (c) exhale (d) whisper

24. sillabub       (a) word formation (b) sweet dish (c) course of study (d) type of argument

25. sirdar       (a) water boy (b) Arabian sword (c) Turkish smoking vessel (d) Oriental military commander

26. stasis       (a) stagnation (b) metrical pause (c) military outpost (d) fixed opinion

27. sternutation       (a) reversal (b) trepidation (c) hardening (d) sneezing

28. stertorous       (a) snoring (b) persistent (c) undecided (d) loud-voiced

29. subvention       (a) trickery (b) secret meeting (c) late arrival (d) financial aid

30. swale       (a) marshy prairie (b) wide path (c) roll of a ship (d) bandage

31. tabescent       (a) purring (b) wasting away (c) accommodating (d) gloomy

32. taxonomy       (a) system of collecting revenue (b) stuffing of animals (c) military science (d) method of classification

33. teleology       (a) investigation of primitive life (b) doctrine of purpose in nature (c) study of sound (d) belief in chance as the determiner of human affairs

34. thalassic       relating to: (a) the Muses (b) the sea (c) geologic formations (d) marriage hymns

35. titubant       (a) resounding (b) honorary (c) percussive (d) staggering

36. topiary       related to: (a) shaping trees (b) earth science (c) wild-beast preserve (d) Oriental headdress

37. triturated       (a) fatigued (b) three-pronged (c) pulverized (d) eliminated

38. umber       (a) scaly skin (b) reddish-brown earth (c) cottage pie (d) shady nook

39. usufruct       (a) exorbitant interest (b) scientific farm management (c) depletion (d) right

to enjoy property of another without changing it

40. vaticination — (a) neighborhood (b) brewing (c) prophecy (d) inoculation

41. velleity — (a) elegance (b) slight wish (c) drapery (d) piece of parchment

42. verbigerate — (a) revolve ceaselessly (b) cause a repeated echo (c) repeat senselessly (d) become evasive

43. verecund — (a) awe-inspiring (b) bashful (c) truthful (d) springlike

44. vermicular — (a) similar (b) slangy (c) farinaceous (d) worm-shaped

45. verrucose — (a) swollen (b) warty (c) respectful (d) twisted out of shape

46. vesicant — (a) causing blisters (b) poisonous (c) relating to a mathematical term (d) glossy

47. virgate — (a) turnstile (b) manly (c) rod-shaped (d) actual

48. viridity — (a) heroism (b) greenness (c) toxicity (d) intensity

49. wimble — (a) gimlet (b) short cloak (c) ruffle (d) head covering

50. ziggurat — (a) winding path (b) type of coil (c) mystic belief (d) pyramidal temple

# Answers

## CHAPTER ONE (Pages 20–21; 21–26)

### Pretest

1. (a) 2. (b) 3. (b) 4. (d) 5. (c) 6. (b) 7. (a) 8. (c) 9. (d)
10. (c) 11. (a)

### A.

1. (b) 2. (c) 3. (c) 4. (a) 5. (b) 6. (a) 7. (c) 8. (d) 9. (d)
10. (b) 11. (b) 12. (c) 13. (c) 14. (a) 15. (c) 16. (a) 17. (c)
18. (c) 19. (b) 20. (d) 21. (b) 22. (d) 23. (d) 24. (a) 25. (b)
26. (b) 27. (a) 28. (d) 29. (b) 30. (c) 31. (d) 32. (d) 33. (a)
34. (a) 35. (b) 36. (f) 37. (b) 38. (c) 39. (a) 40. (a) 41. (d)
42. (b) 43. (a) 44. (d) 45. (c) 46. (c) 47. (b) 48. (a) 49. (c)
50. (b)

### B.

1. (a) 2. (b) 3. (c) 4. (b) 5. (a) 6. (c) 7. (b) 8. (d) 9. (d)
10. (a) 11. (c) 12. (a) 13. (d) 14. (d) 15. (c) 16. (a) 17. (c)
18. (a) 19. (b) 20. (b) 21. (a) 22. (b) 23. (d) 24. (c) 25. (d)
26. (b) 27. (d) 28. (d) 29. (a) 30. (b) 31. (c) 32. (d) 33. (a)
34. (d) 35. (b) 36. (c) 37. (b) 38. (a) 39. (b) 40. (b) 41. (c)
42. (d) 43. (c) 44. (a) 45. (c) 46. (b) 47. (b) 48. (d) 49. (b)
50. (c)

### Add an Initial Letter

1. c 2. f 3. m 4. f 5. m 6. h 7. g 8. s 9. p 10. c 11. s 12. c 13. p
14. b 15. f 16. l 17. s 18. s 19. i 20. c 21. p 22. t 23. t 24. e 25. d
26. t 27. a 28. s 29. a 30. a

## CHAPTER TWO (Pages 28–29; 33–37; 39–41)

### Pretest

1. (c) 2. (b) 3. (a) 4. (b) 5. (d) 6. (a) 7. (d) 8. (c) 9. (b)
10. (a) 11. (d) 12. (c)

### I.

1. (c) 2. (b) 3. (c) 4. (a) 5. (d) 6. (c) 7. (a) 8. (d) 9. (d)
10. (a) 11. (c) 12. (d) 13. (d) 14. (c) 15. (d) 16. (b) 17. (c)

**18.** (a) **19.** (c) **20.** (b) **21.** (d) **22.** (a) **23.** (b) **24.** (d) **25.** (b)
**26.** (c) **27.** (d) **28.** (d) **29.** (a) **30.** (d) * * * **31.** (a) **32.** (c)
**33.** (a) **34.** (a) **35.** (c) **36.** (d) **37.** (d) **38.** (b) **39.** (c) **40.** (b)
**41.** (a) **42.** (c) **43.** (c) **44.** (a) **45.** (a) **46.** (b) **47.** (a) **48.** (a)
**49.** (c) **50.** (c) **51.** (b) **52.** (c) **53.** (d) **54.** (c) **55.** (a) **56.** (b)
**57.** (c) **58.** (d) **59.** (d) **60.** (b) **61.** (c) **62.** (b)

**II.**

**1.** bitter **2.** kept cats **3.** attracting and repelling **4.** pardoned **5.** out
of step with the times **6.** educate ourselves **7.** fraud **8.** embarrassing
incident **9.** women **10.** sullen **11.** genteel phrases **12.** urged **13.** deadlock **14.** early printed books **15.** forbidden **16.** deadly **17.** coin collectors **18.** cure all ills **19.** descendant **20.** rookie

## CHAPTER THREE (Pages 44–47; 47–50; 51)

**I. A.**

**1.** d **2.** f **3.** c **4.** b **5.** g **6.** a **7.** i **8.** j **9.** e **10.** h

**B.**

**1.** (b) **2.** (c) **3.** (b) **4.** (a) **5.** (c) **6.** (c) **7.** (d) **8.** (b) **9.** (a)
**10.** (c) **11.** (d) **12.** (b) **13.** (b) **14.** (c) **15.** (d) **16.** (c) **17.** (b)
**18.** (c) **19.** (d) **20.** (d) **21.** (c) **22.** (a) **23.** (c) **24.** (b) **25.** (d)
**26.** (a) **27.** (b) **28.** (a) **29.** (d) **30.** (d) **31.** (c) **32.** (b) **33.** (c)
**34.** (b) **35.** (b) **36.** (a) **37.** (d) **38.** (c) **39.** (c) **40.** (d)

**II.**

**1.** (b) **2.** (c) **3.** (b) **4.** (c) **5.** (a) **6.** (d) **7.** (d) **8.** (c) **9.** (a)
**10.** (a) **11.** (c) **12.** (d)

**III.**

**1.** (c) **2.** (b) **3.** (a) **4.** (b) **5.** (d) **6.** (c) **7.** (a) **8.** (d) **9.** (c)
**10.** (c) **11.** (b) **12.** (b) **13.** (d) **14.** (c) **15.** (b) **16.** (b) **17.** (c)
**18.** (b) **19.** (c) **20.** (d) **21.** (a) **22.** (b) **23.** (a) **24.** (a) **25.** (b)
**26.** (c) **27.** (a) **28.** (a) **29.** (c) **30.** (b) **31.** (c) **32.** (d) **33.** (b)
**34.** (c) **35.** (c) **36.** (c) **37.** (d) **38.** (a) **39.** (d) **40.** (a)

**Vocabagrams**

**1.** aver **2.** rote **3.** tyro **4.** ruse **5.** mote **6.** rime **7.** rife **8.** dais
**9.** ogre **10.** tacit **11.** venal **12.** gelid **13.** nadir **14.** infer **15.** latent
**16.** recant **17.** writhe **18.** docile **19.** laconic **20.** integral

## CHAPTER FOUR (Pages 61–66; 66–67)

**I.**

**1.** g **2.** e **3.** c **4.** i **5.** f **6.** a **7.** h **8.** j **9.** d **10.** b

**II.**

**1.** (d) **2.** (b) **3.** (a) **4.** (a) **5.** (c) **6.** (d) **7.** (b) **8.** (d) **9.** (b)
**10.** (a)

**III.**

LIKE: 1, 3, 4, 5, 7
UNLIKE: 2, 6, 8, 9, 10

**IV.**

**1.** g **2.** f **3.** j **4.** a **5.** i **6.** b **7.** c **8.** d **9.** h **10.** e

**V.**

**1.** command **2.** credible **3.** incorporate **4.** premonition **5.** amicable
**6.** salubrious; salutary **7.** innate **8.** eventuality **9.** immaculate
**10.** indefatigable

**VI.**

**1.** growth **2.** foreshadowing **3.** greed **4.** outstanding **5.** overhanging
**6.** weariness **7.** worldly **8.** unforeseeable **9.** truth **10.** wordy

**VII.**

**1.** (c) **2.** (a) **3.** (b) **4.** (b) **5.** (a) **6.** (b) **7.** (c) **8.** (a) **9.** (c)
**10.** (b) **11.** (c) **12.** (b) **13.** (a) **14.** (c) **15.** (c)

**VIII.**

**1.** cooperation **2.** periphery **3.** birth **4.** acme **5.** eccentric **6.** anthem
**7.** tenet **8.** phantom **9.** heavenly **10.** adage

**IX.**

**1.** auditory **2.** captious **3.** incredulous **4.** concurrent **5.** progeny
**6.** admonish **7.** rescind **8.** assiduous **9.** intangible **10.** temporize
**11.** adverse **12.** improvisation

**X.**

**1.** (b) **2.** (c) **3.** (d) **4.** (a) **5.** (d) **6.** (a) **7.** (c) **8.** (a) **9.** (b)
**10.** (b)

**Vocabagrams: I**

**1.** acerb **2.** mordant **3.** ignited **4.** remiss **5.** requite **6.** infringe
**7.** overt **8.** simulate **9.** serried **10.** deride **11.** divert **12.** regale
**13.** saline **14.** lambent **15.** asperse **16.** solace **17.** censer **18.** morbid
**19.** salient **20.** impugn

**Vocabagrams: II**

**1.** ferre **2.** fluere **3.** credere **4.** sentire **5.** fidere **6.** paene **7.** venire
**8.** vertere **9.** venia **10.** sacer

## CHAPTER FIVE    (Pages 69–70; 83–87)

**Pretest**

1. post 2. dis 3. di 4. pro 5. in 6. pro 7. con 8. in 9. pro 10. e
11. ex 12. extro 13. suf 14. post 15. ab 16. op 17. retro 18. de
19. ob 20. ant

**I.**

1. de 2. male 3. dif 4. de 5. dis 6. eu 7. dis 8. caco 9. in 10. im
11. hetero 12. ex 13. e 14. extra 15. micro 16. bene 17. de 18. dis
19. mis 20. retro *or* re

**II.**

1. con 2. down 3. over 4. ob 5. be 6. over 7. en 8. sub

**III.**

1. g 2. h 3. i 4. d 5. a 6. b 7. j 8. c 9. f 10. e

**IV.**

1. (a), (d) 2. (b), (c) 3. (a), (b) 4. (d), (e) 5. (c), (e)
6. (a), (d) 7. (b), (c) 8. (c), (e) 9. (d), (e) 10. (b), (c)

**V.**

1. an (c) 2. circum (a) 3. eu (h) 4. peri (e) 5. trans (b)

**VI.**

1. (c) 2. (h) 3. (e) 4. (f) 5. (d)

**Vocabagrams**    (The complete word is given.)

1. construe 2. rescind 3. inured 4. assuage 5. abhor 6. occult
7. erudite 8. surfeit 9. allege 10. embroil 11. inept 12. prestige
13. implies 14. exalt 15. impart 16. benign 17. analgesic 18. malign
19. demur 20. ensuing

## CHAPTER SIX    (Pages 89; 105–109)

**Pretest**

a. 10 b. 2 c. 7 d. 1 e. 9 f. 8 g. 5 h. 4 i. 6 j. 3

**I.**

a. nine b. triumvirate c. six d. thousand e. septuagenarian
f. bicentennial g. four h. first i. quintessence j. ten

**II.**

**a.** 4 **b.** 1959 **c.** 5 **d.** 3 **e.** 10

**III.**

**1.** i ?. a **3.** o **4.** e **5.** c **6.** m **7.** n **8.** k **9.** j **10.** p **12.** d
**14.** f **40.** l **100.** b **1000.** g **10,000.** h

**IV.**

**1.** (d) **2.** (a) **3.** (c) **4.** (d) **5.** (c) **6.** (e) **7.** (d) **8.** (c) **9.** (e)
**10.** (c)

**V.**

**1.** f **2.** i **3.** j **4.** a **5.** d **6.** b **7.** h **8.** k **9.** c **10.** l **11.** e **12.** g

**VI.**

**1.** (a) **2.** (d) **3.** (a) **4.** (b) **5.** (c)

**Vocabagrams**

**1.** dubiety **2.** hecatomb **3.** protocol **4.** myriad **5.** dilemma
**6.** Decameron **7.** sestet **8.** siesta **9.** trident **10.** primate **11.** tripod
**12.** travail

## CHAPTER SEVEN  (Pages 121–127)

**I. A.**

**1.** acquisition, acquisitive **2.** analysis, analytic(al) **3.** antagonism,
antagonistic **4.** contention, contentious **5.** corrosion, corrosive
**6.** eulogy, eulogistic **7.** pursuit, pursuant **8.** resentment, resentful
**9.** revelation, revelatory **10.** subversion, subversive

**B.**

**1.** allegation **2.** allotment **3.** demolition **4.** deprivation **5.** injunction
**6.** existence **7.** maintenance **8.** pronunciation **9.** repetition
**10.** rescission

**C.**

**1.** analogous **2.** apathetic **3.** climactic **4.** crucial **5.** inimical
**6.** heretical **7.** miscellaneous **8.** portentous **9.** presumptive,
presumptuous **10.** prodigious

**II. A.**

**1.** c **2.** d **3.** e **4.** f **5.** b **6.** i **7.** a **8.** h **9.** g **10.** l **11.** k **12.** j

**B.**

**1.** i **2.** d **3.** a **4.** j **5.** c **6.** h **7.** g **8.** e **9.** f **10.** b

**C.**

1. i 2. g 3. e 4. c 5. b 6. h 7. a 8. d 9. j 10. f

**D.**

1. i 2. g 3. j 4. c 5. b 6. h 7. f 8. a 9. d 10. e 11. l 12. k

**III. A.**

1. ologist 2. escent 3. tomy 4. nomy 5. fy 6. ology 7. age
8. tude 9. ory 10. ive

**B.**

1. ology 2. ous 3. tude 4. ure 5. ment 6. ory 7. ology 8. escent
9. ion 10. some

**IV. A.**

1. g 2. i 3. f 4. b 5. h 6. j 7. c 8. e 9. a 10. d

**B.**

1. e 2. g 3. d 4. h 5. b 6. f 7. a 8. c

**V.**

1. g. 2. d 3. h 4. j 5. i 6. c 7. a 8. b 9. f 10. e

**VI.**

1. d 2. h 3. g 4. i 5. b 6. f 7. j 8. e 9. a 10. c

**VII.**

1. o 2. f 3. g 4. m 5. a 6. n 7. d 8. i 9. l 10. h 11. j
12. k 13. b 14. c 15. e

**VIII.**

1. k 2. l 3. d 4. f 5. h 6. g 7. j 8. i 9. a 10. b 11. c 12. e

**Vocabagrams**

1. tangible 2. penal 3. genial 4. arable 5. secular 6. fiscal 7. agile
8. lesion 9. intrepid 10. feral 11. morose 12. decorous 13. stolid
14. exotic 15. truncate 16. insurgent 17. instigate 18. senile
19. endemic 20. mundane

**CHAPTER EIGHT**   (Pages 140–143; 144–145; 146–147; 149–150)

**I.**

1. (e) 2. (g) 3. (b) 4. (h) 5. (f) 6. (i) 7. (c) 8. (a)

**II.**

1. (d) 2. (b) 3. (g) 4. (e) 5. (f)

**III.**

1. (j) 2. (e) 3. (l) 4. (i) 5. (m) 6. (a) 7. (c) 8. (g) 9. (k) 10. (b)

**IV.**

1. (c) 2. (a) 3. (b) 4. (d) 5. (b) 6. (a) 7. (c) 8. (b) 9. (c)
10. (d) 11. (c) 12. (d) 13. (b) 14. (a) 15. (d)

**V.**

1. (c) 2. (a) 3. (b) 4. (d) 5. (h) 6. (f) 7. (g) 8. (e) 9. (n)
10. (o) 11. (j) 12. (m) 13. (l) 14. (i) 15. (k)

**"Occasional Words"**

**A.**

caisson 8; catafalque 11; cortege 7; eulogy 5; plenipotentiaries 2;
protocol 3

**B.**

aggiornamento 4; ecumenical 10; liturgy 8; schema 7; schism 3;
vernacular 5

**"Flash" Words**

1. e 2. g 3. j 4. f 5. i 6. b 7. d 8. a 9. h 10. c

**Vocabagrams**

1. daunted 2. cadge 3. qualm 4. bedlam 5. escalating 6. ribald
7. hubris 8. panache 9. sachem 10. scourge 11. arcane 12. tundra
13. nomadic 14. reticent 15. slough 16. kinetic 17. germane
18. austere 19. perverse 20. heresy 21. cachet 22. detente 23. cavil
24. scud 25. usurp

**CHAPTER NINE** (Pages 152–153; 176–183)

**Pretest**

1. e 2. j 3. f 4. i 5. b 6. 1 7. g 8. d 9. k 10. h 11. a 12. c

**I.**

1. (d) 2. (b) 3. (a) 4. (c) 5. (d)

**II.**

1. (e) 2. (d) 3. (h) 4. (c) 5. (a)

**III.**

1. (b) 2. (d) 3. (a) 4. (c) 5. (b)

**IV.**

1. h 2. d 3. e 4. j 5. a 6. c 7. i 8. b 9. g 10. f

**V.**

1. e 2. d 3. l 4. f 5. b 6. a 7. j 8. i 9. k 10. h 11. c 12. g

**VI.**

LIKE: 1, 3, 4, 5, 9, 10, 12, 16, 17, 18, 20
UNLIKE: 2, 6, 7, 8, 11, 13, 14, 15, 19

**VII.**

1. k 2. h 3. f 4. i 5. b 6. m 7. n 8. a 9. o 10. c 11. d
12. e 13. g 14. j 15. l

**VIII.**

1. (c) 2. (b) 3. (e) 4. (a) 5. (d)

**IX.**

1. (b) 2. (d) 3. (e) 4. (c) 5. (b)

**X.**

1. (c) 2. (d) 3. (a) 4. (b) 5. (d)

**Vocabagrams**

(French) 1. cliché 2. soupçon 3. décor 4. flâneur 5. précis
6. cadre 7. régime 8. tirade 9. ennui 10. timbre 11. malaise
12. svelte 13. adroit 14. outré 15. suave 16. environs 17. crèche
18. tocsin 19. ménage 20. mirage 21. roué 22. canapé 23. chagrin
24. dossier

(Spanish) 1. adobe 2. peon 3. mesa 4. corral 5. rodeo 6. armada
7. gusto 8. sarape, serape 9. rancho 10. adios 11. lariat 12. pronto

(Italian) 1. diva 2. presto 3. trio 4. torso 5. salvo 6. rondo
7. finale 8. cameo 9. patina 10. tempo 11. fresco 12. intaglio
13. forte 14. vista 15. amore 16. solo

CHAPTER TEN    (Pages 186; 190–191; 199–200; 206–209)

**Pretest**

1. (c) 2. (b) 3. (f) 4. (e) 5. (d) 6. (a)

**I. A.**

(a). 5 (b). 4 (c). 8 (d). 2 (e). 1 (f). 3 (g). 7 (h). 6

**I. B.**

(a). 3 (b). 4 (c). 1 (d). 2 (e). 8 (f). 6 (g). 5 (h). 7

**II.**

1. (h) (6) 2. (g) (7) 3. (a) (1) 4. (i) (8) 5. (c) (5) 6. (e) (9)
7. (j) (2) 8. (f) (10) 9. (b) (4) 10. (d) (3)

**III.**

1. (c) 2. (b) 3. (a) 4. (d) 5. (c) 6. (e) 7. (c) 8. (a) 9. (d)
10. (d) 11. (a) 12. (d) 13. (b) 14. (b) 15. (d) 16. (c) 17. (d)
18. (b) 19. (a) 20. (b) 21. (c) 22. (b) 23. (d) 24. (c) 25. (a)

**IV.**

1. uninterested 2. disinterested 3. immensity 4. adapted
5. depreciated 6. deprecated 7. fortunately 8. flouting 9. implication
10. climactic 11. supine 12. venal

**Vocabagrams**

1. ichor 2. reviled 3. nexus 4. eftsoons 5. rugose 6. rancid
7. condign 8. sardonic 9. talesmen 10. lemming 11. almoner
12. spume 13. careen 14. vapid 15. queasy 16. aperture 17. centaur
18. maunder 19. reredos 20. hirsute 21. mutable 22. erstwhile
23. decant 24. nostrums 25. renitent

**CHAPTER ELEVEN** (Pages 212; 220–224)

**Pretest**

1. tell 2. help 3. bereft 4. worthy 5. weighty 6. deem
7. burdensome 8. kingdom 9. kin 10. abode 11. withdraw 12. hang

**I.**

1. (b) 2. (a) 3. (b) 4. (d) 5. (d) 6. (c) 7. (a) 8. (d) 9. (a)
10. (b)

**II.**

1. (e) 2. (e) 3. (d) 4. (b) 5. (c) 6. (b) 7. (a) 8. (c) 9. (c)
10. (b)

**III.**

1. f 2. c 3. b 4. g 5. l 6. k 7. j 8. e 9. h 10. a 11. i 12. d

**IV.**

1. h 2. l 3. e 4. k 5. j 6. g 7. c 8. a 9. f 10. d 11. b 12. i

**V.**

1. worthy 2. befuddle *or* bewilder 3. mislead 4. wandering 5. uplift
6. unbelievable 7. bequest 8. wrongdoing 9. threatening
10. headlong 11. forbid 12. bloody

**VI.**

1. novice 2. archaic 3. worship 4. irate 5. polyglot 6. foreword
7. transitory 8. sympathy 9. hidden 10. deserter *or* defector
11. symbol 12. dolorous

**VII.**

1. division 2. mighty 3. antagonist 4. byword 5. frugal 6. hygienic
7. incendiary 8. scattering 9. dialogue 10. disputant

**Vocabagrams**

1. abet 2. lode 3. rood 4. lief 5. thole 6. churl 7. chore 8. lore
9. swath 10. wroth 11. wont 12. wend 13. offal 14. monger
15. treadle 16. anent 17. bluster 18. writhe 19. nether 20. stint
21. wraith 22. throes 23. sliver 24. fusty 25. meet

**CHAPTER TWELVE** (Pages 226; 233–234; 241–247; 247–248)

**Pretest 1**

1. j 2. a 3. g 4. b 5. h 6. c 7. f 8. d 9. i 10. e

**Pretest 2**

1. e 2. j 3. g 4. i 5. b 6. h 7. c 8. f 9. a 10. d

**I.**

1. (a) 2. (d) 3. (b) 4. (c) 5. (b) 6. (d) 7. (d) 8. (a) 9. (b)
10. (c)

**II.**

1. (e) 2. (k) 3. (j) 4. (l) 5. (g) 6. (i) 7. (c) 8. (a) 9. (f)
10. (h) 11. (b) 12. (d)

**III.**

1. f 2. l 3. h 4. j 5. g 6. d 7. e 8. i 9. k 10. a 11. b 12. c

**IV.**

1. h 2. k 3. j 4. g 5. l 6. i 7. e 8. c 9. a 10. b 11. d 12. f

**V.**

1. (b) 2. (a) 3. (b) 4. (c) 5. (a) 6. (d) 7. (c) 8. (b) 9. (a) 10. (d) 11. (c) 12. (d) 13. (b) 14. (d) 15. (a) 16. (d) 17. (a) 18. (b) 19. (c) 20. (b)

**VI.**

1. a 2. j 3. g 4. f 5. i 6. h 7. d 8. l 9. k 10. e 11. b 12. c
* * * 13. r 14. u 15. w 16. t 17. x 18. y 19. o 20. s 21. p 22. q 23. v 24. z

**VII.**

1. (b) 2. (e) 3. (d) 4. (a) 5. (c)

**Vocabagrams**

(Latin) 1. impetus 2. sinister 3. posse 4. retina 5. stupor 6. avis 7. arbiter 8. limbo 9. cadaver 10. integer 11. arena 12. vortex 13. campus 14. caries 15. censor 16. strata 17. torpor 18. viscera 19. tuba 20. stamen 21. via 22. rebus 23. rector 24. onus

(Greek) 1. icon 2. ethos 3. chaos 4. kudos 5. omega 6. trauma 7. aeon 8. echo 9. delta 10. enigma 11. iota 12. pathos

**CHAPTER THIRTEEN** (Pages 25C; 264–265; 265–268; 269)

**Pretest**

1. e 2. c 3. h 4. j 5. i 6. a 7. g 8. d 9. f 10. b

**"the Twelve"**

1. Jupiter 2. Hera 3. Venus 4. Phoebus 5. Ares 6. Diana 7. Pallas 8. Ceres 9. Vulcan 10. Vesta 11. Hermes 12. Poseidon

**I.**

1. j 2. k 3. h 4. i 5. d 6. g 7. a 8. e 9. l 10. b 11. c 12. f

**II.**

LIKE: 1, 2, 3, 5, 6, 10, 12
UNLIKE: 4, 7, 8, 9, 11

**III.**

1. (a) 2. (b) 3. (c) 4. (a) 5. (b) 6. (c) 7. (d) 8. (a) 9. (a) 10. (b)

**Vocabagrams**

1. oread 2. Medusa 3. naiad 4. Vesta 5. nereid 6. nectar 7. hydra
8. protean 9. Lethe 10. Pluto 11. Minerva 12. Circe 13. aegis
14. Midas 15. Iris 16. Nestor 17. Stentor 18. lotos 19. Hector
20. dryad 21. Charon 22. Gemini 23. mentor 24. Thor


## CHAPTER FOURTEEN  (Pages 271; 292–294)

**Pretest**

1. (b) 2. (d) 3. (c) 4. (a) 5. (d) 6. (b) 7. (a) 8. (c) 9. (a)
10. (d)

**I.**

1. (b) 2. (d) 3. (c) 4. (a) 5. (d) 6. (a)

**II.**

1. h 2. i 3. f 4. j 5. d 6. b 7. e 8. g 9. a 10. c

**III.**

1. (d) 2. (c) 3. (b) 4. (a) 5. (d) 6. (b)

**IV.**

1. (b) 2. (d) 3. (b) 4. (c) 5. (d) 6. (a) 7. (b) 8. (c) 9. (b)
10. (a)

**V.**

1. Armageddon 2. paregoric 3. jingoist 4. panegyric 5. Pecksniffery


## CHAPTER FIFTEEN  (Pages 297; 308–309; 314–318; 318–319)

**Pretest**

1. d 2. i 3. f 4. e 5. h 6. a 7. b 8. g 9. j 10. c

**Can You Dig These?**

1. adulation 2. comprehend 3. concoct 4. connive 5. defalcation
6. delirious 7. disastrous 8. dissident 9. effrontery 10. equivocation
11. exaggeration 12. excoriate 13. incensed 14. lunatic
15. perplexed 16. prevaricate 17. punctual 18. supplant 19. recant
20. pretext

**I.**

1. (c) 2. (e) 3. (a) 4. (b) 5. (c) 6. (d) 7. (c) 8. (a) 9. (c) 10. (a)

**II.**

LIKE: 1, 4, 6, 8, 9
UNLIKE: 2, 3, 5, 7, 10

**III.**

1. acronym 2. fulminate 3. gobbledegook 4. inaugurate 5. inveigh
6. lampoon 7. patois 8. sycophant 9. trope 10. vituperation

**IV.**

1. (b), (c); (e), (f) 2. (d), (e); (a), (f) 3. (d), (f); (a), (b)
4. (a), (f); (b), (d) 5. (c), (f); (b), (d)

**V.**

1. (b) 2. (d) 3. (a) 4. (e) 5. (c)

**VI.**

1. (b) 2. (c) 3. (d) 4. (a) 5. (a)

**VII.**

1. (b) 2. (d) 3. (a) 4. (d) 5. (d) 6. (c) 7. (a) 8. (b) 9. (d)
10. (c)

**VIII.**

1. e 2. f 3. h 4. a 5. j 6. b 7. i 8. c 9. l 10. k 11. d 12. g

**Vocabagrams**

1. amenities 2. in the press 3. list them 4. surmise 5. impale
6. decade 7. curate 8. opts 9. carte blanche 10. melange 11. albeit
12. encomium 13. Hades 14. sadism 15. argot * * * 16. guerdon


OUR OWN BATTERY OF TESTS
 (Pages 321–329; 332–337; 337–368)

**I. A.**

1. (a) 2. (c) 3. (c) 4. (c) 5. (a) 6. (c) 7. (b) 8. (a) 9. (d)
10. (b)

**I. B.**

1. (b) 2. (a) 3. (d) 4. (c) 5. (b) 6. (a) 7. (c) 8. (d) 9. (a)
10. (d) 11. (d) 12. (c) 13. (b) 14. (d) 15. (c)

**II. A.**

1. (a) 2. (c) 3. (c) 4. (b) 5. (d) 6. (a) 7. (c) 8. (c) 9. (e)
10. (d)

## II. B.

1. (d) 2. (b) 3. (a) 4. (c) 5. (d) 6. (d) 7. (c) 8. (a) 9. (e)
10. (b) 11. (e) 12. (b) 13. (d) 14. (e) 15. (d) 16. (a) 17. (c)
18. (c) 19. (b) 20. (a) 21. (e) 22. (e) 23. (a) 24. (b) 25. (e)
26. (c) 27. (b) 28. (d) 29. (d) 30. (a) 31. (b) 32. (e) 33. (e)
34. (b) 35. (e) 36. (c)

## III. A.

1. (b) 2. (a) 3. (d) 4. (d) 5. (e) 6. (d) 7. (b) 8. (b) 9. (a)
10. (d) 11. (c) 12. (a) 13. (e) 14. (a) 15. (e) 16. (b) 17. (d)
18. (e) 19. (b) 20. (d) 21. (a) 22. (e) 23. (c) 24. (e) 25. (b)
26. (e) 27. (a) 28. (c) 29. (a) 30. (e) 31. (e) 32. (d) 33. (d)
34. (d) 35. (e) 36. (d) 37. (d) 38. (a) 39. (b) 40. (c) 41. (b)
42. (d) 43. (b) 44. (c) 45. (b) 46. (c) 47. (a) 48. (b) 49. (a)
50. (e)

## III. B.

1. (b) 2. (d) 3. (b) 4. (b) 5. (a) 6. (c) 7. (e) 8. (c) 9. (a)
10. (d) 11. (a) 12. (d) 13. (e) 14. (c) 15. (c) 16. (d) 17. (e)
18. (e) 19. (e) 20. (c) 21. (b) 22. (e) 23. (c) 24. (c) 25. (b)
26. (d) 27. (b) 28. (a) 29. (d) 30. (a)

## IV. A.

| | | | | |
|---|---|---|---|---|
| 1. (c) | 11. (a) | 21. (b) | 31. (c) | 41. (c) |
| 2. (b) | 12. (d) | 22. (b) | 32. (a) | 42. (a) |
| 3. (a) | 13. (b) | 23. (d) | 33. (a) | 43. (d) |
| 4. (d) | 14. (d) | 24. (d) | 34. (c) | 44. (d) |
| 5. (c) | 15. (d) | 25. (d) | 35. (b) | 45. (a) |
| 6. (a) | 16. (c) | 26. (c) | 36. (d) | 46. (d) |
| 7. (b) | 17. (a) | 27. (b) | 37. (a) | 47. (a) |
| 8. (d) | 18. (d) | 28. (d) | 38. (a) | 48. (a) |
| 9. (b) | 19. (a) | 29. (c) | 39. (c) | 49. (d) |
| 10. (c) | 20. (a) | 30. (b) | 40. (c) | 50. (c) |

## IV. B.

| | | | | |
|---|---|---|---|---|
| 1. (a) | 11. (a) | 21. (b) | 31. (a) | 41. (b) |
| 2. (c) | 12. (a) | 22. (c) | 32. (a) | 42. (a) |
| 3. (c) | 13. (d) | 23. (d) | 33. (a) | 43. (c) |
| 4. (b) | 14. (c) | 24. (a) | 34. (c) | 44. (d) |
| 5. (d) | 15. (b) | 25. (c) | 35. (d) | 45. (d) |
| 6. (d) | 16. (c) | 26. (a) | 36. (c) | 46. (c) |
| 7. (b) | 17. (b) | 27. (a) | 37. (c) | 47. (c) |
| 8. (b) | 18. (d) | 28. (c) | 38. (d) | 48. (b) |
| 9. (c) | 19. (d) | 29. (b) | 39. (b) | 49. (d) |
| 10. (a) | 20. (c) | 30. (b) | 40. (b) | 50. (b) |

## IV. C.

| | | | | |
|---|---|---|---|---|
| 1. (c) | 11. (c) | 21. (b) | 31. (b) | 41. (b) |
| 2. (d) | 12. (b) | 22. (b) | 32. (a) | 42. (d) |
| 3. (a) | 13. (d) | 23. (d) | 33. (c) | 43. (a) |
| 4. (d) | 14. (a) | 24. (a) | 34. (b) | 44. (c) |
| 5. (d) | 15. (d) | 25. (b) | 35. (b) | 45. (c) |
| 6. (d) | 16. (b) | 26. (d) | 36. (c) | 46. (c) |
| 7. (b) | 17. (a) | 27. (d) | 37. (d) | 47. (d) |
| 8. (c) | 18. (a) | 28. (d) | 38. (a) | 48. (c) |
| 9. (d) | 19. (c) | 29. (b) | 39. (c) | 49. (c) |
| 10. (d) | 20. (b) | 30. (a) | 40. (a) | 50. (b) |

## IV. D.

| | | | | |
|---|---|---|---|---|
| 1. (b) | 11. (b) | 21. (d) | 31. (b) | 41. (a) |
| 2. (c) | 12. (b) | 22. (c) | 32. (d) | 42. (d) |
| 3. (d) | 13. (a) | 23. (a) | 33. (a) | 43. (a) |
| 4. (d) | 14. (c) | 24. (c) | 34. (c) | 44. (a) |
| 5. (c) | 15. (c) | 25. (a) | 35. (d) | 45. (c) |
| 6. (a) | 16. (b) | 26. (d) | 36. (c) | 46. (d) |
| 7. (b) | 17. (a) | 27. (d) | 37. (b) | 47. (c) |
| 8. (a) | 18. (c) | 28. (b) | 38. (a) | 48. (b) |
| 9. (b) | 19. (d) | 29. (b) | 39. (c) | 49. (a) |
| 10. (d) | 20. (d) | 30. (a) | 40. (c) | 50. (b) |

## IV. E.

| | | | | |
|---|---|---|---|---|
| 1. (b) | 11. (c) | 21. (c) | 31. (d) | 41. (d) |
| 2. (c) | 12. (d) | 22. (a) | 32. (c) | 42. (c) |
| 3. (a) | 13. (c) | 23. (a) | 33. (c) | 43. (a) |
| 4. (b) | 14. (c) | 24. (b) | 34. (b) | 44. (d) |
| 5. (c) | 15. (b) | 25. (d) | 35. (c) | 45. (a) |
| 6. (d) | 16. (a) | 26. (b) | 36. (b) | 46. (b) |
| 7. (a) | 17. (b) | 27. (b) | 37. (a) | 47. (d) |
| 8. (b) | 18. (a) | 28. (d) | 38. (a) | 48. (b) |
| 9. (d) | 19. (a) | 29. (d) | 39. (a) | 49. (d) |
| 10. (a) | 20. (c) | 30. (a) | 40. (b) | 50. (b) |

## IV. F.

| | | | | |
|---|---|---|---|---|
| 1. (a) | 11. (a) | 21. (b) | 31. (d) | 41. (d) |
| 2. (c) | 12. (d) | 22. (b) | 32. (a) | 42. (d) |
| 3. (c) | 13. (d) | 23. (b) | 33. (a) | 43. (c) |
| 4. (d) | 14. (b) | 24. (c) | 34. (b) | 44. (c) |
| 5. (b) | 15. (b) | 25. (a) | 35. (d) | 45. (a) |
| 6. (d) | 16. (b) | 26. (c) | 36. (b) | 46. (b) |
| 7. (a) | 17. (d) | 27. (c) | 37. (d) | 47. (b) |
| 8. (c) | 18. (a) | 28. (c) | 38. (a) | 48. (c) |
| 9. (c) | 19. (d) | 29. (a) | 39. (a) | 49. (a) |
| 10. (c) | 20. (a) | 30. (d) | 40. (c) | 50. (a) |

## IV. G.

| | | | | |
|---|---|---|---|---|
| 1. (a) | 11. (d) | 21. (c) | 31. (a) | 41. (a) |
| 2. (b) | 12. (b) | 22. (b) | 32. (c) | 42. (b) |
| 3. (d) | 13. (d) | 23. (c) | 33. (d) | 43. (d) |
| 4. (c) | 14. (a) | 24. (a) | 34. (d) | 44. (b) |
| 5. (b) | 15. (c) | 25. (b) | 35. (a) | 45. (a) |
| 6. (d) | 16. (a) | 26. (d) | 36. (c) | 46. (b) |
| 7. (c) | 17. (c) | 27. (a) | 37. (b) | 47. (d) |
| 8. (d) | 18. (d) | 28. (c) | 38. (b) | 48. (c) |
| 9. (a) | 19. (a) | 29. (b) | 39. (c) | 49. (d) |
| 10. (a) | 20. (d) | 30. (b) | 40. (d) | 50. (a) |

## IV. H.

| | | | | |
|---|---|---|---|---|
| 1. (c) | 11. (c) | 21. (a) | 31. (d) | 41. (a) |
| 2. (b) | 12. (b) | 22. (d) | 32. (a) | 42. (c) |
| 3. (b) | 13. (d) | 23. (b) | 33. (d) | 43. (a) |
| 4. (a) | 14. (a) | 24. (b) | 34. (c) | 44. (a) |
| 5. (d) | 15. (c) | 25. (a) | 35. (a) | 45. (d) |
| 6. (b) | 16. (a) | 26. (c) | 36. (b) | 46. (c) |
| 7. (b) | 17. (b) | 27. (d) | 37. (d) | 47. (b) |
| 8. (a) | 18. (a) | 28. (c) | 38. (d) | 48. (a) |
| 9. (c) | 19. (c) | 29. (c) | 39. (b) | 49. (c) |
| 10. (d) | 20. (b) | 30. (a) | 40. (c) | 50. (b) |

## IV. I.

| | | | | |
|---|---|---|---|---|
| 1. (c) | 11. (c) | 21. (c) | 31. (c) | 41. (d) |
| 2. (b) | 12. (d) | 22. (a) | 32. (a) | 42. (a) |
| 3. (a) | 13. (c) | 23. (a) | 33. (c) | 43. (b) |
| 4. (b) | 14. (b) | 24. (d) | 34. (a) | 44. (d) |
| 5. (d) | 15. (d) | 25. (b) | 35. (d) | 45. (b) |
| 6. (c) | 16. (a) | 26. (d) | 36. (a) | 46. (c) |
| 7. (d) | 17. (b) | 27. (d) | 37. (c) | 47. (c) |
| 8. (c) | 18. (d) | 28. (b) | 38. (b) | 48. (b) |
| 9. (b) | 19. (c) | 29. (c) | 39. (c) | 49. (c) |
| 10. (a) | 20. (c) | 30. (d) | 40. (d) | 50. (d) |

## V. A.

| | | | | |
|---|---|---|---|---|
| 1. (c) | 11. (d) | 21. (a) | 31. (c) | 41. (c) |
| 2. (a) | 12. (d) | 22. (c) | 32. (b) | 42. (b) |
| 3. (c) | 13. (c) | 23. (c) | 33. (a) | 43. (a) |
| 4. (b) | 14. (a) | 24. (c) | 34. (b) | 44. (b) |
| 5. (a) | 15. (c) | 25. (c) | 35. (d) | 45. (a) |
| 6. (d) | 16. (d) | 26. (b) | 36. (a) | 46. (b) |
| 7. (c) | 17. (c) | 27. (d) | 37. (a) | 47. (c) |
| 8. (b) | 18. (b) | 28. (b) | 38. (d) | 48. (a) |
| 9. (d) | 19. (b) | 29. (c) | 39. (c) | 49. (d) |
| 10. (b) | 20. (b) | 30. (d) | 40. (d) | 50. (b) |

**V. B.**

| | | | | |
|---|---|---|---|---|
| 1. (a) | 11. (b) | 21. (d) | 31. (d) | 41. (d) |
| 2. (d) | 12. (a) | 22. (d) | 32. (b) | 42. (a) |
| 3. (b) | 13. (a) | 23. (c) | 33. (a) | 43. (a) |
| 4. (a) | 14. (d) | 24. (c) | 34. (c) | 44. (c) |
| 5. (c) | 15. (c) | 25. (a) | 35. (d) | 45. (b) |
| 6. (d) | 16. (c) | 26. (b) | 36. (c) | 46. (a) |
| 7. (b) | 17. (a) | 27. (a) | 37. (a) | 47. (c) |
| 8. (a) | 18. (b) | 28. (c) | 38. (b) | 48. (b) |
| 9. (b) | 19. (a) | 29. (b) | 39. (c) | 49. (d) |
| 10. (c) | 20. (b) | 30. (b) | 40. (d) | 50. (d) |

**V. C.**

| | | | | |
|---|---|---|---|---|
| 1. (b) | 11. (d) | 21. (c) | 31. (b) | 41. (b) |
| 2. (c) | 12. (c) | 22. (b) | 32. (d) | 42. (b) |
| 3. (c) | 13. (a) | 23. (d) | 33. (b) | 43. (b) |
| 4. (d) | 14. (c) | 24. (b) | 34. (b) | 44. (d) |
| 5. (a) | 15. (d) | 25. (d) | 35. (d) | 45. (b) |
| 6. (a) | 16. (b) | 26. (a) | 36. (a) | 46. (a) |
| 7. (a) | 17. (c) | 27. (d) | 37. (c) | 47. (c) |
| 8. (b) | 18. (d) | 28. (a) | 38. (b) | 48. (b) |
| 9. (a) | 19. (b) | 29. (d) | 39. (d) | 49. (a) |
| 10. (c) | 20. (a) | 30. (a) | 40. (c) | 50. (d) |

# INDEX

All words, phrases, and expressions that are defined or explained may be found here.

Prefixes and combining forms that serve as prefixes are followed by a short dash (de-); suffixes and combining forms that serve as suffixes are preceded by a small dash (-ness). Roots and similar word elements are italicized (*vent*).

Special subjects and topics are listed in small capital letters (PREFIXES). Where references are distributed throughout the book, as in the case of ANGLO-SAXON, FRENCH, GREEK, LATIN, etc., only a few representative and important examples are cited; the missing references are covered by the catchall Latin word *passim*, "here and there."

# INDEX

# INDEX

## A

*etymos,* 120
eu-, 16, 80, 143
eulogy, 143
euphemism, 16, 40, 143
euphony, 80
euphoria, 80
euphoric, 143
-eur, 117
eureka, 241
-euse, 118
evanescent, 111
eventide, 211
ex- (Latin), 18, 19, 71, 143
ex- (Greek), 71
exacerbate, 59, 143
exaltation, 72
exasperate, 59
excoriation, 300
excruciating, 235
exculpate, 230
exemplar, 238
exhilarate, 80
exhort, 40
ex officio, 238
exorbitant, 71
exorcise, 72
expatiate, 55
expedite, 18
expertise, 128, 132
ex post facto, 229
*ex quadra,* 96
extirpate, 71
extra-, 72, 73
extrasensory, 73
extrasensory perception, 73
extravagant, 73
extro-, 72
extrovert, 72
exultation, 72

**F**

Fabian(ism), 273
*facere,* 114

facsimile, 238
factious, 16
factitious, 15–16, 160, 187
factotum, 238
fait accompli, 155
fakir, 167
farrago, 184
fatuous, 30–31
faute de mieux, 156
faux pas, 156
feasible, 116
feckless, 118, 196
FEMININE NAMES, 118
*fer,* 58, 129
*ferre,* 55
*ferv(ere),* 80
*fēt,* 95
fetish, 160
fiat, 235
*fic,* 114
*fid,* 59
fin de siècle, 156
fingerling, 216
firstling, 216
flagitious, 196
"FLASH" WORDS, 147–148
flaunt, 205
fledg(e)ling, 216
flotsam, 52
flout, 205
*flu, flux,* 55
fluctuate, 55
flume, 55
flux, 55
folknik, 117
forebode, 213
foreboding, 213
forensic, 279
forsooth, 216
forte, 159
fortnight, 97
fortuitous, 205
fortunate, 205
forum, 279
fossil, 307
FOSSILIZED METAPHORS, 307

# H

# I

# Index of Writers Quoted

*Of a good beginning cometh a good end.*

JOHN HEYWOOD, *Proverbs*